PASOLINI

A BIOGRAPHY BY

ENZO SICILIANO

TRANSLATED FROM THE ITALIAN BY

JOHN SHEPLEY

PASOLINI

RANDOM HOUSE NEW YORK

Library of Congress Cataloging in Publication Data
Siciliano, Enzo, 1934–
  Pasolini: a biography.
  Bibliography: p.
  Includes index.
  1. Pasolini, Pier Paolo, 1922–1975—Biography.
2. Authors, Italian—20th century—Biography.
3. Moving-picture producers and directors—Italy—
Biography.   I. Title.
PQ4835.A48Z8813   858'.91409   [B]   81–48294
ISBN 0–394–52299–0   AACR2

Manufactured in the United States of America

Typography and binding design by J. K. Lambert

9 8 7 6 5 4 3 2

First American Edition

Moi! moi qui me suis dit mage ou ange,
dispensé de toute morale, je suis
rendu au sol, avec un devoir à chercher,
et la réalité rugueuse à étreindre!

—ARTHUR RIMBAUD

ACKNOWLEDGMENTS

This book has been written with the loving assistance of the Pasolini heirs, in particular Susanna Pasolini Colussi, Graziella Chiarcossi, and Nico Naldini, who permitted the author to examine the files of un-published Pasolini writings and the whole vast body of bibliographical material in their possession. To the Pasolini heirs go his thanks. The author also wishes to thank Laura Betti, who gave him access to the Pasolini Archive assembled by her for the publishing house of Garzanti. His thanks go also to all those who through personal memories, whether from chance recollections or texts and letters held by them, have allowed him to reconstruct to the greatest possible extent the life of Pier Paolo Pasolini. He is particularly grateful to: Alberto Arbasino, Adriana Asti, Anna Banti, Mariella Bauzano, Gaspare Barbiellini Amidei, Giorgio Bassani, Dario Bellezza, Giovanna Bemporad, Attilio Bertolucci, Bernardo Bertolucci, Alfredo Bini, Gianni Borgna, Cesare Bortotto, Giulio Cattaneo, Suso Cecchi d'Amico, Vincenzo Cerami, Pietro Citati, Sergio Citti, Ninetto Davoli, Federico Fellini, Marcella Ferrara, Franco Fortini, Augusto Frassineti, Cesare Garboli, Livio Garzanti, Sergio Graziani, Paolo Lepri, Dacia Maraini, Nino Marazzita, Fabio Mauri, Ferdinando Mautino, Elsa Morante, Alberto Moravia, Ottiero Ottieri, Silvana Mauri Ottieri, Piero Ottone, Niccolò Pasolini Dall'Onda, Toti Scialoja, Vittorio Sereni, Luciano Serra, Tonuti Spagnol, Giacinto Spagnoletti, Antonello Trombadori, Paolo Volponi, Andrea Zanzotto, Giuseppe Zigaina. The author would also like to express his gratitude to Laura Mazza and Valerio Magrelli, who helped him in searching newspaper files.

E. S.

CONTENTS

THE OSTIA
SEAPLANE BASIN

You reach the Idroscalo, the seaplane basin at Ostia, by leaving the highway running north along the sea toward Fiumicino for a road that cuts across fields and garbage dumps. After a piazza, some low houses, a bar, you turn left as though heading back for Rome. When I went for the first time in September 1976, there on the field, behind a wooden fence, stood the gray construction sites of three or four buildings.

After an intersection the asphalt once again runs parallel to the coast.

It was an afternoon of sirocco and low clouds, the air heavy and stifling. On a rudimentary soccer field next to a whitewashed out-building with dressing rooms, they were playing an informal game: men and boys ran puffing across a patchy meadow, over scattered puddles of water. A net separated them from the road. This was in the direction of the sea. Rain clouds billowed over Rome, and on that side the road skirted deep ditches, weeds, and a seemingly endless sequence of trash heaps.

Once you had passed the playing field, the shantytown emerged as the trash heaps were joined by some small houses aligned along a new road staked out at right angles to the old one.

The only inhabited house was one still under construction. The others, with doorways of a certain charm, little plaster columns, cardboard nailed over the windows, were scattered and isolated in the mud, amid ruts that ran nowhere.

In the middle of these tracks stood three bare and taut saplings, hard to account for, around a bench of dark stone, on whose seat the wind stirred a handful of dust.

As in a Pasolini film, a woman came out of the unfinished house, saying mournfully, "There's a bomb, a bomb, get away from there, the carabinieri are coming." A little boy was running around the edge of a hole, inside of which, along with tin cans, broken dishes, and garbage, there apparently was something that may have resembled an explosive device. The emergency squad of carabinieri arrived. But the woman had already turned her attention to us.

I had gone there with some members of the Communist Youth Federation of Rome. They were preparing a videotape in memory of Pier Paolo Pasolini, a few of the places in his life, a brief account of his works.

The woman, examining us with two little rude and inquiring eyes, now said, "Did you come about him?" And she pointed to the bench. "He sure yelled that night. 'Mamma, mamma, they're killing me.' That's what he kept yelling, poor man."

Having said this, she peered at us, almost as if to measure the degree of credibility in her words. Then she went away.

Whether this testimony of hers was a lie or the truth, there was no way of telling. They were words long transcribed in a script prepared over the course of several months, dictated by her naïve aspiration to feel herself in some way a participant in an event cut on a grand scale from life.

She hurried away toward the child and the carabinieri, suddenly indifferent to her own credibility, caught up by something else.

The bench had been placed crosswise on the trampled earth, to mark the spot where Pasolini's corpse had been found—a step away from the fence, still standing with its pink and green boards, one of which had been used to butcher him. The wind was bending the slender trunks of the saplings.

Beyond an elevation, almost a curve in the road along which a truck came chugging, was another small field where young boys were running and shouting. It was not a regular playing field, but a strip of narrow ground between a line of distant shacks and this beaten track that perhaps led to them. Another soccer match, another contest.

Let us try to imagine it. The body thrown down where the bench now stands. The car parked over there. The houses plunged back at intervals into a chilling disorder. The darkness, broken by a row of lampposts—too far away to give anything more than an uncertain gleam of light on the open space between the paved road and the small field.

Il Messaggero of Monday, November 3, 1975, reported the words of Maria Teresa Lollobrigida, forty-six-year-old wife of the construction worker Alfredo Principessa, forty-eight years old: "'I was the one who found the body. We came here in our Citroën at six-thirty Sunday morning. We always come here on Sunday, and after lunch all of us work on our summer house. The land is state property. The air is good in the summer. When we got here I noticed something in front of our house. I thought it was garbage and I said to my son Giancarlo, "But just look at these sons of bitches who come and throw garbage in front of the house." I went over to see how I could clean the place up and I saw it was a man's body. His head was cracked open. His hair was all smeared with blood. He was lying face down, with his hands under him. He wasn't well dressed. He had on a green sleeveless undershirt, blue jeans dirty with car grease, brown boots that came to his ankles, a brown belt. I told my husband we should go back immediately and tell the police. At six-forty we were all at the police station.'"

The newspaper account may not do justice to Maria Teresa Lollobrigida's salty tongue. What we learn is the position of Pasolini's body: face down, his hair smeared with blood, the undershirt, the boots, the brown belt.

His face was disfigured, one ear torn away or almost. The newspaper photographs show his lean and battered body lying on the ground, the right arm under the chest. Other photos show it supine, with members of the police homicide squad standing around it. The hands and fingers are badly scraped; there is something maimed in the smothered and resigned expression on the face; the chest is swollen and shapeless, no longer as slender as it had been before.

At about one-thirty in the morning on Sunday, November 2, 1975, a carabinieri patrol car noticed a gray Giulia 2000 Alfa Romeo GT speeding on the Lungomare Duilio in Ostia. The police car set out in pursuit.

The Giulia 2000 showed it was aware of being followed by accelerating its speed—it skidded, grazing the sidewalk. Pursuit was hot, until finally the police car succeeded in running the Alfa against the fence of a bathing establishment.

Inside was a boy who tried to escape on foot. He was seized by carabinieri from other cars. He turned out to be Giuseppe Pelosi, seventeen years and four months old, with a police record for auto theft and acts of juvenile delinquency. He had been released from Casal del Marmo, the Roman prison for minors, for the third and most recent time on September 13, 1975.

The automobile in which he had been caught belonged to Pasolini.

During the interrogation, Pelosi asked for the return of his cigarette lighter, the pack of cigarettes left in the car at the moment of his capture, and a ring set with a red stone and inscribed "United States." The detail seemed unimportant, but was nevertheless included in his statement.

Around four in the morning, the boy cracked. He seems to have cried out, "Mamma, what have I done? What have I done?" Then he fell asleep.

The carabinieri telephoned Pasolini's home, where they spoke to Graziella Chiarcossi, daughter of a cousin of Pier Paolo's. She had been living with him and his mother for years, having left her family in the province of Friuli, and was employed under contract by the Faculty of Arts and Letters at the University of Rome. Graziella got in touch with Ninetto Davoli. Ninetto had had supper with Pasolini at the Pommidoro restaurant in the Tiburtino quarter— it was only a few hours since they had parted. Up to that point, the Giulia 2000 had not been stolen.

It was the small hours of the morning and Pasolini had not come home. True, he usually came back late. But this time there was the telephone call from the carabinieri, and the automobile stolen and recovered with the thief at the wheel. Ninetto Davoli went to the carabinieri. No news of Pasolini. Toward seven in the morning, a bulletin came from police headquarters in Ostia: a corpse had been found in the vicinity of the seaplane basin. The carabinieri asked Ninetto Davoli to accompany them to the site. With Pasolini's disappearance, anything was possible.

It was Ninetto who recognized the corpse, lying face down in the dirt, as that of Pier Paolo.

Pelosi had asked for the lost ring, and the ring had been found near the dead man by the police while they were inspecting the trampled area of the dirt road and small playing field.

Next to one of the metal pipes that served as goalposts, they found

Pasolini's bloodstained shirt lying in a heap, and two pieces from a wooden plank, also bloodstained and smeared with brain matter.

The newspapers reported that around noon on November 2 Giuseppe Pelosi confessed that he had killed Pasolini.

At first the boy insisted that he had been lent the GT by a friend, then that he had found it, key in the ignition, in a parking lot near a Tiburtino cinema. But when challenged as to the presence of the ring beside the corpse, Pelosi began to recount how around ten o'clock the previous evening, while loitering with some friends under the arcades of the piazza in front of the railroad station, he had been approached by a "faggot," a gentleman between thirty-five and fifty, at the wheel of the GT automobile.

There is no question but that Pelosi was a hustler. The arcades of the station are like a temple of eros that casts an aura around the rituals of arrival and departure. The sense of irregularity and uncertainty suggested by journeys just ended or about to be begun acts as an aphrodisiac and nourishes the anonymity that these more or less furtive encounters demand.

Pasolini had no use for furtiveness, either in erotic matters or anything else. What must have attracted him in the station arcades was the mixture of humanity, the varied and chaotic spectacle, the sort of metropolitan slum that convenes there, drawn by the mercenary offer of bodies. Did he frequent this place habitually? It has been suggested that he went there in search of material for the novel, provisionally entitled first *Petrolio* and then *Vas*, which he had been working on for over two years. The lengthy sections, some complete and half-revised, that remain of this large work-in-progress may lend a certain support to this hypothesis, given the background of documentation provided in Pasolini's fiction, but there is no literal allusion in it to this Roman piazza.

It was also suggested that Pasolini had previously met Pelosi—known to his friends as "Pino la Rana" (Joey the Frog)—but there is nothing to prove it. So all there is to go on for the moment is Pasolini's arrival in the Piazza dei Cinquecento, once having left Ninetto Davoli at the doorway of the Pommidoro restaurant, and his encounter with Pelosi.

Pelosi has all the physical characteristics of the "Pasolini type," of the street hustler, or *ragazzo di vita*. Photographs in the newspapers the morning after the discovery of the corpse at the seaplane basin show him standing in the street, leaning against a tree, in jacket and tight jeans, his narrow forehead framed by curls, his hands in his

pockets, with a little smile that hovers between frankness and roguish-
ness. But when his face is not smiling, there is something closed and
sad about it, a lack of expression.

That Pasolini should have singled him out is not surprising,
knowing how faithful the writer was, obsessively so, to his own visual
models. The choice of faces for his films clearly demonstrates it. Pino
Pelosi might well have appeared in the *Decameron* or the *Arabian
Nights*. After the murder, Enzo Ocone, production director for Pasolini's last films, went through all the screen tests for extras in the
crowd scenes, convinced that the boy must have been one of those
screened by Pasolini. Though the search was in vain, Ocone's dogged
effort confirms the degree to which Pelosi belonged to the Pasolini
iconography.

Pelosi's story was brief. The "faggot" at the wheel of the GT
drove toward him. He moved away toward the bar-kiosk in the
Piazza dei Cinquecento. A few minutes later the GT was right behind
him. The "faggot" got out, came up to him and offered him a ride,
promising him a "nice present." No concrete proposition, but Pelosi
had understood what was being asked of him.

They left in the car, stopping at a trattoria near the San Paolo
basilica. Pino drank a beer, and ate a plate of spaghetti and a quarter
of a chicken; the "gentleman" ate nothing.

Between eleven and eleven-thirty, the two got back in the car;
they stopped at a gas station on Viale Marconi, then immediately took
the Via Ostiense in the direction of the sea. During the ride, said
Pelosi, the "gentleman" spoke of a secluded field—they would go
there and "do something," twenty thousand lire ($25) as a reward.

What happened next, based on the report produced by the carabinieri,
is recounted as follows in the sentence of the juvenile court of Rome
handed down by the presiding judge, Alfredo Carlo Moro, on April
26, 1976: "Pelosi added that the man brought him to the playing
field; that he [Pasolini] took his [Pelosi's] penis in his mouth for a
moment but did not finish the 'blow-job'; that he made him get out of
the car and came up behind him, squeezing him from behind and trying to lower his trousers; that he [Pelosi] told him to stop and instead
he [Pasolini] picked up a stake of the kind used for garden fences and
tried to put it up his behind, or at least he stuck it against his behind
though without even lowering his trousers; that he, Pelosi, turned
around and said to him 'You're crazy'; that Pasolini by now was

without his glasses, which he had left in the car, and on looking him in the face it seemed to him so much the face of a madman that he was frightened; that he tried to run but stumbled and fell; that he felt Pasolini on top of him, hitting him on the head with a stick; that he grabbed the stick and flung Paolo away from him; that he again started running, and again was caught and struck on the temple and various parts of the body; that he noticed a plank on the ground, picked it up and broke it over his head; that he also kicked him once or twice 'in the balls'; that Paolo seemed not even to feel these kicks; that then he grabbed him by the hair and struck him again on the nose; that he no longer saw what he was doing and repeatedly hit him with the plank until he heard him fall wheezing to the ground; that he ran in the direction of the car carrying the two pieces of board and the stake, which he threw near the car; that he got immediately into the car and fled in it; that he did not know whether or not in his escape he had run over Paolo's body with the car; that he had not run over Paolo's body deliberately nor been aware of doing so because he was in a state of shock; that he had stopped on the road at the first water fountain to wash himself and remove the bloodstains; that during these events he and Paolo had always been alone."

This bureaucratic prose, culled from the police report, betrays excitement and displays obvious gaps and contradictions. Pelosi, when stopped by the carabinieri, did not look as though he had just emerged from a brawl. There were almost no traces of blood on him, nor were his clothes in disorder. In view of this, the court held that the defendant's full confession "need not prevent a search for the essential truth"—the "truth" as to times, movements, and the mechanics of the event.

In particular it was the police investigation itself that dissolved the credibility of Pelosi's story.

First of all, there were clues suggesting the presence of third parties in the struggle on the dirt road and field at the seaplane basin.

When Pelosi was stopped by the carabinieri, a green sweater was found on the back seat of Pasolini's car. Though a little shabby, it was still in good condition, the kind of cheap sweater sold in the stalls of neighborhood markets. It would not have fitted either Pasolini or the boy.

Also found in the car was the orthopedic sole of a right shoe, this too belonging neither to Pasolini or Pelosi. Nor, like the sweater, could it have been in the car before that day. Graziella Chiarcossi told the police that she had cleaned Pier Paolo's GT the morning of October 31, and she had seen neither sweater nor sole.

Not found in the car, however, were the package of Marlboro cigarettes and the lighter that Pelosi had asked for at the time of his arrest. And yet he insisted he had left them there. The court surmised that a third person "had picked them up in the confusion and carried them away with him."

Other conclusions arrived at by the homicide squad: "In the soil of the penalty area near the left goal of the informal soccer field [at the seaplane basin] footprints were found that had certainly not been left either by Pasolini's shoes or Pelosi's." These were prints made by rubber soles, probably sneakers.

The court sentence reads: "It is to be excluded that the photographed footprints could have been left on the ground by the boys who were playing soccer the morning of November 2. As shown by the police report (vol. 6), the surveys of the site were carried out at seven-thirty in the morning, and in any case before the arrival on the scene of the boys who later played soccer."

There were not only the prints of the sneakers, "but numerous other footprints," also in the goal area—all in all, how many people were there that night on the playing field at the seaplane basin? The question cannot be answered, but it is important that it can be raised.

Another clue: on the roof of the car, on the side of the passenger's door, there were slight incrustations of blood—blood, according to the examiner's report, belonging to Pasolini.

If Pier Paolo's head had struck the roof of the car, there would also have been, as in all such cases, imprints of hair in addition to the traces of blood. Had it been blood that had spurted, the traces would have had much greater consistency. Nor could they have been left by Pasolini's hands if, as Pelosi says, Pasolini never approached the car during the struggle. The hypothesis is that those stains were left by the hands of an attacker.

But who was this attacker? Was it Pelosi?

Pelosi states that after the fight he got in the car and drove away— if this is true, he got in the other door and not the one over which the bloodstains were found.

This would support the hypothesis that there must have been at least one other person with "Pino the Frog," someone who got in the car by opening the door on the passenger side, instinctively steadying himself by placing a hand on the roof.

Assuming that the bloodstains were left by Pelosi's hands, then Pelosi, having left Pasolini dying on the ground, must have run to the car, started to get in, accidentally put his hand on the roof, and realized he had made a mistake. To make his getaway, he had to enter the car by the opposite door—thus he would have closed the passenger door and gone around to the driver's side. Had this happened, he would have left other traces of blood, perhaps slighter ones, both on the right-hand door of the GT and on the wheel. But such was not the case.

The sentence concludes: "There are only two possibilities: either Pelosi had blood on his hands and entered the car from the passenger side, and another person was driving the car at the time that it ran over Pasolini's body and then as far as the fountain where Pelosi washed himself (though it seems unlikely that Pelosi's accomplices went with him as far as the fountain); or the accomplice with blood on his hands got in the passenger's seat by opening the left-hand door, while Pelosi, who did not have blood on his hands, got behind the wheel. In either case, it seems certain that some other person who had participated in the assault got in the car with Pelosi."

This thesis—that there was more than one attacker—is supported by the fact that there was almost none of Pasolini's blood on Pelosi's body or clothes; while Pasolini, before receiving the kick in the scrotum that brought on a violent internal hemorrhage, had had an equally violent external hemorrhage from his head wounds: "it was not a simple discharge of blood, but actual 'spurts' of blood." This is shown, as I said, by the quantity of blood with which the shirt left lying on the ground was soaked.

The investigation ascertained that Pelosi had a little of Pasolini's blood on the left cuff of his tight-fitting jersey (a stain measuring three centimeters), on the bottom of his right trouser leg, and under the sole of one shoe. Had the struggle been the hand-to-hand one described by the boy in his "confession," all of his clothes should have been soiled, not only with blood but with other matter as well, as examination showed the stick and the two pieces of plank that had served him as offensive weapons to be. But Pelosi emerged from the struggle unscathed.

Pasolini was left lying on the ground with his face disfigured, deep wounds in his skull, one ear almost torn off, his hands scraped, his nails crushed. Pelosi had only a small cut on the left side of his forehead over his eyebrow, caused by his slamming on the brakes as the police car forced him off the Lungomare Duilio. Pelosi had hit his forehead on the wheel of the Giulia GT—that was all.

Gaps and incongruities emerge in the boy's words from the moment he begins telling of his first encounter with Pasolini at the arcades of the Stazione Termini.

The assembled testimony makes it clear that when Pasolini arrived in front of the bar at those arcades, he did not get out of the car. He talked cautiously and suspiciously to a group of male prostitutes, saying he was waiting for a friend. When they tried to get closer to him, reaching out to take his hand, he locked the door and rolled up the window.

Meanwhile, one of the boys, Seminara by name, went into the bar, called Pelosi, and suggested that he approach the Giulia GT.

At this point, Pasolini's suspiciousness faded and he opened the door for the newcomer. (Was it because of Pelosi's iconological correspondence to a physical and aesthetic obsession?)

Pelosi got into the Giulia GT. The car drove away from the Piazza dei Cinquecento and was gone for half an hour. During that time Pelosi persuaded Pasolini to return to the station, and also made him promise to take him home to Tiburtino III after the encounter was over. Though a minor, the boy drove on the sly; he and two other boys were the joint owners of a compact; at that moment he happened to have the keys and had to hand them over to the others.[1]

On returning to the Piazza dei Cinquecento, Pelosi asked his friends to keep out of sight of the man in the Giulia GT; he used the excuse of the car keys to speak to them, but what he said is not known.

At this point the GT departed in the direction of Ostia.

Was it Pasolini who was already familiar with the Idroscalo or was it Pelosi? No one knows whether Pasolini had ever been there before. The court sentence contains the hypothesis that Pelosi knew the place: not by chance would he have found the fountain in the Piazza Scipione l'Africano in Ostia, where he was able to wash the blood from his hands and the bottoms of his trousers, while parking the car in a secluded street like Via delle Caserme. In any case, it was at the time of the second departure from the Piazza dei Cinquecento that the seaplane basin must have been designated as their destination, although we do not know by whom.

Stops along the way: the Biondo Tevere trattoria on the Via Ostiense; there Pasolini was known, and recognized. Then a gas station: there too Pasolini was recognized by a chance customer. It would seem to have been an evening like any other. A boy eats a plate of spaghetti with oil and garlic in a trattoria, and a car is filled up with gas at an automatic pump.

Could there also have been an automobile following the Alfa GT, and waiting unseen during the stops? The notion of a trap, put forward by several persons, takes on substance in the legal findings. These findings reveal cracks and contradictions in Pelosi's "confession"—they direct the investigation to the contents of the confession itself and emphasize what its words disclose by omission.

On Monday, May 3, 1976, Franco Rossi, reporter for *Paese Sera*, published a letter that had been delivered to him unsigned (the lawyer Nino Marazzita, representing Pasolini's next-of-kin at the trial in the juvenile court of Rome, received a similar one). The letter delivered to Rossi states that on the night of Saturday, November 1, 1975, Pasolini's GT, having left the Piazza dei Cinquecento, was followed by a car with a Catania license plate: in it were four persons well known to the boys who hung out under the station arcades.

It was one of these boys who wrote the letter, which reads: "We knew those four very well because they're always coming and beating us up and screwing us out of the money we earn by our work. And they tell us we've got to quit working because we're ruining the piazza for them and their women."

And again: "The court judges have done a very bad thing in sentencing Pelosi, because all he should have got was three years for stealing the car seeing as how we street boys, not to say hustlers, know that Pino Pelosi is absolutely innocent. Those four threatened to kill him if he said a single word about it."

A trap. The emotional reaction to the killing of Pasolini was enormous, and the idea that he had been caught and killed in a "political" trap spread immediately among a great many people. The polemicist, the public accuser of those in power, of the regime that had ruled Italy for thirty years, had been "liquidated," violently silenced, and silenced in the most sophisticated and shameful way—on a playing field on the outskirts of Rome, by the hand of a boy prostitute whom he was trying to "fuck in the ass."

Not a pistol shot or a burst of machine-gun fire in the morning as he got into his car at the door of his house—none of what has become the usual pattern of political crime in the dark and turbulent seventies. A diabolically casual *mise-en-scène*, convincing and perfect in its way, was to be reserved and staged in such a manner that he would be found mired up to the neck in his own "well-known masochism," his capacity for "self-punishment."

This interpretation, which exploited a certain existential vulnerability of Pasolini's, provoked a response from Alberto Arbasino: "What do they mean, masochism! Self-punishment! There's a limit! In fact, there are two. One: respect for your own public image when engaged in a political battle: at such times you can't even allow yourself the simple luxury of being caught behind the bushes with your pants down. And our friend knew this all too well, just as the most reckless *cavalieri del lavoro** know all the tricks and turns to keep from getting 'caught in the act.' The other: that the slightest regard for literature, the slightest affection for the titles of one's books, would keep them—this is really stronger than anything else!—from becoming newspaper headlines, even being used as tasteless puns, especially on the occasion of one's death! The whole thing is fishy, and all the more so with all these neat little theories, little school essays with more references than a maid, cook, and mother's helper. Never in Italian judicial history has everything appeared so logical and definitive and without room for change in just a few Sunday hours."[2]

A trap. In the face of a trap, Pasolini's existential vulnerability would have become moral strength. To strike at Italian culture through Pasolini could be to light a fuse, with unforeseeable consequences. The power structure, which Pasolini had been attacking with his "Corsair" and "Lutheran" articles in the *Corriere della Sera*, has subtle ways to hush things up—the establishment in such cases takes only minimum risks. Or it takes its risks on another level, by complicating and falsifying the facts—but then we have the massacre in the Piazza Fontana in Milan, the *Italicus* train massacre.† It exploits, without having any need to ask, all the resources of the far right.

All the same, there would appear to be a trap in this situation. It is possible to advance more than one supposition as to its nature. As of now, the only fact we know is that Pelosi is most certainly keeping silent.

A trap sprung by four pimps setting out from the Stazione Termini

* An honorary title, like "Commendatore," bestowed for some kind of meritorious service. Such titles, however, can sometimes be bought.—Tr.

† Ultra-rightist bomb explosions occurring respectively in 1969 and 1974. —Tr.

on a typical underworld mission of retaliation that then turned into a crime? Anything is possible. Thus, the idea of a "political" murder takes on substance only in a figurative, metaphorical sense, in the sense that any human act can and should be divorced from simple chance and seen within a rational context. This murder becomes "political" because of the importance of the murdered man's public image.

This being said, the only certainties that throw light on the night at the seaplane basin are the multiple and mortal wounds on Pasolini's body, for which Pino the Frog does not seem to be the only one responsible.

The GT arrived at the seaplane basin, and parked in the darkness. Pino Pelosi says that he lit a cigarette and smoked it. Then Pasolini stroked his genitals—"He took my penis in his mouth for about a minute." There was a moment of oral intercourse.

After this, still according to Pelosi's verbal testimony, the boy postponed asking for the twenty thousand lire agreed upon: "I thought I should ask him for it when we were all finished." So Pelosi knew that the encounter was not yet over. At this point, what could have happened between the two?

Pasolini must have loosened his belt, unzipped his fly, and prepared to make love. Pelosi says he himself got out of the car and leaned against a wire fence. "Why?" he was asked in the course of the proceedings. He answered, "Just to take a look." To take a look at what, in pitch darkness?

Pelosi insists that Pasolini got out of the car and followed him with a stake, with which he tried to make erotic contact—this produced the trauma, the transport of rage that led Pelosi to kill. But there were two phases to the struggle, not one as Pino the Frog states. Here the boy's silence becomes impenetrable and guilty.

Next morning, in a cell in Casal del Marmo, he said to his first cellmate, "I've killed a man, Pasolini to be exact." He had still not said so to his interrogators, still not "confessed"—and he added, "Anyway they'll soon find out, they're not jerks, those guys."

Meanwhile he had not confessed, and the investigation had been briefly recessed. Only later was he to declare that he had killed in legitimate self-defense. That man, that "faggot," had attacked him, attacked him with a stake, which he had tried to stick "up his ass."

It was pitch-dark. The trap could have been sprung while Pasolini, still inside the car, was bending over the boy's crotch—they could have grabbed him from behind and dragged him out of the car. Pelosi could have got out and gone to the fence, turning his back on what was happening, "just to take a look."

The struggle began there, seventy meters from the spot where the corpse was found. Pasolini was struck violently on the head, and his wounds bled copiously. He had time to take off his flannel shirt, use it to wipe some of the blood off himself, and drop it in a heap by the goalpost of the playing field. The shirt is not torn in any way, it was not ripped off him. Pasolini unbuttoned it and took it off.

With what weapons was he struck? On the trampled earth of the Idroscalo, a stick and two pieces of board were found, at a distance of fifty-six meters and ninety meters from the corpse, respectively. They were not heavy enough to have produced the head wounds that Pasolini received. He was probably hit with something else.

Anyway, at this point his face was streaming with blood. The scalp teems with blood vessels, and the lesions are such as to suggest that the arteries were damaged as well—there must have been flaring ruptures. Such spurts of blood must surely have spattered the attackers or attacker—certainly not Pelosi. And Pasolini must have fought back —the scraped condition of his hands suggests it.

His attempt to stanch the blood with his shirt marks the end of the first phase of the struggle. A pause, a gap. Then the dash of seventy meters, the last seventy meters in Pasolini's life.

If the head wounds constitute the culminating moment in the first phase of the struggle, a kick in the testicles was the decisive one in the second. Pasolini must have lost consciousness—the blow had given him a deep hematoma in the lower abdomen. Judge Moro's decision supposes that the kick "was dealt by one person while others held the victim to receive the coup de grâce."

Pelosi has said that he beat Pasolini with the stick and the plank, which broke in two between blows; he said that he then gathered them up "by instinct" and threw them away while running to the car. But before this flight there was another one: Pasolini's flight from the soccer-field goal to the spot where he finally fell. A lock of his hair was found on the dirt road. They followed him, overtook him, grabbed him by the hair. This may have been the moment of the kick in the scrotum.

And then the flight of the automobile. Pelosi insists he was not aware of driving over Pasolini's lifeless body lying on the ground. It was this that actually killed Pasolini—his heart burst under the pressure of the GT's tires.

So Pelosi didn't see it—and yet the body was not a negligible obstacle. Pelosi says he was beside himself, in a daze. But meanwhile he had thrown the stick and two pieces of wooden plank far from the corpse. Nor did he appear to be in a daze half an hour later in the presence of the carabinieri, to whom he was able to give answers that were precise in their way, though of course at variance with what he later said had happened. He was preoccupied with the cigarettes, the lighter, and the ring found next to the dead man's body like a prearranged countersign of the murder.

The Giulia was set in motion deliberately to crush the dying Pasolini—naturally the body did not take up the whole width of the road. There were still more than eight meters by which the car could have avoided running over him.

Instead the car hit the body and "finished it off." During the interrogation, Pelosi said, "All I wanted to do was to get away. I didn't think he was dead, but at that moment, since the main thing was to go and get my car, I didn't care that if I left Pasolini there, he might die of his wounds."

He fled, leaving his ring tossed on the ground. Pelosi insisted that in the struggle it was pulled off his finger. But the ring fitted tightly on his finger—in the morning there was still a red circle left on the skin. It would have had to have been pulled off in the course of a hand-to-hand fight from which Pelosi could not have emerged completely unscathed.

Pasolini was a strong, lean man, accustomed to a weekly physical workout—playing soccer was his passion, his distraction, his relaxation. An adolescent joy suffused him when he talked about it; he took an active pleasure in playing with men in his own film crew, or with the boys he met in the shantytowns. He played aggressively, with enthusiasm and spirit. His body could not have weakened and broken down during a fight like the one described by Pelosi.

Pelosi does not say exactly when or how he lost the ring. The ring was there, next to the corpse. But a dying man, reduced to semiconsciousness by a kick in the genitals, could not have had the strength to pull a tight-fitting ring from the finger of a boy in the grip of a homicidal fury.

The absurdity of this clue, this indisputable proof of guilt, has given rise to the most diverse suppositions. All of them lead to one question: was a homicide staged in such a way that the culprit would unquestionably turn out to be this boy from Tiburtino III, who because he was a minor would get off with a relatively light sentence?

Why did Pelosi, once caught, mention the lost ring to the carabinieri? Why throw out such a clear hint of his own guilt?

But this hint, tossed out in such an obvious way, may indicate a role quite different from the one I have described so far. What may emerge from the night at the seaplane basin is a Pelosi diabolically shrewd, diabolically informed, but also a Pelosi stupidly and ominously deprived, who killed by himself while in the grip of a baleful semi-consciousness. What may be revealed is one of those "unhappy youths" of whom Pasolini himself wrote: "There is no group of boys that you can meet on the street who could not be a group of criminals. There is no light in their eyes: their features are the counterfeit features of robots, with nothing personal to distinguish them from within. Stereotyping makes them faithless. Their silence may precede an anxious request for help (what help?) or it may precede a knifing. They are no longer in control of their acts, one would say of their muscles. They are hardly aware of the distance between cause and effect. They have regressed—under the outward appearance of better schooling and a higher standard of living—to a primitive rudeness. If in one sense they speak better—that is, they have assimilated the degrading standard Italian—in another they are almost aphasic: they speak old incomprehensible dialects, or even keep silent, every so often bursting out with guttural cries and interjections, all of them obscene in nature. They don't know how to smile or laugh. They are only able to leer or guffaw."[3]

Is Pelosi thus a criminal who doesn't know he is one because he cannot control his own muscles, because he doesn't know "the distance between cause and effect": a monster, a robot hatched out of Italy's economic development, out of the Italian age of "prosperity"? He certainly had better schooling than his parents; he has eaten better than they. But this boy has paid a dreadful price for such gains: he has regressed to "a primitive rudeness." He is beguiled by what glitters. He has killed a man, and half an hour later, paralyzed by his own myths, all he can talk about is a ring, a ring set with a red stone and stamped with an inscription that obviously leads him on to other myths, to unexplored dreams "made in U.S.A."

Despite his deed, he cannot be accused of having any specific, individual impairment. His impairment is a social one—it is collective.

This means, then, that Pasolini, on the last night of his life, was caught up with a stereotype. Pelosi seemed to be one of those boys with curly hair and a narrow forehead whom he had hitherto so often encountered—but in truth he wasn't. His "silence" may have deceived the author of *Ragazzi di vita*; he interpreted that silence as "a request for help," and from it received "a knifing." This is the only explanation that can dissolve the all too plausible hypothesis of a trap.

So here we have Pelosi appearing to Pasolini under the arcades of the Piazza dei Cinquecento.

"First of all, you are, and should be, very nice-looking. Not necessarily in the conventional sense. You may even be rather short and actually somewhat skinny in build, and your features may already show signs that in later years will inevitably become your mask. But your eyes must be black and shining, your mouth rather large, your face quite regular, and your hair should be short at the neck and behind the ears, while it wouldn't bother me at all if you had a big, high, belligerent mop, maybe even a little exaggerated and comical in front. I wouldn't mind if you were rather athletic, and thus had narrow hips and firm legs."[4] This was the Gennariello of the short treatise of the same name, which Pasolini had begun writing in the spring of 1975 and left unfinished. The text was didactic in purpose; its goal was to save from "anthropological genocide," in those pockets of Italy where it was still possible, the naturalness and humanity of subproletarian boys.

Pelosi, to some extent, may have corresponded physically to the portrait. But Pasolini had by now moved away from that ideal image. In an article entitled "Abiura dalla *Trilogia della vita*" (Repudiation of the *Trilogy of Life*), dated June 15, 1975, he had expressed his "hatred" for "the bodies and sexual organs of the new generations of Italian young people and children." He had written that he would never again be able to show those bodies and sexual organs in a film in the same favorable manner in which he had represented them in the *Decameron*, the *Canterbury Tales*, and the *Arabian Nights*. There was anger in his words, the anger of disenchantment, a "retroactive" anger.

"For some years I had been able to fool myself. The degenerating present was compensated both by the objective survival of the past and the consequent possibility of re-evoking it. But today the degeneration of bodies and sex organs has taken on a retroactive significance. If those who *then* were thus-and-so have been able *now* to become thus-and-so, it means they were already like that potentially: therefore even their mode of being *then* is henceforth devalued. If the young people and children of the Roman subproletariat—who incidentally are the ones I projected into the old and resistant Naples, and later into the poor countries of the Third World—are *now* human refuse, it means that *then* too they were potentially so: thus they were imbeciles obliged to be adorable, or wretched criminals obliged to be holy innocents, and so on."

The conclusion, in the collapse of this ideal that for years had inspired the poet of *Ragazzi di vita* like a religious credo, was extremely bitter and scorching: "Life is a heap of insignificant and ironic ruins."[5]

Among those ironic ruins there was death. At this point one wonders: once this particular Gennariello, whether a true or false one, had appeared, what happened to make the repudiation of his body lose its hold on Pier Paolo's senses?

The call of sex is peremptory, as we know. One wonders if on that November night all that acted was that call, or did it go so far as to act on Pier Paolo for the terrible and appointed purpose of murder?

The night of the Idroscalo has yet to be pierced. By now it is clear that the search for its *truth* within a pattern of guesswork will be vain. What counts, and occupies the screen in the foreground, is its *reality*.

Not that truth and reality are opposed to each other, but the second absorbs the first. Pier Paolo is dead, and the circumstances of his death would seem to be a tight combination of chance and necessity, wiping out all the newspaper reports and blurring the images of Pelosi, the stick, the plank split in two, the ring with the red stone, the sweater left in the Alfa GT.

One recalls the dream sequence in *Accattone*: naked young bodies, half buried under rubble; the sun bleaching everything; a feeling of decay and irresolute anguish; a hallucinatory silence.

This then is the vague, shabby terrain where his death was consummated. The three saplings and the bench, dedicated to the poet by Laura Betti—someday, uprooted, they will disappear.

The landscape of huts, mud puddles, and garbage seems untouched: a place of discard and waste, a place of rubble. In its horror, the Idroscalo is also a place of compassion, a religious place. Its features are illuminated now by the destiny that was completed here.

As we have seen, Alberto Arbasino refused to consider the matter in the light of a macabre and sophisticated *mise-en-scène*. But that is just wherein the question lies: that the *mise-en-scène* should have been possible with such precision, such perfection.

There is a chilling fatality in the fact that Pasolini should die here, at the point where the bench and trees were later planted, on this stretch of uncertain terrain, with its hovels and nearby soccer field.

The fatality is chilling even if it were proved that Pasolini had been led onto that excavated site by a trap.

Moravia has said that on first seeing it, he recognized the place as though he had seen it before: "In fact, [Pasolini] had already described it in his two novels *Ragazzi di vita* and *Una vita violenta*, as well as in his first film, *Accattone*."[6]

This coincidence, which is a sign of destiny, and which in no way detracts from any hypothesis that can be formulated as to the crime, requires an explanation, or if not an immediate explanation, a verification. Pasolini's life and work religiously contain its meaning and mystery.

PART ONE

CHAPTER 1

TAL COUR
DI UN FRUT

A QUOTATION

"That he lived always in his own presence, *on the point of the sword*, while being enchanted by the life, isolated in closed and marvelously nostalgic episodes, of his village, was perhaps due to his being in part a foreigner."

A page of autobiography, the truest that Pasolini ever wrote about his youth in the northeastern Italian province of Friuli. He never collected it in a book, and it has remained confined to an issue (no. viii) of *Botteghe Oscure*, the magazine published by Marguerite Caetani and edited by Giorgio Bassani. The title of these pages is "I parlanti" (The Speakers), and in them Friuli becomes the magical and "foreign" place for the discovery of language and history. Pasolini had written a portion of this piece in 1948; he published it in 1951.

The noble Ravenna blood of his father (in his imagination: an old palace in the heart of Ravenna, worn and faded as in an old print, and then, after a quick and mournful vision of the sea—Porto Corsini—an interior, red and melancholy in its nineteenth-century ostentation, where an old countess, his distant relative, converses with Carducci) had merged with the Casarsa blood of the Colussis (in its turn, in his imagination: an old quarter of the town, gray and submerged in the densest penumbra of rain, peopled with difficulty by antiquated peasant figures, and deafened by the timeless tolling of the bell).

But his grandmother, his mother's mother, had come from Casale Monferrato; a Piedmont painted a vivid pink as in his childhood atlas, and which enveloped in a bright and precious sheath the motionless vicissitudes of his grandmother's family: an asylum, a dancing party, his grandmother as a young girl combing her hair, an emptied house, swollen and blackened by poverty. But from the hills of Monferrato, which he had never seen, there blew into his life a calm, fresh breeze, preserved as though artificially in a memory with no further function, outlived. It was at this point, when he thought of the name *Monferrato*, a warlike name, to which some rigid feudal event—learned accidentally and with happy pride at school—was then attached, that Poland presented itself to his by now traditional imagination. His mother's great-grandmother had in fact been a Polish Jewess—from whom his mother had inherited the name Susanna—married and brought to Friuli by one of his ancestors, a soldier of Napoleon. The Poland that thus automatically and happily appeared to his boyish eyes was of a mouse-gray color, and was shot through with the hues and music of the Risorgimento: all of a sudden it was ripped asunder and at its center appeared the old image of his great-great-grandfather, who in the midst of an expanse of snow as white as lime, kills his horse, rips open its belly, and takes refuge inside to escape the freezing cold.

Let us now leave this fanciful and loving re-creation of the family mythology. I would hope that its music may remain as a melody echoing beyond what I am about to tell.

What was in the mind of this "foreign" child, dreaming his family's exploits over the colors of his school atlas?

TAL COUR DI UN FRUT

Tal cour di un frut—in the heart of a boy. What was in the heart of the boy Pier Paolo Pasolini, born in Bologna on March 5, 1922?

An elegant little boy, his eyes dark and melancholy; his bangs combed neatly on his forehead; a white sailor blouse with geometric piping on the hem and collar; the plump legs encased in white cotton knee socks; patent leather shoes; velvet knee-length pants. Or again: a hat with a rounded brim, and an open fur coat: the geometric patterns of the lining must have been in bright colors, Art Deco. Pier Paolo looks two years old, three at the most. The painted backdrop in the photographer's studio counterfeits a park, a balustrade, and an avenue of plane trees. The little boy is posed standing on an upright, upholstered chair—his mother holds him by the arm.

Susanna Pasolini, neé Colussi, looks in the photo like a young girl. She could be thirty-three (she was born in 1891) and yet in the position of the head, in the lively eyes, in the way she wears her clothes, she shows the vital freshness of a youth barely savored. Her hair is cut short, but not shingled around the ears, and parted on the right; at the throat, a string of pearls; coat of rabbit fur with sloping shoulders, wide collar, studiously left unbuttoned, left arm relaxed in pocket. In this abandon there is a feeling of not belonging, combined with possession, which arouses suspicion in the careful observer. The fur coat is worn with irresistible fragility, with more than a trace of exhibitionism, and also with a jealous sense of ownership.

The coat comes to the knee; underneath, a hobble skirt with a long row of buttons on the side; black stockings visible at the ankles; high-heeled open shoes with straps. Susanna holds the little boy to the right, arm in arm. Her haughty appearance is explained by this proximity to the child—she is presenting him, putting him on display, using him as a defense. Her well-defined lips, accented with lipstick, are set in a moue that proclaims all the pride and joy invested in a son that a mother can feel.

Melancholy arose in the heart of this boy. The melancholy is there in a photograph of him at an even earlier age, sitting on the lap of his Pasolini grandmother, an old woman with flaring nostrils and flattened nasal septum, similar to Pier Paolo's. Old Signora Pasolini resembled her son Carlo Alberto.

These photographs speak of a petit-bourgeois social milieu, Italy in the first years of fascism.

Nineteen twenty-two was the year in which Mussolini came to power. Pasolini was born in a country whose face was changing, a country that was destroying or strengthening its Risorgimento tradition (depending on which of two opposed viewpoints one accepted).

The reality of fascism was, as we know, petit bourgeois—a whole social structure was obliterated in it. On one side, the large landowner and manufacturers obliterated themselves; as did, on the other, a by no means negligible portion of the urban and peasant proletariat— the first in the hope of foiling the "Red peril," the others in the hope of possibly ameliorating uncertain conditions of labor and employment that had become chronic. But Italy was separating itself by accelerating leaps and bounds from Europe; the Europe from which she had sought nourishment during the nineteenth-century period of fine Romantic and post-Romantic hopes, and many people, a great many, accepted the Blackshirt coup d'état with the idea of using it as a tool for their own particular interests.

That was not the way it turned out. No one dominated fascism, in the sense that no one can dominate his own negative drives if he does not recognize them as such. It is no paradox to say that the ubiquitous Italian petite bourgeoisie was expressing in the dictatorship a methodical rejection of history, and its ideology was a solvent that was to produce what has been called "consensus."

The fascist dictatorship was not a harmless invention or a temporary sickness of the spirit. It was the common denominator, political and ideological, for a country that was suffering at every level from a violent inferiority complex, and which found in this abrupt turn to the right, in populism and autarky, the excuse or the point of departure for not telling itself necessary, unwelcome, painful truths.

For the Italians to acquire antifascist consciousness was no simple matter. It was made possible either by "class" motivations—though the proletariat conscious of its own function and its own ethico-political intentions was then numerically small and thus surrounded on all sides—or by the exclusively cultural motivations and reflections of an elite.

Pier Paolo Pasolini arrived at antifascism by the paths of culture, when the Resistance was already at its height. His father was a fascist.

CARLO ALBERTO PASOLINI

The son of Argobasto Pasolini Dall'Onda, Carlo Alberto was born in Bologna in 1892. Orphaned on his father's side, he remained close to his mother, a woman of decided character. Discolored old photographs show a harsh, unsmiling face, the mouth tight-lipped between the cheeks like her son (and as Pier Paolo himself was to be); slender and elegant in her way, she wears a brocade dress with an aristocratic brooch of small diamonds pinned at her throat (in this photo, from the 1890s, Carlo Alberto, about four years old, brandishes a little whip).

Aristocratic vanity was one of Carlo Alberto's traits (as also, to a certain extent, repressed and revealed only at fleeting moments, it was one of Pier Paolo's). In a photograph, Carlo Alberto, not yet eighteen, seated on a light upholstered chair (dark double-breasted jacket with broad lapels and buckled at the waist, striped white trousers, patterned shirt with starched white collar and dark satin necktie, rings on right index finger and left little finger), with his strong bone structure and prominent features, looks like a quick sketch of his son.

Other photos: a rebellious forelock, a profile caught by the imprecision of the lens in such a way that the cheek is markedly hollowed, the eye ringed, the sideburn a light curved brushstroke. Or again: on an Adriatic beach, he wears a one-piece, half-length bathing suit, and holds a lighted cigarette between the index and middle finger of the right hand resting on his waist; the left is hidden behind his back—a swaggering pose, hair ruffled by the breeze. His body, though not slender, is lean and strong-limbed in every part, the crotch conspicuously bulging, pectorals and calves taut, eyebrows frowning— a thoroughbred Italian, not only in the undeniably low-slung hips but also in the psychology of total physicality he exudes.

The young man had inherited some family property, but he seems to have squandered it all—there is talk of an uncontrollable passion for gambling.

Reduced to poverty, he took up a soldier's life and departed for Libya. He was in the infantry. In 1915, Italy intervened in the European conflict. For meritorious service in the zone of operations, Sergeant Pasolini was promoted to second lieutenant. During that period, at Casarsa in Friuli, he met and fell in love with a girl named Susanna Colussi.

That such a man could become a fascist is not surprising; it would be surprising if he hadn't. Fascism was biologically part of Carlo Alberto Pasolini: it was part of his vanity, of his obvious vitalism, of the look of suspicion in his eyes, and it was part even more of his ruined social position, of his aristocratic origins reduced to the desolate realms of the petite bourgeoisie. His having become a soldier is an unmistakable sign, because of the authoritarian, antidemocratic tradition that the Italian army stood for at that time, and because of the way such a career provided an answer to the fate of economic degradation.

Carlo Alberto Pasolini lived the rest of his life in a dream of military ideals, even after his discharge. He was the "officer" in the family, as also in his wife's family, which became to all intents and purposes his own; he never relinquished the proud role of the "count." He aroused respect, even when he undermined his own authority by drinking.

And yet, weak and harmlessly fatuous, he was a generous man, inspired by strict standards from former times. He was crazy about his son, and demonstrated his love for him in conflicting ways. In short, he was one of those Italian fathers brought up on false masculine and patriotic values in which the little gold nugget of personal honesty had nevertheless been deposited.

THE COLUSSIS

There is evidence of the Colussi family in Casarsa in the coat of arms on a lintel over the portal of a long passageway leading to the court-yard of an old house, today much restored, whose rustic beauty is buried under its whitewashed façade. There remain the low arch and this coat of arms: a cartwheel at the center of an oval, in its turn framed within the perimeter of an upside-down spearhead. Below, the device reads: IACO DI COLUS—MDCV.

A peasant family—the cartwheel illustrates it. And Casarsa is full of Colussis, as attested by the many tombstones in the cemetery carved with that name.

After Vincenzo, who at the age of nineteen emigrated to America, Susanna was the second-born but favored child. The third was Chiarina, a spinster, and, says her family, a Communist from the start: she led a wandering existence in Cirenaica before settling down in San Vito al Tagliamento. Next came Enrichetta, who married a Naldini; Gino, an antiques dealer in Rome; Giannina, the youngest, a lively spinster and great storyteller—an elementary school teacher, she taught Pier Paolo. The legend about her speaks of strong attach-ments to women, even escapades in the 1940s and 1950s with girls on motorcycles among the poplar groves of the plain on both sides of the Tagliamento. Lean and wrinkled, her voice strident, her laugh dry, with dyed hair, and penetrating and suspicious eyes, Giannina is ready to read on your face sins that you haven't committed.

Enrichetta, on the other hand, has a sweet smile: her hair is white, and her figure, which has acquired the comfortable softness of a good wife and mother, exudes a positive sensibility.

Susanna still resembles Giannina. Before getting married, she too

driven to marriage by essentially practical considerations. In this double coercion lay the origins of a resentment, at first latent, then gradually more explicit, that was to mark her relationship with her husband, and lead to his desperation, his search for other women, his quarrels with his wife, his desertions, and his returns to the family.

Over the years, Carlo Alberto "adored" his wife even as he quarreled with her. Increasingly stylish, she whiled away the time with cosmetics, making herself more attractive than ever—probably in order to deny herself to him and keep him ensnared at the same time. An unconscious courtship, but one that made life in the house unbearable.

Carlo Alberto pursued his military career, and the family accompanied him when he was transferred: Bologna, Parma, Belluno, Conegliano, Sacile, Cremona, Scandiano, and again Bologna. Pier Paolo was born at the first stop on this circuit. That summer, Carlo Alberto went on leave, and the family paid a visit to Casarsa.

There was endless disagreement between husband and wife. Susanna's smile may have acted as a challenge to Carlo Alberto. He would desert her from time to time, and then come back. To Susanna, these desertions were deadly insults, but she was also able to find an explanation for them.

Some time later Susanna took her niece Annie, daughter of the Naldinis, into the house. Annie lived with the Pasolinis wherever they went—she studied, and looked after her little cousins. (Guido, the second son, was born in 1925.) Once when Carlo Alberto had been gone from home for a week—they were in Bologna, it may have been 1933 or 1934—Susanna said to Annie, "He has to have women." Did she mean that the two of them no longer had sexual relations?

Husband and wife slept in the same bed. Still, it is conceivable that Susanna refused herself to Carlo Alberto.

Susanna's love was all for her sons—especially for Pier Paolo. It was a love that immediately had something unhealthy about it. Susanna invested every ideal in Pier Paolo, but also a rapture that was essentially erotic in nature. The resentment she nourished toward her husband was, with the growth of their son, obviously enhanced—the boy satisfied every emotional need in the woman's fertile imagination. The matriarchal pattern of the Colussi family was repeated in intensified form within her. Susanna never considered betraying Carlo Alberto with other men, but her imagination betrayed him daily with Pier Paolo. And Pier Paolo reciprocated her passion.

A typewritten half page, found posthumously among his papers (perhaps a statement dictated for some interview), reads:

Whenever I'm asked to say something about my mother, to recall something about her, it is always the same image that comes to my mind.

We are in Sacile, in the spring of 1929 or 1931; my mamma and I are walking along a path in a field somewhat outside the town; we are alone, completely alone.

Around us there are bushes, beginning to bud but still with the look of winter; the trees too are bare, and through the long line of black trunks we can see the blue mountains in the background. But the primroses are already out. The edges of the ditches are covered with them.

This gives me an infinite joy that, even now as I speak of it, overwhelms me. I squeeze my mother's arm tightly (indeed we're walking arm in arm) and bury my cheek in the modest fur coat she's wearing: in that fur coat I smell the odor of spring, a mixture of cold and warmth, of fragrant mud and of flowers still without fragrance, of house and countryside. This odor of my mother's modest fur coat is the odor of my life.

A childhood memory can mingle reality and dream. These lines contain the Proustian transcription of a recurrent love. The warmth of the fur coat, the boy's face burying itself in it, come to stand for an undoubtedly incestuous tension. But Pasolini never drew back from such a risk of his imagination and sensibility. To the last day of his life, he accepted its repercussions, its torments, even its absence.

Another photograph. It may be a street in Casarsa: it is winter, the trees are bare, there is faint sunlight. The child Pier Paolo is wearing a short white fur coat and leggings that cover his shoes. Susanna, her face tilted, smiles at him. Relations between mother and son were always of the most tenderly excruciating kind. In his last years Pier Paolo would place his arm across Susanna's frail shoulders, and Susanna would beam with happiness: there was an interchange of diminutives and pet names.

These lines appear on a sheet of squared notebook paper, written on both sides and signed at the bottom, "Bologna 1939, 10 March, Pier Paolo":

Mamma, you look sad:
it is the monotony of little everyday things
that in sadness bows

your forehead, and in sadness
pinches your lips. And you, mamma,
were born to be a skylark:
to give a little peck with the beak here
and one there,
and then to go fluttering in the sky
without getting too tired;
or else like a little butterfly
to fly here and there
over the meadows,
to forget the lily
and the iris,
in drinking the nectar of the rose!

But don't be sad,
you're more beautiful when caressed by laughter!
Smile, since life,
the dear life you've given me,
gives joys as the meadows give flowers:
when one wilts
another blooms.
If you used to laugh
dandling me in your lap,
now you laugh at me when I take you in my arms
and whirl you around in a waltz!
And aren't you then like the chestnuts,
which in autumn are the last to fade?

One can perhaps detect echoes of Pascoli in these verses, but it hardly matters. More important is the direct evidence of a filial sentiment that, once crystallized, remained forever the same. It is that of a seventeen-year-old boy surely nourished by the "poetry of tradition," who had surely shed "tears . . . over a Cinquecento octave," who had thrilled to "the verse of an anonymous symbolist poet,"[1] but who had also codified a lasting image, impervious to time, of his "artless, eternally young" mother.

This image could have been suggested to the son by the Bovaryism of the mother herself. It is certain that he made of it a shield of sublime virtues for himself, especially in adolescence.

His memory dictated these other lines—the straightforward title is "Un'educazione sentimentale":

Who was I? . . .
. . . I was barely delivered into a world
where the devotion of an adolescent
—good like his mother, improvident
and daring, monstrously shy,
and unaware of any conspiracy of silence
that was not ideal—was a humiliating
sign of scandal, ridiculous
sanctity . . .[2]

Such was his "sentimental education." The "monstrously shy" adolescent appears in another photograph dressed like a little Russian, in Cossack trousers and boots, with a violin under his right arm, the bow in his hand, his left hand on his hip. It is 1936, and the Pasolinis were living in Scandiano, while Pier Paolo attended school in Reggio Emilia. He was studying the violin but gave it up after a few months to devote himself to the piano. (Music was only a brief interlude.)

The shyness is barely suggested in his smile, a smile that spreads across the triangulated cheekbones (similar to Susanna's). Another kind of shyness is to be seen in a photo taken with his father at the Piazzale Michelangelo in Florence—he, the boy, wears knickers and a jacket perhaps too large for him; his hair glistens with brilliantine and droops over his half-closed eyes. It is the same boy of the fifth *ginnasio* form in a class photograph, who looks smaller than his companions, still undeveloped, with a peasant sadness in his eyes that may come from Susanna—herself sad and dreaming over her state of being a "little girl" for life.

In 1960, in the volume *Donne di Roma*, a series of texts to accompany 104 photographs by Sam Wagenaar, Pasolini wrote: "How tiny my mamma is, tiny as a schoolgirl, diligent, scared, but determined to do her duty to the end." Susanna—faithful to "her duty," "to the end," and hardworking, "diligent," "scared," or "sad," because of "the monotony of little everyday things"—is the Susanna who is the victim of her husband and whom the passion of the son intends to save.

The shameful stain on Susanna's purity that Pier Paolo wants to redeem is the one produced by paternal vehemence. Vehemence and violence (which later in life drinking was to transform into misanthropy and paranoia) were qualities of the male who takes advantage and exacts demands.

The story of the marriage between Carlo Alberto and Susanna now quickly becomes converted into the story of how Pier Paolo tolerated or deciphered their union—and all by the unacknowledged, unconscious will of Susanna. One can say that Pier Paolo never permitted his own ego to house the image of his father. As a boy, he did not realize it; later he was completely aware of it.

I have never used a single word
used by my fathers (except to send them to Hell).
Their criminality and their hatred for reason
are pure and simple burdens in my life.
I too have naturally made
a long journey in the womb of my mother, and I arrived
like a barbarian, unintelligible and supplied with every excellence
—of a strange and inadmissible maturity—on this earth.
I was not welcomed with love. I was not looked on with filial eyes.
No one was astounded by my bitter knowledge.
The eyes of fathers were on me . . . But enough of this story.
They're dead, accompanied by my curse, by my indifference,
or my pity . . .[3]

And yet Carlo Alberto was always proud of his son. He could be said to be so in accordance with the petit-bourgeois code, by which one is proud of one's children if they illustrate the code in operation. But one does not love them for what they are. Carlo Alberto loved the fact that his son had succeeded in his studies; he could hardly love—and a crisis occurred when he could no longer ignore it—his homosexuality. He must have detested it, since it represented both a tangible rejection of himself, and converted the companionship between mother and son into a totally mysterious eros. It was the conspicuous—obsessively conspicuous—way by which the son placed under accusation not only his virility but his actual presence and existence.

FATHER AND SON

In an interview with Dacia Maraini, Pasolini offered frank and dispassionate clues to his relations with his father.[4]

"In the first three years of my life he was more important to me than my mother. He was a strong, reassuring presence. A truly affectionate and protective father. Then suddenly, when I was about three, the conflict broke out. Ever since then there was always an antagonistic, dramatic, tragic tension between him and me."

At the age of three, the crisis. Before then, his father had even seemed "cheerful." Subsequently he becomes "violent, possessive, tyrannical." From the age of three on, the tension is "antagonistic, tragic"—father and son are rivals.

The crisis explodes while Susanna is pregnant with Guido. "When my mother was about to give birth, I started to suffer from smarting eyes. My father made me hold still on the kitchen table, opened my eye with his finger, and put collyrium in it. It was from that 'symbolic' moment that I began not to love my father."

Everything is clear. "I remember my mother being pregnant and myself asking, 'Mamma, where do babies come from?' And she, sweetly and gently, replied, 'They come from the mamma's belly.' That was something that of course at the time I didn't want to believe."

Of course, he had to believe it. At least he understood its obscure meaning—and the rivalry with his father knew no bounds.

A report difficult to check: that Pier Paolo had surprised his father and mother in the primal scene, right there in the kitchen. One might induce that it was not by chance that in his memory he identifies the "kitchen table" as the place where his father had painfully inflicted on him the repetition of that scene by pouring collyrium into his eye (*eye* and *collyrium* can easily be read as sexual symbols). What matters, however, is not the possibility of a psychoanalytical interpretation of the facts (from the "smarting eyes" to the administered collyrium)—everything is so transparent as to seem predisposed to such an interpretation. What is important is to understand the whole story as the result of a self-analysis that lasted throughout his life. It is significant that Pier Paolo should have made such a decisive crisis revolve around the birth of his brother, Guido. The mother gives birth to a new son, and the firstborn gives birth to a neurosis.

In this same period, Pier Paolo feels himself physically struck by the bodies of the boys playing in the square in front of the house. He says, "I was attracted by their legs, in fact precisely by the hollow of their knees. I had called this feeling of love Teta-veleta. A few years ago Gianfranco Contini pointed out to me how in Greek *tetis* means sexual organ (whether male or female) and how Teta-veleta would be a 'reminder' of the kind used in archaic languages. I had this same feeling of Teta-veleta for my mother's breast."[5]

During the crisis, his father, from having been loving and protective, turns "antagonistic and tyrannical"—in his son's childish fantasy, he becomes a rapist. And at this point, if the journey toward the mother had been inevitable and unconscious, it was now suddenly a journey being made in broad daylight. The discovery of the Teta-veleta unveiled the truth: "Ever since then my whole life has hinged on [my mother]."

Next year he began to dream of losing her—of running after her up a staircase. He was neurotically upset by the fear that his heart was ceasing to beat in his chest—and this happened for the first time at the age of four, while his father was "in trouble" over debts. "My mother had gone back to being a schoolteacher. In that period I slept in the same bed with her."

At that time he also discovered Susanna's "antifascism," and this gave him something else to hold against his father. The Pasolinis were in Belluno, and the king was visiting the city. The population welcomed him with a certain hostility. Susanna, "who was antifascist and naïvely for the king, shouted alone in the silence 'Long live the king!' I remember this 'Long live the king' very well. But I hadn't realized that the crowd was hostile. I had only noticed the beautiful childish voice of my mother."

On the other hand, he says of his father's political ideas, "My father was a passionate, sensual, disorganized man, and once he had embraced law and order, he was serious about it. He became a fascist nationalist."

Rivalry between father and son. His father wants him to be a literary man, a poet. He had had a brother, likewise named Pier Paolo, who had written poetry and had died at the age of twenty, drowned at sea. "Until the age of sixteen I wanted to be a naval officer. He [his father] said I should be a literary man instead. Later on, of course, his encouragement got thrown back at him."

Why "back at him"? Pasolini's reply, at this point, is to some degree disingenuous: "Because he ascribed an official character to poetry. He didn't think it could be destructive, scandalous. He was thinking of Carducci, of D'Annunzio."

Through poetry and culture, Pier Paolo freed himself from the moral world of his father, and gave voice to that of his mother ("My mother for me was like Socrates. She had and still has a vision of the world that is certainly idealistic and idealized. She truly believes in heroism, in charity, in piety, in generosity. And I absorbed all this in an almost pathological way").

This liberation served to fling in his father's face a completely "scandalous" personal myth: poetry as a vehicle to express against him, and against every face of authority, the truth of being "different," the truth of the relationship with Susanna, the tragic corollary of the childish Teta-veleta, homosexuality.

Finally, the "story of the marriage." "My whole life has been influenced by the scenes my father made in front of my mother. Those scenes produced in me the wish to die."

Susanna, delicate and passive, could appear in those scenes as the victim, the one who succumbed. Carlo Alberto scolded her for trifles, "a misplaced glass, an unwashed towel, too much salt in the food . . . He scolded her for having her head in the clouds. But it wasn't so. The fact is that he was a fascist and she wasn't. The two of them never talked about politics, but my father knew that my mother thought of Mussolini as a *culatta*, i.e., 'rump,' 'big buttocks,' as my grandmother called him, à la Gadda. In any case, to be in the clouds for him meant to be a nonconformist, opposed to the laws of the state, at odds with the views of the authorities."

Thus what was under discussion, in a constant state of crisis, was a notion of authority, an actual scale of values. In this disorder, where there was a clear sense of violence in the marriage tie, the only way out seemed naturally the neurotic "wish to die." The solution through expression was to come later—even though Pier Paolo had begun writing poetry at the age of seven, and failed Italian in fifth grade for writing a composition that was "too poetic."

Tyrannical at home, Carlo Alberto treated his subordinates kindly, and Pasolini explains this discrepancy in behavior by paranoia and drunkenness ("it's typical of paranoiacs, and of men who drink"). In any case, the life of the infantry officer Carlo Alberto Pasolini was not a happy one—it was wracked in Dostoevskian fashion by his passion for his wife ("my father was madly in love with my mother but in a mistaken, passionate, possessive way"). The agony was resolved in wine, in gambling, in a downward drift that the outbreak of the Second World War temporarily interrupted. He left for the front, was a prisoner of war in Kenya, and returned to Italy at the end of 1945.

He was overwhelmed by the drama of Pier Paolo, by the "scandal," and accepted it with grief. It brought him to a kind of insanity. He drank more and more, and at night cried out that his wife did not love him. He died in Rome of cirrhosis of the liver on December 19, 1958.

Pier Paolo spoke of him in a poem, but by a slip that was never corrected he deferred his death for a year, to "a sunny winter day in '59."

The lines, dated January 30, 1963, have been published as an appendix to *Il padre selvaggio* (The Savage Father), the scenario for a projected film that was supposed to have been shot in Africa but never was. (Pasolini writes: "It was the trial of [the film] *La ricotta* for contempt of religion that kept me from filming *Il padre selvaggio*. The pain it caused me—and which I've tried to express in these simple lines of 'E l'Africa?' [And Africa?]—still hurts me.")

The lines include a conversation between Pasolini and the producer Alfredo Bini, a wholly dreamlike conversation in which the factual matters that prevented the realization of the film are contained:

I had spent too much money on needless refinements,
and, what's more, I'd stepped on the toes of innocent bigshots,
them too, in their glorious private lives.
I listened to him. He wasn't exploding, yet:
even his mercenary soldier's throat was a boy's throat,
and even there muffled tears were mingled with the rebuke . . .

The face of his producer friend, in his anger, seems to swell "with hysteria," to become red "like a prepuce of blood"—and to split in two:

. . . that other one there, who by osmosis
had emerged from Bini's ribs, was my father.
The father not mentioned, not remembered
since December of '59, the year he died.
Now there he was, an almost benevolent master:
but immediately he turned back into my contemporary from Gorizia,
red-haired, hands in his pockets,
heavy as a paratrooper after mess-hall . . .

The metamorphosis does not stop. Like Banquo's ghost, the father reappears, taking possession again, "with the gray skin of the drunk and dying," of Bini's "red" features. The latter no longer needs to speak and explain why the film cannot be shot. The reasons for the condemnations, the reasons for the contempt charges . . .

Ah, father by now not mine, father who is nothing but father,
coming and going in dreams,

at will,
like a wild boar hung on a hook, gray with wine and death
coming forth to say terrible things,
to re-establish old truths,
with the pleasure of one who has experienced them,
dying in the cheap old conjugal bed,
vomiting blood from your guts on the sheets,
being transported for a night and a day
in a coffin to inhospitable Friuli
on a sunny winter day in '59!
The world is the reality you always paternally wanted . . .

So the conflict between father and son did not cease. Though dead, the father returns to be embodied in forms of authoritarianism that prefigure "reasons of force majeure," those repressive forms of life (Pasolini labeled them as "bourgeois") that prevent the truth from being uttered. And this truth is the truth of the body, and thus of the soul. But the body that speaks is the one that has suffered violation and it demands words that count as cursing, the cursing that liberates all the vital energies—the cursing of "true" religion.

The father is the one who tyrannically tries—in his hysteria he has even become "a prepuce of blood"—"to re-establish old truths." They are discredited truths, to be rejected, discarded: truths that history has turned or is about to turn into lies. Life is elsewhere.

Thus in that event, however it may actually have taken place— which Pasolini's imagination recounts as a *smarting of the eyes* and *his father's violence in treating him for it with collyrium on the kitchen table*—in that event lay the nucleus, the germ, of the poet's creative neurosis. From it emerged the need for a gesture that would sublimate his violent response to that violence. At that point the vocation of Pier Paolo Pasolini was fixed, as a need to give voice to the unfulfilled and implacable aspect of the paternal "rape."

Paul Valéry says in "Le cimetière marin": ". . . *rendre la lumière suppose d'ombre une morne moitié.*"

What the shadow that had suddenly settled on existence had hidden would have to be brought to light—to the light of the word, to the light of expression. Thus only a life burnt out and reduced to ashes would be able to be absolved, pardoned in another life.

The father, by his "tyrannical" and "violent" gesture (and it was a gesture of love, since he wished to cure his son of an ailment), was transformed into a *stepfather*: the tragedy that explodes in the son is that of an emotional compensation that no longer occurs. The appearance of the mother at this point, though central and decisive, though she absorbs *all of life* into herself, is a surrogate appearance, a substitute one. The mother is an avenging figure, a symbol of revenge. The real loss is that of the father—and it is a fatal one. (Every time father and mother quarrel, the son feels himself irresistibly drawn by death.)

Out of the suffering of this *disappearance*, the poet will be "called," but the child will be marked forever, *tal cour di un frut*.

Father transformed into stepfather; son transformed into stepson. His destiny is that of Orestes, or Hamlet. In the struggle against authority, which the *stepfather* physically represents, the personal motive will be symbolized by the political one ("something is rotten in the state of Denmark"), and vice versa.

The public aspect of Pasolini's poetry will take the form of a struggle against all repressive and authoritarian conventions—conventions that are contained within the father's "old truths."

But it is significant that these "old truths," almost dismissed, paper flaking away in ashes, should turn out to be harmless in dreams. In *Pilade* (Pylades; posthumous version), we read:

> *In no other way does one love better than in dreams:*
> thus we will love our unforgettable fathers
> by dreaming of them. And we'll tell each other our dreams . . .[6]

And again, also from the lips of Orestes:

> I'll go to pray at the tomb of my poor father.
> I haven't forgotten him, *he is now in my dreams,*
> and in dreams he speaks to me with words of grace . . .[7]

Was Pasolini able to say that his father, dead at last, spoke to him "with words of grace"? Probably yes. By now "the terrible, / bloody, pure, desperate love" (still from *Pilade*), born of hatred, had been revealed for what it was.

We might ask ourselves: what kind of relationship would Pasolini have liked to have had with his father?

The answer is suggested by another of the tragedies written as in a rapture during the spring of 1966—*Affabulazione* (Affabulation). That spring, as we will see, Pasolini was convalescing—a violent hemorrhage of a gastric ulcer had kept him in bed for a little over a month. (Might we interpret this convalescence as a second birth? The illness had been a serious one, for a few days his condition had been acute—one after another, he wrote the first drafts of six tragedies; and I do not think it was by chance that the subject of the father-son relationship returns repeatedly to the fore in them.)

In *Affabulazione* it is a father in crisis who wishes spasmodically to make his relations with his son real, to overcome his hatred and rejection. He decides to offer him his own nakedness, his own sex organ "useless . . . as in masturbation," "when the boy feels in his grasp a father's sex, / but devoid of the privilege and the duty to fertilize, / like a great tree without shade."

What Pasolini asked of his father was to be that *great tree without shade*: a father without charisma, endowed with a greater charisma, the kind that is usually assigned to divinity. A father to whom sex does not pertain. A father who does not fertilize materially, but fertilizes in the spirit.

At this point, the real father, the *stepfather*, was transformed into a possible father, into an ideal. And the son's "terrible, bloody, pure love" found a solution—if only a literary one.

CHAPTER 2

THE TIME OF THE
ANALOGICAL

CHILDHOOD, ADOLESCENCE, GUIDO

At the nursery school in Belluno, the nuns had the children dig a hole in the garden: they said there was a treasure at the bottom. Pier Paolo dug for several days until he grew tired of it. In his disappointment, he refused to go back to the school—and he had his way. He was a capricious, stubborn, naïve, credulous, easily enthusiastic child, as he himself says. But he was also shy and awkward. He was intoxicated by the pattern of colors in the geographical atlas, and made marvelous imaginary journeys over it. He liked to listen to stories and fairy tales, and Susanna told them.

In first grade in Conegliano he was one of the best in the class. At the school they gave prizes to the best pupils, and he won a prize, a medal with a green ribbon. He went home and showed it to his mother. He had a fretful need for scholastic achievement. The child was an enthusiast for study and knowledge, as Susanna wanted him to be. But he also applied himself very seriously and carefully—in this too he was stubborn.

He confesses to having begun to tell "lies." Susanna tells him not to go out in the street to play, and he goes—but keeps silent about it. He confesses that in this way he enjoyed musing on his own lies.

He attended second grade in Casarsa. It was the moment when he "discovered" Friuli, his mother's soil. For the first time he was living in a house of "his own," and no longer had the temporary feeling that his father's military billets must have given him.

Uncles, aunts, grandmother, cousins. He fell in love with his cousin Franca. Grandfather Colussi died that year, and the family distillery vanished, leaving no trace.

Third grade is Sacile. This was when he wrote his first poems. They are "exquisite" poems, already Petrarchian, with complicated meters. Pier Paolo used to say that he had kept a whole chest full of juvenile writings. Then fourth grade in Idria, where the teacher took a dislike to him—he suffered from this. He confesses that at this time he had become "somewhat of a smart aleck," something that threatened to turn others against him.

He read. He read books of adventure, the cowboy Morning Star, Salgari—marvelous stories. He would have to reach the age of fourteen before discovering other reading matter, and then it was *Macbeth* that was to open a completely different world to him. At that point his passion for books was to be born, second-hand books bought at the stalls of the Portici della Morte in Bologna.

For fifth grade, he was back in Sacile. His third-grade classmates had grown, and he found it harder to get along with them. He felt excluded and was ill at ease. He failed his fifth-grade Italian exam. It was a blow—he had become confident of always succeeding in written composition.

In October he passed the exam, and began to attend the *ginnasio* in Conegliano. He took the train from Sacile to Conegliano. He left home very early and when he arrived at school there was no one around. He was alone with his books and his lunch-time sandwich wrapped in paper.

The rest of the lower *ginnasio* he spent in Cremona. There his childhood ended—he was twelve. "The summer of '34 began, a period of my life ended, I concluded one experience and was ready to start another. Those days preceding the summer of '34 were among the best and most glorious of my life" (this from the interview with Dacia Maraini). Pasolini says he mourned childhood, the "heroic period of life," "desperately" for thirty years. It may have been his arrival in Rome that erased it from his imagination.

From Cremona the family moved to Scandiano, and for a year Pier Paolo attended school in Reggio Emilia. Then, from 1936 on, he went to secondary school and the university of Bologna, where the Pasolinis had finally returned. The timid boy who entered secondary school was fond of sports. In Cremona he had taken fencing lessons. The year in Scandiano had been the year of music. It was in Bologna that he sank his roots in literature.

Meanwhile he was a Catholic, and as with many Italian children, his religiosity was tinged with superstition. He took communion if his cousin Annie urged him, or if his school work was too hard. In his pocket he kept a blunt-pointed pen nib, and when he was called on to recite, he squeezed it in his fist. It was his good-luck charm. He lost this ritualistic religiosity of the Italians around the age of fourteen. His encounter with literature, with Shakespeare's *Macbeth* to be precise, was a decisive factor.

In the meantime he was drawing family portraits and painting small landscapes. He drew his mother making up her face. Susanna's passion for clothes and cosmetics could hardly fail to strike him.

But beside him there was Guido.

Guido had been born in Belluno. He was an exuberant child, with the same exuberance as his father. He was a strong-limbed boy, on the whole smaller than Pier Paolo. There was a vague resemblance between them: the same lips, the same nose, but Guido's eyes were not as widely spaced as Pier Paolo's. There is a photograph of the two brothers together in a little pedal-driven automobile. Guido's hair is lighter, but the soft, frowning look is shared by both.

But Guido "was a normal boy" (Pier Paolo's words in the Maraini interview). For example, he suffered from the quarrels between mother and father, "but he didn't make a tragedy of it." He admired Pier Paolo because he was good in school, because he was bigger, and because he was stronger. But he also loved him very much. The two brothers were friends, though they often quarreled as brothers do.

Guido's secret suffering was rooted in Susanna's ardent passion for Pier Paolo. The younger son tried to do his best in school, but he did not succeed in being a good student like Pier Paolo. He failed to achieve high marks every year at promotion time. It happened that a Latin translation by Pier Paolo—at the Liceo Galvani in Bologna— had been circulated in the classrooms because of its excellence of syntax and form, worked out with such detail as to make it an example for emulation. Such glories were not for Guido. The boy had to suppose that the reasons that moved Susanna to prefer Pier Paolo were essentially scholastic. And so he gave his all. He derived considerable frustration from the effort. But he was saved by his vital nature, an innate generosity. He loved hunting, and spent his whole allowance on trap shooting.

A photograph shows him in short pants, leaning against the trunk of an oak, rifle in hand, intent on his aim. He is almost a child: there is an air about him more adolescent than his years. Likewise in two photographs from 1943: one in March, jacket and pants a little wide and shabby—a garden in Casarsa, at the back of the house, a hoe. Another in summer, short pants, undershirt, socks falling down around the heavy shoes, a green branch in his left hand, a six-shooter in his right: he has wavy hair, a proud look in his eyes.

A family episode contains a hint of Guido's suffering, of the secret frustration that afflicted him. It was 1943. Guido, Pier Paolo, and Susanna were living in Casarsa. Something important had happened to Guido, and Susanna dismissed it. Guido had a fit of despair and weeping, to the point of throwing himself on the floor. It was a dramatic scene.

Pier Paolo felt a veiled sense of remorse for this situation. The privileged position he enjoyed with his mother, when he compared himself with his brother, made him uneasy. In Bologna, a few years before, Guido had defended him furiously. Pier Paolo had been insulted, Guido had heard what was said of him, and a violent fistfight between boys had ensued. Guido's nose was broken. Pier Paolo was solicitous with care and affection. Guido said he would never have thought that his brother loved him "so much."

GROUPS OF FRIENDS

It was easy to love Pier Paolo. With the years his magnetism increased, both in the family and at school.

On the back of the class photograph for the second year of secondary school (the students are all photographed wearing straw boaters cocked to one side on their heads), one can read such sentiments as these: "To the kid with the sad smile of a man tired of life." "May you excel in music as you excel in the art of literature." "O chaste and puritan Pasolini." "When I think of Pier Paolo I think of a brave fool filled with charity for everything and everyone." Or else: "You have two demons in you: beware of the third." And again: "To the mighty halfback."

Pier Paolo was good in his studies, but he also went in strenuously for sports, for soccer, first as a halfback, later as a forward. He was studious and athletic, but a "puritan." And the detachment he displayed in matters of sex was another reason for a subtle ascendancy over his companions.

He had, from high school on—as Franco Farolfi has written[1]—a Socratic influence over his friends. He was naturally their "teacher," suggesting to them extracurricular reading: *The Pickwick Papers*, *Taras Bulba*, Dostoevsky. Or else he guided them to the cinema, to the discovery of John Ford, or won them over by his athletic spirit. It seems that he never backed down from any challenge, even if the challenger were stronger or taller than himself.

To Farolfi, "His life was a game and a friend would accept spontaneously his authority and initiative, which were born of fantastic strength in perpetual motion." Besides Farolfi, Ermes Parini, whom Pier Paolo jokingly called Paria ("pariah"), was a close friend at the *liceo*. Parini died in the Russian campaign, for which he had enlisted as a volunteer, and Ermes was the partisan name that Guido Pasolini took in his memory. Pier Paolo's school rival was Agostino Bignardi, future secretary of the Italian Liberal Party. The race was close, neck and neck. Pasolini did not like to lose.

Once the *liceo* was over, the circle of friends became more exclusively literary. It included Francesco Leonetti, Roberto Roversi, Fabio Mauri (some years younger, but already gifted with keen intuition), his sister Silvana, Luciano Serra, Fabio Luca Cavazza, Mario Ricci, Sergio Telmon, Achille Ardigò, and Giovanna Bemporad. The young people took camping and bicycle trips; in winter they skied in the mountains. Pier Paolo was a good skier.

There are photographs from a bicycle race through Emilia and the Romagna in the summer of 1939: at Gradara, Ravenna, Riccione. The *liceo* is barely over.

These small groups of friends that had formed at school came together in response to a persistent need for culture and knowledge. Their relations with fascism were such as can be imagined. The social milieu to which these students belonged was naturally fascist. Precisely, however, because of the cultural interests they were nourishing, they began to feel suspicious and skeptical about the regime. They took part in the *littoriali*, the sporting and cultural events staged by the party, but in those surroundings they kept guard over and clarified feelings and ideas that were acting to drive them away.

A letter to Franco Farolfi from 1941 is a late but direct testimony on this state of things. Pasolini writes: "Cultural *prelittoriali*. I took part in the *prelittoriali* on Stylistic Criticism, coming out first, and praised by such eminent critics as Bertocchi, Guidi, Corazza, etc. I should have gone to San Remo to take part in the *Littoriali*, but they've been suspended this year, to my great rage and envy. Best of all: soccer tournament between the Faculties. I was captain of the arts team."[2]

Pier Paolo was thus enrolled in the Arts and Letters faculty. The shades of Carducci and De Bartholomaeis still wandered through the lecture halls of the University of Bologna. Roberto Longhi,* bursting with energy, with methodological and stylistic innovations (both in his relations with students and in his writing), was the center of attention. Carlo Calcaterra held the chair in the History of Italian Literature—he taught the classics, from Tasso to Alfieri, in a pedestrian manner. Pier Paolo resisted.

"I'm now caught up in the whirl of a new occupation, the exercise of Italian: Tasso's *Rime* after [the insane asylum of] Sant'Anna: the bibliography is immense, I've now put in altogether four hours of work in the library, just taking notes and seeing what books there are on this subject. This is the classic university assignment, carried out with a pure sense of rhetoric and erudition, which I abhor and, in an act of courage, intend to demolish to Prof. Calcaterra's very face when I deliver my report. What do I, worshiping Cézanne, hearing Ungaretti loud and clear, cultivating Freud, care about these thousands of yellowed and aphonic lines of minor Tasso? I often go to play basketball: I'm no good at it, but I enjoy it a lot. Sports are really my pure, constant, and spontaneous consolation."[3]

This excerpt from a 1940 letter to Farolfi already says everything about Pasolini's character and cultural interests. The tenacity in carrying to completion a job undertaken; the rejection of methods that appeared to lead away from more pressing aims; the "act of courage" in exposing one's own truth, well aware that it does not arise from the occasion but from convictions that no one can make light of; the contrast between knowledge and erudition; the deep passion, almost in a need to adjust to natural inner rhythms, for athletics; finally, the use of the adjective "pure" to indicate the inestimable value of life, its uncontaminated source.

Every summer, from July to September, the Pasolini boys went to Casarsa. From there Pier Paolo sent letters, poems, confessions. He speaks of girls.

---

* Roberto Longhi (1890–1970), a leading Italian art historian.—Tr.

Yes, there are many girls in these letters (to Farolfi, to Serra): girls going by on bicycles and calling out a greeting. There are a few snatched kisses. There is the story of a certain "Nerina, a typist; with an unusual head of natural blond hair; slender; from a good family." Pier Paolo writes: "I've had a little bit of a crush on her. Many evenings I've walked her home from her office. I've enjoyed the sweetest promises of love. But now (see how I'm governed by common selfishness and laziness!) I've given her up because of her impossible office schedule, which had forced me to miss basketball, the soldiers' club, and study. Maybe she'll get a new job and so change her schedule: then I'll find some excuse to start up with her again" (letter to Farolfi, 1941).

These girls are a sort of screen within friendship, the means by which to stay close to his friends. For what chiefly interests Pier Paolo is "friendship." In July 1941 he writes to Serra: "Our friendship lies outside literature, otherwise it wouldn't be friendship: the literature we do together exists insofar as there exists a friendship that unites us."[4]

If, in his letters, he underscores every event with a marked disappointment in life ("Casarsa has disappointed me, but then everything disappoints me while it's happening, and when it's over I lament it: now everything that the countryside can give me I can have: peace and quiet, girls, mental concentration, fields, idleness, drink, and in reality all this is in my possession, but it's sporadic, diluted by a stream of arid and empty hours."—to Farolfi, 1940), this feeling is then projected against thoughts derived from a book (Hölderlin, Kleist), a film, a Beethoven symphony heard on the radio, or else from a hike in the mountains or a swim in the river.

From San Vito di Cadore, on May 31, 1941, he sends Luciano Serra an account of a solitary excursion to the Forcella Grande pass: "In 2 hours I did what they assure me should have taken 3½: I mean walking or marching."

He is happy in his "silence," his "solitude"—once he is on the heights, once he has rested, and the air has turned gray, the sun having disappeared in the clouds, he is frightened and comes running back for dear life. "I had had the same sensation as a child, when I was left all alone in the green waters of the Tagliamento, while all around me it was absolutely deserted, and it seemed to me that my feet were being seized by the fierce and silent god of those whirlpools. Naked and dripping, I dashed out of the water, with barely restrained, and happy, cries."[5]

Youth, its ardent and conflicting emotions—everything is at its height. And there is also that denial of existence that Leopardi was able to divine with such perspicacity in the adolescent mind—the point at which "the youth" has not yet "laid aside his tenderness toward himself," has not yet "grown accustomed and hardened to setbacks," and is therefore ready to turn all his vital energy "to procuring unhappiness for himself."[6] This is the completion of the embryonic state: the whole potential of a character ready to develop.

Again to Luciano Serra, on July 22, 1943: "Peace and quiet have taken on the face of a girl from Valvasone, fat and good-looking, somewhere between a magnolia blossom and an apple. I kiss her and squeeze the breath out of her every evening, and all she asks of me in return is to keep her happy. These are nice evenings, Luciano."

A little later in the same letter: "I'd like to be in the Tagliamento and to hurl my gestures one after another into the shining hollow of the landscape. The Tagliamento is very wide here. A huge torrent, rocky, white as a skeleton."

He tells of arriving there the day before by bicycle with a friend named Bruno. There were some "foreign soldiers": they watched with curiosity the two boys diving "into that cold and for them mysterious water." Then a sudden storm came up—"it was a storm as livid as an erect penis. We fled—dressing in a hurry—but the wind stopped us in the middle of the bridge. The Tagliamento had disappeared, as in the midst of the fog." There is a whirlwind: the sky goes black, then yellow, finally completely white and calm. In the sudden quiet, "three or four gypsy wagons" appear—"like us, they were fleeing the storm, which by now was roaring, with a few shudders of raindrops, toward Codroipo. Inside a celestial-blue wagon a gypsy boy played continuously on a trumpet."[7]

This is an enameled piece of prose, whose style of representation shows it to have been subtly worked up. Pasolini had already read Sandro Penna, Attilio Bertolucci, and Alfonso Gatto, and one can well understand how their writings would have appealed to him. But the gypsy boy playing his trumpet in the celestial wagon, the storm cloud "livid as an erect penis," indicate in retrospect a specific imaginative symbolism. It is not unthinkable that the girls of whom Pier Paolo wrote were not actually girls.

His friends were unaware of his homosexuality, though signs of it must surely have appeared. If the boys organized amateur theatricals and Pier Paolo sometimes struck a languid pose, this was not interpreted as anything more than a game.

It seems that in their high-school days Agostino Bignardi had told Pier Paolo about the trial of Oscar Wilde. The story upset him. He was upset by the idea that what could occur naturally on the stones of the Tagliamento could actually lead to a trial.

Adolescent boys comparing their genitals and indulging in mutual masturbation are facts of life in the country, a ritual that seeks out the quiet backwaters of rivers and streams. These are things that can be experienced innocently, or with retrospective feelings of guilt, or they can be stratified and crystallized in the unconscious in such a way as to build one's whole sensibility on them.

Swimming in the Tagliamento and taking shelter among the willows along its banks, the open and "pure" relations with boys from the surrounding area, the constitution of a universe in which natural and biological rhythms were complied with beyond any moral barrier —all this may have consolidated in Pasolini his instinctive vision, replete with human suffering, of the world, the vision already woven of longing and nostalgia, that suffuses *Poesie a Casarsa*.

His homosexuality is still involved with abstractions or lyrical symbols. In a letter to Farolfi in 1940, Pasolini writes, with poeticizing touches that have little in common with the writer he was to become:

> ... Let us go, my tender flock:
> the mountain is wide, damp the woods.
> I will make you my slaves, and the most handsome
> (which among you?), hair shining,
> will stand upright beside my cup.
> It is spring. I am the prince. Let us go.

And again:

> Impuberal virgins, and do not dare to look me in the face:
> the immodest secret of my adult life is bashful!
> I will tell you, to the sound of my flute,
> of the dark violence, of the nocturnal naked escapades just passed.

Another passage from a letter to Farolfi in the next year, 1941, betrays symptoms of an ego that is shedding its skin, an ego that is drawing back in suspicion from itself, in the need to reach an age of adult emotions, under the lengthening shadows of obscure demands: "To break the chains that bind me to the past by an act of pure will? That's what I'm trying to do. I want to kill a hypersensitive and sick adolescent who is also trying to pollute my life as a man, and is already almost moribund, but I will be cruel to him, even though at bottom I love him, because he has been my life up until the beginnings of today."[8]

Transparent words. Even more transparent when one ponders the decided schism that the boy is aware of in himself. That he is able to speak of his other self in the third person leaves no doubts. (It almost suggests a trace or pattern of schizophrenia.)

Thus Pier Paolo, certainly unwittingly, was sending his friends appeals for help, simulated confessions. Literature has the gift of suggesting what is most disagreeable to the mind—here it is a question of scarcely veiled confessions, of verses whose only interest is psychological.

On the other hand, it was literature that held the circle of young friends in Bologna together, the burning desire to write, to "make a name for oneself."

In 1941 there was an incident in Bologna. Pier Paolo gave some candy to a little neighbor boy. The boy's father accused him of pederasty. Pier Paolo swore he had no perverse intentions. What may have aroused suspicion was his extremely soft manner, his attitude of loving kindness.

LITERATURE

Pasolini wrote his first poem at the age of seven, in Sacile. His mother had shown him "how poetry can be actually written, and not just read in school."[9]

Here, too, Susanna was the central figure. She showed Pier Paolo a sonnet, written by herself, the theme of which was her love for him—and the poem ended, heaven knows by what sequence of rhymes, with these words: *"di bene te ne voglio un sacco"* ("of love for you I've lots").

The little boy, stimulated by the example, and even more—one might say—by his mother's love, wrote his first poem a few days later. He confesses to having used the words *"rosignolo"* and *"verzura"**— he had not, of course, read Petrarch. "I don't know where I had learned the classicistic code for selecting choice words."[10]

* More "literary" forms of *usignolo* (nightingale) and *verdura* (greenery). —Tr.

Adolescence brought him to the epic poem, the verse drama, to his natural familiarity with Foscolo, Leopardi, Carducci, Pascoli, and D'Annunzio. The cultivation of literature took, one can say, its normal course.

But now we come to Bologna. It is the academic year 1938–1939— at the Liceo Galvani, a substitute teacher of art history reads aloud in class a poem by Rimbaud. He was the poet Antonio Rinaldi (Pier Paolo always remained his devoted reader, and found in his verses, somewhat peripheral to the hermetic climate by which they had been nourished, those anomalies that fired his critical inspiration). *Macbeth* and Rimbaud were his early discoveries. Then it was the turn of contemporary Italian poets. The decisive reading was Tommaseo's *Canti del popolo greco*. And with this we are already in 1943.

But it is necessary to go back to June 22, 1942, the day on which four students in the Faculty of Arts and Letters—Pasolini, Leonetti, Roversi, and Serra—founded in Bologna a magazine with the name *Eredi*. "Heirs" of what? Of that tradition of modernism represented by the names of Ungaretti, Montale, Cardarelli, Luzi, Gatto, Sereni, Sinisgalli, Bertolucci, Betocchi, Penna, De Libero.

Serra[11] tells how the four boys cultivated a burning desire to be poets. They spent their evenings in long animated discussions, eating chestnut cake and drinking Sardinian wine. Pasolini had a passion for the theater and arranged performances: Synge's *Playboy of the Western World* and the one-act plays of Thornton Wilder. The boys had been much impressed by the performance of *Our Town* with Elsa Merlini and Renato Cialente—a production that was remembered even in the postwar period as exemplary for a theater free of the academic.

Literary communion was interrupted in the summer, but exchanges of letters helped to keep it alive.

Pier Paolo was jealous of his friends. In a letter to Serra, on August 29, 1941: "Remember, all of you, *Eredi*, our days together; for your friendship, I've sacrificed many others, there are many acquaintances that I haven't followed up, for fear of getting sidetracked."

Pure youthful terrorism; but for him friendship was everything, it drew forth the deepest sentiments. At the "poetry" meetings called by the friends in Bologna, Fabio Mauri, for example, was sometimes absent because he preferred to go out with girls. Pier Paolo would scold him on those occasions: "If girls can take the place of poetry, it means poetry isn't much loved."

It is clear that the choice did not lie in the terms suggested by Pasolini. In him something else was speaking: the ideal of the small, Socratic group, the ideal of a community of faith in which eros, at the moment when it is obliterated, becomes stronger and involves everything, absorbs everything.

After *Eredi* came *Il Setaccio* (The Sieve).[12] *Il Setaccio* was conceived by a painter named Italo Cinti—all these youngsters had intellectual energies to squander—and it was the magazine of the Gioventù Italiana Littoriale of Bologna. They were still bound together by the fasces; it had that simple associative function, antifascism having not yet become clear in their minds. This was in 1942, and the first half of 1943. Art, literature, music, poetry, theater, cinema, even politics were the subjects put through the "sieve." Fabio Mauri wrote about de Chirico; Cavazza about cinema (he gave a negative review of the film version of *Malombra*, directed by Mario Soldati); Giovanni Mascio appraised the work of film-makers such as Duvivier; the names of Lang, Pabst, Murnau appeared.

Il Setaccio published translations from Sappho, Goethe, and Hölderlin (the translator was Giovanna Bemporad, who for racial reasons signed herself Giovanna Bembo), from Machado (a great passion of Pasolini's), and from Baudelaire.

Ardigò discussed aesthetics; Luigi Vecchi, who was Catholic, expounded pauperistic and evangelical ideas that came together in a vague "external" Marxism. Pasolini published Friulian verses and Italian verse dialogues that anticipate the atmosphere of *L'usignolo della Chiesa Cattolica* (The Nightingale of the Catholic Church). But he was also writing literary criticism—on Ungaretti, on Luzi, on Luciano Anceschi's anthology *Lirici nuovi*. He seems driven by a need for "human communication"—in Ungaretti he isolates "an illogicality of dream," "a rhythm of pure and simple teaching."

Better defined, albeit in its adolescent acerbity, appears a reflection on the role of the intellectual and writer in that moment of war and moral crisis. Pasolini wrote about this in "I giovani e l'attesa" ("Young People and Expectation," November 1942); in "Ragionamento sul dolore civile" ("On Civilian Suffering," December 1942); in "Cultura italiana e cultura europea a Weimar" ("Italian Culture and European Culture in Weimar," January 1943—Pier Paolo had attended the congress organized by Nazi Germany in the autumn of 1942; Vittorini was among the other Italians who went); and in "Ultimo discorso sugli intellettuali" ("Final Discourse on the Intellectuals," March 1943).

From "I giovani e l'attesa": "We feel that our further search will have to be carried out in solitude: friends or groups of friends will never cease to exist, because human sympathy and reciprocity of feelings will never be lacking, but we consider the period of reviews, of trends, in short of 'isms,' to be not only over but very remote . . . As we are not fascists, and if, without changing the meaning of the word, we can call ourselves Italians, so we do not want to call ourselves, generically, either moderns or traditionalists, if modernity or tradition do not signify anything but living acceptance of real life."

In "Ragionamento sul dolore civile," Pasolini explains how much his words are framed by the terror of war and its struggle, but he discards all rhetoric and insists on the virtue of solitude ("this poetic solitude, this ivory tower, exists, but it is no sin. It is no sin because from this desert of ours—where we are alone—we do not go astray, dispersed by an unseemly, rhetorical pity toward the men around us, but rather we raise them, *as part of our very nature*, to a love that from being egotistical—without betraying itself, but rather remaining steadfast in the tradition of its sole existence—becomes civilized").

In the article on the trip to Weimar, the antirhetorical ideal becomes precise: "Tradition is not an obligation, a road, and not even a sentiment or a love: one must by now understand this term in an antitraditional sense, that is, of continuous and infinite transformation, i.e., antitradition, traversed by an immutable line, which is similar to historicity for history. It is therefore completely antihistorical, that official tradition which is now being glorified by a false propaganda in all nations as the only resolution for the present European political and social condition."

These statements should serve to indicate how at that moment Pasolini was cultivating a personal nonfascism of his own. In retrospect he testified[13] that he was no longer a "natural" fascist from the day on which he heard Rimbaud's poem read by Rinaldi. But he was not a militant antifascist. Giovanna Bemporad, Jewish and therefore persecuted, was the first to speak to him of a political opposition to the regime.

Bemporad, as a very young girl, was a sort of literary prodigy. Already known for her translations from Greek and German, her precocious literary culture and singular life-style had made her a kind of "hippie" before the fact: ragged and eccentric clothes, absent-minded disorder, and quite anomalous behavior in a girl not yet twenty. Pier Paolo sought her out—she was attending the Liceo Galvani in Bologna—and invited her to contribute to *Il Setaccio*.

The two became friends, and even met frequently at her home in Bologna—a huge room, with a vast table overflowing with books. On one of these occasions Giovanna asked Pier Paolo, "Are you a fascist?" And she spoke to him of antifascism and of the tragic liabilities of the regime.

At the *liceo* there had been no lack of teachers who had made non-conformist statements, but it was probably the relationship or confrontation with his peers that worked to accentuate in Pasolini a tendency, and carry to conclusion a process of clarification that had already been begun by reading and reflection.

It was not by chance that Pasolini, in a letter, had advised Farolfi to read Enzo Paci's book *L'esistenzialismo*. Nor was it by chance that the book was able to contribute to a moral growth that included a negative judgment on the political regime of the country. Existentialist thought succeeded in exposing the "bitter side" of living, beyond fascist vitalism and the glorification of triumph. Thus, in "Ultimo discorso sugli intellettuali," Pasolini wrote: "Intellectuals can give substance to their faith in countless other ways than by propaganda (or, worse, silence) . . . of them, as of notaries or stonemasons, it is rightful to demand that they show their faith in no other way than by intensifying the work that lies within their competence."

Intellectual work is thus first of all a "trade," whose ethical value resides in the arduous and difficult fidelity to oneself. This is Pasolini's true commitment, his morality.

The submission of literature to "propaganda" and to politics seemed treason at that moment to Pasolini.

This is Pasolini's nonfascism of those years. It is made clear in the long "private" conclusion, set off by parentheses, to the same article of March 1943:

My mother and I are sitting in the room that sheltered first her child-hood, and then mine. And here inside this room, from the darkness of the night we hear a voice echoing: it is a boy who pauses before the door of our house and calls to a friend. And for once that cry does not arouse in me nostalgia for the past, for myself as a boy, or vague trembling, but recalls me with new sorrow to the moments we are living. For an instant it brings more vividly before my eyes the faces of my father and my dearest friend, whom the war has taken from me. It is two years since

I have seen the first. Of the second I know nothing, and I spend my saddest hours imagining him in Russia, wounded, missing, a prisoner. . . . And here before me I have the sorrowful gaze of my mother; and I would like to express all this, but it is not possible: it is too vivid, violent, painful.

But what else can one read in these words? The farewell to childhood and its myths. The conquest of the "bitter side" of existence has not been simple.

In 1941 Carlo Alberto Pasolini had been sent by the army to East Africa. There he was to be taken prisoner by the British. Pier Paolo writes to Farolfi: "My father left the day before yesterday for Rome, from where he will proceed to A.O.I. [Italian East Africa]: I won't describe to you, since you can well imagine it, the state of affairs that has descended on us."[14]

In the same year Ermes Parini left for Russia. Again in a letter to Farolfi: "Departure of Paria and Melli. Very sad hours with no cause for hope: I feel depressed and with no wish to do anything, very undecided whether or not to volunteer and go myself."[15]

The following summer he was in cadet corporal training, for paramilitary exercises that took him to Porretta in July. He wrote to Serra: "I am sick and tired of living: this is one of those vague moments when poetry comes back like a distant memory, it is the only sense present and certainly it is that of one's own human solitude. . . . Today my mother came to see me, and she left a little while ago. Thinking of her I feel a sorrowful pang of love; she loves me too much, and I her. I am a poet because of her. The other day she wrote me a letter that brought a burst of sobs to my throat."[16]

Fascism fell on July 25, 1943. Serra, at the officers' training school in Caserta, writes of some of his doubts, doubts he shares with others. Serra speaks of guerrilla warfare, and Pier Paolo replies: "What a lot of speeches you make about 'guerrillas' and 'guerrilla wars': I don't know whether to laugh or get angry. If you care so little about your own blood, save it for now, and if need be shed it for something better than a guerrilla war with those worthy Croats. Italy will have need of blood, and how: but it is my soil that should get bathed. It has need of a flow of blood—or of tears—to destroy a whole century of monarchist, liberal, fascist, and neoliberal mistakes. Italy needs to remake itself completely, from the bottom up, and for this it has an extreme need of us, who, with all the fearful lack of education of all ex-fascist youth, are a fairly well-prepared minority. . . . Even for my particular and very private poetic experience, these days are immensely important. Freedom is a new horizon, which I daydreamed about, yes wished for, but that now, in its very unripe appearance, reveals such unexpected and moving aspects that I feel as though I've become a boy again."[17]

His nonfascism of a few months before had sketched in Pasolini the idea of renewal. Italy was soon to be bathed in blood and tears, but he divined that the irreparable suffering would lead to a great change. The letter to Serra also states: "I have felt something new developing and asserting itself in me, with unexpected significance: the political man that fascism had unlawfully smothered, without my having been aware of it."

In the winter of 1942–1943 Susanna decided to evacuate to Casarsa because of the bombings that were striking all large Italian cities. Pier Paolo was thinking of taking his degree with Roberto Longhi in art history, with a thesis on the Baroque. Meanwhile he published *Poesie a Casarsa*.

POESIE A CASARSA

As Attilio Bertolucci remembers it, a volume of Provençal lyrics, published by Zanichelli, with good Italian translations printed in italics at the bottom of the page, circulated in the university classrooms on Via Zamboni in Bologna as study material for students of Romance philology. It may well have acted as a model for Pier Paolo in composing, typographically as well, his own first book.

Poesie a Casarsa saw the light of day on July 14, 1942. It was printed in Bologna by the Libreria Antiquaria Mario Landi. In the same year, the *Eredi* group as a whole made its debut with the same publisher: along with Pasolini, there appeared *Sopra una perduta estate* by Francesco Leonetti, *Poesie* by Roberto Roversi, and *Canto di memorie* by Luciano Serra.

The Pasolini volume, forty-six pages in three hundred numbered copies, plus seventy-five for private circulation, bears the dedication "To my father"—a deliberate gesture that should be read, apart from the occasion itself, as a by no means obvious expression of love. Pier Paolo was well aware of the extent to which his poetic and literary passion aroused pride in Carlo Alberto, and he may have divined that in that pride was mingled the acute heartache of not entirely possessing his son's love.

The book appeared, and about two weeks later Pasolini received a postcard from Gianfranco Contini: he liked the book and would review it. "Who could ever describe my joy? I went hopping and skipping through the arcades of Bologna. And as for the worldly satisfaction that one can aspire to by writing poetry, the satisfaction of that day in Bologna was more than enough: now I can always do very well without it."

Contini's review was not printed in *Primato* as promised, but in the Swiss *Corriere di Lugano*, on April 24, 1943. "Fascism—to my great surprise—did not admit that in Italy there were local particularisms, and dialects of stubborn unwarlike people. So, my 'pure tongue for poetry' had been mistaken for a realistic document proving the objective existence of poor peasants, eccentric or at least ignorant of the idealistic existence of the Center."[18]

Contini pointed approvingly to "this slim volume" as "the first accession of 'dialect' literature to the breadth of today's poetry, and therefore a modification in depth of that attribute." He added: "One need only imagine oneself standing before its poetic world to realize the scandal it introduces into the annals of dialect literature."

This critic was the first to use a word that was to mark the whole human and literary course of Pasolini's career as a writer: "scandal." By his stylistic expressionism, Contini foretold a destiny; and this word, which may have seemed slight in its very emphasis, or as exaggerating a negligible state of things, now reads like a horoscope.

Scandal: the scandal lay first of all in the very use of dialect, the dialect of the right bank of the Tagliamento, *di cà da l'aga* (on this side of the water), tinged with the speech of the Veneto—a special Friulian, avoiding the fixity of local slang by which written Friulian had hitherto been marked, according to the traditional practices of a Colloredo or a Zorutti (the first in the seventeenth century, the second a Romantic).*

The Friulian of *Poesie a Casarsa* was scandalous because born of a literary koine, a common language determined by the need of imparting the dignity and necessity of written language to one that up until that point had been oral. His study of Ungaretti and the hermetic

---

* Ermes di Colloredo (1622–1692) and Pietro Zorutti (or Pieri Zorut—1792–1867) were Friulian dialect poets.—Tr.

poets,* along with the Provençals, and such Spaniards as Jiménez and Machado, provided Pasolini with a tone, a resolution of similarities, that in *Poesie a Casarsa* rids the familiar landscape of twentieth-century dialect poetry of its echoes of Pascoli and D'Annunzio, along with the padding that accompanies second-rate versification.

In calling this language of Pasolini's a "literary koine," I mean to suggest its autonomy within our literature, and not to set boundaries or limitations to its freedom.

But Contini speaks of contents—he alludes "to that center of spiritual exercise of man over his own body that creates the book's equilibrium."

The tortured narcissism of these poems, their concealed and at the same time obvious homoeroticism, the urgency of achieving a painful maturity ("I want to kill a hypersensitive and sick adolescent who is also trying to pollute my life as a man, and is already almost moribund, but I will be cruel to him"—the letter to Farolfi is from the summer of 1941, when Pasolini was working on *Poesie*)—all this was bound to create "scandal" in a provincial tradition like the Friulian.

According to Serra,[19] in the summer of 1941 Pier Paolo wrote him letters in which he transcribed some poems written in Italian, in the style of Leopardi—Pier Paolo's intention was to include these poems in a volume to be entitled *Confini*.

Confines, borders—a theme rooted in hermeticism as its negative opposite. To the poetics of absence (to its ethical and political implications) could be added, as a negation of the negation (by derivation and contrast), a poetics of detachment or of the "border," by salvaging an "extreme" reality from the farthest reaches of the human.

One morning in the summer of 1941 I was out on the wooden balcony of my mother's house. The hot, gentle sun of Friuli beat down on all that cherished rustic material. On my eighteen-year-old beatnik head of the 1940s; on the worm-eaten wood of the stairs and balcony supported on the granular wall that went from the courtyard to the big bare room of the loft. The courtyard, even in the sunken intimacy of its sunshine, was a kind of private street, because there the Petron family, since before I was born, had had a right of way: their house was there, illuminated by its sun, a little more mysterious, behind a wooden gate even more worm-eaten and venerable than the balcony; and there you glimpsed, still amid that

---

* "Hermetic" was the term applied to the "difficult" and obscure poetry written almost in opposition to the shallow rhetoric encouraged by fascism. Ungaretti, Montale, and Quasimodo were seen as its leading figures.—Tr.

sunshine of others, the heaps of manure, the trough, the beautiful weeds surrounding the kitchen gardens: and far in the background, if you stretched your neck, the foothills of the Alps, still blue and unsullied, as in a painting by Bellini. What did people talk about before the war, that is, before everything happened and life showed itself for what it is? I don't know. There were surely conversations about this and that, of pure and innocent affabulation. People, before being what they really are, *were* equally, despite everything, the way they are in dreams. Anyway it is certain that I, on that balcony, was either drawing (with green ink, or with a little tube of ocher oil paint on cellophane) or else writing verses. When the word ROSADA rang out.

It was Livio, a boy from the Socolari family, the neighbors across the street, who had spoken. A tall, large-boned boy. A real peasant from those parts. But polite and shy, full of delicacy, the way certain sons of rich families are. Because, as we know and Lenin says, the peasants are petit bourgeois. Still Livio certainly spoke of simple and innocent things. The word *rosada*, uttered on that sunny morning, was only an expressive touch in his lively speech.

Certainly that word, in all the centuries of its use in the Friulian region on this side of the Tagliamento, *had never been written*. It had always been simply *a sound*.

Whatever I was doing that morning, painting or writing, I surely stopped doing it immediately: this is part of my hallucinatory memory. And I immediately started writing verses in that Friulian speech of the right bank of the Tagliamento, which up until that moment had been only a *collection of sounds*: first of all I began by writing the word ROSADA.

That first experimental poem has disappeared; the second, which I wrote next day, still exists:

Sera imbarlumida, tal fossàl
a cres l'aga . . .[20]

_____

(Luminous evening, in the ditch
the water rises . . .)

The story, to use a Pasolinian adjective, is certainly wholly "affabulated," but that in no way diminishes its value as testimony—a complete moral universe shines through. Pasolini here decants his vision of the peasant and Christian world, he develops a symbolism of purity and innocence. In this vision both the "blue and unsullied foothills of the Alps" and the artless voices of the rural speakers stand out, including the voice of young Livio. It is his lips that ignite the semantic reverie. The poetry from "on the borders" appears within its physical and linguistic geography: the Alps are in the background, as is the Tagliamento. Everything seems simple, and inherent to the atmosphere of innocence lit by a sunny morning.

In "I parlanti,"[21] Pasolini retraced in Proustian fashion the routes of his journey to the heart of the mother tongue.

Life with children, conversations gathered from their lips and from those of their families (the writer learned survey techniques and methods of expression from Ascoli and D'Ancona, authors of the classic works of Italian linguistics):

Stefano's mother was leaning against the edge of the bed, taking part in the conversation with charm and vivacity, aided by the warmth of her dark eyes and the unconscious habit of bowing her head in the gesture of an embarrassed but not timid child, and in speaking she covered her mouth with her swollen hand (another source of sympathy), certainly to conceal, at least in part, her regional errors of speech, certain soft Veneto *mi*'s instead of the Friulian *jo*, certain soft *th*'s that replaced the resonant *s* and gave her words an indescribably girlish intonation.

What excites Pier Paolo most is the creativity he observes on the lips of these peasants, the breaking of rules, or rather "the attention to the rules of honor of the language . . . without being afraid to vary it by personal or hazarded inventions." He is excited also by the distortion of certain words: the most conspicuous example is the use of *incredibile*, "incredible" for *sceptico*, "skeptical" and *incredulo*, "incredulous."

Friuli unrolled before his eyes (beginning in that year of 1943) like a field to be covered and scrutinized in its length and breadth. "In western Friuli, especially Basso, it was possible in ten minutes by bicycle to pass from one linguistic area to another more archaic by fifty years, or a century, or even two centuries."

The bicycle became a means for intellectual work, and it all must have brought an immediate joy of expression. But

in this immediate joy, which he sought from one village feast to another, from one group of young people to another, there nevertheless still persisted a depth of anguish, a fearful sensation of never being able to reach the center of that life that unfolded, so painfully saddening and enviable, in the heart of those villages.[22]

To write poetry in Friulian linked the poet to the nucleus of that "life," but at the same time it conspicuously indicated his distance and difference from it. Only a "foreigner" would have been able to distinguish accurately between one sound and another, one word and another, as they fell on his virgin ears.

I came into the world in the time
    of the Analogical.
        I worked
in that field as an apprentice . . .[23]

This is what Pasolini, in perfect awareness, wrote at the beginning of the 1960s in *Una disperata vitalità* (A Desperate Vitality). The "Analogical," which governs *Poesie a Casarsa*, aims at escaping the detailing of daily experience. Pasolini was not yet the poet pursued by "an immoderate desire for confession,"[24] but rather by an opposite immoderate desire—for transposition, for lyrical simulation.

Still, the field of his "analogies" is already a small one. The confession is not explicit, but torturously close—even though the music of Casarsa repels it, pushes it "to the confines," in the longing for a lost homeland (a homeland of poetry, a "Provence" of the imagination—the epigraph of the book is taken from Peire Vidal).

Ciantànt al mè spiéli
ciantànt mi petèni . . .
al rît tal mè vùli
il Diàul peciadôr.

Sunàit, més ciampànis
paràilu indavòur . . .

———————

(Singing to my mirror,
my comb singing . . .
the Devil sinner
laughs in my eye.

Ring out, my bells,
drive him away . . .)

There are no analogies in the lines of *Una disperata vitalità*, only a cruel account, thickening like a scab over a wound, of days lived in the village and countryside, and of the anguish there concealed. Everything is clear, everything is uttered, literary exquisiteness is relinquished—the feeling is exposed, along with a devouring and annihilating passion:

I remember it was . . . for a love
that invaded my brown eyes and plain trousers,
the house and the country, the morning sun and the sun

of the evening . . . on the fine Saturdays
of Friuli, on . . . Sundays . . . Ah, I can't
even utter this word of virgin

passions, of my death (seen in a dry
ditch, swarming with primroses,
among gold-stunned vines, behind

dark houses against a sublime blue).

I remember that in that monstrous love
I succeeded in crying out with pain
for the Sundays when there should have shone

"over the sons of sons, the sun!"

In my miserable bed in Casarsa, I wept,
in a room that smelled of urine and laundry
on those Sundays that shone with death . . .

Incredible tears! Not only
for what I was losing of splendor
in that moment of yearning immobility

but for what I would lose! . . .

And one day after lunch, or one evening, shouting
I ran
through the Sunday streets, after the soccer match,
to the old cemetery across the railroad tracks,

there to commit, and repeat, till blood came,
the sweetest act of life,
all alone, on a little mound of earth
with two or three graves
of Italian or German soldiers
nameless on the wooden crosses
—buried there since the time of the other war.

And later that night, amid dry tears,
the bleeding bodies of those poor unknowns
dressed in gray-green uniforms

came to cluster over my bed
where I slept naked and spent,
to soil me with blood until daybreak.

I was twenty, not even that—eighteen,
nineteen . . . and a century had already passed
since I was alive, a whole life

consumed by the painful thought
that I would only be able to give my love
to my hand, or to the grass in the ditches,

or perhaps to the loam of an unguarded grave . . .
Twenty years, and with its human story, and its cycle
of poetry, a life had ended.[25]

Spiritual exercise of the body. But I said homoeroticism: what made
the literary metaphor of the "confines" all the more real, or destroyed
it as such, was the torment of masturbation, of "being different."
Much as they might have wished it, those twenty years did not
succeed in being forgotten—this is the dramatic content of *Poesie a
Casarsa*, its true originality of expression.[26]

CHAPTER 3

THE "PURE LIGHT"
OF THE RESISTANCE

"Forty-three is still one of the most beautiful years of my life: 'mi juventud, veinte años en tierra de Castilla!' "[1]

Susanna was then living with her sons in Casarsa. The seasons went by "like the shadows of clouds over the stones of the Tagliamento," as Pier Paolo wrote to Farolfi. And he added: "The war has never seemed to me so disgustingly horrible as it does now. Have they never thought about what a human life is?"

"One of the most beautiful years of my life"—a joyous cry based on the poems of Machado.

There was the beauty of the discovery of Friuli—a discovery no longer conducted with dictionary in hand. (*Poesie a Casarsa* had been written with the Pirona Friulian-Italian dictionary at his elbow.) At home on his maternal soil, Pasolini now wrote naturally in the spoken dialect; he came closer than ever to the contents and style of the speakers' live voices.

The Friulian plain is uniform in its bluish light, uniform in its irrigation ditches bordered by poplar trees, in the balanced grid of its vineyards. Much more complex, however, is its linguistic geography, all inlets and gulfs, in which the speech of the Veneto comes and goes, with a richness of phonic perspectives to astonish and ensnare a philologist. Pier Paolo, pedaling his bicycle, allowed himself to be astonished and ensnared.

On the night of July 25, 1943, he wrote VIVA LA LIBERTÀ on a wall, and almost spent the night in jail with his brother and a friend, Cesare Bortotto. He persuaded the carabinieri warrant officer to let them go by a long string of dialectical arguments. The *maresciallo* kept repeating disconsolately, "I have no orders." To him it seemed more than the right thing not to talk of freedom.

On a walk during the summer with his cousin Nico Naldini, Pier Paolo came to Versuta, two kilometers from Casarsa. Versuta is a village of only a few houses, south of the Pontebbana. Pier Paolo fell in love with one of those houses, a typical Friulian peasant dwelling. A long construction of gray stone, a stable, a wooden balcony. The peasant woman, Ernesta, rented him a room. It was to be a kind of studio in the country, a quiet retreat for a life of reading and reflection. Pier Paolo and Nico loaded a cart with books, and, again on foot, for two kilometers transported volumes of Du Bos, Cecchi, Bartolini, and Longhi, together with Greek and Latin classics. It was a way of living a life of choice and elevated culture in the middle of an arcadian linguistic paradise.

In that summer of 1943, Pier Paolo was still planning to take his degree with Longhi. In Versuta, the two cousins went in for rural archaeology. Nico was fourteen years old, but he was already following Pier Paolo's lead in adventures of the spirit. By rubbing the neutral-colored wall of an abandoned village shrine with an onion, they brought to light three figures from an old fresco.

The army summons arrived to break the golden equilibrium of this arcadia. On September 1, 1943, Pier Paolo had to report to Pisa. His service lasted a week. September 8, the day of Italy's truce with the Allies, caught him there.

The Germans promptly seized the unit to which Pasolini had been assigned. The column of recruits was marched away to a train for deportation to Germany. As they passed along a canal between Pisa and Leghorn, the man next to him said, "Watch out, when the guard goes up ahead, I'm going to jump in the ditch. Come along, if you want to." Pier Paolo, who had released the safety on his rifle, ready to fire at the Germans, threw himself in the ditch. In rags, beside himself, in terror of still falling into the hands of the Nazis, he covered at least a hundred kilometers on foot. He had with him material he had collected for his graduate thesis, and lost it, but arrived safely back in Casarsa.[2] Looking back, he found the fear was horrifying.

This was his only war experience. "From then on my life was spent in hiding and being hunted—and very much in terror, since at the time I had a decidedly pathological fear of death—constantly haunted by the idea of getting caught in the end. Which was what happened to young men on the Adriatic coast who failed to register for conscription or were avowedly antifascist."[3]

And still this was one of the most beautiful years of his life.

That summer his eroticism had been expressed with more facility than in the past—at a bend in the river, a kind of pond, where youths from the villages around Casarsa went swimming.

It seems that a few years earlier Pier Paolo had been making love with a young boy behind a hedge when a woman saw him and scolded him. For a while he lived in terror of being reported to the carabinieri. But at the time nothing came of the matter. His erotic happiness that summer could not have been complete—it must have been marred by fear and feelings of guilt. But the youthful promiscuity in which it expressed itself gave a lift to his spirits. For Pier Paolo, that happiness, or happy game, prolonged his adolescence, and if the need for maturity once so acutely felt ("I want to kill a hypersensitive and sick adolescent who is also trying to pollute my life as a man") was atrophied, there was compensation in a burst of intellectual and literary expression.

He wrote poetry, in Italian and Friulian. He was also to write a theater piece, *I turcs tal Friùl* (The Turks in Friuli). The manuscript is dated May 1944. It is an instinctively Christian, peasant epic—a eulogy of community solidarity and innocence.

Friuli is on the borders, and has been marked by various invasions in the course of its history. Many armies have crossed it and made it the scene of legendary resistance—from the invasion by Attila's Huns to the passage of the Austrian armies throughout the nineteenth century and up until the First World War. The region's strong linguistic identity could not help but develop in the psychology of its inhabitants a feeling of being alien to these repeated storms of war.

The Turks, too, had appeared in Friuli. A stone tablet on the wall in the church of Santa Croce in Casarsa is proof of it. The stone reads:

On the day of September 30, 1499, the Turks were in Friuli and passed through the town, and we, Matia de Montico and Zuane Coluso, made a vow to build this holy church if they did no harm, and by the grace of Our Lady our prayers were answered, and with the commune's help we built this church, which we comrades Bastian de Iacuz and Zuan de Stefano Gambilim decorated with paintings on September 7, 1529.

Obviously the community epic was to be combined with the pride of a family epic—the presence in the written evidence of this "Zuane Coluso," or Giovanni Colussi, who by a spoken vow had sponsored the building of the church. It is therefore the vow, and the re-creation of that fear of the foreigner, that becomes theatrical material in Pasolini's imagination. To this was added the correspondence with the present. Like the Turks, the Nazis were threatening the Friulian communities with roundups and deportations.

There was constant fear of such incursions. Guido was already a member of partisan groups, first Communist then nationalist, and he was hiding weapons in the house. Once he had to run away, and he confessed to his Aunt Enrichetta that he had hidden a pistol and cartridge holders under the floor of his room. She just had time to throw them into the garden before the house was searched.

Another time it was Pier Paolo who had to hide. He and Nico took refuge in the bell tower of the main church of Casarsa. They were up there for three days, looking out over the plain. Pier Paolo had brought Francesco Flora's history of Italian literature along to read.

In *I turcs tal Friùl* the model of the village feast gives more content than form to the long one-act text. It is an ordinary evening. While people are pursuing their regular tasks, a messenger arrives in the village to say that the Turks have crossed the Isonzo River and are spreading terror; they have almost reached the Tagliamento. The Colussi family, leaders of the village, discuss what to do. Pauli, the elder son, is prepared to leave things to fate; Meni, the second son, organizes a band of resisters. Their dismayed mother, Lussìa, foresees tragedy. And the tragedy occurs. The Turks withdraw from Friuli and the village is saved. Zuan Colussi has made a vow to build a church to the Virgin if the community is spared. But in the red glare of the sunset the steady chanting of the enemy is heard, and the young men of the village return bearing in their arms the lifeless body of Meni, killed in his generous devotion to the common good.

It would be all too easy to read this text autobiographically, to see there a presentiment of the tragedy that befell the Pasolini family with the death of Guido. But there is more to it than that. The contrast between the two brothers was a real one. Pier Paolo's passion for freedom, his rejection of Nazism and fascism, was not translated into action—or at least not into the kind of action represented by armed struggle. In Guido, on the other hand, the attraction to armed struggle was a violent one—a violent wish and need to lay down his life in the war of liberation. In the text of *Turcs*, "the two brothers, Meni and Pauli (we are continually reminded of the two actual brothers), do not seem to be two dichotomous presences, but two souls fused to the point of interchangeability."[4]

In "La religione del mio tempo" (The Religion of My Time), the poem in which Pasolini was to relive with painfully adult hindsight that youthful phase, he writes:

The honest, rough, blindfolded youths
from uncouth families who went
migrating through the docile

woods or flooded zone
comforted the solitude
of my poor bed, of my street.

History, the Church, the vicissitudes
of a family, are thus no more
than a little sweet-smelling and naked sunshine

that warms an abandoned vineyard,
a few rows of hay amid the consumed
groves, a few houses deafened

by the sound of the bells . . . the boys
of old, they alone alive, when filled
with springtime they had their hearts

in the most beautiful ages, were both
dreams of sex and images drunk
from the old paper of the poem

that from volume to volume, in silent
fevers of supreme originality
—they were Shakespeare, Tommaseo, Carducci—

made every fiber of my being tremble in unison.[5]

There was a naïve, romantic fury in the boy Pier Paolo, the fury of a poet who believes without hesitation in the capacity of poetry to educate, as though it alone could give vitality to a people, to a community. Dialect transformed into language, if it is used to express great sentiments and not merely figurative rustic maxims, if it creates history and culture through the form and style of a poet—that dialect, that language, is equivalent to a weapon.

These were convictions dictated by a vague historicism, combined with a dispassionate *amor de loinh* (love of song). Pasolini sought to encourage a tradition of local culture in which poor peasants, marked by centuries of subjugation, could recognize themselves and become men. The wonderstruck archaic quality of expression and custom, characteristic not only of the Friuli "this side of the water," but of other rural areas as well, might somehow be redeemed. It was to this mission, not that of arms, that he felt drawn. Family clairvoyance aside, *I turcs tal Friùl* forms part of a related plan to "establish a culture" and create a Friulian "school" of poetry.

A poetry and a culture are not born of nothing. They take shape from examples, and from those examples a language descends and a style is formed. This process was very clear to Pasolini's imagination. And the book that he perhaps kept chiefly in mind for this purpose was *I canti del popolo greco* (Songs of the Greek People) by Niccolò Tommaseo (edited by Guido Martellotti and published by Einaudi in February 1943). The choral quality of these "songs," the hundred voices that there speak to each other, the hundred stories there interwoven (of love, of death, of war), make up the fresco of an ideal world of the people, transcribed in a vibrant, fluid language.

The contents of these *Canti* appealed to the young poet's gift for "dialect"; they fed his nostalgia for a universe that could be expressed through a language as yet untouched by pen and ink. Pasolini was to define this "position" in his 1952 essay "La poesia dialettale del Novecento (Dialect Poetry of the Twentieth Century), in which he speaks of the "author of *Poesie a Casarsa*": "Perhaps, in order to bring Friuli to a level of awareness that would make it capable of being represented, one had to be sufficiently detached from it, marginal, not be too Friulian, and, in order to adopt its language with freedom and a sense of virginity, not be too much of a speaker. The 'return,' that essential vocation of dialect, ought not to have been carried out *within* the dialect, from one speaker (the poet) to a speaker presumably purer and more fortunate, and in an absolutely immediate way with respect to the spirit of the *inventum*. Rather it should come about for more complex reasons, both internal and external, and be accomplished from one language (Italian) to another (Friulian) that has become the object of mournful nostalgia, sensual in origin (in all the breadth and depth of the term), but coinciding besides with the nostalgia of one who lives—and knows it—in a civilization that has reached a linguistic crisis, the desolation and violence of a Rimbaldian 'je ne sais plus parler.' "[6]

To go back to the "mother tongue," then, seems to such a "foreign" poet the only way to express all the romantic and passionate moments of existence. But this tongue is not undertaken for itself; it is used to revive old models, all the illustrious models, neither slang nor dialect, possible.

This, then, from Tommaseo's *Canti*:

From the lookout the sentry shouted:
"To arms, boys, get yourselves together,
For ten thousand Turks are coming down on us."
Mitromara shouted to the barracks:
"Take heart, boys, show your courage today.
Let's scatter the Turks; here they'll find their graves."
They roared like lions, and seized their swords:
They charge the Turks, storm them, and blow them away.

It is little more than a brief episode, and there is no way of telling if it may have been an example for *I turcs tal Friùl*. But it is important to know that at this time *I canti del popolo greco* was one of Pasolini's favorite books.

Echoes of this diligent reading can also be found in the epic family *canti* included in the second part of *La meglio gioventù*, and they are precisely echoes, not direct copies. Echoes that mingle with those of the lyrical-epic songs of Italian popular poetry ("whose center of diffusion is Piedmont and are inexplicably scarce in Friuli"[7])—in short, a fusion of form and content which, for Pasolini's critical and didactic imagination, would have provided Friulian literature with that self-awareness that in his judgment it lacked.

SCHOOL IN CASARSA

I have mentioned "didactic imagination." In Pasolini the idealistic tension of the teacher was very strong—the sublimated form of a homoerotic drive. This tension also nourished a possible conception of literature, willed in a sense by the poet's desire for a "return to a language closer to the world."[8] He did not, however, mean to discover the world individually, but as part of a community, as the member of a chorus. The school was formed to that end.

He was helped by the exceptional wartime conditions. Because of the danger and uncertainty of railway travel, some students in Casarsa stopped going to the *ginnasio* in Udine or Pordenone.

Pasolini opened a school for a handful of students in his home in Casarsa. Along with the Italian, Greek, and Latin classics, he taught the children how to write Friulian poetry: the pure lyric and the villota.

The villota lasts "only an instant"—"at the base of this sudden capacity for 'revelation' lies almost always a concrete and as though liturgical sense of guilt. And in the light of this *Sehnsucht* [yearning] —almost as though the sense of poverty and injustice were freed from the assumptions of necessarily cheerful resignation—the world of the surrounding Friulian village appears veiled by a profound sadness, with its gray stone houses grouped on a desolate hilltop, or in the middle of empty marshlands, or amid the green mulberry groves of the underground streams."[9]

Closed, passive, prone to renunciation, though an original linguistic island, Friuli seemed to Pasolini to be inhabited by a people "both northern in its moralism, and southern in its lyrical abandon, both clumsy and agile, harsh and cheerful, living in a sort of political substratum, so to speak, a rustic world in itself, and noble in its way. Without a great democratic communal tradition (such as the 'diocese' of Aquileia), and without a great Risorgimento tradition, this people nevertheless has none of those social vices that specifically characterize people devoid of such traditions. Or at least one notices only a vague suggestion of those vices, perhaps where the poverty is grayest and coldest, as in the 'depressed areas' of Carnia or the lowlands, but if this involves the action or conformist political choice of these populations, it does not undermine an innate nobility and uprightness of custom of theirs, something as remote perhaps in time as their surviving Ladino."[10]

In this setting, among these people, Pasolini initiated his own "action." The pupils were very young, and, as Pasolini later wrote, "accepted promptings and aesthetic pressures with the necessary influence from me as though these were essentially unquestionable. In short, they found their tradition there."[11]

The school needed teachers, and Pier Paolo asked his friends in Bologna to help. Giovanna Bemporad came. She arrived with her personal and literary legend. An erratic creature, she wore white makeup on her face so as to look pale; she shunned life by courting inexpressible aesthetic sublimation. Pier Paolo's feelings toward her were subtly critical and at the same time concerned. In life one must have one's papers in order, he told her softly and persuasively. She answered him with intellectualized protestations of recklessness.

They spoke of sex, of love. Once while they were taking a walk together, and Pier Paolo said something that sounded to her like a hazarded advance, Giovanna, as always scorning the conventions, replied, "I'm a lesbian." Had Giovanna sniffed out what was "different" about Pier Paolo? Was she, with unconscious irony, hyperbolically throwing it back in his face by taking it on herself? Probably not. But Giovanna's sensitivity may have discerned the "weak link" in Pier Paolo's eroticism. Pier Paolo claimed to be a virgin. His virginity astonished his contemporaries—what did not astonish them was his obvious innocence.

They taught in the morning. Afternoons they walked in the fields. They talked a lot about poetry and books, but even more, as between well-read young people, about life and death. Death was an obsessive, necessary, and artificial presence in Giovanna's imagination.

The feeling of eternity carried the conversation between the two friends toward the areas of faith and religion. Giovanna professed herself an atheist. Pier Paolo appeared to be attracted aesthetically by Catholic ritual. He liked the singing of the choir boys, the odor of incense, the melancholy scene of the evening recital of the rosary. The afternoon walk frequently ended in church, simply to witness the service. Pier Paolo showed no devotion toward it, but he was intoxicated by the sound of Latin being artlessly murmured by Friulian lips. If anything in the Catholic liturgy struck him, it was perhaps the latent sense of sin and not a sense of the sacred.

One evening he took Giovanna to read a passage from the *De Profundis*, in the text kept in the sacristy: *Si iniquitate observaveris, Domine,/Domine, quis substinebit?** Certainly the idea of sin pursued

* "If thou, O Lord, wilt mark iniquities: Lord, who shall stand it?" Psalm 129, Douay-Rheims Version.—Tr.

him and troubled his conscience, and a possible dialogue between himself and God, attempted many times by literary means in those years, in both Italian and Friulian, was probably inhibited by the anguish of his guilt. If his summer encounters with boys on the white riverbed of the Tagliamento were partially liberating, winter necessarily brought obstacles, and along with the obstacles a painful examination of conscience.

At the same time, there were large family gatherings, with much eating and drinking; there were bicycle races. At home in the evening (Giovanna ate with the Pasolinis and slept at the house of some of their relatives), they held a contest in writing villotas. Pier Paolo composed them one after another. They taught their students these songs. Another diversion: they both loved Foscolo, and versified the unfinished parts of the *Grazie*. And between the two it was a point of honor to write the perfect hendecasyllable. Giovanna was more bound by neoclassical formalism, Pier Paolo freer in invention. They told themselves that they would be the poets of their generation.

The story is idyllic in tone. The poet would lift his mother in his arms, whirl her around, and call her "Cicciona" (Fatty)—Susanna, who was as light and slender as a reed.

One of his villotas ran:

Zovinuta blancia e rosa
con chel stras di vestidin,
la to musa dolorosa
a someja al me destin.

———

(Pink and white maiden
in your ragged little dress,
your sorrowful face
resembles my destiny.)

Giovanna Bemporad had composed the music for two other quatrains celebrating the five hundred years of the Casarsa parish church:

O Glisiuta tal to grin
quanciu muars c'a àn preat!
Sincsent ains che nu i savin
di vei cà patit e amat.

O pais dai vecius muars
vuei beas tal Paradis,
dis tu, a lour, cu li ciampanis,
c'a si pensin dai so fis.

———————

(O little church how many of the dead
have prayed in your bosom!
For five hundred years we have been able
to mourn our suffering loved ones here.

(O village of the dead of old,
blessed today in Paradise
tell them with your bells
to remember their children.)

Secular music, also by Bemporad, for this other quatrain:

Dols orient imbarlumit
tal seren color di rosa
jot suridi plan la sposa
tal so omp indurmidit.

———————

(By the faint light from the east
with its serene rose color
see the bride smile softly
at her sleeping man.)

To get Giovanna to change her "monstrous clothes," which made
soldiers and little boys whistle and follow her in the street, Pier Paolo
designed a suitable outfit: "black corduroy skirt, white blouse, black
string tie, pink and gray knee-socks, old rose sweater."

A game. But it was a game that took the form of a judgment, and
the judgment became clear when, after the war, Giovanna published
her poems and some translations in a volume entitled *Esercizi*. In *Il
Mattino del Popolo* of Venice, September 12, 1948, Pasolini quoted
Cocteau: "The gestures of the tightrope walker must look absurd to
those who are unaware that he is walking over the void and over
death." Giovanna's absurd habits and ways seemed to Pier Paolo to
be psychological and creative defense mechanisms, and the poems in

Esercizi "not yet entirely free of a kind of D'Annunzianism and of a certain corporeity acquired by the Italian language through an overly literary tradition." Still, Pasolini found in Bemporad a positive aversion to bourgeois customs, even if this was based on intellectual preconceptions. And the "disorienting imprudence" of the "high" tone of her lyric poetry—this in itself seemed to him somewhat positive.

He wrote to Serra on January 26, 1944, Giovanna having left Casarsa: "I spent many wonderful poetic days with her, and had marvelous conversations, but in return she certainly caused me a lot of trouble in the village."[12]

In the meantime, he was avidly reading Dilthey, Schopenhauer, Gide's *Immoraliste*, Daniello Bartoli's *Uomo al punto*, Villiers de l'Isle-Adam, Barbey d'Aurevilly. Lautréamont's *Chants de Maldoror* acted, in its way, to fix in Pasolini's mind the destructive symbol of the crucified Christ, the Christ of scandal, which was later to appear in *L'usignolo della Chiesa Cattolica*.

In the little classroom in the Pasolini house in Casarsa, Giovanna Bemporad's listeners were carried away by her reading of Foscolo's *Sepolcri*. Guido Pasolini was there too, and wide-eyed he followed the reading and discussion, wholly enthralled by the "beautiful" idea of dying for the fatherland.

Pier Paolo explained Leopardi's *Consalvo*, and translated Marlowe's *Doctor Faustus* as part of his English teaching. Meanwhile, he was planning a graduate thesis on Pascoli, which would need to be discussed with Carlo Calcaterra, the Longhi plan having gone up in smoke[13] and since it was impossible for him to attend the university without interruption.

The children paid the school a small fee, which helped to pay the rent for the premises where the lessons were held. This led to bureaucratic complications. The Board of Education in Udine, acting on information it had received, warned Pasolini not to proceed with his teaching.

From January to February 1944, the children disbanded. Giovanna Bemporad left just at this time. But a small group of friends had been consolidated, among them the violinist Pina Kalz, the painter Rico De Rocco, Riccardo Castellani, and Cesare Bortotto. The future Academiuta di Lenga Furlana was taking shape.

The first *Stroligut di cà da l'aga*, the "almanac from this side of the water," the right bank of the Tagliamento, was dated "Ciasarsa—

Avril MCMXLIV." Written in Casarsa dialect, it was a little magazine of prose, poetry, and poetic accounts of everyday life.

Il Stroligut was successful—it provoked discussions in the small circle of Friulian philologists. A number of dialect poets submitted their poems to Pasolini. Nico Naldini, outside the classroom, wrote four prose poems, but did not have the courage to show them to his cousin. It was his grandmother who showed them to him.

One Sunday morning Pier Paolo asked Nico to go for a walk with him. Nico, fifteen years old, felt uneasy, although he was on intimate terms with his cousin.

"For what reason did you write? To imitate somebody or out of a personal need of your own?"

The relationship between the two cousins took a turn. Pier Paolo spoke of style and of the sacrifices it requires; he spoke of Ungaretti, Penna, and Montale. He gave the adolescent boy Joyce's *Portrait of the Artist as a Young Man* to read, and Alfredo Gargiulo's essay on D'Annunzio. He spoke to him of Sereni and Caproni, and of the *Conservatorio di Santa Teresa*. Nico thus began to join in the conversations between Pier Paolo and Pina Kalz. He listened to them talk about music, but also about Freud's *Three Essays on the Theory of Sexuality*, which Kalz was reading in the original German, and Pier Paolo in selections prepared for a university course.

Naldini's case was certainly not unique. In Pasolini's imagination, the little circle in Casarsa ought to be transformed into a poetry "workshop," along the lines laid out by the *lenga furlana*, the Friulian language. Everyone was welcome at this "workshop." It was not to be simply a small group of the privileged and educated. On the contrary, the educated were expected to let themselves be suffused by the humors and juices contained in the common language, the language of the people.

This led to the second *Stroligut di cà da l'aga*, "Ciasarsa—Avost MCMXLIV." It opens with the prayer from *I turcs tal Friùl*, printed with no other indication but the simple heading "Prejera." Also by Pasolini, a "Discors tra la plèif e un fantàt" (Conversation between the Parish and a Young Man), the theme of which is the absence of "history" in Casarsa. The note in italics accompanying the text reads, "Everyone knows that except for a fire, a plague, and the Turkish invasion, the five hundred years of our parish have nothing else to record. Its history is all there, work, pray, suffer, die."

One can see if one likes a foreshadowing of neorealism in this urgency to read native history "from below" and in the details of country life. The documentary (here linguistic) approach is combined with the autobiographical. The use of reason is held in abeyance —the investigation starts from such fortuitous and raw material as can be extracted from the spoken language. The ideology, if there is one here (and there is), postulates a "regression" through the discovery of the "world." Catholic humanity and suffering—that Catholicism of simple people that has nothing to do with Rome or the glory of the Church, and is characteristic of the entire lower Po valley (all the way to the gray stone houses of Friuli)—acts here as a solvent, if not as evidence of faith in transcendence.

Now, the peculiarity of such an attitude—anticipating as it does what was to be postwar neorealism—consists in the attention paid to language, in combining with a primary factor—the potential relation between spoken and written language—an idea of literature that is essentially not a neorealist one.

In the same *Stroligut*, there is a villota by Pasolini:

Oh Signòur, misericordia
da la nustra zoventùt,
essi zòvins no val nuja
con la Patria a ni à perdiùt.

———————

(O Lord have pity
on our youth,
to be young is worth nothing
when the Fatherland has lost us.)

Then prose by Castellani and verses by Bortotto, "lontan dal so pais e dai so amics" (far from his village and friends). Clear and simple prose pieces by Naldini and Ovidio Colussi. Then once again an article by Pasolini, "Memoria di un spetaculut," the detailed account of how he had entertained the community of Casarsa with concerts given by Pina Kalz, the classical music interspersed with villotas. A small group of children had sung these texts.

Brief dialogues, music, songs—the performers traveled through the countryside surrounding the parish of Casarsa: "Ciant dai miej fantàs" (Song of My Young People) was the title of the "spetaculut." A great success. They came home by the light of the stars, with much ceremonial drinking and intoxication, during a summer that was no longer a happy one. This form of popular celebration was created by

Pier Paolo in a spirit of antifascist "resistance." And it did not remain without political implications.

In a letter to Serra in May 1944, Pasolini writes. "The war stinks of shit. Men are so disgusted that they could start laughing and say 'It's not worth it!' But they're waiting, for what I don't know: for the rottenness to go away. I walk alone in the fields, I walk and walk, through an empty and endless Friuli. Everything stinks of gunfire, it all makes you sick when you think that those characters are shitting on this land."[14]

On May 29, he writes to Serra about being arrested over some leaflets. "Pina, Luciana, Gastone and I have been arrested with great hullabaloo, accused of having distributed those little circulars, of which you saw an example that had been found in my aunt's store."

Serra had been a guest in Casarsa, and had left the day before this happened. Pier Paolo, Pina Kalz, and the others had been suspected of antifascist propaganda. The real author of the pamphlets had been Guido, but it was precisely because of his activities that the attention of the authorities was drawn to Pier Paolo.

The letter concludes: "Our innocence emerged so fully that now the accusers are apologizing to us and accusing each other."[15] Though Pasolini stresses his own innocence and displays scorn for "the rhetoric of that leaflet!," it can only be for the reason that mail was being censored. It is now clear, however, that the "school" and the "public entertainments" had turned out to be politically dangerous enough to jeopardize the personal freedom of those involved.

More than once in this period, Pier Paolo and Guido slept in Versuta rather than in Casarsa.

GUIDO AND PORZÛS

As early as September 10, 1943, Guido, with one of his friends, had risked his life trying to steal weapons from the Nazis at the Casarsa airfield. In one of these exploits his friend barely escaped alive. They distributed leaflets and wrote on the walls of houses in the village: THE HOUR IS NEAR.

At the end of April 1944 Guido passed the examination for his high-school diploma. On May 5 he wrote a long letter to his prisoner-of-war father explaining his doubts about choosing a field of study at the university. Susanna would have liked him to study medicine ("actually I don't lack the aptitudes for it, a steady wrist, a sure hand,

and a certain inclination for that kind of life"), but he feels drawn to politics and philosophy ("I think Political Science would suit me better, but Mamma has a kind of horror of politics and I really wouldn't want to disappoint her like this"). He ends by asking: "What do you think? I'll do what you say."

The letter goes on:

We are all well, Pier Paolo is still staying quietly at home, I'm at home too, but not too "quiet" (though I still haven't received that *postcard**). Try as I may, I can't keep off the subject of politics, in this I'm a terrible hothead (ideas and concepts in Italy have changed a lot in recent times . . .) and I'm really desperate at the thought of acting in opposition to your way of thinking. All the same, I'm sure that if you were here you'd have no hesitation about which side to take . . . Pier Paolo does what he can to hold me in check and I admire him for his generosity (I'm convinced he does it only to spare Mamma grief) and feel that I love him very much, unfortunately many times I let myself be carried away by my emotions . . .

His "emotions" in fact did carry him away. Free now of the obligations of school, revolted by the idea of being called up in the fascist army, with Nazi surveillance having become more stringent, and even going against the need "to spare Mamma grief," Guido left for the mountains; he left by train one early morning.

Pier Paolo accompanied him to the station. To throw the police off the scent, the two brothers bought a ticket for Bologna. Instead, Guido went to Spilimbergo, and from there to Pielungo, where he joined the Osoppo partisan division.

It was a morning on which unawares
a sea light dreamed on the eroded horizons;

each blade of grass as though struggling to sprout
was a thread of that huge and obscure splendor.

We came in silence along the hidden embankment
by the railroad, light and still warm

from our last sleep together in the bare barn
that had been our refuge amid the fields.

* I.e., conscription notice.—Tr.

Behind us Casarsa turned white and lifeless
in the terror of Graziani's last edict;

and, struck by the sun against the shadow of the mountains,
the station stood empty: beyond the sparse trunks

of the mulberry trees and the brushwood, alone
on the grassy tracks, the Spilimbergo train was waiting . . .

In the white color of the air and earth,
I watched him leave with his suitcase,

in which a volume of Montale was jammed
among a few clothes and his revolver.

His jacket, which had been mine, a little tight
at the shoulders, the boyish nape of his neck . . .

I went back along the burning road . . .[16]

What had led Guido to this decision? Pier Paolo's letter to Serra,
on August 21, 1945, is crucial for a direct understanding of what his
brother's death meant to him: "You remember Guido's enthusiasm,
and the sentence that hammered in my head for days and days was
this: He wasn't able to survive his enthusiasm. That boy had a
generosity, a courage, an innocence that are not to be believed. And he
was so much better than all the rest of us; I see his living image now,
with his hair, his face, his jacket; and I'm seized by such an unspeak-
able, unbearable anguish."[17]

Guido left at the age of nineteen to join the nationalist partisans of
the Osoppo-Friuli Brigade. Susanna accepted her son's decision
bravely. She knew that his choice to be a partisan represented
maturity and that it would do no good to oppose him. His *nom de
guerre* was Ermes.

He wrote home, addressing his letters to his mother and calling
her "Dearest Fatty," and signed himself "Amelia." In code, and in the
guise of a woman, he recounted his life in the mountains. For example
(the letter can be dated October 23):

Up there, where "I" have decided to devote myself to winter sports, it
will be snowing in a few days. I *absolutely* need winter gear, heavy

sweaters, ski cap, woolen gloves, knee socks, and another pair of heavy shoes (the ones I have are in bad shape). So either you, or Giannina along with Signorina Pina, should bring all these things you know where, right away! There's no problem for a woman taking the trip. Pier Paolo needn't worry . . . When you go through Udine, don't forget to buy lots of "Mom" [insect powder]—I need it more than bread! Also bring plenty of soap.

Elsewhere he thanks them for the packages he has received, and worries about his brother—he hopes he'll write to him, and also write a few songs in Friulian for him and his friends. "Send me *Poesie a Casarsa* and *Stroligut* immediately and whatever you can send me written by Pier Paolo . . . A friend of mine can't do without it."

Again: "I'm sorry to have given you the idea of coming to see me— the trip is really very dangerous and uncomfortable. It's a good thing Pier Paolo stopped you."

Meanwhile, as the bombings of the railroad hub of Casarsa intensified —all the historic center of the town was destroyed—Susanna and Pier Paolo moved permanently to Versuta.

> With a few peasants around me
> I lived the glorious life of one haunted
> by the frightful edicts . . .[18]

This "glorious" life was one of study, while the life of the community was dispersed by the increasing ferocity of the war.

There in Versuta, Pier Paolo had met Tonuti Spagnol, a fourteen-year-old boy, the son of peasants. He gave him lessons, taught him to write verses, and Tonuti wrote a few poems. In his essay "La poesia dialettale del Novecento," Pasolini devoted a sentence to him: "And one might mention Tonuti Spagnol, who started writing as a 'sonarel,' peasant boy, showing signs of being, in a few brief lyrics, an example of sensitivity and intonation, just where uneducated poets of his type are all sentimentalism and ear."[19]

Before Ninetto Davoli, Tonuti was Pier Paolo's true love, a love that was to end in later years when the boy became a man and the "fragrance" of Versuta a painful memory.

Anyway, Pier Paolo wrote to Guido, and also sent him some poems, and Guido-Amelia replied as follows to "Dearest Fatty":

I've received Pier Paolo's letter and it's brought great peace to my heart, I'm really very grateful to him. In an extraordinary way his poetry has interpreted my state of mind on certain windy days made milder by the sun: . . . I was up there on a high summit, with below me the plain, all the way to the sea, to Istria; and the villages (the roofs of the houses red) filled the plain, which was still green (but the green was pale and faded). I followed eagerly with my eyes the white bed of the Tagliamento: at a certain point the countryside was covered with a slight blue haze . . . You were all down there and maybe you were thinking of me. Ask Pier Paolo to write me again, when he has time. It gives me great joy.

In the same letter he adds: "I *must* have books of modern and contemporary history—among others, Omodeo's *L'età del Risorgimento italiano*."

Guido liked girls. Among his papers at home, they found a greeting card full of erasures and left unfinished, in an unaddressed envelope: "My dearest Wilma: It's been ages since I've heard from you. Sometimes, when I think it over, I end up wondering if I've known you, and your memory ends by mingling with the sweet unreality of so many other beautiful dreams. But there also still remains the reality of all the things about *you*, which surround me and overwhelm me with a tremendous and desperate longing."

The First Osoppo-Friuli Brigade operated in an area situated some twenty kilometers north of Udine, where it found itself alongside the Second Garibaldi Brigade. The Garibaldians were Communists, the Osoppians adherents of the Action Party. The zone, the Attimis-Subit valley, was also infiltrated by bands of Slovenes, who were making nationalist propaganda and setting forth territorial claims to these borderlands.

Since October 1944 the Allies had been stalled south of Bologna, and the Italian resistance struggle was preparing for a long, hard winter. Wherever they could, the Nazis and fascists mounted violent attacks on the partisan bands. In this critical situation, the Communists and Italian nationalists signed a friendship pact on this Friulian border. They formed the Garibaldi-Osoppo Division.

The Division received word that the Allies were disarming the partisan groups in the liberated regions. To the Osoppians, "the news made no difference"—their goal was the liberation of Italy. This was not the position taken by the Garibaldians. At this juncture, a mission sent by Marshal Tito himself proposed the absorption of the Garibaldi-

Osoppo Division into the Slovenian army. Sasso, the commander of the Division and a Garibaldian, hesitated; Bolla, the Osoppian deputy commander, refused outright.

The Tito mission was undecided whether to try again or to take action against the Italians.

On the night of September 26–27, 1944, the Germans, with an armored train, attacked the partisan positions between Reana and Tricesimo. The attack was a heavy one—Garibaldians and Osoppians disbanded, dispersed, and fell into the hands of the enemy. The Slovenes, though they could have, did not lift a finger to help, and the worst fate befell the Italian nationalists, who suddenly found themselves in conflict with their own Communist comrades-in-arms.

Guido, in a long letter to Pier Paolo, dated November 27, gives a detailed account of these episodes:

The Garibaldian leaders (when we meet them on the road) do their utmost to demoralize us and get us to take off our tricolor badges. A Garibaldian commissar in Mernicco aims a pistol at my head because I yelled in his face that he had no idea what it means to be "Free Men," and that he was arguing like a fascist federalist (indeed in the Garibaldian ranks you're free to speak well of communism, otherwise you're treated as an "enemy of the proletariat"—no less!—or else an "idealist sucking the blood of the people"—what crap!—). We hold up our heads and declare that we're Italians and fighting for the Italian flag, not for the "red rag."[20]

The surviving Osoppians, Guido among them, gathered in the Prosenicco-Subit-Porzûs area and regrouped. They re-established contact with the Garibaldians. There were rumors that the latter had united with the Slovenes, but the rumors were denied.

Then on November 7, the anniversary of the Soviet October Revolution, the announcement came that the Italian Communist units were being combined with the Slovenian troops. There was considerable disappointment, among even the Garibaldians themselves. Again, as Guido writes: "Many are weeping with rage and don't want to replace the tricolor star with a red one. Some have managed to pass over to the Osoppo and they tell us that the Garibaldian commissars have launched a campaign of intimidation among the units."

The order arrived from Marshal Tito that the Osoppo Brigade would have to vacate the area, "unless it consents to join the Slovene ranks." The Osoppo responded by starting a newspaper, *Quelli del tricolore*. Guido, in his letter, asks Pier Paolo to write an article or to send some poems. He says: "You must be an Italian speaking to Italians."

It was in this atmosphere that the horrible episode of the Italian Resistance known as the "Porzûs massacre" unfolded. Guido Pasolini was to be killed there "by a fraternal enemy hand."

It all happened for complex reasons, among which the "Slovene question" acted as a fuse. By now it has been ascertained—it was broached in the course of the two trials (the first held in Udine in 1945, and even more so at the second trial, in Lucca, 1951–1952) that helped to unravel the tangled skein of events and in historical studies that have since been conducted on the case[21]—that the Osoppo units were used for definite anti-Communist purposes by the local nationalist leadership of the Resistance. This led to a conspicuous misunderstanding, on the part of the Communists, of certain actions— specifically those inspired by the rigid soldierly ideals of Commander Bolla, otherwise known as Francesco De Gregori, a fervent monarchist, under whom Guido Pasolini served.

There was talk of contacts with Nazis and fascists—and these took place, through the archbishop of Udine, for purposes of a reconciliation or truce, without producing any actual results. But because of this, and since the local Communist leaders were misinformed, they were able with frightful irresponsibility to engage in a show of force that ended in a massacre. Commander Bolla's Osoppo Brigade was accused of treason.

On February 7, 1945, a column of some hundred *gappisti*, members of the Gruppo d'Azione Partigiana, most of them very young and unaware of the true purpose of the operation, climbed to the heights of Porzûs. In the afternoon of the same day, Bolla, Gastone Valente, a commander who was supposed to replace him and who was known as Enea, and Elda Turchetti, an alleged spy, were killed. The three had been handed over to be shot after being tried by a kangaroo court. Fourteen other members of the Osoppo Brigade, including Guido Pasolini, were taken prisoner and killed in the days that followed. They were not liquidated on the heights but below in the plain. There was talk of their having been beaten to death with hammers, but although this story gained currency in people's imaginations, there is no truth in it. The executioners did not inform their victims of the fate that awaited them.

The prisoners, having been brought to the plain, were assembled for the "political hour" on the evening of February 8. There was an interruption: since the subject being discussed was justice, Guido yelled that as far as justice was concerned, the only kind known to the Communists was a "bullet in the back of the neck." No one bothered to answer him.

In the following days the fourteen were slain in small groups, a few at a time. Guido seems to have succeeded in escaping from the hands of his executioners a few minutes before he was to have been shot.[22] A burst of machine-gun fire caught him in the shoulder and right arm. He took refuge in the house of an old peasant woman named Libera Piani. He asked for help, without explaining his wounds. The woman comforted him, offering him coffee with milk and brandy. Two Garibaldians came in and said they would take the boy to the hospital. Guido, much weakened, was dragged out bodily.

They took him to the house of Lina Madaloni, where the head of the National Liberation Committee of Dolegnano was lodged. Here a third Garibaldian arrived. He recognized Guido Pasolini and said to the others, "If you let him get away, I'll kill you." He went out to look for a bicycle.

He came back and loaded Guido's now almost lifeless body on the frame of the bicycle. He assured the others that he was taking him to the hospital in Cormons; instead he took him back to the spot from which he had fled. They made him lie down in the grave that had already been dug. A battalion commander seems to have finished him off with a pistol. The incident took place in Bosco Romagno, near Novocuzzi, probably on February 10.

Reports of the slaughter were immediate and confused. It was thought to be a Slovenian attack, then one by fascists. A few days later Garibaldians and *gappisti* were summoned to explain. The Friulian Communist Federation ordered an investigation. The local National Liberation Committee was threatened with a split, which was averted only by the arrival of the Liberation at the end of April.

The break within the partisan association took place later, in the midst of the cold war, at the time of the trial in Lucca. The "Slovenian question" returned to the limelight: there were accusations of treason, of attacks on the territorial integrity of the State. The trial was the occasion for a violent anti-Communist campaign, to which the Italian Communist Party reacted by insisting that the episode be seen in the harsh political perspective of the Friulian borders—the threat of a Slovenian occupation had embittered people's minds during the months of the partisan struggle. The fascists had, sometimes successfully, fomented splits within the armed antifascist resistance. The Yugoslavs, for their part, had acted irresponsibly, almost as though their intention was to exacerbate the conflict.

The court decision in Lucca, by which thirty-six persons were convicted, explained the events by the rivalry and animosity that had arisen between Garibaldians and Osoppians over an ideological disagreement.

Historians maintain that it represents a bitter page in the class struggle that developed alongside the war of national liberation: the anti-Communist, tactical deployment of the Osoppo units could only have led to tragedy. The aim was clear: to play a few dangerous cards in preparation for what would later be the political confrontation in liberated Friuli. It may seem to some that this interpretation serves to eliminate personal responsibility, but such is not the case. The guilty parties were singled out by the sentence, and the guilt falls both on certain local Communist leaders, and to a greater extent on those *gappisti* on whose initiative the massacre was carried out.

The Lucca decision, in any case, left no room for further controversy. Even while handing down prison sentences, it freed all the defendants of accusations of treason and attacks on the territorial integrity of the State.

It was from Cesare Bortotto that Pasolini, on the afternoon of May 2, 1945, learned with certainty that Guido had been killed at Porzûs. He was walking with his cousin Annie on the Versuta road, when Bortotto, returning as a partisan from the mountains, told him the facts. Pier Paolo was petrified. Susanna Pasolini was to receive the official notice a few days later.

For mother and son, Guido's death was "like a huge, frightful mountain." Of this mountain, Pier Paolo wrote to Serra on August 21, 1945: "The farther we get from it now, the higher and more terrible it looks to us against the horizon."[23]

Guido had died "on the borders." These "borders" revealed to Pasolini a tragic reality, one hitherto hidden behind the veil of linguistic problems. The world of the "borders" could even demand the sacrifice of human lives, and thereby eliminate any literary consolation.

The event, on the one hand, radicalized the idea of death in Pier Paolo's existential experience; on the other, it drove him to seek, if not political justification, at least the political path whereby the misunderstandings and ethnic conflicts (magnified by fascism and the war) that had produced so tragic a result as this massacre might be dissolved.

By now the bombings had wiped out the Casarsa of his youth, the Casarsa "of his dreams." The church, on whose walls old frescoes "with somewhat cold blues and vaguely Gothic forms" showed through, lay in ruins. In May 1945 it was the real Casarsa that was disclosed to Pasolini's eyes, and this initiated in him a progressive approach to local political life.

The excitement of the Liberation, and the months that followed it, demanded of a great many people, even the most absentminded intellectuals, a specific public commitment. In Pasolini, this commitment shunned vague question-begging—it was lived on a day-to-day basis and in the midst of controversy. In *La ricchezza*, at a distance of twelve and fifteen years from that time, he wrote that he had arrived "at the days of the Resistance / without knowing anything of them except their style." That "style" was "pure light"—and "pure light" was Susanna's later despair as well.

Came the day of death
and of freedom, the tortured world
recognized itself in the light as new . . .

That light was the hope of justice:
I didn't know which: Justice.
Light is always the same as other light.
Later it varied: from light it became uncertain dawn,
a dawn that grew, widened
over the Friulian fields, on the ditches.
It illumined the struggling farm hands.
Thus the rising dawn was a light
outside the eternity of style . . .[24]

The lines allude to a transition that had occurred: the "eternity of style" combines the literary illusion of *Poesie a Casarsa* and the first issue of *Stroligut*; the "rising dawn," the awareness of concrete problems produced by the postwar period.

If we look for evidence of this transition, two texts on Guido's death, found among Pier Paolo's posthumous papers and certainly intended to be read aloud, tell how the pain and sense of being petrified became sublimated in his mind and transformed into a balanced judgment of what had happened.

The first must have been prepared immediately after the Liberation, perhaps for the first ceremony commemorating the victims of Porzûs. The certificate of Guido's death, sent to Susanna by the Command of the Fourth Osoppo Division, and signed by Commander "Emilio" of the Fourteenth Brigade, bears the date of June 21, 1945. That was the day on which Guido's body was brought back to Casarsa and buried there. Pier Paolo most likely wrote this piece for the occasion (one would suspect that Carlo Alberto was not present: there is not a word about his grief).[25]

I am not speaking because I hold any office or any special merit, but only because I am the brother of one of these martyrs. The extent of my mother's grief, my own, and that of all these brothers and mothers and relatives, I don't feel up to expressing at this time. Certainly it is too great a reality, that of knowing them to be dead, to be contained in our hearts as men. They are dead, carrying away with them the whole past of their families, our whole past, and they have left us alone on this earth that seems to us so foreign. Speaking for my brother, I can say that it was the fate of his enthusiastic body that killed him, and that he could not survive his enthusiasm. The ideals for which he died, his gentle tricolor, have transported him into a silence that now is no longer ours. And all his heroic comrades with him. And only we, their relatives, can mourn them, even as we do not deny that we are proud of them, even as we remain convinced that without their martyrdom there would not be sufficient strength to react against baseness, and cruelty, and egoism, in the name of those ideals for which they died. We alone can mourn them, we who knew how they spoke, how they laughed, how they loved us. We alone can mourn them, we who know how alive they were, and how desperately they wished to return to us, to their homes, to the lives they cherished. Other people, no, they cannot mourn them except in passing; for other people this can only be a tragic episode, a necessary martyrdom. It is proper and human that it be this way. But we do not ask society for tears, we ask for justice.

The second text is from two years later, and it, too, was probably delivered during a memorial ceremony. Pasolini is by now a militant in the ranks of the left, but his militancy makes him subtly polemical.

Sunday in Subit (the weather having made it impossible to reach the upland pastures of Porzûs) a ceremony was held in memory of Bolla, Enea, and their comrades, murdered by a gang of degenerate Garibaldians. As the brother of Ermes, one of the martyrs, I must first of all thank the organizers of this moving pilgrimage and all the guests, whose loyalty has been truly comforting. Two years have passed since the day of the massacre, but I am still unable to face that "infinite obstacle" that guards my brother's life and his sacrifice from our uncertain interpretation. Too much generosity died with him, a twenty-year-old boy, and there is too much purity in the death he deliberately faced. Yet of one thing I can be sure, that it is legitimate for me to speak in his name. And in his name I must say unfortunately that the ceremony in Subit was lacking in sincerity; in sincerity, I say, not in good faith. The deaths of Enea, Bolla, and my brother, of D'Orlandi and all the others have been interpreted on a level of patriotism (to what general extent this is not the occasion to note), instead of on a level of morality. For this reason the poor victims of Porzûs were not once again present among us on Sunday and were only an abstract pretext. I believe that their relationship with the Garibaldians who murdered them was nothing less than a relationship between Good and Evil; they thus died in the name of that Spirituality that is also inherent in communism or even in the worst of men. If we want them, in the name of this Spirituality, to go on living among us, it is of THEM we must think, not of the human symbols for which they gave their lives. Look at my brother and his friend D'Orlandi; on that tragic day they were returning to Porzûs from Musi, and having been informed of the betrayal by some of their comrades who were trying to escape, they did not wish to turn back, and their heroic decision to go to the aid of their commander led them to martyrdom. How can we, their families, now consider that martyrdom pointless because Italy must sign an unjust peace and lose part of its territory? In that martyrdom itself lies an incorruptible goodness.

The point is clear: a polemic against those who, if only to accept a peaceful compromise with Yugoslavia, put the ceding of the Carso hinterland before any "moral" evaluation of the massacre. In preserving "morality" as the expression of a civic feeling, Pasolini released the trauma suffered over the death of his brother from the sphere of the private. But this death became an emblem, the fountain of light in the rising dawn, "outside the eternity of style."

CHAPTER 4

FRIULIAN EPOS

LIFE IN CASARSA

In Casarsa— . . . in old Casarsa, with its dozen dilapidated houses of the sixteenth century, the porticoes, which, in those areas aged with the generations, ingratiate by their structural traces of inner orchards, kitchen gardens, livestock folds, pens, and low stone walls, not infrequently display in the center the soft blues or blackish tones of some crude Renaissance painter. Here people speak a gray and solid Friulian that is still intact and exemplary in its archaic quality. They speak this Casarsese in old families of small landowners, in which marriages between relatives have not been unusual, and who by tradition are attached to the church. This explains on the one hand the survival of certain traditions otherwise unaccountable at this highway junction, and may on the other justify the impression of anyone who catches in this speech something like the gray odor of incense, a monotonous Sunday boredom, an echo of liturgical choruses sung in the penumbra of the apse by boys and old men, their hair combed, by Catholic tradition, with a part on one side and a forelock standing up over their wooden and irregular faces.

Beyond the station, having traversed the long and dull avenue of the lingua franca that unites the two villages, one comes to San Giovanni. What joyfulness, if not always expressed, surely hangs always in the air of San Giovanni! What a constant possibility for happy encounters with gatherings of people ready for the warmest and most excited comradeship!

There are certain summer evenings when, having passed through three or four villages by bicycle, one happens to ride through San Giovanni and to feel there in all its calm stretch of lights, of songs sung half aloud, of sounds lost in their throbbing echoes within an atmosphere of dust and dew, the genius of the peasant summer. There is no hamlet that can compare to San Giovanni for freshness of inspiration in bringing together groups of friends amid the shadows of the large piazza, in thronging the streets, in raising sudden shouts from some orchard lost in the warmth, in evoking snatches of song hummed from afar . . . The echoes of laughter, of challenges, of fists playing *morra*,* never cease.[1]

With the war over, Sundays were more beautiful; work was joyous, and there was the joyous possibility of breaking everyday habits. Pier Paolo was living in Casarsa, having given up Bologna for good. Bologna remained a place for study, for meeting friends, and little else. Maternal Friuli had filled his imagination to the brim. And the two poles of Catholic ritual and of uninhibited and happy peasant festivity were embodied in the character of the two places between which his existence unfolded—Casarsa and Versuta, or rather the hamlet of San Giovanni.

Pier Paolo organized a film club in Casarsa. Fritz Lang came to show his films, and as an actor and director put together a theater company with which he staged some contemporary works, including Eugene O'Neill's one-act play *The Rope*. Community life seemed to extract Pasolini from the shadows of his conscience: Guido's death, his troubled inner tranquillity.

Because of his son's death, Carlo Alberto Pasolini was granted an early return from the prisoner-of-war camp in Kenya. By late autumn of 1945 he was in Casarsa. In that same autumn, on November 26, Pier Paolo received his arts degree with honors. His thesis, discussed with Carlo Calcaterra as required, was entitled *Antologia della lirica pascoliana (introduzione e commenti)*. The originality of the anthology —chosen on the basis of criteria not far from those of Croce's distinction between poetry and nonpoetry†—lies in its linguistic

---

* Game in which each of two players shows some of the fingers of one hand while shouting a number; the one who calls the number equaling the sum of the fingers shown is the winner.—Tr.

† The dialectical interaction between aesthetic and extra-aesthetic tendencies in a given poet's work, or in the human spirit itself. Croce developed the distinction in 1886; in 1923 *Poesia e non poesia* became the title of a collection of essays, translated in 1924 as *European Literature in the Nineteenth century*.—Tr.

emphasis. Though the style is determined by its academic purpose, marked, however, by a discriminating choice of adjectives, it is not hard to detect an autobiographical line in the text. Pasolini discerns in Pascoli the poet who possesses the language "through the native and mother dialect"; he dissects the writer of an "ordinary Romance modern Italian, almost dialect, that is to say minor." He enjoys comparing him to Tommaseo for "a kind of dull and montonous style, of disagreeable delicacy, too lacking in sensuality."

Through this he probes the repressed romanticism of the *Myricae* and the *Poemi conviviali*: "The effort at knowledge availed itself of speech as the only sure means; and to have discovered an image, an original connection, was to enter more deeply into the indifference of the unknowable world." Halfway between the religious desperation of Rimbaud and the existential "terrible inquietude" of Rilke, Pascoli was not to live his own *saison en enfer*, i.e., the heartbreaking absence of God, to its ultimate extreme, due to the slothfulness of a literary and moral tradition from which he was able to free neither himself nor the Italian culture of his time.

What is autobiographical about this? An autobiographical content, though inexplicit, is present. In this graduate thesis a poetics is implied that has begun to take shape, seeks confirmation, and assumes the form of a critical plan.

Confirmation was also provided by what life was able to suggest. In his active participation in the community life of Casarsa—the theatrical performances or sharing in village feasts, in the collective Sunday "transgressions" on the public dance platforms that on feast days seemed like floating rafts in the midst of a crowd half-mad with joy—beyond the natural expansiveness of youthful exuberance, there was also a touch of willfulness. He who tries to live the life of other people so intensely often wants to flee from his own. Pasolini's inner life was, to himself, a brightly illuminated scene—what was happening there demanded compensation. Casarsa life, enjoyed in all its possible forms, was certainly a compensation, but a compensation that in its turn demanded an excess of clarity and light. The primal scene opened on another scene, one theater called up another. Thus, intellectual reflection draws nourishment from existence.

His friends, of course, were summoned to these scenes. But Pasolini did not require simply their presence. He gave of himself, and encouraged and judged them with a passion that was generous to the point of risk.

Giovanna Bemporad returned for a visit. The girl had settled in Venice after the war, another stop in her continual wandering. She spent a few holidays in Casarsa, and there Pier Paolo pressed her to participate in the village dances and drinking bouts, in the hope that she might free herself from the martyrdom of her aestheticism.

In a letter dated January 20, 1947, he wrote to her (Giovanna must have spent New Year's with him):

I did not salute your images; that wish of yours seemed to me too ego-tistical. Can it really not have occurred to you to have me say hello to our poor little group of New Year's friends in Casarsa instead? Do you absolutely refuse to pardon them for the crime of not writing poetry? I know, now you feel insulted; forgive me. People are stupid, base, con-fused, but there is an aspiration in them, an inferiority complex that can still be considered a residue of abstract goodness; this is something worth-while and should not be overlooked by those of us who have a conscience. Basically you have a very romantic concept of the poet, and you want to have yourself forgiven for too many things because you write poems, i.e., have something divine about you. But you're still not so superior to others not to feel hurt if they don't forgive you ...

Eleven days later, obviously in response to a letter of explanation, Pier Paolo wrote again:

Thanks for your good letter. Just when you seem lost in a murky and fatal darkness, you come out of it with artlessness and candor; you have your lovable comebacks. When will these comebacks be reflected on the outside? And when will your face, your glasses, your stockings shine with kindness? When will you sing the Settima* silently, without insult-ing others by declaiming it aloud? ...

Beyond the occasion, these words clearly demonstrate the pedagogic spirit that animated Pasolini, not only in his relations with his friends but also toward the Casarsa community. This spirit was the expression of a feeling that every intellectual, in his opinion, ought actively to cultivate in himself ("those of us who have a conscience"). In these very words, however, one can see the reflection of what was leading Pier Paolo both toward active politics and teaching school. For a moment Friuli, and Casarsa in particular, represented the place for him to carry his epic destiny to completion.

* Seventh-day Requiem mass.—Tr.

ACTIVE POLITICS

The first commitment was to Friulian autonomy. On October 30, 1945, Pasolini joined the *Patrie tal Friul* association, established in Udine by Tiziano Tessitori. The association's political program was openly in favor of autonomy.

This was a difficult time for Friuli. Caught between Yugoslavia's expansionism and the residue of fascist rhetoric, the program of the autonomists was a confused, not to say hysterical, one. A debate was in progress about whether to promote Pordenone to a province, a Friulian province for the area *di cà da l'aga*. Pasolini spoke up on the question, and in elaborating his own rejection of this possible solution, he clarified the meaning of his own idea of autonomy. His contribution, entitled "Che cos'è dunque il Friuli" (So What Is Friuli), appeared in *Libertà*, an Udine newspaper, on November 6, 1946.

"Pordenone is a linguistic island almost in the heart of Friuli, and this is not a mere circumstance, a negligible circumstance—it is simply the result of a different history, and thus of a different (in the sense of mentality) civilization. . . . The Duchy of Pordenone, directly dependent on Austria, lived for too long a time autonomously in the bosom of the Patriarchate of Friuli, and when this ended, it passed, already too de-Friulianized, under the rule of the Republic of Venice. . . . It is enough to board a train (for instance, the one that goes through Casarsa at seven in the morning) and compare the students and clerks from Pordenone with those from Casarsa, and especially with those from Codroipo and Basiliano." The fact is that "Veneto" behavior looks quite different from "Friulian."

In this phonic and linguistic determination (which seeks to rise to the level of anthropology and collective psychology), Pasolini's autonomistic conception stands out: "Sentimentally and irrationally, we . . . feel that Friuli is not the Veneto; it is Italy, to be sure; but one should blush even to say so, almost for fear that the opposite proposition might exist and be formulated."

Friulian autonomy ought therefore to be pursued for the purpose of strengthening, not weakening, the Italian frontiers: "There is no better way to oppose the underhanded expansion of the Slavs than a Friulian Region that is conscious of itself, electrified by the dignity conferred on it by right of its clearly differentiated language, customs, and economy."

While the Constituent Assembly was debating the future regional arrangement and planning the Friuli-Venezia Giulia region, Pasolini published two front-page articles in *Libertà*, on December 31, 1946, and January 26, 1947. His target in the two pieces was a double one: on one side the sentimental regionalism of those who used the protection of Friulian customs only as an excuse for political and cultural immobility; on the other, the positions of the left, in particular the Communists.

The Christian Democrats on the one hand were supporting Friulian autonomy, or rather supporting the parochial intemperance of the Friulians as a barrier against the twists and turns of pro-Slavism; on the other hand, the Communist Party—and we are already in 1947, that is to say, at the rupture of the democratic solidarity of the Committee of National Liberation—opposed autonomy. Togliatti's policy at the time was one of "unity," of national cohesion.

But Pasolini, who begins his article of December 31, 1946, with the words "Being Communists ourselves," does not hesitate to interweave his polemics with the official line of the Communist Party; and on January 26, 1947, he writes: "It would be above all up to the left . . . to ensure that the new regional bodies (Friulian, Veneto, Lombard, etc.) do not become dens of local interests, of parochialism—in a word, of reaction; but that on the contrary they be the most immediate and natural field of social progress. . . . Do the Communists fear the rekindling of bourgeois and clerical conservatism in the Region? No, it would actually be more a question of its blessed indolence; and the suggestion or installation of a new mentality capable of transforming prehistory into history, nature into consciousness, would depend on them. For our part, we are convinced that only Communism at present is capable of furnishing a 'real' new culture . . . a culture that will represent both morality and a full interpretation of life."

In the official Communist position Pasolini saw tactical expediency —the Communists were against autonomy out of abstract opposition to the Christian Democrats, for reasons of political alignment. But a year later, he was to insist, on February 28, 1948, in *Il Mattino del Popolo* of Venice, again on the front page, that he had done his utmost many times "to demonstrate that the foundations for a *leftist* interpretation of autonomy existed and were even rather solid." At this point, however, he found himself resigning from the Movimento Popolare Friulano—which he had also helped to found in January 1947. (This movement had been hastily transformed, when Parliament voted regional autonomy for Friuli on June 27, 1947, into an association in support of the Christian Democrats, a secular arm, between Udine and Pordenone, of the party that was setting out to win the April 18 elections.)

But by now Pasolini was a Communist intellectual,[2] and for him political problems took shape within the dialectic of the party. Some have found it disconcerting that he had approached the Italian Communist Party as early as 1946. After all, he was the brother of Guido, who had been killed by the Communists at Porzûs. One might give a simplistic interpretation of that gesture, taking it for pure provocation. But Pier Paolo saw in Communism a dialectic and rational weapon. As he wrote in his article of January 26, 1947, it was a way of "transforming prehistory into history, nature into consciousness."

One could maintain that this was an illusion, and this is not to say that he was not even aware of the illusory character of such a faith. But the effects of reason, as he was now convinced, could not be detached from the wellsprings of feeling. This intuition saved him, once and for all, from banal Marxist orthodoxy. In Pasolini's Communist choice, his "populist" idealism, which was being enhanced and consolidated in these very years of 1943–1945, should not be underestimated. The urgency of redemption or social regeneration had become acute in the Friulian countryside during the Nazi occupation and the partisan struggle.

The Communist cell that Pasolini joined, probably in the course of 1947, was in fact the one in San Giovanni di Casarsa, a cell marked by a violent anticlerical controversy (understandable given the diehard clericalism that tinged public life in nearby Casarsa). In the 1946 elections, San Giovanni gave 700 votes to the Communists, 420 to the Christian Democrats.

The Christian Democrats were harshly anti-Communist; on the other side, the Communist militants, where they existed in large numbers, reacted with equal forcefulness. The Communist Regional Federation in Udine tried many times to soothe the harshness of the Communists of San Giovanni, but in vain. When, in 1949, Pasolini became secretary of his cell, the arguments were becoming more violent and cutting, since, though the members were anticlerical and opposed to the Christian Democrats, they had not divorced themselves from Christian principles.

On the little square in San Giovanni, to the left as one arrives from Casarsa, there is a small loggia in the Veneto style: two ogival arches on the front, one on the side; the same number of windows on the upper story, elegantly ornate in the manner of the fifteenth century; similarly ornate is the cornice of the little structure, evidence of a happy communal civilization. Under this loggia—a stone bench runs around it—bulletin boards are placed for the wall posters of political parties. During the period in which he was the local secretary, Pasolini wrote texts in Italian and in dialect for the Communist board. It was the time of the signing of the North Atlantic Treaty, the time of the Peace Congress in Paris (attended by Pier Paolo in the delegation with Mario Lizzero); it was also the time when Pope Pius XII was excommunicating Communists. Here are Pasolini's responses:

Appeal to Christians for peace.
Clergymen of all the Churches were present at the World Peace Congress in Paris. There were Anglicans, Orthodox, Protestants, Calvinists, and CATHOLICS. The Abbé Boulier, a Catholic priest, gave his allegiance to the Congress and pronounced lofty, fresh, and moving words. An appeal to all Christians was issued from Paris, and from it we transcribe these words: The kingdom of God is the kingdom of peace. The Christian cannot deny the advent of this kingdom if he has not decided to work for it in the present world. In 1949 the Christian is incited by propaganda to give his approval to war in the form of a crusade against Soviet Russia. In the name of Christ, our common teacher, we implore every Christian to understand that such a crusade would be a crime against humanity and one with which he cannot burden his conscience.

The texts in dialect are less general, more subtly ironical:

Black souls.
What is this political policy that the priests are carrying out against us poor people? They're the ones who ought to think as we do; it seems to us that our feelings are Christian enough! Christian Democrats are amazed if the Communists go to mass, when instead the Communists might be more amazed in seeing the Christian Democrats go to mass with their souls as black as coal.

Or:

The satisfactions of a fool.
Two men were talking in the courtyard of a house. One of them said that it was better not to get involved in politics and to let the world go on as it had to, since it had always been this way and always would be, that the bosses had always existed and always would exist, and so on and so forth. The other lost patience and said: "We Communists don't think

like that. One shouldn't let oneself be led by the nose by those who have done so up until now, and it's time to put a stop to it!" And the first answered: "At least now we have freedom." And the other: "What freedom, to die of hunger?" And the first: "And why not? I may be dying of hunger but I can go to De Gasperi* and tell him 'You're an idiot.'" Replied the Communist: "These are the satisfactions of a fool."

In a dialogue between a Christian Democrat and a Communist, in which the latter recalls the Gospel teaching "to love one's neighbor, not to do unto others what you would not like to have done unto you, and many other things," the conclusion is:

Don't you see that if the fear of God exists it's for ourselves alone, and those who are against us haven't even one religious principle, because they're so sly that they're always on the side of right, and they're full of iniquity and without any scruples, and we who work every day and who haven't much strength left are the first to be blamed, and this is the Gospel of the rich! But every so often the priest tells us that it is harder for a rich man to enter Heaven than for a camel to go through the eye of a needle. That's our consolation.

These wall posters go back to the spring and summer of 1949. Pasolini's Friulian years were about to come to a dramatic end and these polemics, political and Friulian, played a part in it. One should point out the cultural and intellectual plane on which the writer was moving in formulating them. A great distance lies between *Poesie a Casarsa* and these texts. The sublime idea of the "eternity of style" has suffered a complete decline, and Pasolini's perception of the peasant moral universe has been given over to the concrete. Above this universe, as common denominator, an equation is set up between Christianity and Communism, between Gospel doctrine and Marxist doctrine.

Populism and Manicheism ("good" people on one side, the "bad" on the other) constitute the points of reference of Pasolini's reasoning (with the well-founded suspicion that in order to win uneducated readers to his side he deliberately employs the style of the moral fable). Along with this, he speaks "from the left" of Catholic values.

So much was happening in 1949. The papacy of Pius XII was at

* Alcide De Gasperi (1881–1954) was the first prime minister of the new, postwar Italian Republic and of six successive governments, 1945–1953.—Tr.

its height. It had transformed Catholicism into an ideology, which it sought to impose as custodian, guarantor, and chaplain of society. A different idea shone through Pasolini's wall posters—an idea that considers religion as a form of restless human conscience, by which to reflect on spiritual errors and "faithfulness." The same communion with Marxism, in the light of this, could be contemplated and experienced without one's faith being shattered.

These posters were tinged with peasant good sense. At a distance, they seem in a way like "Romance" *haikai*, Brechtian fables inspired by the Gospel dictum of charity. But something else is depicted here— the archaic feeling of rural community life. That life is the locus for a ceaseless discovery of relationships, in which the individual finds the possibility for an existential base and a positive public role.

POLITICS AND CULTURE

The wall posters of 1949 mark the climax of Pasolini's political activity in Friuli. He had become a political figure in the region. A photograph shows him among the founders of the Communist Provincial Federation of Pordenone in 1948—he is on the flag-decked platform, on the other side of the table, among official representatives of the party.

There was in him a precocious vocation for leadership. This should not be taken in the negative sense: the cultural ideas for which he became the spokesman were what placed him in the limelight.

He gave lectures, held meetings and debates, and wrote front-page articles for various daily newspapers of the region. As for literature, he was no longer merely the promising writer and philologist printed in *Il Stroligut*.[3] He was contributing to *La Fiera letteraria*, drawing the attention not only of Friulian writers but also of other young writers outside his narrow provincial sphere.[4]

In 1947 he had shared in the "Libera Stampa" prize of the Ticino canton in Switzerland. Gianfranco Contini was on the jury. A number of friendships consolidated Pasolini's position on the national level. Enrico Falqui invited him to contribute to *Poesia*, and asked him for essays for the literary page of *Il Mattino di Roma*. In Venice, on March 29, 1947, he won the Angelo prize, an award for poems in the Friulian and Veneto dialects organized by art critics and painters. The jury was headed by Giuseppe Marchiori.

He had painter friends. He himself painted, using oils, as well as such natural materials as herb juices and coffee. His adolescent passion for painting had by no means become dormant. Among his artist friends, Giuseppe Zigaina deserves particular mention. Zigaina and Pasolini had met in Udine, on the occasion of a group exhibition in 1945 in which they were both included. Their friendship was not simply the result of their coming from the same region. Zigaina, from Cervignano, would accompany Pasolini on bicycle trips for linguistic research in the villages of the plain. The two were militant Communists, and their party duties often brought them together.

From this association came a small volume, *Dov'è la mia patria* (Where My Homeland Is). It contained poems by Pasolini, written from 1948 to 1949, and drawings by Zigaina, and was published by the *Academiuta* in 1949. Here we have strophes gathered from the lips of "speakers"—and the "spoken" original is scrupulously kept intact—from Caorle, Valvasone, Cordenons, Pordenone, a whole linguistic geography transcribed in the rhythm of the poet.[5]

Zigaina's post-Cubism was juxtaposed to the Romance-language experimentalism of Pasolini. Post-Cubism was the style by which the Italian realists, in those years of intellectual excitement, were discovering Europe; it was also the style in which political faith and moral truth came to be synthesized. It was, in short, an epic style—that same epos that Pasolini was imaginatively pursuing in the Friuli scenario.

> Do you remember that evening in Ruda?
> When we gave ourselves together to a game
> of pure passion, measure of our raw
> youth, of our as yet little more
> than childish hearts? . . .
>
>   . . . one alongside
>
> the other, we shouted the words
> that, almost not understood, were sure
> promise, love expressed and revealed.

These are a few tercets from *Quadri friulani* (1955).[6] By the time Pasolini wrote these lines, Friuli was for him the distant background of poetic memories. He was recalling a political meeting he had held with Zigaina in the little square in Ruda, among "day laborers in holiday clothes," "boys coming by bicycle/from the nearby villages." It was also the memory of a shared passion, mirrored in Zigaina's painting:

The swollen and festive air

of your first pictures, where the green
was almost a childish green
and the yellow a hardened wax . . .

In this painting bursts of imagination are fused with "a greenish/ stench of grass, of dung, stirred/by the wind . . ." It is the life of the fields in its exalting complexity, but it is also the indication of a new culture, in which post-Cubism ended by being incinerated by the naturalism of the Po valley, by a Panic, almost mystical sensitivity to the physical and existential fact. The "hardened wax" in Zigaina's painting was the equivalent of the hardened uvula of the Friulian "speaker."

What was the outline of this "new culture"? Pasolini did not hesitate to work out a plan of it, to participate personally in what in leftist jargon was called "cultural work."

"Is there a new culture, a progressive culture? This is the question that the worker and the peasant would like to put to me, but it is a premature question. Culture in Italy is still bourgeois." These words are taken from a talk at the First Congress of the Communist Federation of Pordenone that Pasolini was not able to give, but which was published in a bulletin entitled *Per la pace e per il lavoro* (For Peace and Work) in March 1949.[7]

Of the "critical" attitude of the intellectuals in the presence of the bourgeoisie, one cannot ask anything beyond the "polemical" side— "on the creative side, instead," everything "is still very uncertain."

Pasolini knows that it takes a "long time" to create art, and his remarks have the tone of an antidote when one thinks of the demagoguery of those years.

There is a "bourgeois" literature that satisfies the huge majority of the population, one composed of bad taste, hypocrisy, puritanism, pornography, and sentimentality; but there is also a bourgeois literature that is opposed to and lies outside the taste of the bourgeois and bourgeoisified masses, and is all intelligence, richness, fantasy, audacity, impartiality . . .

An alignment of right and left exists even in literature, and for purely literary reasons, but those who are on the left in literature are not always on the left in politics, etc. There is thus a double set of relations between literary avant-gardism and political avant-gardism.

The literary man is not generally at the service of capitalism as he once was at the service of the nobility or the kings; his service is indirect and his choice is due to the influence of a bourgeois environment of which he has not become aware from a social point of view. Generally the literary man is ready to betray his class . . .

What for the Marxist was an immediate and direct connection between "structure" and "superstructure," between economic class basis and expression, in Pasolini's words becomes a complex relationship, shading into a set of facing mirror images. "Those who are on the left in literature are not always on the left in politics"—this is the reverse of Lukács's thesis on Balzac. But it is a daring reversal: the intentions of the ego do not always match its secret, or its nature.

Pasolini seems to call into question, as he was to do later in the years of *Officina* and after, the "progressive" design of neorealism, and though he indulges in a few moralisms,[8] his arguments allow the periscope to revolve in the broadest range.

What is now asked of the intellectual is not an easy or a comfortable thing: it involves a renunciation. May he too carry out that introspective, inner, diaristic examination, which is in fact the vital exercise of the man of thought, though especially and immensely individual, without which it is impossible to be an artist; but try to be, in this work of his, more objective and more, let us even say, Christian, and take his place in human history. At first this historicism of his will perhaps not be faithful to Marxism-Leninism, it will presuppose some idealism, some Catholicism, some anarchy, some humanitarianism, but also life and the will for renewal. And it is this, I think, that is asked today of the literary man: this is what basically Banfi and Marchesi meant when they stated that the Communist literary man should be completely free to do as he liked in literature and still remain a loyal comrade in politics.

Beyond these words, one sees not only Labriola or Croce. There is the experience of European decadentism, understood positively as a moment not to be rejected in a realistic vision of cultural problems.

PEDAGOGY

Nineteen forty-seven. Valvasone, twelve kilometers from Casarsa by open road. A group photo: a secondary-school class—boys in short pants, others in long pants, gym shoes, sandals, with or without socks, clothing thrown together as was happening everywhere in the impoverished Italy of the postwar period, dim smiles, candid smiles; three girls in black smocks, neater than the boys, and thus showing a modest awareness of being almost women.

This is Professor Pasolini's class. The teacher stands among his pupils, wearing a dark double-breasted suit with a white shirt and necktie, his hair parted over his forehead on the left.

Following the episode of the private school in Versuta, closed "by order of the higher-ups," Pier Paolo was now teaching literature in the state school, but he had not relinquished his personal method. "To see my students using Latin was like seeing beggars in top hats. They were pathetic. We were pathetic."[9]

He traveled by bicycle from Casarsa to Valvasone. Along with the prescribed program, he read poetry (and enchanted his students as he read). He read Chekhov, the stories of Verga, the *Spoon River Anthology*, the words of American Negro spirituals, and, later, Ungaretti, Montale, Saba, Penna, Cardarelli.

He encouraged the children to compose verses, to explore the possibilities of a written use of the Friulian dialect *di cà da l'aga*. He himself improvised for them.

Darzin (Arzene)
"Dulà vatu?"
"A Darzin."*
His voice is a whisper.
The young mechanic
bends over the handlebar
with his hair in his eyes.
His blue overalls bring
the sky to earth . . .
The wheel murmurs
on silken mud . . .
There's Arzene.
The boy raises his head:
the broad curves of the road . . .
the fields . . .
the church suspended on the embankment . . .
He has arrived
in his blue Arzene.

* "Where are you going?"/"To Arzene."

"Bundì Pauli,"* laughing,
he squeezes the brake.

The well on Sunday
White boat
on the green and yellow sea
of the sun, Domanins vanishes.

A little old woman
turns the wheel at the well
in the empty piazza.

Helmsman
of that becalmed boat
the little old woman labors,

lost in the green
and yellow light of the sun.
The hours strike.[10]

Impressionism, landscape, the influence of Pascoli (in the use of a simple rhyme, which keeps time as though folding the suggestion of rhythm back on itself)—these Pasolini poems, composed for his pupils, are like five-finger exercises for the piano student.

The young teacher showed how all of life, what one sees and feels flowing in the heart, can become something else in words and in the accentuated scanning of a line. And the life is that of the surrounding villages, Arzene, Domanins—the one lived by the old woman straining to draw water from the well, or the life of the mechanic on his bicycle, with his blue overalls, and his hair in his eyes.

In the image of those overalls, whose color "bring[s]/the sky to earth," one can read something else, a private element of sensual trepidation, beyond the refinement of a five-finger exercise. Certainly the poet, with his anxieties, did not obliterate himself in teaching school.

This teaching left an imprint. Andrea Zanzotto recalls: "In pointing out Pasolini's experiments to his colleagues, the principal, Natale De Zotti, whose subordinate he was, called him 'an admirable

* "Buon giorno [Good day], Paolo."

teacher.' "[11] Pasolini at the time was conducting experiments in *active pedagogy*, bringing the "benumbed Latin grammar book" to life.

Zanzotto again: "He set up a little garden in the school courtyard and taught the Latin names of the plants; he drew placards with colored figures . . . and made up fairy tales like the one about the monster Userum, so that the children would enjoy learning the adjective endings *us, er,* and *um.*"

Such pedagogy certainly had unconscious, psychoerotic roots—the teacher-pupil relationship is in any case a relationship imbued with eroticism. "Pasolini, being an excellent teacher, knew all the same that he had to change the cultural and social canons in order to be at (relative) peace with himself, and to be able to forgive himself his pedagogic love-violence," Zanzotto comments.

Perhaps, however, he tried other paths in order to "forgive himself" this form of exclusive loving violence. They were paths that outflanked the contingent, wholly psychological, wholly personal problem, and tended to transpose it into the fields of expression. They were the paths of the novel: fantasy and testimony, imaginative projection and autobiographical fact.

Pasolini had an inkling that the narrative fable might help him to escape a tormenting, extremely private obsession. His life in Friuli was dominated by the unconfessed anguish of knowing himself to be *different*. His teaching colleagues, like his friends in Bologna, had glimpsed no trace of this difference. The secret was well guarded, but that did not keep it from seeking to be demonstrated and expressed.

AMADO MIO

The spring of 1948 brought a happy burst of creativity. Seventy-five pages, single-spaced, four chapters in prose—the title, *Amado mio*. The folder containing them bears, between title and date, the words "unfinished novel."

Amado mio is a love story. Desiderio, the hero with an all too programmatic name, is consumed with passion (a true case of love at first sight) for a young boy, Benito, during a village festival. Benito at first rejects him—then he submits, with perhaps something more than a kiss. Later he rejects him once again.

Desiderio is desperate. It is summer, and he again meets Benito (whose name, in Gidean fashion, he changes to Iasìs) at a bend in

the Tagliamento where the boys go swimming and spend happy mornings and afternoons. Sunday dances, drinking bouts; fields drenched
by sunlight, by the darkness of the night, by the faint light of dawn;
bicycle races through the lowlands; a swim in the sea at Caorle, in
the quiet splendor of an early September day. After his long refusal,
motivated by unacknowledged shame, Iasìs will say—at the very end
of that day at Caorle, they are at the cinema, where on the screen
Rita Hayworth is singing "Amado mio" to an audience of frenzied
boys—Iasìs will say, "Tonight."

Everything is told, represented. Pasolini wrote a true Alexandrian
idyll, like something from the *Palatine Anthology*, on which he im-
printed the happiness of a season innocently lived in the most
complete eros.

These pages illustrate the joy that the Tagliamento, the river
whose limpid current merged in his mind with dead acacia branches
and promiscuity among youths, represented for his existence and his
éducation sentimentale.

Something inexpressible: the fifteen, sixteen years of a boy, under-
pants wet and closed modestly with a pin, stumpy hands, immature
limbs, exaltation over an invoked virility—all this Pasolini lets flow
in smooth prose, a prose ever exact, never languid or allusive.

Unhappiness in love seems to be the inevitable pattern of homosexual relationships. In the unexpected conclusion, in Iasìs's surprise
answer, "Tonight," and in the erotic vortex in which it is uttered,
Amado mio suggests something different. It is the novelty of acceptance—with no shadows to darken it—of one's own nature, one's own
destiny, a destiny promising, in human fashion, equal measures of
happiness and pain.

Desiderio sheds bitter tears but attains the "inexpressible." He had
taken the boy with him in the moonlight behind the bushes near a
village dance-floor; then to the stones of the river, where the light
glowed more than ever. Iasìs had always had in his eyes a thread of
regret—it is just this dismayed trepidation, in a boy who is all willingness, that Pasolini succeeds in showing, and he arrives at this by
all the means of a consummate storyteller.

Desiderio went up to him and embraced him. Benito lay still on his
back, looking up. Desiderio kissed him again on the mouth; when he
removed his lips, Benito was still lying there, motionless as before. And
Desiderio again kissed him, three or four times. They were interminable
kisses. But all of a sudden Benito broke loose and ran toward the concrete
blocks, he clambered up and from there began watching the fishes darting

in the water, which was as transparent as air. Once more Desiderio slowly went up to him, and together they gazed at the fishes.

Wherein lies the concreteness, the truth of this story?

It is the concreteness of a psychological truth—the distance, not only of years, but of education and culture, between Desiderio and his friend. The names of Tommaseo, Nievo, Gide, Goethe are mentioned throughout the text. In the grip of despair on the riverbed, when Iasìs seems to reject him for good, Desiderio reads the *Canti del popolo greco*, and there discovers the mirror of his own sorrows:

> ... I will tell the air to greet you for me
> and say that for you a youth is dying ...

The names of Kafka, Dostoevsky, Proust recur as well, not as literary emblems, but rather in accordance with a counterpoint that seems almost to go beyond literature.

No, it is the difference in age between the two characters, which Pasolini indicates and narrates, that makes love bitter and difficult. Desiderio is an adult, he is carried away by the innocence of his Iasìs; but that innocence, just because it is such, cannot help but defend itself from the threat of its own extinction. This is an obscure but rooted feeling, which can only be obliterated in a kind of rite, as part of a collective redemption.

The excursion to Caorle. The day goes by pleasantly: the swim in the sea, the boat. Desiderio and Iasìs had left at dawn—Iasìs had never seen a beach. With them go a friend named Gilberto, Desiderio's companion in studies, and a little boyfriend of Gilberto's. The four of them meet other young boys whom they know, and they all go to the spot where the Livenza River empties into the Adriatic.

When it comes time to return, Desiderio wants to go back on foot. He is eager to be alone with his boy, and is hoping to make love.

Here they are running along the sandy shore, when a horrid spectacle looms up before them:

> In the curve traced by the beach inland along the right bank of the Livenza, the tide had regurgitated a huge and disgusting pile of garbage. Farther inland and at the edges, naturally, lay the lighter refuse, masses of seaweed, starfish, bones, shells; closer to the sea and river, the heavier: the remains of dogs, cats, birds, unrecognizable carcasses, stripped skeletons that whitened like silk and silver under the sun. Some, however, were still fresh and emitted a treacherous and insistent stench. The dogs lay

with their mouths open and curled back, the palate of an awful, Indian red color, the fur stiff, the ears like parchment.

In this repugnant landscape baking in the sun and more painted than real, Iasìs utters his final, decisive "No." "It's better if we don't see each other again," says Desiderio. And Iasìs "remained silent, while the blue of his eyes scarcely dimmed, or shone too brightly."

It is the most utter despair, the farewell that brings tears. But now comes the cinema, and the initiating and restorative rite.

It is an open-air cinema. The moon is out. The boys are yelling with joy, but Desiderio's heart is "aching."

Perhaps it was that striking difference between the audience and the firmament, that awful picket fence in such direct contact with the moon; perhaps it was that beautiful youth with the beautiful brown hair who turned to his friends and shouted the exploits of his own adolescent sex organ; finally perhaps, or especially, it was that phallic aura that an outsider like Desiderio sniffs in every slightest aspect of unknown places, that native, collective, and almost folkloristic eros that becomes fragmented and shattered as in a prism in the crowd of strangers in holiday clothes. But Desiderio was a single aching wound.

The lights go out, the audience holds its breath, and the film begins, "the most beautiful film Desiderio had ever seen."

Before the image of Gilda something wondrously shared enveloped all the spectators. The music of "Amado mio" was devastating. So much so that the obscene remarks shouted across the audience—"Watch out your buttons don't pop!" "How many times you gonna do it tonight?"—seemed to merge in a rhythm in which time seemed finally to be assuaged, to grant a respite with no happy ending. Even when Iasìs, embraced by Desiderio, rested his head on his shoulder, and in that atmosphere of consummated orgy beyond time, before death, Desiderio's heart seemed finally to melt, it was an emotion at a level where tears became frozen. Rita Hayworth with her huge body, her smile, her breasts of a sister and a prostitute— equivocal and angelic—stupid and mysterious with that nearsighted gaze of hers, cold and tender to the point of languor—sang from the depths of her postwar, roman-fleuve Latin America, with a divinely caressing inexpressiveness . . .

Everything becomes a symbol of Desiderio's "tragic resignation": the "peasant" beauty of the actress, a "post amorem" exhaustion. Instead, just at that point—the obvious effect of the "consummated orgy beyond time," an inescapable rite—Iasìs whispers "Tonight."

Critics will find plenty of room for comment. The landscape of the marine undertow, the orgiastic vision of the film—the impelling expressionistic expansion of the images, the essayistic sorcery suffused with lyricism—all this is material that points broadly ahead to the author of *Ragazzi di vita* and *Una vita violenta.*

There are moments when *Amado mio* seems like a preliminary drawing for the small Friulian fresco that was to come (I am referring to *Il sogno di una cosa*): dance floors and cornfields, groups of boys on the lowland roads, and skies painted with a wholly Veneto taste for light. But Pasolini perhaps never again produced such a crystalline declaration of his own eros, in a vein of total abandonment and Panic joy—and this is something completely new.

It is like reading the headings of a book of illuminated Persian manuscripts, the last of which contains the unforeseen conflagration—the wholly personal intuition of an eroticism that explodes and takes comfort in the celebration of itself. And the usual features of homosexual literature—along the lines of a much pondered *Nourritures terrestres* by Gide—disappear at this point. There is Rita Hayworth on the screen, with her "huge body," epiphany of unknowable nature, terminal point of a highly recognizable physical tension ("Watch out your buttons don't pop," etc.)—the woman, a "peasant," with her languor, suggests, redeems, apotheosizes.

It would seem to be she, at the moment when she takes off a glove "with delicate lust and furious patience," who drives Iasìs to say "Tonight"—and that moment was "a cry of joy, a sweet cataclysm."

Clinically, I believe one can speak of an arrest of the libido at the adolescent phase. But the projection of the father throbs in it insidiously. Desiderio with his arm squeezes his boy's shoulders, and the latter rests his head on Desiderio's shoulder—the relationship is unmistakable. The writer is most certainly here divided, he is one and the other, the father and the boy, united by a passionate urgency that seeks expression before the irresistible epiphany of the female. *Gilda* and Rita Hayworth, needless to say, constituted the symbol of a boundless sexuality—a "postwar," as Pasolini acutely observes, or "*roman-fleuve*" sexuality.

But the becoming one of father with son and vice-versa—a union desperately awaited and strategically postponed for the whole story—

takes place in the dark womb of the cinema, almost as a multiplication of the female and maternal symbolism. The woman is there, an illusory priestess on the screen, singing and dancing, flattering, urging.

At this point, I offer a hypothesis. The incompleteness of the story lies not within itself. It lies in what life has enclosed there as a symbol—the incomplete relationship with the father image that Pasolini contained within himself.

At the time he composed his text, following Cavafy as much as possible (the Greek poet is also included in the quotations), and complied with his "slave penis" freely and unequivocably, he found himself caught in the impossibility of going beyond the (wholly fantastic) hypothesis of an embrace between the "father" who was within him and the "son" that he likewise was. The result was a desperate need for love, for physical love, the need for a warmth and rapture always refused and always, secretly, desired. In this uncompleted narrative—an incompleteness, I repeat, more supposed than actual—Pasolini concealed, by one of those unforeseeable, scorching, and immediate projections of life into art, the meaning of his own obsession: to become father to his boy, so that the latter would mirror, by returning his embrace, all his unsatisfied longings as a son.

A family episode took place at this time. Nico Naldini had acquired a copy of Umberto Saba's *Canzoniere*, the first volume to contain all the poems by the author of *Trieste e una donna*. Pier Paolo asked to borrow it.

Returning home one day, he found it open on his desk. His father had marked the sonnet from the "Autobiografia" sequence that reads:

For me my father had been the "murderer,"
until at the age of twenty I met him.
Then I saw that he was a child,
and that the gift I have I had from him.

On his face he had my pale blue smile,
a soft and crafty smile in misery.
Always a pilgrim, he went about the world;
more than one woman loved and nourished him.

He was light and gay; my mother
felt all the burdens of life.
He escaped from her hand like a balloon.

"Don't be like your father," she admonished.
And later I understood it in myself:
They were two races in age-old conflict.

Carlo Alberto was trying to reappropriate his son for himself, a son who had been divided because of the mother and in the mother. In Saba he had read something deeply gratifying to himself ("he was light and gay"). Heaven knows if he succeeded in following to the end the road that his "age-old conflict" with Susanna had opened to his son.

In *Amado mio* Carlo Alberto is not the "murderer." In a moment of happiness it so happened that Pier Paolo abandoned himself to the image of the beneficent father. It was a dream, a fleeting moment, one probably linked to the emotion felt during an actual screening of *Gilda*. It must have been the summer of 1947, and indeed in a cinema in Caorle.

In Caorle the summer cinema glowed with electric light under a pitch-black night, whose endless curtains were lowered behind a picket fence, the temporary enclosure for the seats . . .

These are the first lines of an essay that Pasolini published in *Il Mattino del Popolo*, December 11, 1947, and actually entitled "Amado mio." The essay recounts in the first person "the cry of joy, the sweet cataclysm" aroused by seeing the film. Identical phrases from the newspaper recur in the typewritten text. There is Rita Hayworth, there is the excitement in the audience, there is a young boy named C. The fictitious invention must have been a liberation, to the point of seeming too explicit. The Alexandrian idyll was locked in a drawer and consigned to its "unfinished" state. The feast of the body that it had represented was to be harshly paid for.

THE DAYS OF THE
DE GASPERI DECISION

These were years in which Italian literature was being called upon to produce the novel of the people's exploits. Literature wished to unite its own destiny with the discovery of the outlying areas—both historical and moral—of the country. This was the generous illusion of neorealism, though its most singular fruits are lyrical and at the same time documentary—transfigured autobiography. I am thinking of Carlo Levi's *Christ Stopped at Eboli*. Neorealism was a moment of lively controversy; it was also a moment of renewed literary experimentation, and Elio Vittorini and Cesare Pavese were its Castor and Pollux. Pasolini lived these controversies from a distance; he lived their reflection in Friuli.

Pier Paolo had already tried to write prose before *Amado mio*. A few essays and narrative accounts (dreams, nightmares) were published in *Libertà* from 1946 to 1947. But there were earlier and more significant attempts.

Funeral in September. Office of the Dead in Casarsa. A burial in Casarsa. Storm that clears the air. Detached, white clouds in the sky. Naturally all the fields are shining. On the road to Ponte a Borgo Meonis. Under the clouds groups of people amid glittering puddles. Men in their Sunday suits and old women with kerchiefs and black skirts. The priest bustles up, to join the people who speak softly, etc., with a group of little acolytes, like him dressed in white cassocks with black ornaments. Candles and crosses. The group disappears through the portal. It rains in clear sunlight. The children from the orphanage arrive, with a flag, etc. Here come Aldo and Giovanni out of the portal, carrying a wreath, and followed by four men who carry old Cesarìn's coffin on their shoulders . . .

A brief, typewritten page, included in a folder of verses (all dated before 1944 and entitled *Lapidi* [Stones]).[12]

A telegraphic, noun-riddled prose, already almost "cinematographic" —precisely in this sense, inspired by epic images. The peasant epos is in Pier Paolo's heart. His intellectual and political tension may be seeking to resolve it in the form of art, in the novel of group exploits to which literature was about to devote itself.

It happened at the beginning of 1948. On January 7 about three thousand people demonstrated in San Vito al Tagliamento to demand that the "De Gasperi decision," promised for two years, be implemented. The "De Gasperi decision" was the political arbitration handed down by Alcide De Gasperi in 1946, by which a series of payments was allotted to tenant farmers as compensation for the disruptions and damages inflicted by the war on the peasant economy. The "decision" also provided for the hiring of the unemployed.

The San Vito peasants continued their agitation until January 12. The landlords promised to hire one hundred and twenty unemployed farm workers, a compensation of 4 percent for the land improvements that had been guaranteed them. The Camera del Lavoro demanded that six hundred workers be hired, a 50 percent compensation for those improvements.

On January 13 the negotiations broke down. Simultaneously the court in Udine was ruling on what part of the province the "decision" was to be applied to—in principle it involved only tenant-farming areas of the countryside. In the region of Udine, part of Carnia and part of the Cervignano area would fall under the "decision"—one fifth of the territory. For the remaining four-fifths, the court commission decreed slight benefits.

A new phase of the struggle began. In the countryside of San Vito al Tagliamento, committees formed by tenant farmers and unemployed farm workers presented themselves at the various agricultural agencies to obtain individual agreements, independent of the Udine ruling. This action continued to expand, for it was also strongly supported by the trade union. On the other side, the police intervened with a great show of force to prevent any demonstrations.

So far, despite acts of repression, concrete results had been obtained —one unemployed worker was to be hired for every five hectares of land. On the morning of January 28, when the tenant farmers' committee appeared at the villa of the Rota estate, serious unrest erupted. The administration gave no sign of life. The demonstrators forced the gate, entered the house and found no one, not even the servants—only a dog and a cat. It seemed that the administrator was in Codroipo.

The carabinieri command post asked for help from the army and police in Padua and Mestre to deal with the occupation. Meanwhile they tried to keep the demonstrators to the back of the house, the side opposite the one where the gate had been forced. The carabinieri were met by about a hundred women who drove them off with blows and kicks. They returned after a short while with an armored car, soldiers, and police. The demonstrators barricaded themselves inside the enclosure of the villa. The armored car dislodged a gate but was stopped by a new onslaught of women. The demonstrators erected barricades and once again obliged the forces of law and order to withdraw.

That evening, on hearing that the Rota administration would adhere to the tenant-farmer agreements already signed by other employers, the peasants gave up the villa.

The next day similar demonstrations took place in Cordovado. There, too, agreements satisfactory to the farmers were reached. Nevertheless the police attacked the demonstrators with truncheons and tear gas. In protest, a new demonstration was proclaimed on January 30, in which five thousand people joined. At this point, an official was sent from the prefecture in Udine to guarantee the peaceful continuation of the remaining negotiations.

The invasion of the Villa Rota had a sequel in the courts: thirty people were tried and twenty-two convicted. The demonstrators, having entered the house, were charged with theft—a pair of socks and a shirt; one of them had exchanged his old worn-out shoes for a pair of heavy socks.

Around this episode of peasants asserting their rights, Pasolini built the novel of his Friuli. The novel was to see the light many years later, in 1962, "duly cut, restored, varnished, and framed," with the title *Il sogno di una cosa* (The Dream of Something). The "dream" (Marx's word in a letter to Ruge in 1843) was the hope of social regeneration that men preserve with difficulty and shame beneath their consciousness.

The 1962 version is a novel composed of a series of freely linked sketches telling the slender story of three Friulian boys in search of work, who live their youth in a free and easy fashion: dances on Sunday, wine drunk in abundance, love, the sorrow of death. The demonstration in January 1948 is a sort of conclusive moment of truth, the one in which political passion (their Communism is innate) is sanctified through the physical clash with the guardians of bourgeois justice. Hunger, the need for work, the contested hope of existence are enriched at that point by a fatal content.

The epic quality of the book draws substance from its picaresque design, from the sense of adventure that ruffles the existence of the three protagonists. Pasolini arrived at this structural and stylistic solution after writing *Ragazzi di vita*, and *Il sogno di una cosa* should be read as the mythical and peasant background of the "Roman" novel.

It started out somewhat differently, as is shown by the unfinished drafts, dated 1948 and 1949, and not accidentally entitled *La meglio gioventù*,[13] the title under which Pasolini later collected the most successful of his Friulian poems, a true epos, in retrospect, of his own youth.

In these drafts, two other plots, linked to the story of the mass demonstration and combining with it to make up the novel, are woven: the story of a young priest who organizes an after-school program for the peasant children, and that of a young woman, a militant Communist and intellectual, who composes the Sunday wall posters for the cell to which she belongs.

The priest, Don Paolo, in his activity as a teacher, conceives a secret homoerotic passion for a young boy; the woman, Renata (in the other draft she is a man, named Renato), through her Communist faith establishes a spiritually complex relationship with the priest. Both tend to emerge from the political and ideological schematic patterns to which they are supposedly consigned, and to overcome them by their need for a moral freedom that politics would hinder.

In the outline of the two characters, which remains incomplete due to considerable gaps in the story, one can see the divided image of Pasolini himself. Don Paolo and Renata are a duplication of his Christian and didactic fervor, and of his political passion. There is in them a curious "evangelical" drive that threatens to transform them into plaster saints, and it was probably his awareness of this that prompted the author to eliminate them from the final version of the book.

Along with this, especially in Don Paolo, a more insidious auto-biographical element comes to the surface. The priest—in a diary whose entries are interspersed in the narrative—shows clearly the extent to which homosexuality was capable of arousing conflict and crisis in Pasolini's mind. If happily lived in some moments, it was also the cause of lacerating guilt feelings, of bitter outbursts. The young priest seeks comfort in the text of Saint Paul's epistles,[14] and writes:

"To remain in the flesh"—to love with the flesh, obviously. But why is it necessary for me to love with the flesh? My God, haven't I suffered enough "for the flesh"? . . . I had no lack of encouragement to do so.

Or again he recounts a youthful experience beyond the pale of shame.

While everyone was asleep, I went walking through the deserted streets. My violet shirt, light-colored pants, my hair just cropped, and everything damp with sweat—but my age prevented me from worrying about this. I was too occupied in my wholly special observation of the arcades, the windowsills, the electric wires, the paving stones of the sidewalk . . . I was heading for a lonely bridge over the river, which for some days had been my favorite goal, replete with I don't know what alluring attraction. When I reached it, I leaned in broad daylight on the parapet, and looked down. . . . I stayed there a few minutes, enjoying myself; then I raised my head again and, looking around, noticed a detail that had hitherto escaped me: on a side street that skirted the river, but much secluded under a grove of acacias, stood an old urinal, surrounded by a sheet of rusted iron. The thing was new to me, since in my village structures of this kind did not exist. So I approached, and going inside, I saw before me only a mere slab of yellowish marble, wet from a continual dripping of water. There was a sharp and persistent stench of ammonia, and I, very excited, and as though on the point of committing something forbidden, was about to urinate in that place I had never before seen. But now all of a sudden I heard voices approaching. The two men who were speaking were already inside as I was about to run away; now I could no longer get away and I had to stay there, in the middle, between the two men, against the marble slab, and bowing my head in shame, I waited for them to leave . . . When I found myself again alone and free by the parapet at the river, I realized that I was completely overcome by a new, intoxicating, spasmodic palpitation. . . . In that strange city, my modesty had received a shock so violent and unexpected that even that pleasure that I had already discovered, that pleasure different from anything else, seemed to me to reclothe itself in more compelling attractions. I was as yet unable to decipher them, I was simply thrown into the midst of their violence. But my thoughts, the fiercely logical thoughts of a child, began to connect themselves in line with a practical, interested order. By now I was seeking a way to obtain once again for myself that offense to my boyish modesty. And as was natural, a plan formed immediately in my mind, on which for some time the temptations and curiosities of that different adult atmosphere, all imbued with sin, had been impressed. I would pretend to be looking at the river as usual, and as soon as someone else stopped at the urinal, I would go in too . . . So for two days I devoted the first deserted and burning hours of the noonday to plotting my course from that urinal to another similar one that I had discovered near the Market. As I stood before the sultry marble slabs, I often happened to hear the buzz of bluebottles, of horseflies, or of some stray wasp.[15]

A stifled agitation, the feeling of sin and transgression—here the buoyancy of *Amado mio* is lacking.

The body, the body, is the source of everything and it has to be made to disappear. Some nights I wake with my eyes wide open, and I raise myself on my elbows—I even stay this way for ten minutes or a quarter of an hour, with my eyes fixed on the "thing." I see it perfectly, in its slightest details, exposed in an awful light, engraved on a slab . . .

The fear of being discovered, the fear that your flesh may betray you to the eyes of others, that it may reveal your secret, fearful identity. The confession is plainly obvious in these pages from Don Paolo's diary.

But Don Paolo, as I said, is also a teacher, and in this, rather than in pure faith, his anxiety finds comfort.

Means are needed, mediations. I've read something of modern scholastic methods (activism) that avail themselves precisely of "means" that are not the pure speaking relationship of the teacher, by sacrificing the latter's traditional authority for the active participation of the children. It is essentially right, however . . . to make the children study willingly, make them "enthusiastic," something quite else is needed besides adopting a more modern and intelligent method. It is a question of nuances, of risky and exciting nuances . . .

The method of Montessori and the positivists certainly has its good points: but this belief of theirs in external applications and gradual and foreseeable improvements, their optimism that does not reckon with the mystery and the incongruence that are at bottom the concretions of freedom . . . By barely changing the terms, the same defect is implicit in the educational thinking of the idealists, they too do not take concretely into account contradictions, the irrational, the gratuitous, and the pure living quality that lies in ourselves. . . .

Only he who knows what it means to love, who is always aware of Divinity, can educate . . .

I am full of ideas, all too committed. I've painted some large signs representing the most abstract grammatical rules by tricks, symbols, and amusing surprises. I've thus introduced colors and images into the dry subject matter . . . The children are rather unsuspecting of these deviltries, but their eyes say that they are curious and enjoying themselves . . .

Here too it is not the character speaking, but the writer, barely disguised. It becomes clear how Pasolini sublimated in teaching the "loving violence" by which he had been wounded, in such a way that the Catholic flavor of some expressions sounds almost like an exorcism. Christianity was part of his moral reasoning, the part that obliged him to interrogate himself (albeit in the guise of a country priest) on the unrelenting demands of the body ("The body, the body, is the source of everything and it has to be made to disappear").

But his psychological subtlety, his critical intelligence were not content in merely sharpening the feeling of corporality to the point of tragedy. Rational demands for historical examination became increasingly evident in him, in his ideological conceptions and in his imagination. It was this that produced the conception of Renata, the bourgeois girl who becomes a Marxist and *betrays her own class* ("her class was never to forgive her for it, even the best of them").[16]

In Renata the idea of social regeneration is explained, even a will to failure that transforms itself into an ethical imperative: "Now I cannot do anything except understand them [the tenant farmers and day laborers], go back among them and from there return to the level of consciousness. This is what's difficult."

But this summons to "understand" the poor and the disinherited, to "go back among them," what is it if not the irresistible call of an anthropological unconscious?

Don Paolo's diary also observes:

I've noticed how much better the youngsters of the people are than those of the bourgeoisie. It is an absolute and substantial superiority, allowing no reservations—like the beauty of a landscape or the freshness of a fruit. Later, while the young people of the bourgeoisie, in getting older, will improve, their minds strengthened against decay and regression, those of the people, as adults, will increasingly become nonentities, nonexistent, a lump of monotonous and never clarified experiences. They descend the slope of humiliation.

A corrective element appears: decadent aestheticism, a bewitched sensitivity to beauty, even the merging of it with death. Don Paolo, in fact, does not stop with sociology and psychology. The young priest, in accordance with *l'esprit de la décadence*, goes over into action. He wants the beauty of these peasant boys to be kept intact. At the climax of the novel, the demonstrations over the "De Gasperi decision," he is killed by a shot fired by the police while shielding the body of a young demonstrator with his own. He dies a sacrificial victim, designated as such, it would seem, by his own despair.

The author seems to suggest that this annihilation is a solution of fate. But it is the kind of solution that writers adopt to transpose roles that are all too vivid or obscure in their imaginations into the realm of the unconditional, the inevitable.

What to say at this point? That the autobiographical element, at the moment it revealed itself, cast doubt on its own ultimate truth, rebuked it in the death of the character; or, observing the matter with the advantage of hindsight, that it arrived at a disconcerting prophecy.

But Pasolini, in this phase of his creative life, by using the prose of the novel, was more concerned with gaining objectivity than with his own subjectivity.

The Friulian epos should have resolved the split in his ego, the gap between politicization and his feeling of guilt. This epos was to have been the pure representation of the poor and happy peasant life, perfumed by the primroses in the ditches, drenched by the freshness of the brooks. But in some way the split remained a secret, painful, incurable ulcer.

BOUNDLESS FRIULIAN INTIMACY

When he came back, I was in Casarsa, an evacuee along with my mother—I was lost as in a boundless intimacy that made of Friuli its idle objective center. . . . Thus he ended up in Casarsa, in a kind of new confinement, and his death throes, lasting a dozen years, began. One by one he saw my first little books in Friulian appear, he followed my first small critical successes, he saw me get my graduate degree in literature, and meanwhile he understood me less and less. The conflict was dreadful —if someone were to fall sick with cancer and later recover, he would probably have the same memory of his illness that I have of those years.[17]

Carlo Alberto Pasolini, a repatriated prisoner of war, found his whole world changed. Not only was Italy no longer fascist, but his son Guido had died in the struggle against fascism, and his son Pier Paolo was actually a militant Communist.

For Carlo Alberto, the horizons of his physical existence had also changed. No longer Bologna, but Casarsa; no longer the impoverished petit-bourgeois interior, but a peasant interior, a still more tangible sign of degradation, resounding with dialect voices that to him were alien. His son had even become a poet of those voices—a son in a manner of speaking, more a Colussi than a Pasolini.

Pier Paolo lived his "boundless intimacy" with his mother—the tragedy that had befallen Guido must have made that intimacy even more indissoluble and mysterious. The father's return violated it. Carlo Alberto's flayed heart must have been aware of the meaning of this violation. His harshness increased as he followed, grudgingly and lovingly, his son's public successes. He kept newspaper clippings. He had a room built on the ground floor for the *Academiuta*.

This son, for whom he might have dreamed a humanistic future, was disobeying one of the commandments of the Italian petit bourgeois who devotes himself to literature—he was betraying the supposed lofty style of his class, rejecting cultivated language, and talking about "little homelands."

Carlo Alberto, divided in his love, could not forgive Pier Paolo this treason. He did not forgive him in the depths of his heart, in the secret recesses of his mind. And sometimes he exploded—obsessed, accusing, raving.

From the "boundless intimacy" of Friuli, he was tragically excluded. This exclusion was one reason for his illness.

Carlo Alberto Pasolini's "long death throes" thus began, and for Pier Paolo they were also a horrible illness. The father treated his illness with wine, until finally he killed himself. The son took the road of expression, with the ancient conviction of poets, for whom the word is the only possible therapy for the evils of life.

On December 6, 1945, Pier Paolo wrote to Silvana Mauri, an old friend from his Bologna years: "My father's return has thrown me into a state of mind that is confused but less intolerable than in recent months." Again to Silvana, on February 5, 1946: "My life is not very calm, but it certainly would be if my father were not in such an awful state. The doctors call him paranoiac."

The father was keeping an eye on the son—his excessive love drove him to read in secret what his son was writing. But so much love deprived him of all his courage—even when it came to politics, he stood in awe of him. All this, of course, instead of improving his condition, only made it worse. Carlo Alberto, when his crises were upon him, would yell that he was being hounded and hurl dark accusations.

About homosexuality Carlo Alberto may have had his suspicions. Perhaps he didn't want to know. Perhaps, as frequently happens with strong and virile men, the possibility of homosexuality in his son did not alarm him, and in the beginning he was unable to grant it any importance.

The reason for his anguish lay elsewhere—it was precisely his exclusion from the world of Casarsa (he did not get along with his sisters-in-law, especially with Giannina) that reawakened in him the themes of past resentments. What he resented was Susanna and her rejections of him. But this resentment in turn provoked that of his son, a vicious circle that went on endlessly.

Carlo Alberto had no friends in Casarsa, and, locked in his pride as a former army officer, he did not make any. Everything became for him a fuse for his obsession, even Susanna's domestic chores, or the lessons that she gave to supplement the meager family budget. There were tearful scenes. He blamed Susanna for Guido's death, he accused her of reducing him to despair.

His attacks became more and more frequent in the course of 1947. Carlo Alberto fell prey at first to a deadly silence; he would hold his tongue for three or four hours and then begin to shout insults; in a frenzy, he would throw himself cursing on the floor. He wanted to die, and they restrained him by force, since he was threatening to commit suicide.

Then he would burst into tears, and the tears finally gave way to drowsiness and sleep. In early January of 1948, the symptoms grew more acute, the insults more heated—enraged obscenities flowed from his lips. Pier Paolo decided to have him examined by a psychiatrist in Udine. This announcement drove Carlo Alberto almost mad; he said that mother and son were out to destroy him, but he would defeat them, he would put them "to rout."

To document for the doctor the kind of things his father said in his moments of fury, Pier Paolo compiled five typewritten pages of his disconnected ravings. They are brief tirades of lucid and caustic bitterness. In his son he hates the intellectual; in his wife he looks with horror on a peasant cunning that is plotting his downfall. He commiserates with his son, prey to his mother's "deceits," but he accuses him of blindness; he despairs because Guido is no longer there, since Guido would have taken his side. He throws in Susanna's face that she is no wife to him.

The medical diagnosis spoke of paranoidal mania.

But Pier Paolo's "boundless intimacy" in Friuli was not filled solely by Carlo Alberto's outbursts, or by the passion that Susanna's visible discomfort increasingly kindled. There was the happiness of youth, friends, the holiday dances—as well as old friends from Bologna. Silvana Mauri, to be exact. His relationship with her was fond and intense; she was a concerned and loving presence. Silvana was close to Pier Paolo immediately after April 25, 1945, at the moment when the tragic truth about Guido's fate was disclosed. She accompanied Pier Paolo to the uplands of Porzûs to visit the scenes of the massacre.

The close and loving relationship between Pier Paolo and Silvana continued for years, until it dwindled in Rome after 1950. But, as shown by the letters he wrote her—dispassionate letters—their closeness represented for him something deeply rooted in feeling. As with Giovanna Bemporad, it had emerged from a meeting of minds, and become transformed.

This loving friendship inevitably had its difficult moments. In a letter of August 15, 1947, Pier Paolo accuses himself of having given Silvana "acute pain," of having expressed himself in forms "of sadness and protest."

The relationship runs along the crest of words left unsaid, but explicitness cannot help but emerge: "Ever since we first met, you will have understood that behind my friendship there was something else, but *not very different,* an attraction that was even fondness. But something insurmountable, let us even say monstrous, has come between me and that fondness I feel."

The words underlined by Pasolini already say much. But that is not all. In the spring of that 1947, Pier Paolo had made a trip to Rome, his first, as the guest of his maternal uncle, the antiquarian. He met a few intellectuals, and was much taken by Rome. Silvana had joined him there. The letter continues: "Recall something else, Silvana, and then you will finally understand. Think back to the two of us in that restaurant in the Piazza Vittorio eating our pizza, and remember the warmth with which I defended that homosexual girl friend of yours. Don't be alarmed, for heaven's sake, Silvana, at this word—remember that the truth is not in it, but in me, that finally, despite everything, I am amply compensated by my *joy* [in English], my joy which is curiosity and love of life. All this is good for only one thing to you: to explain to you some of my drawbacks, some of my lack of understanding, some of my vagueness and false innocence, which perhaps (I say perhaps) have hurt you."

The anguished truth, caught in the net of everyday familiarity, is revealed. And yet (from the same letter): "you are the only woman toward whom I have felt and feel something that is very close to love."

In the Piazza di Spagna in Rome, Silvana had seen a small notebook sticking out of Pier Paolo's pocket; she would have liked to read it but he stopped her. It was a diary, and probably contained something more than a confession.

A mortification, an affront disrupting love. This produced on August 15 a letter to repair the damage, a letter inviting Silvana to enter into a "vital confidence," into the "little chamber of the ego." "That way I'll be able to offer you the love I bear you without feeling the confusion of a child caught in the act."

The confession, besides, was by now necessary. Pier Paolo had gone with the Mauri family to Macugnaga in the mountains. There there were more silences on his part, and obviously more unspoken appeals by Silvana—this mutual uneasiness must have changed into cruelty.

The wish to be released from the anguish of a lie took shape for Pier Paolo in a dream, as revealed in the same letter. "Like a flash of lightning, I remember now that I must have dreamed of you last night: in fact we were in Macugnaga, but a happy, marmoreal

Macugnaga, a Macugnaga without Monte Rosa or the stream. In the corner of the living room, one can see that I fermented in my poetic memory the smell of the wood, the heat of the divan and table, until it turned into a kind of substance of marble or ambrosia, in which you and I argued calmly and enjoyably."

Enriched by the truth, a truth casually alluded to but at the same time unequivocably highlighted, the relationship between the two maintained its intensity.

All his life, Pier Paolo had significant relationships with women, relationships that were always spirited and sometimes exclusive. They were relationships in which friendship came to be combined with a bundle of emotions that the friendship transformed. Though here one cannot speak of love or sex, there was an undeniably strong emotional tension. It would be a mistake to think of these relationships as belonging to that realm of sticky gossip that sometimes unites homo-sexuals and women. Or that they had anything to do with the search for a replica of the mother image. Susanna, in the tormented rapture that bound her to her son, never suffered an eclipse and left no room for surrogates.

There was in Pier Paolo an overbearing virile component, eroded and ulcerated by the conflict with his father. Perhaps the father who had betrayed Susanna and left home for a few days at a time (as had happened before the war) to seek elsewhere the physical satisfaction that married life either denied him or provided only in miserly, grudging doses, may have fixed in him a neurotic nostalgia for women.

His future sexual behavior may present the reverse symbol of this nostalgia. Pier Paolo, who went out night after night on the hunt for boys, refrained, in accordance with a dichotomy that is not difficult to grasp, from bringing any of them home, the place reserved for Susanna and his love for her.

This was to be the Pasolini who had ripened his own erotic destiny within himself, until it became his pattern. Already, however, at the time of his Friulian "intimacy," his unconscious was elaborating a female image differing from the maternal one and not to be placed in conflict with it.

Among the epigrams of 1958, the one dedicated "To an Unborn Child,"[18] testifying to a physical relationship with a woman, expresses something else ("first and only unborn child, I have no sorrow / that you can never be here, in this world"). Pasolini used to say that this had been his single experience of heterosexual eros—with a "little girl, and already a mother," who had "come from Viterbo":

> . . . she was the fastest:
> she ran to the window of my car, shouting,
>   so sure of herself I couldn't undeceive her:
> in she got, made herself comfortable, cheerful as a boy,
>   and told me the way to the Via Cassia . . .

There is no difference between this and the homosexual contacts in the form to which Pier Paolo was most accustomed—the car stops, the boy gets in, and away they go to some more or less secluded spot. The "little girl" prostitute is seen with the same eyes.

I think that in Pasolini's imagination woman was to have a different role, the role that two figures, in some way complementary, in *Teorema*, suggest—the mother and the servant, in both of whom freedom and devotion are inextricably mixed.

The way these two figures mirror each other—and their fate is resolved in the apotheosis of the servant—suggests that Pier Paolo considered woman as a creature endowed with a mysterious privilege, or, conversely, endowed with no gift of intellect, but being instead the ultimate flowering of nature, a sibyl mediating between man and the dark and paradisaical earth of the mothers, or of the mother.

That he should have conceived a difference between "woman" and "mother" does not seem absurd—he needed to distinguish Susanna from all other women, so that she could sustain the weight of all his love and preserve it pure and uncontaminated. This writer once heard him say that women, with a few exceptions, did not have "souls"—he exemplified the exceptions by referring to certain women who had given birth; obviously in his opinion they could be likened to the symbol of Susanna. When he maintained that women were devoid of "souls," the embittered reader of Saint Paul's Epistles or of Baudelaire's *Mon coeur mis à nu*[19] must have been speaking in him. He did not mean anything degrading, he meant that they were messengers between life—and life is to be a man, and alone—and that area of the spirit where this life finds nourishment, restoration, justification, truth: the mother.

As for the character of the servant in *Teorema*, it is no accident that the role was played in the film by Laura Betti. For all its insufferable moments, Pasolini in the last years of his life kept up his relationship with her with singular and impassioned loyalty.

It was also the "boundless intimacy" of Friuli that made Pier Paolo experience his homosexuality in difficult ways, with suffering. The feeling of freedom of his early encounters was replaced by a different feeling, and the alarming torment of his father's presence could hardly have failed to be part of it. One can suppose that in his unlimited trust of Susanna, Pier Paolo could count on her understanding. He could not count equally on Carlo Alberto's. His sense of sin and guilt, judging by the contents of what he was writing, was acute in him. The dense and astonishing output in the unpublished *Diaries* (1945–1949), from which he was later to extract the completed whole of *L'usignolo della Chiesa Cattolica* (The Nightingale of the Catholic Church), testifies to conflict and anguish.

From these pages one could gather a copious harvest of quotations, among them "slave penis," "being lost" ("my life lost on its course"), repeated to the point of saturation. Indeed, torment prevails over any feeling of fulfillment.

> The greatest torture is "giving in,"
> I stand at the dark crossroads of sin,
> and I give in . . .

Or again:

> I give in . . . Restrain me, life, at the brink.
> Or do you want to erase this creature
> from the marvelous pattern of regrets? . . .

> Who blames me?
> Come, Accuser,
> point your finger in my happy face.

His "joy" is always disturbed by an accusing presence, or by the anxiety of solitude.

Odor of my bed, the bed of a poor young man, odor of the Angel or of the Dandy that I sometimes am, when faraway in an overcivilized city atmosphere I tell myself the fragments of the story of my Joy.

These fragments seem to gravitate toward two poles: the truth or a lie:

> To lose yourself or pretend. Duty,
> celestial inheritance, light of childhood,

blazes on the humiliated belly.
I lose myself and pretend. And I entrust myself . . .
object of my scorn and of my pardon,
example of the alive and envied
youth in the image of youth . . .

O I'll shout my case to strangers:
I'll no longer be the face of the prism,
and my solitude will be
sung. And if among the listeners
pitying the boy who is losing himself
the lie should shine like a sun,
I will see my destiny entire,
and the omen . . . Duty . . . I'll be a dead man.

The shadow of Gide is present, present in this need for "confidence," for explicitness. It is the Gide of *La Porte étroite* and *L'Immoraliste*, the Gide who wonders how to go on with his existence with the unheard weight of the "lie" and the "fiction" on his heart. Why not confess his "shame" and "temptation" to those who love him?

But in Pasolini this anguish seems to be vented by a "joyous" trick: "O I'll shout my case to strangers," "my solitude will be sung." In these words lies the hope of being able to express his own "difference" by freeing it from the reins of the "celestial inheritance" of duty—and the "belly" will no longer be "humiliated."

The pleasure, however, of such a cry, of such a full song, the pleasure for his own "heart laid bare,"[20] speaks less of the other face of Gidean immoralism than of the dandyism of Baudelaire—of a poet who deliberately poisons his own life in order to acquire a freedom beyond the limits of morality, beyond all good and evil.

He knows that

if he fears his ghost, or if his unfulfilled
flesh makes him a child,
he is enamored of nothing but his sex.

And he also knows that he is

always in the man, never in the god.
But is there a god in this unknown flesh?

And yet,

I'm happy to be a sinner because my sin in broad daylight is a shadow of marble! I'm happy to know that I'm exposing myself, error upon error. You, LOVE OF THE SON, give me enough light to comfort me secretly for my errors.

Sometimes writing a poem a day, typing it on half a sheet of onionskin, Pasolini was confessing his own "error" to himself, while letting himself be overcome by despairing lust.

From late 1947 through all of 1948—to judge by the verses written, collected sheet by sheet with meticulous care, divided into folders each with its own table of contents as though ready for the printer— was a long period of anguish, more acute than in the past. Very likely the crisis that his father was going through caused Pier Paolo a violent loss of balance. Even though life seemed to absorb him completely, and his creativity was running extremely high—in his projected novel, in his poetry—the "boundless intimacy" concealed traumas and inner slumps that were to take on the character of fate.

In a letter to Silvana Mauri—and it is a decisive letter,[21] written from Rome in 1950, when everything had happened, the Friulian epos forever over, his homosexuality exposed to public outcry—Pier Paolo was to say, with his eyes on the past, that the "descent" had begun "in '47," later to become "ruin." "I don't yet succeed in judging myself, not even, easy as it might be, in judging myself badly, but I think it was inevitable."

The same letter says: "I was born to be calm, balanced, natural: my homosexuality was something added, it lay outside, it had nothing to do with me. I've always seen it as something beside me like an enemy, I've never felt it to be within me."

The verses in the 1948 *Diary* speak precisely of this "enemy"—an enemy that lays siege, deceives, offers fleeting solutions and immediate joys ("an extreme inner joy was the only way out," says the same letter to Silvana)—in any case, it was an enemy with which it was impossible to struggle, useless to do battle.

If Pier Paolo achieved a few victories over it, managed to soften its attack, he was able for the moment to do so by having recourse to the Catholic temper of his native culture. Such was the relationship, for instance, with Tonuti Spagnol.

On April 3, 1947, Pier Paolo writes to Tonuti from Rome, and speaks of his trip: "I went to the Vatican to see the Museums. Just imagine, at the entrance to the Sistine Chapel (the ceiling of which was painted by Michelangelo—remember when I showed you the pictures in school?) there's a corridor as long as from the Colonél house to Versuta, all very carefully painted and decorated." His letter to the peasant boy shows the loving solicitude of the teacher to take the upper hand and silence "the enemy," but also a vein of quietly Catholic paternalism.

Catholicism. Pasolini had not yet subjected to criticism the Judeo-Christian idea of the indivisible unity of conscience. This phantasm was undermined, placed in jeopardy from one day to the next by a different and personal reality—a reality of neurosis, where the split was actually occurring. On one side, his homosexual drives; on the other, the need to censure them and to pretend. The pretense was absorbed within him by the resources of pedagogy.

Nevertheless, the "boundless intimacy" of Friuli had been scarred.

CHAPTER 5

AS IN A NOVEL

RAMUSCELLO

A dispatch from the carabinieri of Cordovado, Territorial Legion of Padua, October 15, 1949: "From public rumor, since the matter has aroused scandol [sic], this command has learned that the above-named Pier Paolo Pasolini of Casarsa about ten days ago went to Ramuscello, where [he enticed] minors."

So it was "public rumor" that protested. Someone overheard a conversation that two or three boys were having among themselves—two or three boys from Ramuscello, a hamlet on the outskirts of San Vito al Tagliamento. It had been on September 30, the feast day of Saint Sabina, and there had been dancing in the village to celebrate. Pier Paolo, along with his cousin Nico, had gone to dance.

For the past year Pier Paolo had been living a more desperate, and more open, homosexual life. The reasons for this, according to his own words, lay in the need to get away from his unhappy family situation—Carlo Alberto's increasingly frequent attacks—and the need to overcome, if only temporarily, a personal literary crisis. Friuli was becoming too small for him. In a letter to Tonuti Spagnol, from Rome,[1] he wrote: "I've been enjoying myself this time, and am getting used to an intellectual and social life that, alas, is just not to be had in Versuta."

The practice of homosexuality made the secretary of the Communist cell of San Giovanni all too vulnerable. The matter had possible political consequences. Summer—the atmosphere of *Amado mio*— had renewed the enjoyment that Pier Paolo found it difficult to do without. He took his chances.

Between July and August of that year of 1949 a priest had tried to blackmail him. The priest had picked a woman go-between, who told Pasolini that he must either give up political life or his teaching career would be ruined. Pier Paolo's reply, also through the go-between, must have been a harsh one.

A local Christian Democratic figure had been involved in a similar situation some time before. Provincial life demands retaliation, it demands that certain persons, once exposed, submit to gossip, even to infamy. "Public rumor" could not stand to see intellectual renown combined with Communist idealism and homosexuality.

The obsessive pattern of the attacks to which Pasolini was to be subject for the rest of his life as a public figure began to take shape in Friuli. Friuli set the stage for the attempted blackmail by the country priest, and onto this was grafted an obscure political intrigue. Nico Naldini had had a casual conversation with Giambattista Caron, the principal of the *liceo* he had attended in Udine. Caron, who had been elected a Christian Democratic deputy in the elections of April 18, 1948, was a cultivated man who read the French spiritualist philosophers. He told Nico that it would be a good idea if his cousin were to stop making Communist propaganda. The posters affixed in the loggia in San Giovanni might produce pernicious reactions. Pier Paolo and Nico gave little importance to this warning.

Then came the Ramuscello affair. It was the day of the feast. Pier Paolo met the three boys—one was sixteen, the others younger. They came to an agreement, an understanding. Nico was also present. But he stayed behind to watch the couples dancing, though Pier Paolo had invited him to come along.

What caught Pier Paolo in those moments was the promiscuity of the dance floor, the sexual excitement induced by wine, and the expectation that was created, in the bodies and overheated tension, between one dance and another—the special intoxication of the peasant festival.

So he and the boys left the wooden platform and went off into the darkness.

He came back and told Nico that it had been an "unforgettable" evening. Later the Ramuscello boys began blaming each other for what had happened, probably mutual masturbation. Someone was listening and reported it. "Public rumor" reached the carabinieri.

The statement by the Cordovado brigadier mentions "impartial persons speaking in good faith" and an "interrogation of the minors"— there is nothing about the parents. This took place on October 14. On October 21, the same brigadier summoned the heads of the families, who "though undecided, have let it be known that they reserve the right to go to court."

But by now "the matter has been made public." The brigadier in his report expresses a supposed neutrality of judgment while stressing the gravity of the situation. Since "there is general indignation," and since Pasolini is a teacher in the secondary schools, "it has been decided to draw up the present statement in three copies."

No lawsuit was brought by the boys' parents. But the informer had spoken and public opinion had given vent to its indignation. Pasolini was charged by the magistrate of San Vito al Tagliamento with corrupting minors and with lewd acts in public. The sixteen-year-old was also charged.

On December 28, 1950, Pasolini was acquitted of the charge of corrupting minors, but he was convicted of lewd acts. The appeals court in Pordenone, on April 8, 1952, was to absolve him for insufficient evidence.

Though in time the "scandol" faded away and people found other things to talk about, emotions for the moment ran high in Casarsa. Pier Paolo was summoned to carabinieri headquarters on October 22. The marshal asked him to explain himself. His answer was, more or less, "I was trying an erotic and literary experiment, under the influence of a book I had been reading—a novel on the subject of homosexuality." He mentioned the name of Gide.

In short, Pier Paolo did not deny it. He shielded himself behind literature—Gide had won the Nobel Prize in 1947. He was under the illusion that he could save himself by appealing to the writings of an illustrious man. But certain statements, certain declarations, took their course. The marshal informed his superiors, and they informed the school board and the press. The *Messaggero Veneto* of October 28 reported this deposition—the deposition of a confessed criminal. *Il Gazzettino* of the same day also printed the item. Newsboys began shouting it in the public square of Casarsa.

If the intrigue had been a political one—as Caron's warning suggests—the Communists fell into the trap. On October 26, the executive committee of the Communist Federation of Pordenone, at the instigation of the Regional Federation in Udine and militants in Casarsa, expelled Pasolini from the Italian Communist Party "for moral and political unworthiness." The local edition of *l'Unità* responded to the insinuations of the *Messaggero Veneto* and *Il Gazzettino* by announcing Pier Paolo's expulsion and abandoning him to "guilt" and to intellectual "deviationism" nourished by reading "bourgeois and decadent" writers.

The decision made by the Communists—though not a unanimous one, since Teresa Degan, one of Pasolini's teaching colleagues, was opposed to it—is easy to explain. In the fierce climate of the cold war, political and moral schematism was obligatory. To Togliatti's party it seemed excessive to put up a public defense for a homosexual spokesman, and Pasolini had not denied the facts.

"As for me, I ought to be condemned for a truly indecent naïveté," he wrote to Teresa Degan a few weeks later.[2]

The idea made headway in the Pordenone Federation that once he was in court, Pasolini, no longer being a Communist, would win his case. Such a Machiavellian notion, however, shows how uneasy the party felt in the presence of the established powers. It was almost objectively incapable of protecting a member placed under an accusation that was considered disgraceful.

For Pasolini, his expulsion from the Communist Party was a traumatic blow. "There was a moment when I might even have drowned in the dungheap of bourgeois hatred," he says in the letter to Teresa Degan. The anger he felt at his dismissal must have called everything into question, including the very fact of having joined the party after the murder of Guido.

But he wrote a letter to Ferdinando Mautino of the Udine Federation in which he rejected his banishment with firmness and dignity. "I am not surprised at the diabolical perfidy of the Christian Democrats; I am instead amazed at the inhumanity of all of you. You yourself know very well that to talk about ideological deviation is a piece of stupidity. Despite you all, I am and will remain a Communist, in the most genuine sense of the word. But what am I talking about? Up until this morning I was sustained by the thought of having sacrificed my person and my career for loyalty to an ideal; now I have nothing more to lean on. Someone else in my place would kill himself; unfortunately I have to live for my mother."[3]

"Despite you all." He was rejecting the party's tactics, its motives of political convenience (or opportunism)—just as he had rejected them at the time of the controversy over regional autonomy. This time, however, they touched himself, his person, his very survival.

"I am and will remain a Communist." It was the "most genuine sense" of his own public commitment that Pier Paolo was trying to save within himself. He knew that his responsibility was above all an intellectual one—it was there that his morality had its roots.

He believed in an ideal, and rejected the dissolution of policy in the area of practice—by now he was no longer a militant. What remained to him was the consistency of his own thought, the consistency governing a combination of noncontingent choices, brought to maturity on the red thread of history. These choices could not be betrayed or eroded by anger or bitterness, or destroyed by the fierce sentiment of solitude and exclusion.

The denunciation robbed him of his teaching position. Not only did it disgrace him in his relationship with his pupils, which had been of the fullest and happiest kind, it also destroyed his economic security.

The letter goes on: "I hope you will work with clarity and passion; I have tried to do so. For this I betrayed my class and what you call my bourgeois upbringing; now the betrayed have avenged themselves in the most ruthless and frightful way. And I am left alone with the mortal suffering of my father and mother."

Mautino, to whom the letter was addressed, knew Pier Paolo well. A party functionary and journalist, as a partisan known as Carlino, it was he who had explained to Pier Paolo what had happened at Porzûs—the Communist ambiguities and the fatal outcome. Pier Paolo felt doubly betrayed, by a comrade and close friend.

Everything seemed to have collapsed. The newsboys had shrieked the event in the public square. Carlo Alberto had come home with the newspaper in his hands. Pier Paolo was already in anguish, in expectation of the worst. And now the worst was there, one step away.

Carlo Alberto shouted the truth about their son at Susanna. Susanna locked herself in her bedroom.

Pier Paolo went with Nico by bicycle to San Vito al Tagliamento in search of a lawyer. Later Nico, Aunt Giannina, and the lawyer spoke to the parents of the boys.

Friends were another resource. Pier Paolo called Zigaina by telephone, and Zigaina came by train from Villa Vicentina near Cervignano. He found the family silent and convulsed. Pier Paolo told him that he wanted to kill himself.

In the letter to Mautino he wrote: "Yesterday morning my mother almost went out of her mind, my father is in an unbearable state— I heard him weeping and moaning all night."

Long days of desperation began. As the weeks went by, the tragedy was revealed in concrete terms: the lack of work, the impossibility of giving private lessons. Pier Paolo was pointed out by passersby as a corrupter of minors. His public experience of being "different" began in the harshest way. Suddenly Friuli had turned its back on him. The "enemy" had taken on a tangible appearance.

> Didn't you realize that the world
> of which I am the blind
> and loving son
>
> was not your son's
> joyous possession,
> soft with dreams, armed
>
> with goodness—but an ancient
> land of others that to life
> imparts the anxiety of exile?

These are some tercets from "La scoperta di Marx" (The Discovery of Marx), the final section of *L'usignolo*, written in 1949—that his mother is being addressed is obvious. Pier Paolo was now living in a "land of others," in "exile."

Moral conventions are cruel, stronger, and more overpowering than the happy and abstract strength of literature. Carlo Alberto adhered to those conventions in their darkest and most backward aspects, and his illness, in the injury he had suffered from his son, grew worse. Life at home was hell.

The days followed one after another, without a ray of hope to brighten them. His economic desperation was complete, and it was necessary to come to a decision.

"In the winter of '49 . . . I fled with my mother to Rome, as in a novel."[4]

A novel. The decision was made without Carlo Alberto's knowledge. Nico and Zigaina were told about it. A few friends lent the money. One early morning, with the sky still dark and frozen snow on the fields, Susanna and Pier Paolo departed by the first train for the south. In Rome there was Uncle Gino, who was to help them. Susanna carried along her modest jewelry, the value of which turned out to be ludicrous. Pier Paolo later confessed that this departure gave him back his happiness. He was snatching his mother from the hell of Friuli and from his father. The provincial framework of Friuli, having turned into a prison, into a kind of obsessive habit all its own, was broken.

This decision had developed slowly. In a letter to Silvana Mauri during those weeks, he wrote: "I'm going away—where? Rome, Florence, maybe even Lebanon, if things take a certain turn. I go more and more off the track, Rimbaud without genius."

The "Rimbaud without genius" left for Rome in a sad winter dawn. He too, *le coeur supplicié*, would be able to sing, fiercely and bitterly, *Mon triste coeur bave à la poupe*. And even, *Il s'agit d'arriver à l'inconnu par le dérèglement de tous les sens*.

Departing, he severed all ties of affection. He even left behind him a girl, a sweetheart. As one of the ambiguities and contradictions by which he was marked, in the last year he had become involved with a young schoolteacher in San Vito. Her name was Maria. Among his papers from that time there remains a note from her. There is no date. The girl invites him to a party at the Workers' Club. She wants to dance the rumba with him. She writes: "I've learned how, you know —of course, not very well. But so as to improve, I'm waiting for you to be my teacher. You're the best of all." The melancholy eyes and plump face—his photographs from those years show how he could be attractive to girls and inspire notes like this one.

He and Maria became engaged. Nico had to go to her and explain the scandal. The girl wept. She was pretty and petite—everyone said what a fine couple they made.

But the Friulian epos was extinguished forever.

ECLIPSE OF FRIULI

Only in the last year of his life did Pasolini return as a poet to the Friuli of his youth—duplicating, along the lines of the controversy he had kindled over the anthropological shipwreck of peasant Italy, in the acquired language of the "little homeland," in the "mother" tongue, the old verses of *La meglio gioventù*. Overcome by a dry and ruthless bitterness, he was to write the verses of *La nuova gioventù*.

In the "historical" poems of *Romancero* (1953), and in the volumes of *Le ceneri di Gramsci* and *La religione del mio tempo*, Friuli remains the setting for tragedy—the death of Guido—or the place for heightened and solitary despair:

> . . . I consumed the hours
> of the best time of life, my whole
>
> day of youth, in loves
> whose sweetness still makes me cry . . .
> Among the scattered books, a few
>
> light blue flowers, and the grass, the innocent grass
> amid the broomcorn, I gave to Christ
> all my naïveté and my blood.[5]

Pasolini rejected Friuli, and at the same time he knew that it represented the time and place of his whole existence. He rejected the place physically, even though the sting of memory was painful.

In some letters written to Tonuti Spagnol from Rome, in 1950 and after, the increasingly transfigured meaning of the sting becomes clear.

> So much life . . . still remains for us to talk about. Yours shines for me in images full of youth—you are in full chanson de geste, my dear Tonuti. Ski-lift, smuggling, and motorcycle (and girls, I imagine). Mine instead cannot be summed up in any way, much less in joyous or expansive terms: that's the way it is, huge, neutral, full of violence whether good or bad— it's a little like Rome. . . . For now I have something to tell you. For this reason, not only will I never be able to forget you, but on the contrary I will always keep you constantly in my deepest memory, like a reason for living . . . There is nothing for which I am so grateful to fate as the fact of having loved you.

These words were written in 1950, perhaps 1951. Everything is immersed in a past with which there is a tenuous link—a happy memory. But by now life is "violent."

On September 25, 1955 (Tonuti has continued to write him of his own poems, of which he is making a collection; Pier Paolo has replied with advice about publication, and has told him of having mentioned his name in the preface to his anthology of dialect poetry), he writes Tonuti a note:

> At the beginning of August I passed through Casarsa, and this time I had a less sad impression than the other times. It seems to me that every-

thing up there has by now settled into sadness, and in this process a little
of the old, immemorial cheerfulness in re-emerging. How wonderful the
greenness of our fields is, and the sharpness of our air. We'll end up
going back, eh Tonuti?

Memories begin to surface. In a brief letter to his friend Cesare
Bortotto, on December 19 of that same year, 1955, he writes:

To my great pleasure you come back to life every so often, and a breath
of air from '43 strikes me, giving me a warm feeling inside—that fearful,
melting air.

On October 5, 1959, again from Rome:

Dearest Tonuti:
For months now I've had your card with Easter greetings here on my
desk. It's shameful that I've let so much time go by without answering,
but aside from the fact that I'm leading not a violent but an extremely
violent life, I find it very difficult, almost painful, to write to you: and
you understand why, our friendship in those years, those summers and
those winters, our early youth, those feelings so absolute, and perhaps the
greatest moment of life. So forgive this kind of impolite silence, which is
actually a terror of looking back . . .

Tonuti had changed, he had become a man. He had done his military service, become engaged, got married, and was working. All this
may have made it more difficult and terrorizing for Pier Paolo to "look
back," but this terror existed and it was named in such a way as to
leave no doubts. In the span of ten years the earlier rejection had
changed into a feeling of fear—"the greatest moment of life" had remained there, closed and impenetrable. Poetry had vanished from
existence, and the present was violent, or rather extremely violent.
In the letter of September 25, 1955, he had also written:

Life is cruel here in Rome, and unless you're tough, stubborn, willing
to struggle, you're unable to survive. To me it seems like a dream to have
had days, weeks, whole months to myself, with no other commitment but
a football match or to go dancing at a village feast.

In short, the moral setting of Pasolini's life had changed.

With even the desire for Friuli dispersed—the land of his mother
had betrayed and repudiated him—Pasolini had on his desk the great

many pages he had written. Poems and a novel—the accumulated sheets of onionskin, the painstaking corrections in pencil. The Friulian poems were to be collected in 1954 under the title *La meglio gioventù* —chosen, sifted, and grammatically clarified, they were to take on a tone of tormented regret (while the title, extracted from the words of the fascist song "Bandiera nera," functions also as a dedication to the Resistance and, implicitly, to Guido).

It took more time to decant the material written in Italian.

Also in 1954 came the publication of a slim volume, *Dal "diario"* (*1945–1947*): sixteen poems, with the addition of a shorter one, "Europa."

The year 1958 saw the publication of *L'usignolo della Chiesa Cattolica*. The author whose name it bore was already the poet of *Le ceneri di Gramsci*. *Il sogno di una cosa* appeared in 1962.

In a writer like Pasolini, one whose work seems little by little to create his life, these two books have something posthumous about them, echoes of survival. But their tone of elegy was marked by the "terror of looking back."

L'USIGNOLO

Nocturnal song, sweetness of the heart; a sound of running water— "angelic" poetry, poetry of "alabaster and quagmire." *L'usignolo della Chiesa Cattolica* is a remarkable book. It is hard to attribute it to a school or doctrine; one can only attribute it to the psychology of its author, to the myths that moved him at the time he was writing it.

In Pasolini's *Diaries*, written between 1943 and 1949, it is all composed and already polished. Pier Paolo submitted a considerable part of it to literary competitions. "L'Italia" was sent to Giacinto Spagnoletti, who included it in his *Antologia della poesia italiana contemporanea*. Some pages from the first section—prose dialogues, particularly those that read, "Che avete, occhi? Ombre di corpi la luna . . ." and "La mia luce"—had appeared in Friulian in *Il Stroligut*, in April 1944 and August 1945, respectively.

L'usignolo della Chiesa Cattolica selects and assembles the whole poetic youth of Pasolini—it represents his rustic secret, his Dionysiac exhaustion. But it is not a youthful book.

The song opens in muted fashion: the rapture of dawns, the tremblings of twilight, "days that fly away like shadows." Brief dialogues, of old women and children, whispered in the fields. The Christian exaltation of the mass, the joyfulness of Sunday. The rituals are sweetly extracted from their natural course. Everything is seen through the starry eyes of a boy. His mother is the light in his pupils. The scene is always in the fields: the coolness of the flowing springs, the quiver of the primroses along the ditches.

After the prelude of early adolescence, comes the conflict, the conflict between sin and salvation, narcissistic virulence and the feeling of the divine, the siege by the "enemy" and the need for sublimation.

Christian faith is here a point of simple readiness: it seeks the truth in the body and suffers the imposition of doctrine. Christianity coincides with nature, and nature expresses itself in sensuality. Sin is also a good, a symbol that redeems pain—it may even be the expression of freedom.

Sex becomes an inexhaustible flowering of life, and life is always innocent beauty.

> You, boy, are a monster,
> you do things in the family
> with remorse, and seize on
> abstruse obstacles.

> But you know (I'm enjoying myself),
> you know and all the same
> do nothing to restrain yourself,
> all outlets are open to you.

The difficult, heightened religiosity of this poetry is contained in the play of opposites: the "corrupt candor," the "mire" and the "ivory," between which, revealed by the glow of the lamp, the "ungirt" body seems almost a mystical offering, the vision of a sacrificial symbol molded of a dewy substance.

Pietro Citati has written that "in *L'usignolo della Chiesa Cattolica* Pasolini abandoned himself to an orgy of psychology."[6] This solitary orgy, illuminated by an uncertain light, takes place inside a confessional booth. The poet is the priest of his own *Confiteor* and of his own absolutions—he succeeds in looking on his own nakedness as a sinner, as though emerging from himself, and in tingeing his own flesh—the luster of ivory!—with melancholy.

The "orgy of psychology" (which denies the nonpsychological modernism of an Eliot or a Montale, and strips Ungaretti's "man of suffering" to the living flesh) aims at a transfiguration of the ego, at changing the fever of sin (or of what is felt to be sin) into a life that is as much life as ever.

> I have the calm of a dead man:
> I look at my bed which awaits
> my limbs and the mirror
> with my engrossed reflection.

> I cannot overcome the chill
> of anguish, by weeping . . .

But there is the prospect of emerging from such sweet sorrows. The poet of "L'Italia" already feels Foscolo's public inspiration: a cheerful song of the future spreads through the strophes, that of a festive Italy with its hopes of the Resistance:

> Italy was reborn with the dawn of the earth,
> virgin perfumed by galls and roots,
> wondrously ignorant of the tongue
> with which, jealous of the morning light,
> I tried to give voice to her Soul.

In a breath of optimism, the swaying pendulum of this precious collection of lyrics, with its highly developed and feverish decadentism, comes to rest.

The "political" perspective bars the labyrinthine paths of *décadence* as a credible remission of all sins—and the political perspective is called the "discovery of Marx." The sins of the flesh, the sins of the intellect—everything is enveloped in a cruel sweetness, candid and tragic.

From participation in the "Passion" of Christ ("Christ wounded,/ blood of violets,/pity of the clear/eyes of the Christians!/Flowering flower, / on the distant mountain, / how can we / mourn you, O Christ?"—where the homosexual interweaving between Christ and his executioners, or where the appearance of a young Saint John, "gentle boy, / light body, / curls of light," show how well the poet had absorbed Roberto Longhi's teachings on "Italian pictorial Mannerism")—from so much autobiographical participation in the Christian mystery of the Passion, to the conquest of reason and history through Marx, there are not only the pages of books—there is the intense party experience that we know. There is, in short, the need to make real and concrete the relationship of the flesh and the senses to peasant life—the need to penetrate, if possible, the concept of existence, and to make life, if possible, adult.

The theme of the transition from Arcady to History binds the poetry of *L'usignolo* in a ring of intelligence. This is the dynamic element that threads the book onto an endless spiral.

The exercise of the intelligence through poetic sensuousness is an obligation of the Pasolini canon, the greatest of risks. Pasolini grasped that only this exercise might bring about his release from the contradictions that marked him. What this book also contains is the boundless strength to elucidate a destiny. One might be tempted to read it in a scandal-minded and mediocre way, unearthing in it traces of "vice" and the troubled and invoked masochism of its author. But the clinical case is overcome by the poetry. The book "recounts" the fate that usually befalls any poet: to go forward in life with daring and sincerity, to the end, without fear of suffering or impropriety.

The exercise of the intelligence, as the conquest of the terrain of History, can also take the form of a perpetual forward flight. The experience of sin, his dismay at the dark forces besieging his heart, drove Pasolini toward utopia, drove him to the hope that only utopia could lift that siege.

This forward flight irremediably shackles him, however, to the longing for an uncontaminated and innocent past. And the past, by its "violent" innocence, besides systematically devaluing the present, may also corrode utopia and reduce it to ashes. These risks were to become part of the intelligence and poetry of Pasolini—his poetic audacity was never to allow him to withdraw in the face of them. But he knew that the price of poetry is very high—high to the point of annihilation.

> We shall be offered on the cross,
> to the pillory, amid eyes bright
> with fierce joy,
> exposing to irony the drops
> of blood from chest to knees,
> mild, ridiculous, trembling
> with intellect and passion in the game
> of the heart burned by its fire,
> to attest the scandal.

Prophecy? Art anticipating life? A "fierce" wish to carry out his destiny on the basis of a prediction that appears imminent?

There are no certain answers to such questions. One could suggest that dandyism *maudit* in Pasolini becomes a need to bear witness to "the scandal." For the moment the scandal is only the proposal, certainly conscious and antimodernist, of "an orgy of psychology" put into verse—a scandal that falls within the literary convention. On the other hand, equally scandalous for that convention is the "discovery of Marx," the landing in the harbor of reason, the "marvelous gift."

The poet who in the classrooms of the *liceo* and at the university had adored the light and shadow of Ugo Foscolo's tercets—

> And bathed with tears
> the bleeding breast
> of the Cyprian youth . . .

—was to whisper to his mother:

> . . . You wrung me
> in the mystery of sex
> from a logical Creation.

In so doing, he was to "discover," alongside "reason," the disruptive force of Christian meekness, and was to learn to savor the mild weakness of the saints who willingly embrace ridicule. And on this he was to impose the corrective of ideology, the passion of the political left, which had once been a passion of Rimbaud's.

"Rimbaud without genius," "poor and a dandy," Pasolini was now ready for the great leap of the poem "The Ashes of Gramsci," ready for the poetry of a different "scandal":

> The scandal of contradicting myself, of being
> with you and against you; with you in my heart,
> in light, against you in the darkness of my bowels . . .

But in the budding sheaf of his *Diaries,* this flower entitled *L'usignolo della Chiesa Cattolica* has gathered, as on a precious stem, a few symbols of his future as an artist. If the happy eroticism of *Amado mio* was to return to the full in the film of the *Arabian Nights,* if the decadent and rational mystery of "La crocefissione" foreshadows the decadent and rational complexity of *La ricotta,* if the moral dy-

namic of Christ, God, and demon will go to make up the allegorical
pages of *Teorema*, the angry and griefstricken gaze of Christ

> removed from itself
> in what burning
> countrysides has
> His eye gazed?[7]

is the same look that Pasolini will engrave on the frames of the *Gospel
According to Saint Matthew*.

The obscure Rimbaud from the Friulian provinces, departing with
his mother in a winter dawn for Rome, "as in a novel," carried with
him just such a burden of creative energy.

PART TWO

CHAPTER 6

THE DISCOVERY
OF ROME

AWESOME MONOTONY
OF THE MYSTERY

Rome 1950. Like the painters of the Renaissance, the Mannerists, or the great Caravaggio, who all came to Rome from the villages of the Po valley to learn secrets of style and secrets of life, the deafening sound of reality, Pasolini in Rome learned a new love and was deafened and overwhelmed by it.

Cesare Garboli has seen a parallel between "the whole destructive experience of the 'Roman' Pasolini" and Caravaggio, the intermediary being Roberto Longhi. In fact, it was Longhi who in 1951 organized the great Caravaggio exhibition in Milan. "With texts in hand," says Garboli, "one would say that Pasolini was working at the time not in the mirror of Caravaggio, but in the mirror of the Roman Caravaggio as he has been depicted by Longhi."[1] For the painter, it had been almost like being shipwrecked in the huge body of Rome. His young Bacchuses or little Saint Johns were petty thieves or tavern boys, his dead Madonna a pregnant whore who had drowned in the river, his Magdalens the country women who came to the city in the early morning to sell fresh cheese in the market. It was a shipwreck for Pasolini, too—and both were vitalizing, splendidly creative shipwrecks. It was a regeneration.

Looking at dates, one sees that the earliest version of *Ragazzi di vita* was published in *Paragone* (the literary magazine founded by Roberto Longhi) in its June 1951 issue. This was the first chapter of the picaresque novel *Il Ferrobedò*. With a few variations as compared to the final text, we read: "It was a very warm July day. Lucià, who was to have his first communion and confirmation," etc.

One is tempted to say that everything was immediately resolved in the word. Lucià, or Riccetto (as he was later to be called in *Ragazzi di vita*), was there immediately, the plastic incarnation of a myth. There was no need to transform him into a little Bacchus crowned with vine leaves. In his body, existence and culture met.

Roberto Longhi, when Pasolini had asked him for a subject for his graduate thesis in Bologna, had not shown much enthusiasm. He had judged this talented twenty-year-old unsuited for the study of art history. All the same, he went along with the idea. Then the whole project was aborted by the war.

Tonality and sense of color through syntax, an ear for dialect as a vehicle of reality, repaid Pasolini in poetry for his apprenticeship in art history.

The young Friulian poet, thanks to the crisis he had endured with the scandal of Ramuscello, discovered himself to be a mannerist and realist by coming to grips with Riccetto. It was a loving struggle, which no longer required any pretense.

In Casarsa, he had felt he was "sinning"—in Rome, he believed that he was no longer doing so. Fate had delivered him from a nightmare, the nightmare he had inflicted on Don Paolo in the first draft of *Il sogno di una cosa*. For this liberation, however, he had paid a high price: lynching. Then flight and poverty. And also a violation of the image of his mother.

Arriving in Rome, Susanna and Pier Paolo asked Uncle Gino for help. Uncle Gino did what he could. He settled them in the Piazza Costaguti, in the ghetto. Pier Paolo was to have a furnished room; Susanna, in order to earn a little money, was to work as a maid for the family of the architect Pediconi, and would also live in the Piazza Costaguti close to her son. There was a child to be taken out for walks, and Pier Paolo could help her with this.[2]

All this was reason for torment, a feeling of bitter solitude. But there in the deepest bitterness, his soul was relishing its happiness. An absolute erotic freedom.

In the letters written from Rome to Silvana Mauri there is a Pier Paolo wearied by destiny, a Pier Paolo who painfully accepts his own homosexuality. It is all true enough, and he may have hoped to be "cured." But this hope lay on the surface of his mind, as on the surface of water that otherwise ran deep. The truth of the words written to Silvana concealed another truth, written this time on the skin, or under the skin, of Arnardo, Lucià, Biondomoro, and all the others who are the first, superimposed faces of Riccetto.

The demon of Riccetto—and of the many "bad" boys who are combined in him—took complete possession of the writer. I would say he flatters this demon, flatters it with "affectionate" bonuses—the ones that can be read in the letters to Silvana, or which are mirrored in the verses of the diary, Roma 1950[3]:

> Whoever, sinning, has felt in his throat
> the fever of the lynch mob, is always pure
> if still he cannot hate, and there still rises
> in his scorched eyes an affectionate
> glow of sweetness and courage.

His psychological split now allows Pasolini a new register of expression—adherence to a new and unexpected erotic reality through linguistic mimesis. The poet who composes the lines of Roma 1950 strenuously trims the old hendecasyllable—he is convinced that poetry after Rimbaud is dead. The creator of Riccetto pursues instead a language to which he is trying to offer the redemption of History.

Having come to Rome, Pier Paolo lived his crystallized homosexual inclination for the poor and disinherited with "the discovery of Marx" in mind. A horizon—"African" Rome—opened before him, and he began to explore it.

Did the tragedy of Casarsa and the flight shift in the slightest the moral and physiological anxiety of the author of L'usignolo?

In Roma 1950 he writes:

> Adult? Never—never, like existence
> that doesn't ripen—it always remains tart,
> from one splendid day to the next—
> I can only remain faithful
> to the awesome monotony of the mystery.

This stasis, accepted as a banner, makes Pasolini the man extremely faithful to his own trauma.

Susanna is obliged to be a "servant," but all this degradation brings boundless compensations.

Roma 1950 continues:

That is why, in my happiness,
I have not abandoned myself—that is
why in the anxiety of my sins
I have never arrived at a true remorse.

In the dialectic of the unconscious, "true remorse" would cancel the feeling of guilt, would translate it into the words of reason. Pasolini does not face such a resolution—he lives the "awesome monotony of the mystery," in which he is:

equal, always equal with the unexpressed,
at the origin

of what he is. But in that "unexpressed," in that "origin," everything coexists, sin and the absence of sin, the feeling of Susanna's degradation and the happiness of having her all to himself, anguish over the lynching he has suffered and its opposite, the fertile and joyous amazement caused by the free expression of his senses.

In Rome homosexual encounters are easy, lower-class boys ready and willing. All that was needed was a little money. Pier Paolo wrote to his cousin Nico in Casarsa, and Nico went to Venice and raised some ready cash by selling the Greek and Latin classics in the Teubner editions and the Laterza Italian ones, books painstakingly collected by Pier Paolo over the years. The "violent life" was off to a whirling start.

AN INADMISSIBLE EXISTENCE

The first months in Rome were very difficult. It was hard to find work. Pier Paolo looked up a few writer friends, with whom hitherto he had only been in contact by correspondence, as was the case with Giorgio Caproni. But Caproni had nothing to suggest.

Silvana Mauri tried to get him private lessons. But it was through journalism that Pasolini succeeded in making ends meet. He worked as a proofreader. He wrote for a wide range of vaguely pro-government newspapers. His expulsion from the Communist Party was a help to him.

On March 9, 1950, he published, on the literary page of *La libertà d'Italia*, his first article written in Rome, a review of Leonardo Sciascia's *Favole della dittatura*.

On May 12, with an article entitled "Romanesco 1950" (in which he reviewed a volume of dialect poems by Mario Dell'Arco), he began his collaboration with *Il Quotidiano*, the newspaper of the Curia, where he was to publish, in addition to literary pieces, journalistic articles that were sometimes signed "Paolo Amari."

He wrote for *Il Popolo di Roma*, *Il giornale* of Naples, *Il lavoro* of Genoa. He printed a few stories in *Il Mondo*. As in previous years, he contributed to *La fiera letteraria*. His pieces for the literary page are often fiction—Pier Paolo would take out of the drawer a chapter from *Amado mio* ("Avventura adriatica" in *Il Quotidiano* of May 31, 1950), or else a few pages from the notebook that was later to be *Il sogno di una cosa*.

But Rome had already captured him: "Rome, with all its eternity, is the most modern city in the world—modern because always abreast with time, absorber of time" (as he wrote in "Romanesco 1950").

Pasolini began to write about street boys or *ragazzi di vita* in the newspapers—colorful sketches in which dialect emerges only in brief snatches of dialogue.

In "Ragazzo e Trastevere" (*La libertà d'Italia*, June 5, 1950): "For myself, I would like to be able to know through what mechanisms of his heart Trastevere lives within him, shapeless, throbbing, sluggish. Where does Trastevere end and the boy begin?"

The literarily transfigured homosexuality of *Amado mio* seems to become raw and real in the promiscuous Rome of little neighborhood cinemas, the human clusters clinging to the hand rails of buses and trams, the ceaseless chatter of street vendors, the bursting vitality of the little shoeshine boys.

The Friulian world and the Roman world shade one into the other —at least through literature. If life in Rome had an immediate alchemistic and strengthening effect on Pier Paolo, literature was weaving more subtle patterns, constantly embroidering on the open fabric of its existence.

Singular transpositions could also take place between the Friulian and Roman worlds, as in the case of "La rondinella del Pacher" (*Il Quotidiano*, September 6, 1950). The ending of this story, set in the Cordovado hills, is similar to the ending of *Il Ferrobedò*, which, as we have seen, appeared in *Paragone* the following year. But the expanded expressiveness of the later version sweeps away the idyllic color of the "Friulian" text, and not only through the Roman dialect intonation of the dialogue. The same poetic world, outside of its incidental geographical setting, is dramatically transformed by focusing the linguistic lens. These boys, first seen as possessing a haloed and honeyed charm, are flooded with a light that poisons them, little marble torsos dug from the mud, aggressive but sick, savage and marked by anemia.

The buses that cross the center of Rome from Monteverde to the Termini station, the circular Red Line, the pissoirs along the Tiber— Pasolini writes of everything: chestnut vendors and kids playing football, boys who go out stealing to buy themselves a blue sweater seen in a shop window, or who descend under the bridges to play the hustler with a "faggot." All around the landscape takes on an air of theatrical decoration, as in the canvases of the great Italian Mannerist painters—the ruins of the Coliseum, the Theater of Marcellus, crumbling palaces of Umberto I with heavy cornices, all are transformed into the signs of a faded Renaissance, while the skies are ablaze with indefinable flashes or crossed at night by hallucinations. "They walked along the Circus Maximus, under an oval sky on whose metallic surface, amid the red and purple vapors that swarmed densely over the city, white cloud banks passed as slender as knives."[4]

Pier Paolo seems to be writing without letup in order to possess as much as he can of the city: after singling out a detail his gaze is lifted above the network of alleyways until it loses itself in the bare fields of the outskirts.

The sun is "frothy and shining," the hair of boys "fiercely and softly waved," little boys run "lightly, their pants rubbed by the thirsty air."

A light-struck world. "Elementary chromolithograph colors, pure tints extracted from the rainbow by the experiments of an oculist, iridescent harmonies like carbonated drinks." Misleading as it may seem, Pasolini goes so far as to bring in the name of Chagall ("the Chagallian groups of passersby in the trolleybuses, in the ruins, a magnesium flash, but reducing the space to cubes, spheres, etc., a masterpiece through enchanting abstract conjecture . . .")—but Chagall is there, evoked by metaphor; he is the painter of a universe of changing colors in flight, and the flight is eroticism in the pure state, the dream state.

Pasolini's writing becomes turgid, its classisistic cadence is broken up, oxymorons and amphibologies thicken and pile up. The most impassioned ecstasy appears side by side with sarcastic scribbling; visceral identification with the objects represented gives way to the violence of refusal, to the harsh resentment of rejection.[5]

The Baroque city *par excellence* seems to ensnare the writer in its coils—it numbs him, possesses him, less through the swarming and shouting of its low-life inhabitants than through the complexity of its style: the Borrominian volute and serpentine line, the marble opalescence of Bernini.

Underneath oozed deadly torments.

In any case, Pasolini needed work, he needed friends; his anguish was not allayed, even though Rome, the very idea of Rome, had changed him. He lived at Piazza Costaguti 14, with a family named Castaldi, until the summer of 1951. His friends were writers and literary men, and little by little the circle was widening.

Arriving in Rome, he had met Giorgio Bassani—he had written him a note. Bassani had answered, and between the two a lasting intellectual friendship began. Neither Pasolini nor Bassani felt at home with neorealism, nor were they willing to accept the subjection of literature to politics. It was not that they rejected the ideals of the Resistance. Democracy in culture signified for both the critical clarification of intellectual processes. Democracy, for both, was the lesson of history, the growth of knowledge for the purpose of freedom.

Bassani was editor of *Botteghe Oscure*, the international magazine founded and directed by Marguerite Caetani. Bassani suggested to Princess Caetani that she hire Pasolini as librarian, but the princess refused. This poet, though cultivated, seemed to her too young, too fragile in appearance.

For *Botteghe Oscure* Pasolini wrote "I parlanti" (might we now call this happy text the impassioned farewell given to Friuli without a shadow of elegy or grief?), and the magazine published it.

Velso Mucci, Libero Bigiaretti, Enrico Falqui—these were a few of the writers and literary men whom Pier Paolo was seeing in these early Roman days. He was in correspondence with Giacinto Spagnoletti, Vittorio Sereni, and Carlo Betocchi.

He had met Sereni on the occasion of the Libera Stampa prize in 1947. He now got in touch with him in the hope that Mondadori might publish *L'usignolo della Chiesa Cattolica*. Sereni was a reader for this publishing house. He wrote a penetrating report on the Pasolini manuscript, but nothing came of it. Pasolini then tried Bompiani, where Silvana Mauri had begun working. But this possibility also went up in smoke.

He had an understandable aspiration to be published. He was submitting his poems to contests. In the summer of 1950, "Il testamento Coran," a short poem now included in *La meglio gioventù*, won second prize in the Cattolica, a contest for dialect poetry (Eduardo De Filippo was one of the judges). The check came to fifty thousand lire [about eighty dollars]. Next year one of his love poems was to tie for the Sette Stelle Sinalunga prize. In 1952 he tied for second place (again fifty thousand lire) in the Quattro Arti contest in Naples. This was a literary criticism prize reserved for beginners, and that year the winner was Leone Piccioni with an essay on Pavese. Pasolini came in second with his article on Ungaretti (which he had found it difficult to place in a magazine[6]), sharing the prize with Franco Rizzo, whose piece was on Gramsci and Giaime Pintor. The judges were Goffredo Bellonci, Gino Doria, Giovan Battista Angioletti, Luciano Anceschi, Mario Sansone, Rosario Assunto.

Angioletti thereafter helped him to get assignments from the literary department of the national radio. Pasolini reviewed books, composed imaginative interludes—an activity he continued until 1954. The editors of the department, assisting Angioletti, were Leone Piccioni and Giulio Cattaneo. There was also Gadda,* and it was here that Pier Paolo met him, a decisive encounter.

Gadda was to accentuate in Pasolini a material sensibility for language and a concern for its unconscious contents. Language, a complex orchestration of *langue* and *parole*, became the terrain on which Pasolini increasingly exercised his critical talent. And Gadda, with the lucent humorism of which he was capable, magnificent in conversation that seemed unintentionally to crackle, was undoubtedly a participant in the development of that sensibility. Still I do not think that the writing of *Ragazzi di vita* owes anything to *Quer pasticciaccio brutto de via Merulana*.

For Pasolini, dialect was above all the privileged language of the

---

* Carlo Emilio Gadda (1893–1973) was the most outstanding experimental novelist of recent Italian literature. His masterpiece, *Quer pasticciaccio brutto de via Merulana* (That Awful Mess on Via Merulana, 1957), imposes a highly structured combination of dialect and stylized Italian on the vehicle of the detective story.—Tr.

poor blessed by God. In Gadda, the rupture of the traditional literary lexicon, its extension to slang, was the basis for an all-inclusive representation of reality (if this representation turned out later to be impossible to achieve, and in its growth damaged the structures on which it rested, it was a question having more to do with metaphysics). In any case, Pasolini did feel toward Gadda a kind of intellectual debt, similar to the one he felt toward Gianfranco Contini.[7] The two have generally been seen as exterting a twin influence on him.

Among his new friends there was also the poet Attilio Bertolucci. Temporarily leaving his family in Parma, Bertolucci had come to Rome to work on a film script. He was living with Luigi Malerba and Antonio Marchi in a house on Via del Tritone, and was a friend of Bassani's. One morning Bassani showed up in the apartment accompanied by a dark-haired boy in a white sweater. Pasolini's long friendship with Bertolucci dates from that moment.

Football matches on the open fields of the city's outskirts, the sea at Ostia in the summer—Pier Paolo went in for sports and had an athletic appearance. With his mop of dark hair, parted on the side, he asked Malerba, who knew a few directors, to help him find work as a film extra. He had a union card, and thus there would be no problem. With his need to survive, he was unwilling to turn down any kind of work, and one thing might lead to another.

In the letter written to Silvana Mauri in early 1950, in which he tells her "you have always been for me the woman I could have loved, the only one who has made me understand what a woman is," he explains: "My future life will certainly not be that of a university professor: by now I have the mark of Rimbaud on me, or Campana,* or even Wilde, whether I like it or not, whether others accept it or not. It is something uncomfortable, irritating, and inadmissible, but that's how it is, and I, like you, do not *give up*."[8]

This is no longer Catholic resignation, but a "Pauline" fury, a fury also nourished by the spirit of decadent revolt. His destiny has by now been revealed: his epos will be a tragic one, a destiny of provocation. The father has been abandoned, and the son has assumed in the face of the world the responsibility for his own load of transgressions. And by virtue of this, he can permit himself everything, from the urinals along the Tiber to the film extra's union card.

* Dino Campana (1885–1932), Italian poet. He led a wandering existence and died insane.—Tr.

Sandro Penna was his companion in many adventures. Penna lived a life of joyous, deliberate poverty, but it was the rich poverty of one who is a friend of painters, and lives on painters by buying and exchanging canvases. Penna's life was an uncertain one, a "strange *joie de vivre*,"* with no explicit sorrows. Boys, the outskirts of Rome, the lukewarm sun of its winters were the figures and landscape for a personal mythology. And we find Pasolini following Penna on these paths. As the weather improved, there were the bathhouses on the Tiber, the famous Ciriola establishment below Castel Sant'Angelo, the favorite haunt of *ragazzi di vita* from all the neighborhoods, though they still did not know themselves as such. So passed a happy season of poverty and dissipation.

He and Penna had a contest, which went on for years: which of them could succeed in "doing" more boys in the same period of time. And Pasolini compiled long lists, and the ironical and curious crux for whoever was listening to him was "how many?" "where?" "why so many?" Pier Paolo never went into detail, but he added a generous dose of gaiety, of openly childish banter, while bewildering his friends and leaving them in the end dissatisfied. He provoked Gadda, and Gadda, ensnared, eager for exact details, turned away with Lombard politeness and remarked, "It's all a matter of generic but also numerical Petrarchism."

Among the literary articles of the period, the review of Penna's *Appunti* and the one of Bertolucci's *La capanna indiana* deserve mention. Here Pasolini is the critic we will come to know—he departs from accepted images to grasp the complexity or buried anguish of a poem that in appearance is colloquial and realistic.

Is Penna a "pure" poet *par excellence*, is he a poet without flaws? To understand him completely, one must go beyond such a scheme. "It is implied life, with its squanderings, its mistakes, its manias, its voids, its humiliations, its baseness, its opacities, that ferments in this poetry of few lines, making them long resound beyond their conclusion."[9] This is precisely the line taken by later critics of Penna, and it was initiated by Pasolini.

* In Penna's own words: "Sandro Penna è intriso di una strana/gioia di vivere anche nel dolore" (Sandro Penna is soaked with a strange/joy of living even in sorrow). *Una strana gioia di vivere* was the title of one of his collections of poems.—Tr.

For his part, Bertolucci might be accused of "joking" about himself. No, it is the "reaction of a love overwhelmed by shyness"—"the best reading of this poetry might be a preliminary one, in the sense that the development of the language proceeds on a priori grounds, in accordance with a constant that is at first uncertain, cut off, betrayed."[10]

Psychological fractures, linguistic fractures. Pasolini was enriching his vision of literature. It was not only Rome and its myth that altered his vitality and sensibility. Pasolini reacted to contact with the cultural fabric of the city through the relations he was establishing with the new literature of the moment.

From 1948 on, the printing of the first edition of Antonio Gramsci's *Quaderni dal carcere* (Prison Notebooks) was in progress. They were published by Einaudi, and Palmiro Togliatti was their unofficial executor. These were the years of Zhdanov*—after its first moments of freedom and openness, the Italian Communist Party moved to a position of Soviet orthodoxy in its cultural policy as well. But Togliatti had the intelligence to make what Gramsci had written while in the fascist prisons an obligatory reference point not only for the intellectual thought of the Communist Party, but for the whole Italian left.

Gramsci's historical and materialist criticism acted as an underground corrective, even an alternative to the rigid principles of "socialist realism." Gramsci was able to represent a sort of *continuum*, albeit in the light of Marxist dialectic, with Croce's philosophy—and generations of antifascists had been raised on Croce.

The problems were not only political, or ethical-political—they were also literary. One question very dear to Gramsci had been that of a "people's national literature." This idea allowed the Zhdanovian rigidity dictated by Stalin's Russia in these years of Cold War to fade and then replaced it.

For example, in Italy there was little discussion of the "positive hero," a required Soviet theme. Instead, there was an ever-growing interest in everything that fascism had rejected as marginal to the country, linguistic and cultural peripheries where the people's soul, though dispersed, had spoken.

Naturally these were the very themes that made Pasolini highly

---

* A. A. Zhdanov (1896–1948), army general and Politburo member who formulated the Stalinist hard line on culture. His policies remained in effect until 1953.—Tr.

sensitive to the reading of Gramsci. Or rather, they strengthened and integrated what he had learned both through his personal experience in Friuli and through Contini (and Gadda). Except that linguistic and moral marginality was for him a physical marginality—a marginality that extended beyond the limits of the Marxist idea of the proletariat. The Romance dialect of Friulian was marginal, but also marginal, very much so, were the Roman shantytowns, Riccetto and his prototypes— and they became the sole example, in Pasolini's imagination, for the concept of a "people's national literature."

I wonder if in this the writer was perhaps aided by his Christian sensibility, by the idea that the more one is rejected, the more he is the vehicle and receptacle of truth. Undoubtedly he was, but he was also abetted by the romantic idea by which the outcast would have, mystically, on his own, the right to transgress linguistic, moral, and political codes. Thus the red rag of revolutionary hope belonged in his hands, and in the hands of all those like him—the *ragazzi di vita.*

To be a Communist was for Pasolini almost a fact of nature. Expelled from the party in Friuli, in Rome he frequented the dance halls on the "red" outskirts of the city. Along with the need for human contacts with his "comrades," there was in Pier Paolo a conviction that capitalism brought about the dissolution and end of everything that was good and real on earth. He believed, with the strength of faith, that it was in communism that the instinct of self-preservation and the will to survive took form. For him, as for Leonardo Sciascia's Candido, communism had "to do with love, and also with making love."

Rome and Marxist historicism—a line that sutured the tradition of Southern humanism to Marx. Mario Alicata was the spokesman for this statement of cultural policy. Although alien to the Croce matrix, Pasolini came to find himself in this sphere, whose dimensions were vast and by no means exclusive. What the Communists proposed was less a rigid philosophy than a policy of alliances. Anthropology and linguistics, psychology and literature—Pasolini's dominant interests— could very well be magnetized within the universe of history, and history might equally well project on them a political rationale.

Pasolini in those years felt strongly that Marxism should not cut itself off intellectualistically from the culture of the masses. In this, let me repeat, his early Catholic and rural upbringing was alive in him. If at this point he was living a conflict—a conflict that marks his literary production, especially *Ragazzi di vita* and *Una vita violenta*—

it was between the Marxist idea that "simple people" should be redeemed from their naïve philosophy of common sense by a higher conception of the world, and the Catholic idea, which that philosophy considers a value in itself, an absolute given.[11]

Rome, the need to describe and know it—this led to "Studi sulla vita del Testaccio,"[12] portions of which Pasolini published in the newspapers. But these "studies," dated 1951, were more than a mere cultural appropriation of the Roman world. Once again, in their meticulous description, they constitute testimony of an urge to write fiction feeding eagerly on itself. The writer, in short, exhausts all other subjects, and the surrender to life is what interests him most.

His friendships were growing in number. And now, too, came the moment for a fixed salary. It was extremely modest, twenty-seven thousand lire a month, for teaching in a special secondary school in Ciampino, the Francesco Petrarca School on Via Appia Pignatelli. The post had been found for him by the Abruzzese dialect poet Vittorio Clemente, an official in the ministry, and it was a salvation.

The school was on the far outskirts of the city, a violent and individualistic world, indifferent to politics. Pier Paolo's pupils were between the ages of eleven and thirteen, children from subproletarian families living a hand-to-mouth existence. Among them was Vincenzo Cerami.

Pasolini, wearing a checkered, rust-colored jacket, taught these astonished children how to combine adjectives and nouns, and how to read poetry. He read them Ungaretti and Dante; he got them to collect the songs and nursery rhymes that their parents had brought with them from their home regions. In this way he was trying to offset the ruthless urbanization to which these families had been subjected either by the war or its aftermath.

The school was in a ruined building, but it looked out over the fields, the countryside, the Alban hills. Pier Paolo began teaching in the last trimester of 1951, in the spring, and he left in the last trimester of 1953, before the posting of marks. The salary allowed him to rent a house and to free Susanna from being a servant with the Pediconi family.

The rented house was at Via Tagliere 3, at Ponte Mammolo, in the vicinity of Rebibbia—an equally outlying neighborhood to the northeast. The Ciampino school was to the south, along the belt of Roman shantytowns. To get there required much traveling, three tram changes going, three coming back. But there was no alternative.

Furthermore, the Ponte Mammolo house could be said to be "under construction." It was a small building left unfinished for lack of funds. Life in the shantytowns was utterly precarious. This gave rise to a new despair, which cast a pall over the erotic joy of discovering Rome.

Rome had changed him:

Rome has made me become pagan enough not to believe in the validity of certain scruples, which are typically northern and in this climate don't make sense . . . Anyone who lives by ethnic tradition in a world inhabited by extroverts, whose secrets and inclinations are sensual and not sentimental, cannot help caring about this relationship, as the concrete form of a life lived on the outer surface, social in the primordial sense of the word . . . For two or three years I have been living in a world with a "different" flavor—a foreign and therefore defined body in this world, I adapt myself to it with a very slow grasp of awareness. A cross between an Ibsenian and a Pascolian (if you see what I mean), here I am in a life that is all muscles, turned inside out like a glove, which always opens out like one of those songs that I used to hate, absolutely devoid of sentimentalism, in human organisms so sensual as to be almost mechanical, where none of the Christian attitudes, forgiveness, humility, etc., are known, and egotism takes legitimate, virile forms.

Having arrived at Roman "paganism" from the "Christian" north, Pier Paolo feels himself transformed:

Here among people much more under the sway of the irrational, of passion, the relationship is instead always well defined, it is based on more concrete facts: from muscular strength to social position. Rome, girdled by its inferno of shantytowns, is marvelous these days: the unrelenting heat, so glaring, is just what is needed to take the edge a little off its excesses, to denude it and thus show it in its higher forms . . .[13]

These are excerpts from a letter to Silvana Mauri, written in the summer of 1952. The inflamed love for Rome gives way to reflection, to a lens that imparts distance—Rome is also an inferno.

The true, wonderful Roman spring, which you know, and the aroma is like an enormous mudguard scorched by the sun, a metal sheet, of wet rags drying in the heat, of scrap iron, of burning slopes of garbage . . . I am absolutely alone listening to a radio, which is playing certain old songs ("Torna piccina mia") on a typical Sunday broadcast, and to some boys playing football. And I'm faced with a Sunday with no plans: I'll go dancing with Mariella. Or else I'll give in to the demon, and go to

Settecamini to watch a match played by teenagers from Pietralata and then go and get drunk with them . . .

These words are from another letter, also written to Silvana, probably in 1953, and they speak again of the strangling siege of anxiety, of a solitude with no escape, and no longer the feeling of banishment and geographical "diversity," but the tormented obsession of eros, which is now just that, identified, identifiable at every moment, even if no longer secret, no longer concealed.

No longer concealed, above all, in the face of his father. Carlo Alberto Pasolini arrived in Rome once the Ponte Mammolo house had been found. He arrived in that house where the walls were still unplastered, without saying a word to his wife and son about their flight from Casarsa, almost as though it had been a normal move. At home he kept silent, but when he happened on a writer, one of his son's literary friends, he opened up—he seemed happy about Pier Paolo's literary successes.

Pier Paolo began working on two anthologies, *Poesia dialettale del Novecento* and *Canzoniere italiano*,[14] and Carlo Alberto, having nothing else to do, acted as secretary and went back and forth to the Biblioteca Nazionale with the borrowed books.

Gadda, who in a way was one of his victims, called him "Colonel Buttonholer." Carlo Alberto talked, and Gadda, deferential and respectful to the point of obsession, was incapable of freeing himself from this chatter. And as usual the author of *Quer pasticciaccio* was not long in coming up with a quip.

But "Colonel Buttonholer" had found in Rome the winter of his existence. His conversations were only the most fleeting signs of improvement. His silence was real and incurable; he drank more and more and always silently. In his son there was no longer a shadow of his adolescent longing for him.

Susanna sometimes prepared a small meal for Pier Paolo's friends. Bertolucci, Caproni, and Gadda came, bringing a flask of Frascati. Susanna was hoping that the new surroundings would bring about a fundamental change in her son. She set her hopes on Mariella.

Mariella Bauzano, mentioned in the letter to Silvana, was a tall, striking girl, a friend of Zigaina's. She had literary interests. She had reviewed *Poesie a Casarsa* for *L'Italia che scrive*, and wanted to meet the author. Zigaina told her that Pier Paolo was in Rome and she looked him up.

Pier Paolo was already living at Ponte Mammolo. Their friendship grew close, intimate. They took trams across Rome, they went dancing and to the beach. They were often together at Giordano Falzoni's, at Amelia Rosselli's. Mariella worked at the Biblioteca Nazionale. As Pier Paolo wrote in the letter to Silvana Mauri, Sunday was their day to be together. Pier Paolo lived by a compelling curiosity about everything, and he exuded physical and athletic vitality over all his surroundings. Mariella was a little in love with him.

One evening, in her home, they began necking. Pier Paolo drew her down on the bed and undressed her. Mariella let herself be touched, but she did not have the courage to touch him. The young man of thirty was aroused, but insufficiently. Next morning, on the telephone, Pier Paolo told her that he was still upset about all that hugging and kissing. That was the last time the episode was ever mentioned. Pier Paolo told Mariella he had had a girl at the beach when he was eighteen or nineteen, and that he had not had any heterosexual relations since.

Nevertheless, when they went dancing, and a flock of boys, boorish and violent as one can imagine, made advances to her, Pier Paolo would say to Mariella, urging but at the same time daring her, "Go ahead, go ahead."

Great freedom, great trust. But what counted between them was a breath of eros, a kind of amorous illusion, different perhaps from what Pier Paolo had experienced with Silvana, because more physical. (Had the violence of Rome acted in this direction, too?)

Alongside a drawing by Zigaina, dedicated to Mariella, Pier Paolo wrote a quatrain, and the lines speak of this illusion, or suggest it:

Cloud with a woman's body.
Woman? Cloud? Your weight,
cloud woman, speaks
to the clouds of a body.

When Mariella met a man with whom to fall in love, the relationship ended. One evening at dinner—besides Pier Paolo, there were Bill Weaver, Giacinto Spagnoletti, Paolo Volponi, and Cesare Vivaldi —Mariella, momentarily irritated, decided to leave. Vivaldi escorted her out, and shortly thereafter the two of them were to marry and stop seeing Pasolini.

Another friendship was with Toti Scialoja and Gabriella Drudi. Scialoja was already painting abstractly and also writing stylized surrealistic prose pieces, many of which had been collected in a volume, *I segni della corda*, in 1953. Pasolini was contributing at that time to *Giovedì*, and wrote a review of Scialoja's book. But the paper folded and the article was never published. Later he sent it to *Paragone*, the magazine edited by Longhi and Anna Banti, but they rejected it. In the meantime, the friendship between Pier Paolo, Toti, and Toti's companion, Gabriella Drudi, was cemented.

Pier Paolo, at the time, had the look of a premature beatnik. In an effort to attract the *ragazzi di vita*, he was competing with them in his physical appearance. Their reward was a pizza or a pair of shoes, that was all. And the boys were little rascals, or little monsters, whom he found beautiful. The features they had in common were curls dangling on their foreheads, a "roguish" smile, a vitality that sprang suddenly out of torpor—the specific traits that were to be combined, years later, in Ninetto Davoli.

The "beauty" of these boys constituted an infraction of every canon, whether the obviously bourgeois canon or the decadent one. Pasolini's conception of this "beauty" was wholly his own. It was a beauty made up of pimples, of dirty ears and necks, of coarse and tender movements. As a conception, it had something expressionistic about it, a pictorial quality that seemed to go along with some of the subject matter of the painter Renato Guttuso.

But Pasolini's originality did not stop with physical appearance. His was a singular linguistic and social experiment, whose significance was to appear in the pages of *Ragazzi di vita* and—in a surprising continuity between literary and cinematographic writing—in the film *Accattone*. First of all, the "discovery of a world"—then its authentication through a style that redevelops its logic and emotions.

The discovery of the urban peripheries had so far been essentially visual—I am thinking of the gas tanks, and of Portonaccio as painted by Lorenzo Vespignani. Pasolini established a linguistic workshop over and above these figurative examples. Roman street slang was of no value in itself from the standpoint of linguistic and expressive value. Pasolini wanted to impart an aesthetic value to it.

The friendship with Scialoja was to break up for cultural reasons. They parted over the realism-versus-abstraction controversy, at a time when neorealism was taking the offensive and condemning with unjustified harshness everything that differed from it. The considerations were political, and were determined by criteria that had nothing to do with culture. Pasolini had even written the introduction for an exhibition of Scialoja's work in Parma in 1954. Still, it was in that very year that their friendship came to an end. The episode is not an idle one. From it emerge the alignments that were beginning to characterize Italian intellectual life, dividing it into opposing, water-tight blocs.

Pasolini made his own side of the argument the subject of the poem "Picasso" (1953), written on the occasion of a retrospective at the Galleria d'Arte Moderna in Rome of the Spanish master's work:

> He—among the enemies
>
> of the class he mirrors, the cruelest,
> as long as he remained within its season
> —enemy by rage and by noisy
>
> anarchy, necessary decay—goes out
> among the people and provides in a nonexistent season:
> feigned by means of his same old
>
> imagination. Ah, it lies not in the sentiment
> of the people this ruthless Peace of his,
> this idyll of white orangutans. Here
>
> the people are absent . . .
>
> The way out
>
> toward the eternal lies not in this willed
> and premature love. It is by remaining
> inside the inferno with a cold
>
> determination to understand it, that one seeks
> salvation.[15]

These were anti-intellectual, populist arguments, but in them there is a flavor of historicism, the need to be anchored to the concrete. There is the urgency to "remain inside the inferno" in order to understand it and not be torn apart by it.

Violent quarrels went on all night. Scialoja accused Pasolini of Zhdanovian commonplaces. Pasolini invoked the "song of the people": themes of slums haunted "by joy and Neapolitan hunger," "infected neighborhoods," and "rude dialect voices." Passion and ideology ended by dividing the two friends.

The year 1953 had brought remarkable practical results. In the spring, Pasolini stopped teaching at the school in Ciampino. For two weeks his cousin Naldini took his place, then he resigned for good.

His new work was the cinema, writing the script for a film by Mario Soldati, *La donna del fiume*. The scenario was written jointly with Bassani.

Ever since his Friulian years Pier Paolo had been persistently tempted by the cinema. Already by 1945 he had written his first film script, entitled *Lied* or *I calzoni*. In 1949 he had the idea for a documentary on the farm workers of San Vito al Tagliamento. He had written new scripts, in the hope that someone would take them, as soon as he arrived in Rome. Some of these he had read to Mariella Bauzano.

Here then was the cinema, a profession that was to enable him to live comfortably, and one he was to pursue with dedication. But his economic situation was to improve through literature as well. The publisher Livio Garzanti, son of Aldo, was interested in new Italian fiction. Garzanti had taken over the old Treves line. Livio, who at the time was editor of *L'Illustrazione Italiana*, was seeking new authors for the periodical and for the publishing house, still run by his father. His consultant was Pietro Bianchi. Bianchi introduced Bertolucci to him, and Bertolucci gave him *Il Ferrobedò* to read, that early chapter printed in *Paragone*.

Livio Garzanti wanted to meet the author. The appointment was in a hotel in downtown Rome. Bertolucci and Pasolini arrived in the lobby; it was a spring afternoon in 1953.

Garzanti spent half an hour in conversation with Bertolucci. Garzanti was a young man with decided cultural interests, but both shy and aggressive at the same time. He suddenly turned to Pasolini and asked him how much he was earning. Pasolini told him that his salary as a teacher was twenty-seven thousand lire.

The reply was "I can offer you twice that sum so that you can finish the novel you've been working on." Garzanti became Pasolini's publisher.

The charm that Pasolini exerted at that time, which explains Garzanti's gesture, stemmed from the combination in him of uncommon critical and philosophical rigor and the decadent existential facts of his life. In Pasolini two anomalous characteristics compensated each other, with exceptional results from both the human and literary standpoint.

April of 1954 saw the Pasolinis change their address. They moved to Via Fonteiana 86 in Monteverde Nuovo. The petit-bourgeois neighborhood, and the opportunity to live in a middle-class apartment, satisfied Carlo Alberto's vanity. Life amid "the Arab houses on the outskirts" was over, on the cracked asphalt streets where spring might be a "blinding copy that makes the evening whiter than the dawn."[16] A prehistory in which he had amassed an incomparable experience had ended for Pier Paolo.

Friuli and Casarsa had been a rural and peasant experience. His time in Rebibbia was an experience of urban marginality.

> Ah, the old seven o'clock autobus, waiting
> at the end of the line in Rebibbia, between two
> hovels and a small skyscraper, alone
> and smacking of chill and confinement.
> Those everyday passengers'
> faces, as though on leave
> from gloomy barracks, dignified and serious
> in the feigned vivacity of the bourgeoisie
> masking its harsh and age-old
> fear of the honest poor.
>
> Theirs was the morning that burned
> on the green of the vegetable fields along
> the Aniene, the gold of the day
> reawakening the odor of garbage . . .

Mornings by bus to Ciampino, the painful decorum of one who works for low pay and feels all hope for the future to be closed to him, the impalpable but aggressive presence of the anonymous city— Pasolini was storing up within himself a disheartened image of life.

> That breathless course between the narrow
> construction areas, the burned edges,
> the long Tiburtina. Those lines of workers,
> jobless, thieves, who got off the bus
> still dirty from the gray sweat
> of beds—where they slept head to foot

with their grandchildren—in little rooms
dusty as wagons, sinister and gay.
Those city outskirts cut up into
identical lots, absorbed by the too hot
sun, amid abandoned quarries,
broken embankments, hovels, building sites . . .[17]

All this was over, and the profound echo of it remained, almost a
burst of lightning from which it would forever be impossible for him
to remain detached. The universe of the damned, the universe of
nonbourgeois freedom, had taken shape in Pier Paolo's imagination
on those urban borders.

. . . Ah, days of Rebibbia,
which I thought wasted in a light
of necessity, and that now I know were so free! . . .

The world became the subject

no longer of mystery but of history.
The joy of knowing it was multiplied
a thousandfold—as every man,

in his humility, knows.
Marx or Gobetti, Gramsci or Croce,
were alive in those living experiences.

Rebibbia, in short, was the true period of Pasolini's human and
intellectual maturing. It was where his youth ended.

The Friulian years are the years of "planning"—of conceiving the
design, more divined than lived and possessed, of poetry and culture.
One might almost say that whatever successes those years produced—
Poesie a Casarsa, L'usignolo della Chiesa Cattolica—were sporadic, if
not fortuitous.

The Rebibbia years transformed an obscure vocation and an
equally obscure destiny, which only a few pages of poetry, precious
as they are, might go to illustrate, into "a living light":

The few friends who came to see me,
in the forgotten mornings or

evenings at the Penitentiary,
saw me in a living light:
a meek and violent revolutionary . . .[18]

This awareness, which narcissism rendered both sick and vibrant, caught fire just at the moment of saying good-bye to the shantytown grouped around the construction site of the new district prison of Rome. The farewell to that plot of scorched grass changed into a burning nostalgia, and literature was nourished by it.

The specific trait of the writer and the man is by now sealed in this oxymoron of "meek, violent," in which he combined the extreme and vitalizing flavor of an ideal "political" mission—human meekness and intellectual violence.

CHAPTER 7

THE POET OF
"THE ASHES
OF GRAMSCI"

LIFE DIMINISHED

The years 1953, 1954, to 1961 were those of Pasolini's most intense work. He wrote and published the best of his output—*Ragazzi di vita* (1955) and *Una vita violenta* (1959), the two books of poems *Le ceneri di Gramsci* (1957) and *La religione del mio tempo* (1961), and the critical essays in *Passione e ideologia* (1960). He was the guiding spirit of a literary magazine, *Officina* (1955–59). He turned out a total of thirteen film scripts. He translated Aeschylus' *Oresteia*, which Vittorio Gassman was to stage (1960). Finally, 1961 was the year of *Accattone,* his first film.

These were years of hectic and parallel activities that resist chronological treatment. One gets the impression of simultaneous whirlpools, of work resolutely executed on several keyboards.

The storyteller lent himself to the cinema, and vice versa. The poet of *Le ceneri di Gramsci* decanted his language into that of Aeschylean tragedy. The organizer of *Officina* was the critic of *Passione e ideologia,* and the latter mirrored with crystalline lucidity the poet and storyteller whom he nourished in himself.

These were also years of furious controversy. Pasolini began to experience persecution in the form of court trials and scurrilous accusations.

If he was a witness of his period, he was not so in the sense one ordinarily is: a witness within the culture of the ruling class. He was, instead, witness and child of a culture in its phase of exhaustion and dissolution—Italian peasant culture. So as not to feel himself defeated, he gave a face to the struggle such as only a poet could have succeeded in doing, clothing not only his intelligence and sensibility, but his person as well, with all the possible legacies that history had to offer him.

He placed his bets immediately—whether consciously or unconsciously, it is hard to say. And public opinion, the press, lighted its own dim lamp on literature. It discovered him as a protagonist.

In all this, however, it would seem that his life was diminished, that Pasolini had no more space or time for himself. Or rather it seems that he increasingly made a ritual out of his· free time, imparting to it a rhythm of fixed habits.

The "inadmissible" life was accepted, not to say exhibited, and thereby took on an appearance of disembodied solemnity, even in the torment and fury by which it was marked. Ever changing, through the continuous and various encounters with which it was crowded, it remained identical to itself, increasingly so, to the point of becoming stalled in a kind of highly mobile eternity.

This life was lived under the banner of objectivity. But the hard work with which it alternated forced it to adapt itself to a marginal schedule, which was always to remain the same: the early hours of the afternoon, especially in spring and summer, when the small playing fields outside the city, the marshes, and the popular seashore establishments in Ostia fill up; the late evening hours, after dinner, from eleven o'clock on—the hours of strenuous nocturnal "cruising"; Sunday and holiday afternoons, when boys swarmed more freely in the outlying streets, or came into Rome from the shantytowns to sniff out adventures.

Rome was anxious and vital in those years. In it there quivered a political opposition that united on the left many students, the intellectuals, and even the vast throngs of shantytown inhabitants. The roads were becoming crowded with small cars and motorbikes. Governmental policy entrenched itself behind Scelba,* behind the anticul-

* Mario Scelba, prime minister February 1945–June 1955.—Tr.

tural dregs of a Christian Democratic Party that in Rome itself was seeking tactical alliances on the right.

Everything seemed clear, blindingly clear—there was good and there was evil. Good and evil could exchange places depending on one's point of view, but once that was established, everything on this side was good and everything on the other evil.

Such Manicheism could not be cultural, but culture—and not only in Rome—was able to make use of this oversimplification, even abase itself in it, and at the same time miraculously escape from its threadbare abstractness.

The publication of Antonio Gramsci's *Prison Notebooks* aroused a new interest in history. Publishers were bringing out timely translations of foreign literary and cultural works: Proust, Freud, Jung. Italian literature, contrary to what was to be written about it in the following decade, experienced a moment of true and unsurpassed vigor.

The novel was the leading form of expression, that "Italian" novel that tradition had made to seem impossible. Gadda was working on *Quer pasticciaccio*; Palazzeschi was still writing with vitality; Landolfi, Moravia, and Brancati each arrived at his creative height, as did Pavese and Vittorini. Through a highly sensitive attention to language (Moravia on one side, Gadda on the other, like two opposite and complementary poles), their kind of novel expressed a pattern of historical awareness, one not so much governed by the idea of a reductive mirroring of reality as by the search for a possible definition of psychological and anthropological forces. Writers were living within an aggressive social fabric, and testing this aggressiveness in their writing.

Gadda aside, Moravia's *La romana* (1947) and *Racconti romani* (first edition, 1954), Pavese's *La casa in collina* (1948), Brancati's *Il bell'Antonio* (1949), and Landolfi's *Racconto d'Autunno* (1947) and *La bière du pécheur* (1953) comprise an essential anthology of this testimony, the artistic quality of which can hardly be questioned.

Alongside them should be listed such writers as Anna Banti and Mario Soldati, as well as new writers like Elsa Morante, who in 1948 published her extraordinary *Menzogna e sortilegio*, and then Pasolini's generation, with Bassani, Calvino, Cassola, Fenoglio, Anna Maria Ortese, Leonardo Sciascia, Natalia Ginzburg, Ottieri, and Testori.

These are also the years from which date the great comedies of Eduardo De Filippo, and Ernesto De Martino's anthropological studies on the magical beliefs of the South. These latter works constitute the most striking novelty (in the fabric of Italian culture), and though unrelated, can perhaps be seen as paralleling, in their concern for a world of the dispossessed, the creative and literary research of Pasolini.

Meanwhile, in 1953 *Tal cour di un frut* was published by Lingua Friulana. Contini wrote Pier Paolo that these dialect poems had given him "unexpected joy."

The anthology *Poesia dialettale del Novecento*, on which Pasolini collaborated with Mario Dell'Arco, was published in 1952, and in 1955 came the companion volume, *Canzoniere italiano: antologia della poesia popolare*. In 1954 the *Paragone* series issued the definitive edition of the Friulian poems *La meglio gioventù*, and Anna Banti expressed the hope that the novel *Ragazzi di vita* would appear in the same series. Nineteen fifty-four was also the year in which Pasolini, in a collection of verse edited by Vittorio Sereni and issued by Meridiana, published *Il canto popolare*, the first sample of the poems to appear in the volume *Le ceneri di Gramsci*.

His contributions, between January and September 1953, to *Giovedì*, a political and cultural weekly edited by Giancarlo Vigorelli (and it was a publication that brought together intellectuals and writers who could not be said to be Communist or leftwing, but belonged instead to the ranks of democratic Catholics), represented a success for Pasolini the literary critic. His articles on the poetry of Ungaretti, Saba, the young poets of the "Lombard line" as described by Luciano Anceschi, or the stories of Gianna Manzini, showed that he was an essayist of unusual penetration.

Carlo Betocchi, writing to thank him for a review, remarked: "In your piece, both of us reveal ourselves."

Pasolini the philologist, meanwhile, in addition to anthologizing dialect texts from both cultivated and folk sources, contributed to *Il Belli* between 1952 and 1954, and his comments, directed to discerning the subtle connections between vernacular and artistic poetry and inspired by a feeling of historical concreteness, aroused wide approval.

When, after the success of *Ragazzi di vita*, Moravia suggested to Mario Missiroli, then editor of the *Corriere della Sera*, that he invite Pasolini to write for the paper, Missiroli, a shrewd spokesman for government conformism, refused, but added, as a custodian of literature: "Tell your friend for me that when it comes to the work he has done on the dialect poets, nothing like it has been seen since the time of Carducci."

I said that Pasolini's life was becoming diminished. This was to be a long process, but it begins at this time. There were practical urgencies, and there was also a life of "literature," in which little by little he became involved, even when his interest was not an immediate one but only that of any writer in search of a public.

He was working "like a slave" on the script for *Il prigioniero della montagna*, a film by Luis Trenker, an assignment he shared with Bassani. The two of them were Trenker's guests in Ortisei during the summer of 1955. A photograph shows Pasolini and Bassani in the mountains—Pier Paolo has the same uneasy smile as always, and a freshness and leanness of body that make him look younger than his more than thirty years.

And 1955 was the year in which *Ragazzi di vita* was published. The novel appeared in the bookstores in April. At the end of July, the prime minister's office reported it to the public prosecutor in Milan for its "pornographic content."

RAGAZZI DI VITA

Pornography. What pornography? A few ellipses. *Vaffan . . .* ("up your . . ."), a few pederasts depicted like silhouettes against the partition walls of certain little neighborhood cinemas, or else the word *cazzo* ("cock"), never fully uttered but allowed to run lightly across the surface of the story.

What was pornographic was the odor of truth that circulates throughout this picaresque book—the sick, oozing vitality of the characters, their outspoken frenzy, the ludicrously brazen plasticity of their bodies.

To understand the "scandal" aroused by the bookstore appearance of *Ragazzi di vita*, the discussions it provoked, and its outstanding success, one must turn to images from the newsreels of the period. A mildly chastened Italy, which was losing its mind over the so-called *maggiorate fisiche*, the buxom girls in beauty contests, quite obvious symbols of a country that was finally eating and producing: large breasts, gleaming stomachs, Rubensian hips. Prosperity took the form of glowing female health—the myth of Pomona came back to life under the stiffened pleats of tailored suits, or declared itself in the "generous" *décolletage* of summer dresses.

The 1950s were years of an old-fashioned society, which reacted hesitantly to European and transatlantic fashions. Men's high-waisted trousers looked clumsy, as did the Borsalino hats worn as in the prewar period. The Italy of that time was not the industrialized country it was to become; for the moment industrialization had only shallow roots in the Po valley. The rest was rural, spasmodically or gently rural, and a certain tone of life in the large cities was rural as well. The Montesi scandal,* which combined politics and judicial weakness, and an embezzlement scandal in Rome involving a prelate, sounded the alarm even in those years over public morality. Against this background cultural life seemed to be an anomaly—no one could tell whether it was being discarded in advance on the path that the rest of the national community was following, or whether it was miraculously drawing oxygen on other levels.

But the flywheel of massification was ready to start turning—the great revolution in Italian customs, their disfigured (or degraded) transformation, was about to begin.

Ragazzi di vita speaks instead of shantytowns, of derailed existences. Pasolini writes of a life that has only the appearance of life: the unveiled bad conscience of a country clinging to moral and social preconceptions. It is the skeleton in the closet—and this skeleton speaks a bullying and disgraceful language.

The urge to go beyond archaic patterns of production, the survival of deep-rooted and dead ethical principles—from here springs the accusation of pornography against a book that has nothing pornographic about it, and in which eroticism is evoked to drive forth a secret, acculturated image of death.

This book carries a disruptive political charge. It lays bare, through the novelty of a highly elaborate style, the existential outskirts of Italian society. This society had just been treated for serious wounds, and treated in haste. It was pretending to be cured, while still harboring its ancient and inveterate ills. The wasted lives of Riccetto and his

---

* A scandal revolving around the unexplained death of Wilma Montesi, a young aspiring actress, which occurred allegedly at a party near Ostia attended by prominent figures in the business and cinema worlds, including the younger son of the foreign minister, Attilio Piccioni, who was accordingly forced to resign.—Tr.

friends became, perhaps beyond the author's intentions, the scorching mirror of those ills. It seemed easy to deny the ills by trying to ban the mirror.

The connection between a work of poetry and the society in which it emerges is undoubtedly mysterious, even indecipherable, but sometimes reactions set in that seem to draw that mystery into the light.

Thus, in the case of *Ragazzi di vita*, it was Prime Minister Antonio Segni's office that took action. Eleven days after being sworn in, he took the trouble to have a copy of the book sent to the public prosecutor in Milan calling for "eventual appropriate action." The covering letter concluded: "The work is found to be of a pornographic nature."[1]

On December 29, 1955, the Milan public prosecutor issued a "writ for the immediate trial of Garzanti Aldo and Pasolini Pier Paolo on charges of publishing obscene material."

After Livio Garzanti had come forward to take his father's place in the proceedings, the trial was held on July 4, 1956. Pietro Bianchi testified, in his capacity as literary consultant to the Garzanti publishing house, as did Carlo Bo and, in writing, Giuseppe Ungaretti. They spoke of "religious values," of "compassion for the disinherited." The public prosecutor asked for acquittal "because the matter does not constitute a crime." The verdict was for acquittal, and the novel returned to the bookstores after being sequestered for months.

The trial turned out for the best. The publisher had succeeded in getting politicians to take a positive interest in the case. The verdict lauded the "climate of calm dignity" in which the proceedings had taken place, and stressed "the magnanimity of the statements by the public prosecutor and the defense."

Pasolini was to be brought to trial many times for his work as a writer and film director. The charges were filed anonymously; such anonymity is a condemnation of itself and there is thus no point in talking about it. What is surprising in the case of *Ragazzi di vita* is that the proceedings were initiated by the political establishment through one of its highest offices.

The shantytowns of Rome, their human and social dregs, constituted a troublesome belt around the capital, an indictment of successive Christian Democratic governments that did not succeed in shaking off the legacies of fascism. The social and urbanistic cancer of these shantytowns had been brought about by Mussolini's dictatorship, and the war and its aftermath had made the situation chronic. The new democracy had pointed itself in the direction of economic prosperity, but this visible sore, a howling human sore, spread increasingly like a tumor.

A book saturated with literary elegance had given voice to all this. Simplistic and even naïve as it may seem today, an attempt was made to silence that voice.

"It's a soundtrack," said Gadda, who liked *Ragazzi di vita*.

Gadda himself, Bertolucci, Giuseppe De Robertis, Piero Bigongiari, Carlo Bo, Cassola, Sereni, Anna Banti, Mario Luzi, and others made up the jury that in early summer of 1955 awarded the novel the Colombi-Guidotti prize in Parma. It was an award that served as a pronouncement against all those, politicians or otherwise, who were rushing to attack the new writer and his outstanding book.

A number of Marxist critics also joined in the attack. Carlo Salinari had written in *Il contemporaneo* of "linguistic equivocation" and "equivocation in content," of a "false *verismo* in the words," and of "clouded inspiration."[2] Some Marxists reacted moralistically to Pasolini's conception of the Roman subproletariat. They set up a sort of scholastic decalogue, according to which Pasolini's work was rejected and denied existence (as being the fruit of a "narcissistic" literary sensibility). After accusing Pasolini of linguistic arbitrariness, these critics went on to question the credibility of the underlying reality presented in the book. The author was said to have been betrayed in his realistic intentions by his own aestheticism.[3]

Even these positions, with their claims based on content, serve only to point out the hidden political meaning of *Ragazzi di vita*. The existence of the urban subproletariat was not merely an aesthetic problem.

But this was the gist that Pasolini must have derived from all that was written and said—his book bore directly on the residues of prefascist and preliberal decrepitude that obscurely afflicted the nation's conscience. This impact emerged not only by dint of reasoned argument, but from an explosive subjectivity, marked by all the stigmas of the great decadent tradition—and also from what in Christian terminology is called "scandal."

It was the vast and strange realms of the unconscious that Pasolini was driven to explore. Across them he projected the "pure" requirement of social justice, but in him this purity was an infernal voice and a vision of hell.

His stormy verbal gift was here quite different from the Félibrian*
one of the Casarsa poet. *Ragazzi di vita* makes a frantically physical
and resonant, not a melodic use of sound.

The novel does not simply portray a reality. But Pasolini's rigorously
literary conception transforms the book into a reality.

"With an obsessive and monotonous tension, Pasolini empties the
world of the shantytowns of everything not animal or brutal. He
eliminates every sigh, every human breath, every glimmer of hope,
every reason that might drive the characters to live rather than die,"
writes Pietro Citati.[4]

This Lautréamontian inferno, where everything is enclosed in the
code of defeat, is also strangely happy. The style transforms it into a
perpetual flowering of images, invests it with an exuberant vitality.
Innocently and with considerable shrewdness, the creator of this
world conveys to the reader the cheerful, shameless thrill of his own
discovery, a discovery both erotic and creative.

His subjectivity triumphs thereby—it is a diffuse eroticism, which
cannot be restrained and opens out onto an unprecedented, and
intensely political, perspective.

Marxists, in fact, were discussing the issue. Did the "Roman dialect"
in which the novel had been written constitute linguistic arbitrariness?

Among the boys he had met in the shantytowns, Pasolini had discovered a "consultant," Sergio Citti. "My walking dictionary of
Roman dialect," he called him.[5]

It was the summer of 1951. Pier Paolo saw Citti for the first time
along the Aniene River at Ponte Mammolo. A few days later he ran
into him in front of a cinema in Acqua Bullicante. The two struck up
a conversation. Sergio was eighteen, and a few weeks before had
been released from the reformatory. He took Pier Paolo for a social
worker and accordingly distrusted him.

"I'm a writer," Pier Paolo told him. Citti, for his part, wrote, or was
thinking of writing, stories. A child of the people, uneducated, gifted
with an unusual verbal imagination of the "underworld" type, Sergio

---

* *Félibrian:* relating to the Provençal writings of Frédéris Mistral and his
followers, who sought to maintain the ancient *lanque d'oc* of southern France
as a current literary vehicle of expression.

talked at length that evening with Pier Paolo whom he discovered to be a quite different sort of person from what he had seemed at first sight. Pier Paolo spoke to him about psychoanalysis, of how eros develops during adolescence. The two ended up on the steps of the neighborhood church, playing *ditate* (mutual blows with the extended index and middle fingers) until the blood came. Later Pier Paolo said he was writing a book about the boys of the shantytowns and asked Sergio to help him.

Pasolini and Citti began seeing each other. They used to go to a pizzeria in Torpignattara, a place called L'Aquila d'Oro (the Golden Eagle). Sergio at the time was earning more than Pier Paolo—he was a housepainter at eighteen-hundred lire a day. It was he who paid for Pier Paolo's pizza. He introduced him to his untalkative and melancholy brother Franco.

These suppers, in which they were often joined by other boys, were the occasion for stories, the eating and drinking interspersed with talk and gestures. Pasolini kept an open notebook in front of him; he asked Sergio for particulars with the punctilious and quibbling manner of a professional linguist.

The supper over, he took the tram home to Rebibbia, or vanished in search of his own adventures. Sergio suggested that they go out together with a couple of girls, and Pier Paolo responded by suggesting that he come along on the hunt for boys. Once, however, he mentioned a certain Franca, but this woman never materialized.

Citti at the time had not given much importance to the fact that his friend "wrote." They lost touch with each other. Later, opening a newspaper, he happened to see a photograph of Pier Paolo—the article was about literary prizes and *Ragazzi di vita* (the novel shared the Viareggio prize in 1955).

Er pasòla or *Giacche Palànce* (the friendly nicknames that these boys called Pier Paolo—the second referred to his hollow cheeks, resembling those of the American actor Jack Palance) had been telling the truth.

Two years went by, and "the writer" showed up again in Acqua Bullicante. He had a white second-hand '600 Fiat, and gave his old clothes to his friends in the shantytowns. He was writing a new novel, and the friendship with Sergio became close: *Una vita violenta* emerged.

Sergio not only became his consultant for underworld slang but also joined in Pier Paolo's work in the cinema (which meanwhile had become exacting). Together they prepared a first draft, which was never used, for Carlo Lizzani's film *Il gobbo* (The Hunchback), in which Pasolini acted a part. As a boy in the shantytowns, Citti had lived the saga of Alvaro Cosenza, known as "the Hunchback" (the climate of this criminal episode is not far removed from that of Pasolini's novels).

Sergio later helped Pier Paolo to work up the dialogue in Roman dialect for Federico Fellini's 1957 film *Le notti di Cabiria* (Nights of Cabiria).[6] Pasolini wanted Sergio to act a part in it, and Fellini agreed, but Sergio preferred to stay on the hind side of the movie camera.

So, was the Roman dialect suggested by Sergio wholly arbitrary? It was a slang cut from slang—the speech of delinquents invented as a code for communication among friends while excluding outsiders; but it was also slang that testified to a tragic ghetto, to a sick marginal human existence.

Pasolini was too good a philologist to deny himself the experience of poetically reinventing it. The "subjectivity" of this language was irresistibly turned inside out and made "objective," his imagination went all out to catch "things," and stylistic mimicry became, in the eyes of the writer, the absolute and matchless moment of their capture.

Thus this slang lost its purely literary intentions, and came to be adopted for purely cognitive ends. It illuminated the virgin world of human suffering in the shantytowns, it was a ray of light cast on the darkness of a hydra's lair. From underworld speech, it changed into a functional language that heightened and defined the opposition of a world, an inferno, to the rest of the world.

One might say in passing that what limits Pasolini's "Roman" fiction is not its use of a partial and arbitrary language, but its ideological programmatics, its temptation to be didactic.

The time of Pasolini's greatest success runs from 1955 to 1959, from *Ragazzi di vita* to *Una vita violenta*.

Pier Paolo worked spasmodically on his new novel. Livio Garzanti had asked for it, and between one film script and another Pier Paolo snatched the time to write the story of Tommasino. Meanwhile the moment of critical recognition had arrived for him (1957: *Le ceneri di Gramsci*), as well as recognition by the reading public. Pasolini had come to the attention of the national public both for his talent and because of the "scandal" aroused by his open and actively pursued homosexuality.

In the midst of controversy, he was not to disavow the requirements of intellectual rigor. "My teachers are Gramsci and Contini."[7]

Linguistics and historical materialism were his working tools, which he threw boldly and disdainfully onto the desks of Italian intellectuals. With striking ease he applied his critical criteria to any problem, literary or not.

The desks of Italian intellectuals were still cluttered by dusty retorts and alembics, by archaic little instruments vainly catalogued in a freshly printed vocabulary. Pasolini, however, could write about fashion, hermetic poetry, or childhood eroticism in perfect keeping with the times. The attention he paid to society was the sign of a different way of understanding "commitment"—a writer's "commitment" was no longer only to political and public battles. It was something different, nuanced and all-enveloping, a way of reasoning about the world we live in.

As I said, these years did not pass idly for Pasolini, nor were the polemics he engaged in idle, the ones that descended on him over *Ragazzi di vita*.

There was a weakness in Pasolini, and the fact was that these polemics, in a subtle and intangible way, nourished in him the need for a novelistic construction that would satisfy those principles of didactic realism hastily skipped over or taken for granted in his first political attack, the picaresque *Ragazzi di vita*.

The didactic impulse was not alien to Pasolini, but in what he had written so far it had doubtless been repressed, or if not repressed, absorbed in the sensuousness of representation and expression.

Una vita violenta is instead an edifying novel. It shows that linguistic experimentation (this was the formula under which Pasolini's work was by now being classified) could lay claim to the projected national people's novel advanced by Gramsci. Pasolini acknowledged these intentions. It was his way of confronting militant Marxist criticism, a confrontation he sought by a provocatory, roundabout strategy.

Tommasino, the hero of *Una vita violenta*, is not Riccetto in *Ragazzi di vita*. He does not seem to burst forth from the mirroring prism of his pointless existence. He is meant to be an entirely rounded figure, the synthesis of a series of experiences that make him "typical."

He is a member of the neofascist party, he is a *ragazzo di vita*, and like all his kind he lives by expedients. He will go to jail. He will be released from jail as a "mature" person who wants to take his place in society. He reckons according to his own needs. He comes down with tuberculosis, and in the sanatorium moves closer to communism. He dies, a sacrificial lamb, during a flood in the shantytowns, trying to save some of the inhabitants.

This outline exposes an ideological limitation—by the time the story ends, it has not been enlightening in even a latent way. This is because ideology here plays a coercive role—the moment it encapsulates and determines the development of events, it offers them as examples of devotion.

This structure (as compared to *Ragazzi di vita*) achieves the effect of backlighting the characters and events of the novel—it renders them in silhouette. *Una vita violenta* seems reduced to silence, a novel in which the behavior of the characters has been flattened in the montage, more sight than sound. Their world appears dreadful and bare, the epiphany of a sickness that lacks any healing compensation.

The lights go on in the orchestra of a cinema and it is "like when you lift a stone and find everything underneath full of worms, a heap of worms entwined around each other, moving and wriggling on all sides, twisting their heads and tails."

Such comparisons in the novel appear to evoke the rhetoric of Dante. They testify instead to a growing and obscure anxiety. The world of the *ragazzi di vita* tends to turn to ashes in the imagination of its author, and he experiences this eclipse in the wish to redeem it through ethico-political prescriptions.

But the word no longer produces such redemptions. *Accattone* and the cinema are just around the corner.

On the conscious level, these were still happy years for Pasolini. He had established lasting ties among real *ragazzi di vita*—these were the friends he was to summon onto the set of *Accattone, Mamma Roma, La ricotta*, and the *Gospel*; they were the friends who sometimes accompanied him to restaurants with writers and intellectuals; they were the friends with whom he played football whenever he could. In short, they were the boys with whom he satisfied his need for male solidarity. He sought them for the humanity of their spirit— the imaginative verbal knowledge of Sergio Citti, the muscular elasticity of Ninetto Davoli.

Sergio and Ninetto were special and extreme examples. Besides, they were to be the friends of his life, the ones with whom Pier Paolo expressed his taste for the vernacular sally, his irresistible bent for colloquial mimicry.

The others, the many, many others who called him simply Paolo, or in Roman fashion *a Pa'*, and whom he treated with extraordinary kindness and gentleness, were to mark throughout his entire existence the countless way stations where he paused in his search for a truth and naturalness of life that little by little eluded him.

With these boys, Pier Paolo was the lucid, fascinating teacher that he had been in Valvasone—he was their hypothetical father. He used to say that these boys were free in their feelings and bodies because they agreed to make love with homosexuals, with a homosexual like himself—they accepted him cheerfully and not with mercenary indifference, even though they did it for a thousand lire, a pizza, or a pair of jeans.

Erotic contact with them occurred once, if it was that kind of encounter. Once it had occurred, the friendship that ensued, if it ensued, forever excluded sex.

This exclusion, which Pasolini ended by considering as a sort of victory over instinct, nevertheless threw the door open to despair, to an unresolvable emotional insecurity. To masturbate them, to perform fellatio on most of them, and then to continue, night after night, in a search that extended quantitatively as far as possible, reduced eroticism to a mechanical replica of itself. This could only act to solidify the neurotic anguish by which his intelligence was besieged.

In time, the siege became more pressing and obsessive than ever. When he temporarily succeeded in freeing himself from it, he emerged into the light exhausted, mute, destroyed.

The indications of this obsession, this silence, can actually be seen in the darkening images of *Una vita violenta*—evidence of a poetic world that was dying prematurely because it had merged too much with the life of its author.

BOLOGNESE WORKSHOP

May 1955, the first issue of *Officina* (Workshop), a bimonthly poetry magazine; editors, Francesco Leonetti, Pier Paolo Pasolini, Roberto Roversi; office at Via Rizzoli 4, Bologna. The cover was of coarse packing cardboard, off-white, a workshop color.

Longhi's *Officina ferrarese* was surely not far from their minds.*

---

* *Officina ferrarese* (Rome, 1934; 2nd ed., Florence, 1956) is Roberto Longhi's study of the fifteenth-century School of Ferrara, in particular the workshop of Cosimo Tura, responsible for the fresco decorations of the Palazzo Schifanoia.—Tr.

It was to be a workshop of ideas, style, and poetry, the center for a "literary discourse" that sought to be important in itself, but did not shun confrontation with history and society.

The magazine ran for twelve issues, until April 1958. Only two issues of a second series came out, dated March–April 1959 and May–June 1959—editorial secretary, Fabio Mauri—black cover with the table of contents printed in white.

The literary partnership of Leonetti, Pasolini, and Roversi, with the later addition of Mauri, went back to the Bologna *liceo* and the days of *Eredi* and *Il Setaccio*. With the passage of time, Pasolini was hoping to repeat the project of "creating culture in the provinces."

The urge to set up an organ of cultural propaganda was not Pasolini's alone—it was shared by Leonetti, and Roversi acted as a catalyst. Meetings were often held in his antiquary bookstore, the Palmaverde, and little by little the group attracted other members: Gianni Scalìa from Bologna; Angelo Romanò, whom Pasolini had met in Rome in the course of his radio work (Romanò was an official at the state radio, and now lived in Milan); and Franco Fortini, also living in Milan. Bologna thus became the midpoint between the extremes of Rome and Milan.[8]

Pasolini went on with his "violent life" in Rome—he said that he considered Bologna, a quiet city that had changed little since the prewar years and was still a favored university citadel, as his own "Porziuncola."*

Long discussions and much correspondence—every critical or creative text was read by all the editors, and the authors were encouraged to correct, expand, rewrite. The circle of contributors was handpicked. Pasolini invited some of his friends in Rome to contribute: Gadda, Bertolucci, Caproni, Bassani, Garboli, Penna, Vivaldi, Volponi. Pieces also appeared by Pagliarani, Sanguineti, Arbasino, and Pasolini's young "discovery," Massimo Ferretti.

A clear separation can be seen between the critical and creative texts. The critical texts are for the most part editorial analyses of the past and present literary situation. The creative ones are by the editors and "guests."

The magazine did not pay its contributors. But Roversi would sometimes send them a few bottles of Lambrusco wine—a thoughtful

---

* Or Portiuncula. A portion of land with a chapel near Assisi, donated to Saint Francis and where he founded his Order.—Tr.

expression of provincial courtesy, perhaps of an old agricultural tradition, and one that should not be overlooked if one hopes to understand the cordial atmosphere that prevailed in the little circle.

The disputes with Fortini came later.

The magazine's "plan of action," in the words of Francesco Leonetti:

. . . We must educate ourselves with the necessary deliberation to pass from the inner, personal world to the social and historical one, from the little world to the big world with its powerful illusion-forces, which are not at all naïve illusions, as some believe who argue, even with artistic sensitivity, in the midst of endless chaos. Indeed neorealism has taught us by its haste what happens when the "little world" does not express itself; it is clear that what is needed instead is a continuous and fruitful transition . . .[9]

What are the implicit contents of this statement? A detached and critical attitude as regards neorealism and the period of the hermetic poets, insofar as this period may have affected neorealism; the manifest proposal to recover the "historical world"; the need to develop a notion of "culture" through which to approach human reality without mystification or soothing consolations; an implied rationalism. Which is to say that if the world seems to be endless chaos, this is because people linger in an illusion, a state of mental torpor that encourages them to feel themselves to be victims, rather than seekers of moral and social goals.

An optimistic tone, a touch of utopia—permissible sentiments in the harsh decade of the fifties.

This touch of utopia was still resisting at the moment when the ideals of the Resistance were succumbing to premature old age—not only because the madness of Stalinism had broken the trusting hope for revolutionary regeneration in more than one intellectual (both inside and outside Italy), but also because there was widespread awareness that historical materialism was changing into a theology much more suffocating than the idealistic kind.

Officina offered a revision of Francesco De Sanctis and Antonio Gramsci, presenting them in a light that was not the usual one, nor in accord with the principles of socialist realism as commonly understood. The magazine revived the subject of decadentism "as a contemporary problem," and reintroduced the historical avant-gardes as subjects not to be thought of as dead and buried. And while it stressed the complete legitimacy of literary discourse as something sufficient unto itself, it did not deny another legitimacy: that this discourse fall into a dialectical relationship with life.

It was in these years that a swift and progressive erosion of the idea of "history" occurred in Italian culture—its place was to be taken by sociology.

Officina, while fully aware of the limitations of Crocean historicism in all its most time-worn expressions, nevertheless went back to the notion of "history," and thereby came to offer an effective and singular interpretation of certain crucial moments in modern and contemporary literature. Pascoli, Leopardi, *La Voce*, Renato Serra, the Crepuscular poets, Spitzer, Lukács, leftist culture of the postwar period—these were some, though by no means all, of the subjects examined by the magazine.

In line with Gramsci, it sought to offer a fresh view of what was alive and what was dead in twentieth-century Italian literature.

Was all this an illusion? Cultural organs seemed immune from possible corruption, and this illusion had the right to exist. But there was a limit.

As Pasolini wrote in 1974:

What is irritating and unsatisfactory about *Officina* is its naïveté, which is also to its credit. Its inability to foresee imminent neocapitalism and the rebirth of fascism is humiliating for its editors. Also humiliating is its "criticism" of values—those of the left—while indulging in a substantial and quasi adulation of these values. In *Officina* there was neither disobedience nor extremism; there was the calmness of reason in the act of rebuilding. But it was not true calm, or rather it was an unjustified calm. In reality, the editors of *Officina*—potentially, only potentially— were preparing to take the place of those they were criticizing, with vitality and rigor, but also with respect. That is, they were preparing to take power . . .[10]

Is this an all too personal judgment? Pasolini was the true driving force behind the magazine—his "naïveté" was refracted onto his friends. It was not that they lacked personality and qualities of their own but their existence as a group irresistibly centered around him.

Francesco Leonetti was patient and tireless in the quest for material. Roversi certainly contributed more, much more, than his hospitality. Pasolini brought with him his experience as a cultural organizer in Friuli, and old ideas from Friuli as well.

The Pascoli of Pasolini's graduate thesis returned in his essay appearing in the first issue of the periodical. And this Pascoli, the plurilingual poet, reread in the light of stylistic criticism, opened a dialogue of several voices on the "decadent" pattern of twentieth-century Italian poetry. Both Leonetti and Romanò devoted articles to the subject, while Sbarbaro, Clemente Maria Rebora, and Ungaretti were called as witnesses in prose and verse.

Plurilinguism evokes the image of the *Academiuta*, and with it the image of the "little homelands" and the "poetics of regression." This last, persistent conviction of Pasolini's expands like a rose, and from the level of dialect is transferred to stylistic experimentalism *tout court*. Pasolini makes it the critical key, and also the rule of prudence, of his own poetry and that of others.

If the twentieth century had raised language "to the level of poetry," the new literature had the obligation to lower it "to the level of prose." This involved "a probably unforeseen readoption of pre-twentieth-century—in the current sense of the term—stylistic modes, insofar as they have by now re-entered naturally within the confines of rational, logical, historical, if not actually instrumental language. Such traditional stylistic modes become the means for a kind of experimentation that is instead, in its ideological awareness, absolutely antitraditionalist, to the point that it violently, by definition, throws into question the structure and superstructure of the state, and condemns, with a no doubt biased and emotional gesture, the tradition that from the Renaissance through the Counter-Reformation and the nineteenth century has pursued its social and political decline, right down to fascism and the conditions of today."[11]

An ambitious program, an ambitious hope. Pasolini published the volume *Le ceneri di Gramsci* in support of this design as well. And Roversi and Leonetti, with their own poems, harped on the same theme. *Officina* was a true school of poetry: the writers who constituted its core shared a singular community of aims. And undeniably the poems of Paolo Volponi, later to be collected in *Le porte dell' Appennino* (1960), were inspired by such a design.

In short, Pasolini, a true leader, had formulated the idea of a literature open to the "problem"—his plan was for a "new post-twentieth-century" or postmodern style, and for it he had aroused some solidarity.

The dream, almost a lucid madness, meant to consider poetry as a potential sword unsheathed against the Italy of the fifties. But the country was already on the verge of an incalculable leap. Others had already sniffed the changes in progress. The economic miracle was a reality, and an understanding of it required other instruments, perhaps another personal history from the one so far lived by Pier Paolo.

The success of *Officina*, proceeding apace with Pasolini's success as a writer and poet, consisted in reviving, in a synthesis of considerable intellectual dignity, cultural values that belonged to a tradition imbued with rural Catholicism. Throughout the difficult course of Italian life, this tradition has played a cohesive, unifying role. Ultimately historicism and decadentism had melted into it, and the ideals of socialism had looked to it for their hopes of renewal. True, this tradition had also nourished fascism, but the latter was the leprosy from which to free, in the name of a new ideal, one's faith in the rational qualities of man.

Pasolini felt all this alive within himself. He did not reckon on what was coming to the fore in the rest of the world, nor on the swiftness with which Italy was to follow suit.

The world was changing: the rule of Stalinism collapsed at the Soviet Union's Twentieth Party Congress when Nikita Khrushchev delivered his secret report. Optimistic faith in Soviet socialism was disintegrating.

Khrushchev in the Soviet Union, John Kennedy in Washington, John XXIII on the throne of Saint Peter—unheard-of developments. The public mind seemed freed from the nightmares of the dark post-war years. The Italian Communists began to conceive national roads to socialism.

To understand a world so suddenly changed required that one not delude oneself. Pasolini's delusion, his "humiliating naïveté," was his belief that he could retain once and for all his literary leadership. The "humiliating naïveté" had its roots in narcissism. The effects of neo-capitalism were rapidly to dispel all certainties—the new "struggle for power" was to make rubble of the arcadian civilization of letters whose final blossoming appears in *Officina*. And the signs of this—uncertain signs but in any case real—were not lacking on the coarse printed pages of that little magazine.

For example, the apparently pointless "polemics in verse" with Edoardo Sanguineti. In the June 1957 issue, as reverse examples of the theses expounded in the essay "La libertà stilistica," Pasolini had collected a "little neo-experimental anthology" (texts by Arbasino, Sanguineti, Pagliarani, Brunello Rondi, Mario Diacono, Michele L.

Straniero, Massimo Ferretti), in which he documented an experimentalism passive in regard to history, with no involvement in the social sphere.

Sanguineti reacted. He sent the magazine a poem written in tercets —a pastiche of the tercets of "The Ashes of Gramsci"—in which he accused Pasolini of having abused his good faith. Sanguineti had submitted a group of serious poems to the magazine, and Pasolini had selected and "arranged" them in a way that blurred their meaning. Sanguineti objected to such liberty being taken with his work; he objected to his poetry being placed "outside History."

There is a good deal of psychology in this "Polemica in prosa" (the title of Sanguineti's pastiche). In it, he addresses Pasolini by the bourgeois *lei*, the formal third person singular:

> You believe in history, you believe in it
> > in the way you believe in it, and you can write
> > of having thereby now renounced
>
> the "security of a mature stylistic
> > world (your words), refined
> > and dramatic as well," in favor of a higher
>
> and actually more historical drama . . .[12]

Sanguineti displayed a certain methodical "coldness," he was "cynically" counting on the potential disruptiveness of his accusations. Pasolini's emotionalism, never denied, was such that it was easy for Sanguineti to stick a pin in it as through a butterfly. The meaning of his pastiche tended to disparage both subjectivity as such and the risk that Pasolini's subjectivity might run (expending all its "passion," all its "ideology") in trying to salvage within itself the strength and violence of certain, perhaps outmoded, means of knowledge. Sanguineti made a show of embracing to his own advantage a line of existential historicism ("the unhappy activity of the unclever 'vanquished' is more historical"), but essentially his attack was a personal one on Pasolini, "who alone is beautiful and who insists on running the whole show."

The whole affair may seem quite unimportant—a combination of naïveté and narcissism on the part of both men. But if we put aside psychology, there still remains the essential and concrete fact, which needs to be examined critically.

On one side, an ideology that considers historical awareness a point of resistance beyond which lies intellectual and social chaos (for Pasolini, there was to be barbarism, the "new prehistory"). On the other, the opposite ideology, by which history is mere occurrence or physiological dysfunction, a dreary swamp where existence sinks "not with a bang but a whimper."

The conflict, in essence, was between a residue of traditional humanism to be revitalized through Marxist historicism, and neo-positivist sociological thinking imbued with existential inhibitions.

This conflict was to be repeated on a broader scale in the controversy between the new avant-garde and its opponents, a controversy that was to scourge Italian literary life in the early sixties. Sanguineti's versified captiousness was a prefiguration, an augury, of those polemics. Sanguineti rejected Pasolini's critical views, but above all he was contesting a leadership.

Among the editors of *Officina* an obscure mechanism was being set in motion that would cause them to disperse just when the magazine was achieving greater success. The first series came to an end. Valentino Bompiani, a well-known publisher, accepted the task of printing and distributing the second series. Due to external factors the little magazine was suddenly forced to cease publication.

Relations with Bompiani were broken almost immediately. *Officina*, in the second number of the new series, had published a group of epigrams by Pasolini, including one on the death of Pius XII, "A un Papa" (To a Pope):

No one asked you to pardon Marx! an immense
    wave breaking from millennia of life
separated you from him, from his religion:
    but in your religion don't they speak of mercy?
Thousands of people under your pontificate,
    before your eyes, lived in stalls and pigsties.
You knew it, to sin does not mean to do evil:
    not to do good, that's what it means to sin . . .[13]

Valentino Bompiani was a member of the Hunting Club of Rome, a center for the Vatican aristocracy. The club, judging the epigram blasphemous, called him on the carpet, and the publisher decided to cease financing the magazine.

A small uproar broke out in the press. Pasolini replied with a new epigram, directed at the Roman nobles:

Non siete mai esistiti, vecchi pecoroni papalini,
  ora un po' esistete perché un po' esiste Pasolini.[14]

(You've never existed, you old papal sheep,
  now you exist somewhat because Pasolini somewhat exists.)

So much for the facts. But the break with Bompiani was simply an external circumstance. Contacts established with other publishers—Einaudi, Mondadori—for the purpose of continuing the magazine, not surprisingly, fell through. The group was already dissolved—the terms under which Pasolini and his friends were joined seemed archaic, and the idea that poetry alone could cement a "cultural operation" appeared obsolete.[15]

In Pasolini's mind the creative function of literature essentially took precedence over the political and organizational one. For his Bolognese and Milanese colleagues, particularly Fortini, who had become very active in the editorship of *Officina*, the dialectic between the two functions was being overturned.

This was the period that witnessed the beginning of the debate between "literature and industry." It had been announced by Elio Vittorini with the publication of *Il Menabò* in 1959, as also by the first polemics of the new avant-garde. The mass media symbolized antitraditional roles for culture, and it was this industry that literature reached out to "take possession" of. This primed a new mechanism for "taking power"—"power" was to be taken over from those who held it in the name of "absolute" literary values. These "values" had no more currency, like devalued money. They were to be supplanted not by new values, but by different "techniques."

Most likely Franco Fortini, in the discussions at *Officina*, had made himself the spokesman for these questions. Fortini, having worked in an industry such as Olivetti, run by Adriano Olivetti in a completely atypical and liberal fashion,[16] was of the whole group probably the most informed on the new trends.

There were heated quarrels. In mid-December of 1958, while the first issue of the new series was being prepared in Milan, a squabble took place between Fortini on one side and Leonetti, Roversi, and Romanò on the other—Pasolini was absent. Fortini was asked to leave Romanò's apartment, where the editors had met to discuss the manuscripts to be sent to the printer. They accused him of interfering with editorial work. The episode is slight, but it shows how much the hidden conflicts in point of view could create the highest degree of tension in their personal relations.

There was literature and its content, but there was also a growing confusion of aims that made the survival of the group still more uncertain. Everything had deteriorated in the space of a year. On June 26, 1957, Leonetti could still write to Pasolini to express his enthusiasm over their common efforts: what awaited them was "a rather hard—and full, lofty—task, and of necessity moderate rather than daring or munificent."

In an epigram written in 1958 and addressed "to the editors of *Officina*," Pasolini echoed him:

> Quixotic and harsh, we attack the new language,
> which we still don't know, and must attempt.

But the same epigram foresaw:

> . . . even the time of life is thinking, not living,
> and since thinking is now without method and word,
> light and confusion, antecedent and end,
> even pure life is being dissolved in the world.[17]

From 1958 to 1959 was a decisive period for the intellectual project represented by *Officina*. Each of its editors seemed to be concerned with something else. Roversi was thinking of a magazine of his own— it was to be *Rendiconti*. Fortini and Leonetti gravitated into the orbit of Vittorini's *Il Menabò*. Pasolini was to drift toward the cinema, while Romanò was to be increasingly caught up in television work.

I said confusion of aims. Pasolini's dominance may have helped to sour relations, even to harden positions. Some words from a letter from Roversi to Fortini, dated November 11, 1959: "Free yourself from the Pasolini complex and its fortunes. They're his, not yours, not ours. Find your own that will be yours, not his, not ours. Don't we want to forsake the roads that lead back to the farm? . . . I'm well aware (and I love you and understand you) that in you (soldier of Thermopylae) rankle the disappointments of the past and the seemingly lost years; that you see certain young (or old) lions running ahead of you and waving their tails. But in the past, commitment was a form of political paranoia, a fanciful and static radicalism, a genuine backwardness. Today, with neocapitalist patterns overcome, and the peat of the experiments of recent years burned, we can really have and seek out the clarity to act. To arrange our own ideas *in the right place* and to verify and communicate them. Rejecting Gorgias to seek Socrates."[18]

One might ask: had the "neocapitalist patterns" really been "overcome"? Had the "peat" really been "burned"? That the "political paranoia" of the fifties had been thawed is not to say that another kind of "paranoia" was not lying in wait. In any case, beyond these considerations, the "Pasolini complex" had caused a decline in the solidarity of the group.

In a letter of May 1, 1959, Fortini wrote to Pier Paolo: "We make a needless package of our critical-aesthetic opinions, the quality of our verses, Pasolini's private life, Bompiani, *Officina*, the pope, confusing—there's never been a better moment to say so—our ass with the Forty Hours,* as they say in Florence. In my opinion, you yourself should be the first to want to keep all these things apart. You are hounded, persecuted, and abused, and I understand your reactions, but to accept the terms of one's opponents means to play their game."[19]

"Confusing our ass with the Forty Hours"—in his harshness, Fortini had hit, almost inadvertently, the sore point of the argument. But Pasolini, by now at the center of too many controversies, neither wanted nor was able to "keep apart" things so apparently different as literature and "private" life. For him, life and literature constituted a whole, now as never before, and from their combination rose his love-hate relationship with his public.

Literature, for many, was no longer itself—it was fast becoming one more aspect of the organization of culture. At *Officina*, albeit in a restricted setting, they were suffering from the trauma of all this change.

One thing remained clear to Pasolini—that his survival as an artist was linked, and increasingly so, to the desperate exercise of his "desperate vitality."

LIFE AGAIN, FRIENDS AGAIN

On December 19, 1958, Carlo Alberto Pasolini died in Rome.

My father suffered, and he made us suffer. He hated the world, which he had reduced to two or three obsessive and incompatible facts. He was a

---

* A devotion during which the Sacred Host is exposed for a period of forty hours on the altars of parish churches. The expression, typically Florentine, is a less prosaic way of saying that one shouldn't mix apples and oranges.—Tr.

man who continually and desperately beat his head against the wall. His actual death throes lasted several months—he had trouble breathing and complained constantly. He had a diseased liver and knew it was serious, that even a finger of wine was bad for him, and he drank at least two liters a day. For the sake of his rhetorical life, he had no wish to recover. He wouldn't listen to us, to me and my mother, because he despised us. I came home one night just in time to watch him die.[20]

There is no reconciliation with the image of his dead father to be found in these words. Once again they describe the scene we know, in which Susanna and Pier Paolo, unheard, offer words of advice, and Carlo Alberto sinks into his sad destiny.

For the moment, seen at the point of its last flicker, Carlo Alberto's existence was very far from Pier Paolo's. If, as he wrote, life at home was "always the same as death,"[21] his creative life, though foundering in anguish, was spreading out in the sunlight of Rome, and it was a life of friends, writers, and boys from the shantytowns.

Bassani, Bertolucci, and Gadda were still among his closest friends, as were now Elsa Morante and Alberto Moravia, Renato Guttuso, Pietro Citati, Cesare Garboli, Niccolò Gallo. And Adriana Asti, Elsa De Giorgi, and Laura Betti.

Pier Paolo passed warily through fashionable literary salons. He was not a salon man, he conducted himself there with cautious irony, shunning all society rituals. Nor did he like artificiality in relations between friends. In the presence of artificial politeness, he became elusive, in his final years sarcastic. An impassioned friendship that lasted for more than twenty years, and on which he expended much kindness and sensitive affection, was the one he cultivated with Alberto Moravia and Elsa Morante. And it was mutual.

Pier Paolo had met Elsa at the time he was still a friend of Toti Scialoja—their humane Christianity, their innate sensitivity to the myths of decadence, may have brought them together. But they were also united by the torment of being truthful beyond endurance. Their friendship contained a conspicuous element of play—the game, for example, of telling each other their dreams and interpreting them, and interpreting their own gestures and those of others on the firing line of psychoanalysis.

The relationship between Elsa and Pier Paolo was marked by a religious feeling for life; the relationship between Moravia and Pier Paolo, on the other hand, by a keen interest in political and cultural matters. Sometimes there was considerable disagreement between them—Moravia's enlightened and cosmopolitan attitude clashed with

Pasolini's underground Christianity. Yet these reactions, rather than bringing about a rupture in their friendship, served to cement it even more. One would explain to the other, unwittingly, his personal qualities of intellect and judgment, and this kept the conversation going in its divergence.

Moravia had a fascinated and quite open interest in archaic civilizations, an interest that impelled him to travel the roads of the Third World of the spirit and not only of the spirit. Pasolini joined him in this, and was his enthusiastic traveling companion in India and Africa.

Moravia and Pasolini symbolized "Roman literary culture." The swiftness of their intellectual reactions, their free and easy approach to the most diverse problems, laid them open to much criticism and aroused against them a certain hostility by the press. Despite this, an instinctive capacity to catch the essential in its most tangible aspects— a capacity they shared—assured their position on the cultural scene.

Moravia had met Pasolini later than did Elsa Morante. Their ties were forged in 1955. Elsa had taken Moravia the "public" poem "The Ashes of Gramsci", at the time it was written, in order to get it published in *Nuovi Argomenti*.

Nuovi Argomenti was the journal of culture and politics edited by Moravia and Alberto Carocci. Its aim was to break anti-Communist and anti-Marxist schematism. Norberto Bobbio's essays on the independence of culture from politics were the most concrete and controversial testimony to this aim. But the magazine was also hospitable to new Italian fiction. It did not publish poetry.

On this basis, Alberto Carocci rejected Pasolini's poem. Although its content reflected the themes of the periodical, it was verse and so was unacceptable. But Moravia put up an ardent defense, and "The Ashes of Gramsci" appeared in the issue of November 1955–February 1956, no. 17–18. It was the moment when the controversy over *Ragazzi di vita* was at its height.

The friends frequently gathered for supper in a trattoria. Moravia and Elsa Morante ate out every night. Pasolini got into the habit of joining them, and Bassani, Penna, Parise, Bertolucci, and Augusto Frassineti were there from time to time.

In winter they usually ate at the Campana in Via della Campana, or at the Bolognese in the Piazza del Popolo, also at the Carbonara in Campo de' Fiori, and in Trastevere, at Pastarellaro or Carlo's. In summer, their favorite place was a trattoria on the Via Appia Antica, a stone's throw from the Porta San Sebastiano, outside the walls. Outdoors, under a makeshift roof, some benches and a few rough wooden planks had been set up; the railroad, the Rome–Genoa line, ran close by. The friends called the place "the trains," and they went there especially to eat fettuccine and lamb cutlets *"alla scottadito"* (à la burned finger).

There were verbal skirmishes between Elsa and Moravia, between Bassani and Elsa. Pier Paolo would come out suddenly with a sharp, biting remark, or more often say something gently paternalistic.

He was never very talkative. He expressed his disagreement, if the occasion arose, fairly and bluntly. He enjoyed the comic gifts of the others, even when it was a matter of amusing gossip, as in the case of Penna, whose tongue was malicious beyond belief.

He was always fond of Elsa De Giorgi, who was not on particularly close terms with his other friends. He devoted occasional evenings to her with a kind of amused submission—and this continued for years. They would go out to supper—in those days to Mario's, a restaurant in Via della Vite.

Elsa De Giorgi, with her sophisticated makeup and striking blond hairdo, radiated a certain theatrical aura derived from the cinema of the forties with its white telephones, when she had had the good fortune to be a star. She always carried a large white refrigerating satchel on her arm when she went out: she could not do without her champagne at the table. Drinking champagne and eating steak tartare, she prattled enthusiastically on about the literary subjects that she enjoyed cultivating. Pier Paolo listened.

His intense and lasting friendship with Laura Betti began around 1958. It was consolidated little by little and always renewed by the tenacity of Laura, who, with her voracious thirst for intellectuality and success, could not help but be carried away by Pasolini's progress. Pier Paolo was caught up by Laura's aggressiveness. She, in return, was caught up by his own, his rapid-fire response to the polemics being unleashed around him. And it was this, at first a game, that once impelled her, while flashbulbs were bursting around them, to take his arm and say in public, as a challenge, but a challenge directed first of all against herself, "He's my husband."

It was the turn of the sixties. In the illustrated magazines, Laura Betti was known as "the jaguar," with her helmet of platinum hair, her eyes shaped by her mascara like two commas pointing toward the temples. She was famous for her violent quarrels with all and sundry, and for her sudden infatuations. Her stage was not only the theater but the street as well—she reigned like a queen over Via del Babuino, where she lived. In her harsh voice she sang songs by writers, whom she sought out and pursued shrilly and vociferously. But she was also pursued by them, and this gave her the satisfaction she desired.

She had invented a new kind of glamour, a different way of being a prima donna, by employing shock tactics compounded of flattery and insults to attract the attention of reporters. This was her face in public; in private, her self-irony did not allow her to take her own image so seriously. She liked to give rather noisy and disordered suppers in her apartment, two adjoining rooms, with the kitchen to the right as you came in. Through these rooms passed a little of everything: the cinema, literature, the press, high fashion, boys from the shantytowns. This mixed orchestration of social life was the sign of a changing society—a society that was tending to legitimize more than one infraction of its former codes.

These suppers—at which Laura sometimes laid the table while auctioning off the bric-a-brac that surrounded her—amused Pier Paolo.

But Laura also had the capacity to become the central figure in the lives of persons to whom she felt attached. She persuaded couples in trouble to get married; she saw to it that ephemeral, if seemingly deep, relationships were dissolved. She seized on many fragments of Pier Paolo's life.

She was friendly with Susanna, and knew how to amuse and captivate her by her own intrusiveness. She understood the importance to Pier Paolo of the table, of meals, and being a born cook in the Bolognese tradition, she set up a "kitchen" for him.

Over the years, Laura's "kitchen" became a ritual, and a metaphor in the vocabulary of their mutual friends. It meant to draw up statements and "press releases," as though they were recipes to be carefully followed amid pots and ladles.

This was the "dolce vita," that truly very easy life, though all too wild, even inelegant and chaotic, which was lived in Rome between the years of the decline of ideologies and the whirl of the "economic miracle." Fellini, in his emblematic film, was to catch its essence, already nostalgic at the very moment it was lived and depicted.

Illusory and domestic, it was an existence within which grave political and social problems tended to be lost or overlooked. In 1960 the Tambroni government imagined a rightist coup—difficult days, public demonstrations. There was the harsh transition to Socialist participation in the government; there were also the opening skirmishes with a bitter, tormented, and tragic future.

Pasolini, with Sergio Citti, was to write a scene for the Fellini film, dialogue placed in the mouths of the homosexual hustlers in the orgy sequence. This was the sign of his passage through the "dolce vita." An infinitesimal sign—on tiptoe.

But Pasolini did not live a "sweet" or easy life. There was too much mortified sweetness in him for him to be able to live it dispassionately. The difficulties were in his heart and they easily projected themselves around him.

He was soon able to count on his fingers the writers with whom he kept up a steady friendship. They were the little band of Roman intellectuals whom we have met, and to which we can add Calvino, Zanzotto, Volponi, and Leonetti. With the others, his relations quickly deteriorated.

The rapid success of *Ragazzi di vita* displeased the narrow literary society of Rome. That narrow society was prepared to raise tempests in every teacup.

In 1957 the volume of poems *Le ceneri di Gramsci* was nominated for the Viareggio prize. It won, but after a long debate, and the award had to be shared with Sandro Penna's *Poesie* and Alberto Mondadori's *Quasi una vicenda*. In 1959 *Una vita violenta* was to be submitted for the Viareggio fiction prize—the judges' rejection was firm and explicit. At the instigation of Giacomo Debenedetti, the novel received the Crotone award that year.

Prizes still played an important role in bringing literary works to the attention of the public, they still represented the selection of quality. The debate over an award was a cultural debate. Psychological and moralistic elements entered into the resistance raised by some to Pasolini's work. But the case immediately became cultural and political, though undermined by gossip.

All this was clear in Pier Paolo's mind. He said his impersonal good-byes to the literary men, "his contemporaries," in an epigram of 1958:

I see you: you're there, we go on being friends,
    happy to see and greet each other, in some café,
in the houses of ironical Roman ladies . . .
    But our greetings, our smiles, our mutual passions,

are gestures in a no-man's land: a . . . waste land*
    for you: a margin for me, between one history and another.
We can no longer really agree: it makes me tremble,
    but it is in us that the world is enemy to the world.[22]

This "enmity of the world" grew within his mind, and took on before his eyes the shape of public persecution. He was nourishing at that time the hope of another private friendship to be cemented through literature.

In those years Pier Paolo had met Massimo Ferretti. Ferretti, born in a middle-class family in Jesi, had been ill since childhood with rheumatic endocarditis. It was from this disease, of whose serious consequences he was aware and from which he was in constant expectation of death, that he was to die prematurely on November 19, 1974. The knowledge of being sick and doomed—though in his appearance there was something anxious, vital, and handsome—produced in him a kind of angry scorn (or "allergy," as he used to say) toward others.

He had met Pasolini in the most natural way. When *Officina* came out in 1955, Ferretti, then twenty years old, had submitted some poems, and Pier Paolo had published them.

They went on to exchange letters, and met frequently in Rome as well as in Bologna. Pier Paolo was much taken by this sick boy with such a strong will to live. In young Ferretti's heart he represented "the only true friendship"—this was what Massimo wrote him in a letter dated January 10, 1959. This signified an insurmountable barrier of feelings.

Pasolini flattered himself that he could cross that barrier.

In the same letter, Ferretti wrote: "I was not horrified by your sensuality. We have absolutely different concepts of friendship. I'm fond of you, but it is impossible for me to think of you as an object of love."

A pass by Pasolini, rejected by Ferretti—this is what may have happened. And it must already have happened some time before. Ferretti, on February 5, 1958, had written: "Your friendship is important to me, and the gratitude I feel toward you goes far beyond the publication of a handful of poems in *Officina*. Your work has

---

* In English in original.—Tr.

opened a new world for me—amid so much confusion, you have been a point of reference for me, a moral example. I mean that your intellectual influence on me has been total and formative, and I have reaped its fruits in the 'particulars' of my everyday life. But I was twenty years old and I made a hero out of you ('You are of the race of those who win'[23]): this has been my one great fault—and when I understood that, even for my hero, passion was not grace, it was natural to react. And I became an indignant philistine, when it would have been so easy to pass it all off with an embarrassed smile."

Obviously, Ferretti's rejection did not simply take the form of "an embarrassed smile." Pasolini must have asked for his love and brotherhood. The young poet was his discovery, and this brought forth in him an intense tenderness, in which shone an erotic spark. The peasant boy Tonuti Spagnol had also been a poet.

It was an absolutely unique case. Pasolini liked to repeat *ad nauseam* that in his eyes the bodies of bourgeois youths evoked nothing but a historical misfortune, a sad destiny: their freshness was illusory. They were all, to his mind, too repressed to admit to themselves the impulses of desire, the raw dreams of eros.

But in Ferretti's presence, Pier Paolo must have felt an acute need for a friendship in which an unexpected light shone—a dedicated relationship, not only intellectual but physical as well, with a person who harbored the same literary faith. From others, those close to him, he hoped for a moment to receive not merely "pity or sympathy," but something more, something that might respond to his inexhaustible demand for love—which was nothing else but "love, naked love, with no / future." He was mistaken, because penetrating and diabolically subtle as he was, his ideas were sometimes exceedingly naïve when it came to the eroticism of others.[24]

This episode in his friendship with Ferretti is thus evidence of nostalgia. Pier Paolo experienced his true mortal discomfort in his relationship with the public. What happened in connection with the awarding of the Crotone fiction prize to *Una vita violenta* in the autumn of 1959 is highly symptomatic.

As I mentioned, the book won the prize in the midst of a literary controversy arising over its rejection by the judges of the Viareggio prize—a rejection blown up both by the press and by society gossip. And there was something else besides.

In August of that year, Pasolini had written a journalistic piece about Italian beaches for a monthly periodical.[25] He had also written about Calabria. The brawl that ensued in the newspapers ended up in court. Pasolini had seen and described the tragic aspects of Calabria, its poor and hungry people. He had written of Cutro, a village a few kilometers from Crotone: "It is really a village of outlaws, as one sees in certain western films. Here are the outlaws' women, here are the outlaws' children. One feels oneself outside the law, or if not the law, the culture of our world, at another level. In the smiles of the young men returning to their cruel work, there is a quiver of too much license, almost of madness."

The mayor of Cutro brought a libel suit against Pasolini, just at the time when *Una vita violenta* had received the prize. It was a painful situation, fed by the rhetoric of southern regional pride, and tinged with politics. This mayor was a Christian Democrat; the Crotone prize, on the other hand, was one of the activities of a Communist administration. The award had been announced on November 12, 1959; the writ filed by the mayor of Cutro is dated November 17.[26] A farce.

The local newspapers railed against awarding the prize to a "defamer" of Calabria; the prefect of Catanzaro sought to have it annulled. Nothing came of the lawsuit.

The storm ended as it had begun, but the event, with its soiled atmosphere of wrangling and abuse, aroused in Pasolini a feeling of bitter deachment from everyday life. And his bitterness flowed from the defeat that his ambitions seemed to suffer, and from seeing himself reduced to a target for obscure resentments. His existence became progressively emptier in the search for a relationship, first of all with his readers, whatever that might be. In this relationship, in the success he garnered, he was aware of something equivocal, something that "humiliated" him. He did not know whether to look on his thousands and thousands of readers "with love" or "with suspicion."[27]

A vicious circle—rejection produced success, the success a new rejection. And life was passing him by, leaving in its wake boundless anxiety. "I spend the major part of my life on the outskirts of the city, beyond the end of the tram line, as a bad neorealist poet would say so as to sound obscure. I love life so fiercely, so desperately, that nothing good can come of it: I mean the physical facts of life, the sun, the grass, youth. It's a much more terrible vice than cocaine, it costs me nothing, and there is an endless abundance of it, with no limits: and I devour, devour. How it will end, I don't know."[28]

THE POET OF
"THE ASHES OF GRAMSCI"

"My poetry is different from that of the twentieth century; it substitutes logic for the analogical, problems for gracefulness."[29]

Pasolini filled the pages of daily and weekly periodicals with statements. His poetics, his view of twentieth-century literature, became items of newsworthy interest.

Formerly D'Annunzio had been able to use the means of mass communications for the purpose of disseminating his own image as a writer, while at the same time defying the good manners of the period. Pasolini seemed to do no less.

D'Annunzio's name soon came up in connection with Pasolini. Pasolini rejected it with excessive scorn.

One difference between the two: the Italian bourgeoisie, in D'Annunzio's time, had not withdrawn its license from the figure of the poet. The conflict between D'Annunzio and society, which indeed existed, was marked by a sort of game on both sides, and if he sometimes played the fool, that is to say violated prevailing codes, this was what society allowed itself, nothing more. For this reason, D'Annunzio knew his own market value, and he had no hesitation in becoming his own impresario.

Pasolini as a poet had no license from society. He struggled mightily to obtain one. He chose, within society, the interlocutor's role that he considered to be favored by future history—the left, the Communists. Pasolini looked to "life" (is there an echo of D'Annunzio in this?). But he was often frustrated in his quest. Those he chose balked at the appeal. To forestall the difficult step, Pasolini the poet descended onto the terrain of rationality, substituting "logic for the analogical, problems for gracefulness" in his verses, and exposing and illuminating his own contradictions But this turned out to be insufficient to gain immediate approval.

What was needed was for him to become, in a different manner from D'Annunzio, his own impresario—with the doggedness of one who does not count as a liability what the public challenges or denies.

He knew in advance that there was no charisma in his destiny, and he made up for this lack by forms of mythomania darkened by negative signs—pathos, the condition of being a victim.

And here I am myself . . . poor, dressed
in clothes that poor people eye in windows

of raw splendor, and who has shed
the filth of the most secluded streets,
of the seats in trams, from which my day

has strayed . . .[30]

This victim figure, beyond coinciding with his life, is a heroic image—it is the image of one who is "different," and who, because of his "difference," is not subject to the rule of the material and economic world. He can claim a freedom to pronounce on the things of life and the world that would be impossible for others.

Mythomania—Pasolini's obsessive loyalty to this image, his obedience to an ideal model of truth. Being "different" became symbolically the protest of poetry against commercialization, against the development of technology, against "anthropological genocide" (of which in these years there had already been an obscure presentiment).

In Pasolini the clinical mythomania that had once stricken Baudelaire was revived—with common features, even technically speaking. Just as Baudelaire, in his polemics against the formlessness of the Romantics, re-evaluated the alexandrine and the closed form of the sonnet, so Pasolini, against the formlessness of neo-experimentalism, re-evaluated the hendecasyllable and the tercet, utilizing within them all the breaks and irregularities of classical composition.

In Baudelaire the traditional instruments of poetry tended to strengthen the communicativeness of the line; likewise in Pasolini, the poetics of "stylistic regression" were to assure compensations in the literary marketplace, a wider popularity.

Livio Garzanti, in a letter dated July 27, 1957, writes (*Le ceneri di Gramsci* had been in the bookstores for a few weeks, not even a month): "Your book is selling well. It's just that I was foolish enough to publish only 1500 copies. I've now ordered it to be reprinted because it's been sold out these past days."

Succès de scandale? Did the echo of *Ragazzi di vita*, and trials and acquittals, encourage the rapid sale of the book?

Many people have insinuated that Pasolini planned his own success, and the statement is true insofar as such a plan had its philosophical side. Pasolini's poetics contemplated a new figure of the poet—new as compared to the one set up by Italian modernism. But not new in relation to D'Annunzio. And this new factor supplants the real poetic results, and involves "the poetry public" (just as D'Annunzio had involved it in his time).

"In Pasolini there is that old fanaticism, between the laud and the hairshirt, that scourging taste for provocation, that marks the nature of heroes, saints, and martyrs, in short all those who live by a kind of ancestral metaphysical protest, and who seem to be depositories of the fatality of life only because they cannot help pushing their fundamental and congenital abstraction to its ultimate conclusion. With this incautious, Faustian tendency to embody in the theater of one's own nature, along with some Michelangelesque nuances, the universal drama of being born, Pasolini combines a highly acute, timely perception of the point at which on one side the 'eternal' (and also 'literary') evils, and on the other the rising and most consoling ideals of our century (read: socialism, 'communism'), meet (and besides how could they not?)."[31]

Cesare Garboli, in this portrait, sets Pasolini's decadentism— mythomania, the victim theme—within the Italian tradition. And he also says that the poet (the poet so marked) does not fade out along the coordinates of the past, but in an unforeseen way comes to stamp those coordinates on the present, by burning all his bridges behind him.

The poem "The Ashes of Gramsci" begins with a slow and doleful music:

It's not like May this impure air
that makes the dark foreign garden
darker still, or dazzles it

with blind patches . . .[32]

This musical quality makes the adjectives flow like notes on a staff, all imbued with a sense of loss, with a funereal pace, with deathly pale splendors. The "lean" cypresses, the "scrubby" grass, the "violet" atmosphere, the "old" mistrust, the "confused" adolescent, the "grimy" little beaches—"a desperate love" for what exists is mingled with the idea of "losing one's way" in the "silence" of "corrupt and sterile" life.

It is a poem of "surviving fate"—"here the silence of death is fate." And the city, which sets the scene, spreading out in "immense semi-circles," fades into a vaguely illuminated architecture.

The English Cemetery in Rome lies along a modest outlying avenue running next to the Aurelian Wall near the pyramid of Caius Cestius. A strip of earth with a knoll, which faces Monte de' Cocci and the Testaccio quarter. Nowadays the street is used as an express thoroughfare, but in 1954 (the date of Pasolini's poem) it was a deserted corner of the city, bordered by cypresses whose brown colors stood out clearly against the gray stones of the Roman ruins. There the sounds of city life were remote, diminished by distance. Gramsci's grave was there, among other tombstones of "lay people," among "wan loops of boxwood, which the clearing / evening dissolves in simple / suggestions of seaweed."

It must have been a serene twilight, with darkness falling swiftly, as happens in southern cities. In that swift passage, however, an idea of the eternal is suspended—a tremor that transports the human mind into another realm from the everyday one, without erasing anything from it.

Pasolini's vitality, in the presence of this vivid twilight, discovered its own dispassionate immobility—the hidden obverse, the disillusion that kindles anguish. The anxiety of history and knowledge, the incessant scrutiny of himself and the world, "lost themselves" among "lost streets," in "a dark scandal of conscience." Gramsci's "rigor," the meaning of that tombstone guarded by silence and dim extraneousness ("patrician / boredom lies around you") came to bear like a scalpel on the abscess of naïveté and sensuality, on the lump of existential risks buried within the poet's mind.

"Rapture of nostalgia" and "poetic light" dissolve the outlines of the world—they block the light of the sunset, the "wind's wet whisper." The individual does not succeed in escaping from his own physiological irresoluteness.

> . . . But since I possess history,
> it possesses me; I am illuminated by it:
>
> but what good is the light?

In Pasolini, the socialist myth flourished naturally, as it can flourish in a Romantic poet who takes his stand with the damned of this world: he feels united with them, he seeks to be their voice. But the fact that he is "different," and the perception of a vagabond destiny that emerges from it, required precise answers from him. Within the framework of leftist ideology, which Pasolini shared, the demand for an ethics of the person—a new morality whereby the individual would be salvaged in his entirety, in his specificity—went completely unheeded.

> I don't say the individual, that phenomenon
> of sensual and sentimental ardor . . .
> he has other vices, and the results of his sins
>
> are called by other names . . .
> But what ordinary prenatal vices,
> and what objective sin, lie
>
> mixed in him! . . .

So if the ideals of the left encourage the growth of collective rebirth, in another sense they themselves strangle the feeling for justice, and not only economic justice, that a man, this man—thief and bandit, homosexual and Negro in his heart—demands be satisfied, both in and for himself.

The originality of "The Ashes of Gramsci" lies precisely in defining the pressing demand for such justice. I believe that it is this, beyond any personal intention or strategy of cultural politics, that constitutes the strength of the poem's impact on the most disparate readers; herein lies its "public" novelty.

> Well protected
> from impure virtue and enraptured sinning,
>
> defending a madman's ingenuousness—
> and with what conscience!—lives the ego:
> living ego, eluding life, in its breast
>
> the sense of a life that is violent
> and painful oblivion . . .

Freedom and necessity appear in opposition, and the ego is prey to unresolved and unresolvable subjection by the historical superego, by the progress of a civilization in which the law of repression holds sway. The utopian liberation of psychic energy is very far away. What is close at hand is the anguish of non-life, of oblivion-life, "violent and painful" oblivion.

Pasolini expresses this tragic condition: being "different" allows him to arrive at the discovery—"How well I understand the whirlpool / of feelings." But to express this he must pay a painful price. In devouring all of existence, and reconstituting it in the form of a liberating message, his poetry spreads into a "deliberately poetic" program[33]—the poet's desperation seems inevitably to lead it to excess and redundancy.

Pasolini expends every stylistic resource to allow the ego to attain the blissful haven of the word. But the ego is represented as an accumulation of lexical, syntactical, and rhythmical detritus. And the life that the poet implores for it—a life of freedom and happiness, where necessity is a historical incrustation of class—barely dawns over all this dense and inert material:

> . . . a craving life that makes a faint
> concert of the raucous roll of trams,
> of human street cries . . .

It is the moral void, the omen of approaching barbarism—the ego remains rubble, the individual is not saved, history dies.

What is there then beyond the "droning pause in which life is silent"?

> . . . wondrous, scorched,

> almost Alexandrian sensuality, illuminating
> everything and impurely glowing,
> is better manifested . . .

The world of the *ragazzi di vita* is about to sink into darkness. One might say it had become "Alexandrian," an "illuminated" world, but already a cemetery. The discovery of Rome and of the "happiness" of the body had burned itself out. For Pasolini the path of "survival" was taking shape:

> . . . But I, with the conscious heart

> of one who can live only in history,
> will I ever again be able to act with pure passion
> when I know that our history is over?

With this question "The Ashes of Gramsci" ends. Pasolini has worked as though over a great fresco with the obsessive rage of one who fears he will not succeed—at moments with enervated softness, at moments by tormenting himself in a parody of his own style. A painful urgency makes of the poem—indeed, behind it appears the narrative design of Pascoli, or the unpolished Carducci ode—something uncommon and anomalous, but also incomplete; it is less a poem than an endless diary sequence.

The final question seems like an infringement. On one side, the instincts, the "aesthetic passion," are onstage; on the other, the image of the hero Gramsci—he the superego, he the father. It is an image that consciousness finds it difficult to restore above the cascading harmonies of the tercets.

No other indication of the conflict remains but the "obscure scandal of consciousness":

The scandal of contradicting myself, of being
with you and against you; with you in my heart,
in light, against you in the darkness of my bowels . . .

Beyond this stasis there is the timeless flow of the Roman world: the trams and the distant cries from the Testaccio; one hears the sounds of an anvil; lying in "aphrodisiac filth," the whores await the soldiers. The ordinary life of the quarter freezes in a *tableau vivant.*

It seems that Pasolini, in reaching the height of his creative potential—and everything seems available to his verse—was aware of an irreparable exhaustion of inspiration. If he speaks of the end of history, what is understood is the actual end of poetry, of his own poetry.

To be sure, the extreme point of risk to which he drove himself, precisely with "The Ashes of Gramsci," was the demand for a new morality for the individual, by seizing on in depth, as a Christian and Catholic, a dramatic deficiency within the ideology of the left. But the demand suffered an immediate collapse—almost as though the effort were greater than the plan. And everything was involved in the collapse: ideals, history, and still more, personal destiny.

This collapse, and the exhaustion of inspiration, call into question the "public" nature of the poem. The demand for a radical change appeared, but the poem seemed not to find a resolution, either in word or rhythm.

And yet "The Ashes of Gramsci" has memorable things about it. There one reads the division in a generous soul that would have liked to see, in itself first of all, a joyous union of happiness with justice and freedom. But this torment and division did not belong only to this soul—they belonged to a whole generation, which believed itself to be one step away from great possibilities. The ideas by which it had been nourished had driven it toward unimagined achievements, and painfully it was discovering that these ideas fell silent before the ever rampant snare of existence. For it life itself became an illusion not to be lived.

Unlike the great Pre-Romantic cemetery poems of Thomas Gray and Ugo Foscolo, it was impossible for Pasolini to think that "e'en from the tomb the voice of Nature cries." If that voice "cries," it is the prelude to an end, to the *finis historiae.*

POLEMICS IN VERSE

Finis historiae. The idea of an apocalypse—this was what separated Pasolini from the Communists. Relations between himself and certain party intellectuals, and between himself and the party press, became matters of extreme complexity after the publication of *Ragazzi di vita.*

On one side, the theological inflexibility of the Marxists:

They are inflexible, they are gloomy

in their judgment of you: those who wear
hairshirts can't forgive.
From them you can't expect a crumb

of mercy: not because of any teaching of Marx,
but because of their own god of love,
the elementary victory of good over evil,

which lies in their acts . . .[34]

On the other, the concrete and urgent problems of cultural revision, posed to all militants, all leftist sympathizers, from the spring of 1956 on with the revelation of Khruschchev's report.

That "terrible" 1956. The Khrushchev speech—then, in the autumn, the events in Poland, the hope that dawned when Gomulka came to power. Then Hungary, the revolt of the Petöfi Club, the liberal declarations of Lukács—and the arrival of Soviet tanks in Budapest. The simultaneous Suez war—unleashed almost as though to freeze everything that was seeking change by the events in Hungary in the *status quo*. A tragedy.

Perhaps, in retrospect, the events of those autumn months can be seen as the explosion of a moral conflict that had long been smoldering in Europe during the ten long years from the end of the war, and which had its roots in the boundaries—political and ideological—that had been arbitrarily drawn in its bosom. Hungary polarized a need for freedom that exceeded the will of the great powers. Nevertheless, the so-called Yalta principle won: an arbitrary stroke of the pen on the map, and the world was divided into two hostile halves.

The distress was profound. If the Soviets, by their intervention in Hungary, squandered a heritage of ideals actually born within the young socialist world by dismissing it as "counterrevolutionary," likewise the Anglo-French intervention in Suez marked an end to the aims of freedom of the Western democracies. The policies of the great powers on the international tightrope entirely ignored the needs of the people. History still appeared as something irreparably remote from the efforts of individuals and the powerless.

Tormented months and years, for the left and the Italian Communist Party. The latter, the target of a campaign of indiscriminate accusations coming from all the other parties, was wracked from within by schisms among intellectuals and by unrest at its working-class base.

As Giorgio Amendola recalls:

All these agitated emotions arose from the fact that a myth had collapsed, one that had held sway over us all, the myth of Stalin. The battle went on in the privacy of the conscience of each of us who had been a Stalinist. One of the elements of our upbringing had collapsed. Each reacted as best he could: some by trying to analyze historically the origin of certain events, some by cursing, but there was really something that shook everyone profoundly.[35]

The cultural tradition of the Italian Communist Party was original in being mingled with the liberal tradition. It was Palmiro Togliatti, in those very months, who condemned in the Khrushchev report the absence of any historical analysis, while at the same time defining the need for "national roads to socialism." It was an act of political brilliance—Stalin's crimes could not be interpreted as mere personal crimes. On the other hand, the blueprint of socialist hopes should not be buried with the corpse of a dictator soiled by horrible deeds.

Even in the midst of violent controversy, everyone was calling on the Italian Communist Party to "change."

All questions of changing our formulations are of little importance. The problem is to see how certain changes are to be made. Sometimes it is better to seek a delay which reflects a sincere effort, in changing a formula, rather than to adopt convenient formulas that make you look good in your opponent's presence but then are not accompanied by deep and self-critical reflection.[36]

Giorgio Amendola's balanced judgment may be right in retrospect about the tumult of those months. But those tumultuous months were a reality. And in that reality Pasolini spoke up.

Pasolini, like others, demanded something of the Communist Party.

He wrote "Una polemica in versi"[37] in the autumn of 1956. Already in the spring of that year, he had pointed his finger, in a critical piece in *Officina*, at the "perspectivism" of Communist cultural policy. He had sparked harsh comments.

The *Officina* text reads:

As for the, so to speak, *tactical* position taken by the Communists, whether in the case of *l'Unità* or *Il contemporaneo*, it would be at this moment like hitting a man when he's down. The crudity and ideological-tactical harshness of Salinari and others was invalidated by what Lukács—in an interview granted to a correspondent from *l'Unità* itself during the proceedings of the Soviet Party Congress—calls *perspectivism*. The naïve and almost illiterate (as well as bureaucratic) theoretical compulsion derives from the convention that a realistic literature should be based on this *perspectivism*—while in a society like ours the state of suffering, crisis, and division cannot be simply removed in the name of an anticipated, compulsory health seen in perspective.[38]

Pasolini was attacking a literature of wishful thinking. He attacked the Communist critics, who had attacked and rejected his pessimism. A heated debate emerged in the columns of *Il contemporaneo*, a controversy that dragged on for some weeks in June 1956, and in which Carlo Salinari shared the spotlight with Pasolini.[39]

Salinari, the following year, made amends in reviewing the book *Le ceneri di Gramsci*: "In its time, our reaction to the accusation of perspectivism was perhaps, as Pasolini writes, disproportionate. But we ought to be allowed the extenuating circumstances of having been seriously provoked."[40]

But Pasolini had not been trying to "provoke" anyone. He was asking instead for ideological courage and a feeling for the truth of existence.

"The hour is confused, and we are living it
as though lost . . ." you whispered to me, bitter,
disillusioned with what you've had

inside you for ten years, so clear
that between world and mind it was almost an idyll:
and it has your weariness—a little vulgar—

the smirk of an old son
of southern immigrants
starving and cringing behind the scowl

of poor newcomers, of naïve doctrinaires.
You wanted your life to be
a struggle. And now here it is on a blind

siding, here the red banners
droop without wind . . .

A meeting on Via Quattro Novembre in Rome with Antonello Trombadori. Trombadori, then editor of *Il contemporaneo*, looked to him like a disoriented militant, worn out by the cruel news of the moment. What was Pasolini asking of him and of the Communists in general?

                    . . . Your pain
at no longer being in the front lines
would be purer, if in the hour

in which the error, even if pure, is overcome,
you had the strength to call yourselves guilty.

In a letter to Trombadori, written on June 7, 1956, explaining what had just been published in *Officina*, Pasolini had anticipated his poem:

Dear Trombadori . . . You are infinitely more agile than Salinari and your uncle. In fact, it was exclusively of those two that I was thinking: certainly not of Muscetta or Gallo or Cases. Salinari and Trombatore[41] are essentially rigid, incapable of feeling, aprioristic. In short, handicapped by a provincial moralism. Not you. And your "perspectivism," even if in appearance more compromising, is in reality more problematical and amenable to development . . . You shouldn't try to deny the reality of any of your moments of crisis, change of mind, and discomfort. Natural and proper, and if you are really honest and sincere with yourselves, pro- ductive, full of promise. It's no longer a matter of doing the usual auto- criticism, carried through without examination. It's something much more serious and important, and I say this to you not as an opponent but as a friend. And a friend sometimes says things much more violently than an opponent, as you know . . .

Pasolini was demanding moral courage from the Communists. In that autumn of dismay, Pasolini asked more: the confession of an "error":

It is to error,
that I urge you, to religious
error . . . In the red sun of the

still sultry autumn noon,
in an air of death, your feast
reopens.[42]

And the "error," once and for all, was that of having "served / the people not in its heart / but in its flag."[43]

Nineteen fifty-nine came, and Pier Paolo published *Una vita violenta*.

In the January 1960 issue of *Rinascita*, the Communist senator Mario Montagnana, in a letter to the editor, almost as though to correct differing opinions that were widespread in the party, delivered a violent attack on the novel: "Pasolini reserves the vulgarities and obscenities, the dirty words, for the world of the poor. One gets the impression that Pasolini does not like poor people, that he despises in general the inhabitants of the Roman shantytowns, and despises our party even more. The hero, Tommasino, is in reality a juvenile delinquent of the worst kind: thief, robber, pederast."

Montagnana's article was disconcerting. Month by month *Rinascita* was expounding the official Communist line, and this piece was said to have resulted from a decision taken at the top of the hierarchy.

What followed, however, was that in its next issue, February 1960, the periodical gave six columns of space to an article expressing the opposite argument. It, too, took the form of a letter to the editor, signed by a distinguished leader, Senator Edoardo D'Onofrio: "I think that one of the reasons that induces some of our comrades to make an incorrect evaluation of Pasolini's novel *Una vita violenta* derives largely from the fact that they do not know the political and social importance of the presence in Rome of a numerous subproletariat."

D'Onofrio's letter explained the reality of this subproletariat, which was already in the process of transformation, and even, to unobservant eyes, in the process of disappearing, and showed how this reality constituted the strength of the novel. D'Onofrio maintained that "the life of our party does not correspond to a fixed pattern, good for all situations. The struggle, the process of development of proletariat class consciousness, is neither smooth nor linear; it presupposes ups and downs, forward and backward leaps. Pasolini does not hide the truth in order to spare the party; he tells things as they were; nor does he claim that one moment in the development of the party in the shanty-towns is the development itself or the result of the development. To prove the truth of what Pasolini says, I could give first and last names and dates."

His defense of the book is "political," based on its content. But D'Onofrio did not stop there—Pasolini's use of Roman dialect, that special and much debated Roman dialect, was for him proof of the novel's truth. Far from "any bourgeois moralist or bigoted influence . . . *Una vita violenta* . . . is . . . an original and remarkable work that deserves to be read."

D'Onofrio's remarks did not settle the issue, but they exposed the fact that within the Communist Party there was not only an interest in Pasolini and the problems raised by his work, but attentive consideration as well.

One subject remained unresolved: Communist inflexibility about the requirements of individual freedom. For the Marxists, the collectivist plan for society could not be challenged by such requirements. For the poet of "The Ashes of Gramsci" they constituted the keystone of utopia.

In the conflict between the reality principle and the pleasure principle, the Marxist did not want to acknowledge the possibility of an equilibrium: "pleasure" was absorbed back into "reality," dissolved and consumed in it. In Pasolini, on the other hand, it was a desperate struggle. His public "provocations" tended to resolve it. But the knot, living flesh of his flesh, remained tight.

SURVIVAL

Maximum effort, total disillusionment. The logical plan for a new world, and the shipwreck of the new in "barbarism."

The "practical aim" of Pasolini's poetry was defeated by the force of things. With the softening of the ideological stance of the left, the Italian economic miracle made culture insensitive to the philosophical problems of individuality and personality. But it seemed that the old liberalism could still express itself around them.

Pasolini, like Victor Hugo, liked to make use of current happenings in his poetry; but by now, a deliberate victim, deliberately provocatory, and faced with the deafness of others, he made a myth of himself. Public opinion gave credit to his image, not to his person,[44] and this led to a crisis. His trajectory was too rapid, his life a sudden blaze— he embraced the fate of survival with equal, singular rapidity.

Poetry then became memory, a dirge for the splendid hopes of the Resistance. Pasolini willed himself to be the poet of that "pure light," and of a vanquished faith.

The "poetic reappearance" of the past is already in "La ricchezza" (1955–1959). It is the present that demands it, a life in the present that appears as an incurable ulcer, and as uninterrupted "sensual regret." But the "regret" also asks to become "religion."

"The Religion of My Time" (1957–1959) represents the "psycha-gogic" turn in Pasolini's poetry: the "victim" becomes a prophet.

> Thus when I look deep into the souls
> of the ranks of living individuals
> of my time, close to me or not too far away,
>
> I see that of the countless possible sacrileges
> that every natural religion
> can specify, the one that remains
>
> always, in everyone, is cowardice. . . .

It is this cowardice that makes man irreligious . . .[45]

The anguish of the rejections he has suffered continues to throb.
And when humiliated subjectivity rises to the heights of myth—

. . . I've never sinned: I'm as
pure as an old saint, but neither

have I had anything; the desperate
gift of sex has gone
up in smoke: I'm as good

as a madman. The past
is all I had for destiny,
nothing but a desolate void . . .[46]

—the feeling of objectivity is obscured by sarcasm, by desolation:

. . . now I refuse
to live. There is nothing else
besides nature—in which moreover only the charm

of death is spread—nothing
of this human world I love.
Everything is painful to me: these people

who supinely follow every summons
by which their masters wish to summon them,
heedlessly adopting the most disgraceful

habits of predestined victims;
the gray of their clothes in the gray streets;
their gray gestures on which seem stamped

the conspiracy of silence over the evil that invades them;
their swarming around an illusory
prosperity, like a flock around a little fodder;

the regularity of their tides, whereby which throngs
and deserts alternate in the streets,
regulated by the obsessed and anonymous

ebb and flow of stale necessities;
their multitudes in the gloomy bars, the gloomy cinemas,
their hearts gloomily surrendered to the wherefore . . .[47]

In the face of this impious world—impious and passive—ruled by "foul pupils of a corrupt Jesus / in Vatican salons," poetry is extinguished and pushed to the margin—in the slackened cadence of the terza rima it is destroyed. The words seem to whirl in skies "of a dazed blue," the skies of mannerism.

Poems of memory emerge, poems of impossible love for boys and their vitality, poems where hope is canceled by the shadows of night. Life belongs to the past, to "maternal Friuli." And if there is a "light of good" in all this shipwreck, this light is in the comforting vision of the mother, in Susanna.

Even while surviving, in a long appendix
of unexhausted, inexhaustible passion
—that almost has its roots in other times—

I know that in the chaos a light of religion,
a light of good, redeems
my excessive love in desperation.

It is a poor woman, mild and delicate,
who almost lacks the courage to be,
and stands in the shadows like a little girl,

with her sparse hair, her clothes now shabby
and almost poor, over those surviving
secrets that still smell of violets . . .[48]

With Carlo Alberto dead, there would seem to be no longer any obstacle to the maternal embrace—in the midst of all the disappointment, disenchantment, and storms of persecution. Pasolini brings Susanna ("my poor sweet little bones") into the myth of himself as victim:

By now, at every hour, everything is for her, the child,
for me, her son, it is finished, and forever:
nothing remains but to hope that the end

will really come to extinguish the implacable
pain of awaiting it. Soon we will be
together, in that barren meadow filled

with gray stones . . .[49]

The Casarsa cemetery, "where passion / keeps the bones of the
other son / still alive in frozen peace"—Guido is there, but there is
no suggestion that Carlo Alberto is there too.

       Soon
we too, sweet survivor, will be

lost at the bottom of that cool
plot of earth: but ours won't be
a stillness, for mingled in it too much

will be a life that has had no goal.
We'll have a sad and difficult silence,
a painful sleep, one that won't bring

softness and peace, but nostalgia and reproof . . .[50]

These lines are from 1960—everything seems truly finished, the
trial of the inner life has ended with no appeal. There remained to
Pasolini the conviction of being able to testify *post mortem* to his
own defeat—a testimony that would sound as a "reproof" to the
"impure" living.

His victim theme was nourished by a neurotic core. The principle
of authority, after the death of his father, had been deeply introjected,
like a lost lump in the bowels; against it the conscious layer of the
ego writhed piteously, drawn by a single need—to pour scorn on it.

The strategy of Pasolini's unconscious seemed animated by blind
and negative impulses, and to confirm the judgments of enemies and
persecutors. But this unconscious was also the scene of an alchemistic
transformation of his negativity.

Intellectual clarity, in Pasolini, was not a mere word, it was
sharpened intelligence, the capacity to scrutinize reality. And the
neurotic knot was dissolved in the positive: it spread energy and light

over the shadows enveloping Italian public life, and held at bay the system of ethical and political censures governing it.

Disillusion did not overcome the poet of "The Ashes of Gramsci"— and "survival" was, finally, an aspect of his personal myth, and not simply a state of irreversible drifting. It was a way of bringing his own epic destiny back to life and renewing it. It was a way of resisting, and becoming the voice not only of the dispossessed subproletariat of the shantytowns but also of all those who by moral and social pressure of all kinds (and from every class) had been driven beyond the possible confines of the world.

CHAPTER 8

CINEMA

THE STORY OF ACCATTONE

"I would not be surprised if all of a sudden he were to set off on a completely new course, and in the most unexpected manner." This was how Cesare Garboli concluded his piece on the book *Le ceneri di Gramsci*.[1]

Pasolini did indeed change course, and to most people's eyes, "in the most unexpected manner." He made a film—he became an internationally famous director.

And yet Pasolini's turning to the movie camera had, as I mentioned, deep roots going all the way back to the Friuli years. As Pier Paolo acknowledged: "I had always thought of making films. Before the war I had thought of going to Rome to attend the Centro Sperimentale,* if I could. This old idea of making films came to a standstill and disappeared."[2]

Then came his friendship with Federico Fellini.

It was a lively friendship, at the time of *Le notti di Cabiria* and *La dolce vita*: a professional collaboration and a deep human attachment.

---

* The Centro Sperimentale di Cinematografia, which opened in 1933 under the direction of Luigi Chiarini, was a school and workshop for film writers, directors, technicians, designers, and actors.—Tr.

They had met by chance in the Piazza del Popolo. Pier Paolo had already published *Ragazzi di vita*, Fellini had already made *I vitelloni*. They saw each other often, and this led to their collaboration on *Le notti di Cabiria*.

Pier Paolo showed Fellini the underside of Roman life, the nocturnal Rome of thieves and hustlers; they explored the cancerous landscapes of the periphery, the urban madhouse of Torvaianica and Ostia.

To Fellini, Pier Paolo possessed the wisdom of a father prior and the inspiration of a moonstruck elf. For his part, Pier Paolo was fascinated by Fellini's psychological complexity.

It was certainly their manneristic creative sensibility that brought them together, their willingness to combine stylistic elements, both having decided not to submit, whether in literature or the cinema, to the sentimental blackmail of declining neorealism.

Fellini created, Fellini was a magician whose realm was the imagination. Pier Paolo let himself fall under the spell.

After the success of *La dolce vita*, Fellini, with the help of Rizzoli Productions, "created" a film company, "Federiz," for a different kind of cinema, one that would revive the market. It planned to produce films by Marco Ferreri, Ermanno Olmi, Vittorio De Seta. The schedule included a new script by Pasolini, *Accattone*. Pasolini also had an alternate subject ready, *La commare secca*. It had been specified that he was to move from the desk to the camera. Other producers were interested in the project, for example Tonino Cervi and Sandro Jacovoni, young themselves and in search of young talent. But Cervi and Jacovoni lost interest in Pasolini, and Pier Paolo went to Federiz.

Fellini had furnished an apartment in Via della Croce in the style of a tavern from *The Three Musketeers* as headquarters for the new company. The director had devoted himself to this enterprise, Pier Paolo wrote, "with the pride and happiness of a boy, also of course a little coquettishly."[3]

Fellini accepted Pier Paolo's project, and Pier Paolo set to work. The choice of faces, actors, places—the idea was for an *auteur* film, everything in the hands of the one who conceives, writes, and carries it through with complete freedom. To begin with, no professional actors—this was a rule to be strictly adhered to. The professional actor carries with him the affectations of his training—his expression can be foreseen. Here, instead, the unforeseeable nature of existence was to become the mark of style, just as in the pages of *Ragazzi di vita* the slang of the shantytowns was transformed into expressive ornament, into reckless and "unique" speech.

"That's how I spent, I think, the most wonderful days of my life."

In the fever of preparation, signs of obstacles and mistrust may have escaped Pier Paolo.

He had with him a small group of collaborators that included Bernardo Bertolucci. Bernardo, the son of Attilio, was then nineteen, and the cinema was in his blood. He wrote poetry, but he wrote it as though waiting for the decisive moment that would see him with his eye glued to the camera. Pier Paolo took him on as an assistant, and it was a choice that determined a career.

And so days of excitement went by. Then the test: Fellini asked Pier Paolo to shoot a couple of scenes in order to try out the troupe. It was September 1960.

"They were marvelous days, in which the summer still burned in its purity, with only a slight abatement of its fury. Via Fanfulla da Lodi, in the middle of the Pigneto, with its wretched little houses and cracking walls, was grandiose in its granularity, in its extreme insignificance—a poor, humble, unknown little street lost under the sun, in a Rome that was no longer Rome."

A small troupe. For Pier Paolo the task of being a director was "extraordinary." He had immediately decided on his stylistic model: Dreyer's *La Passion de Jeanne d'Arc*, "a norm of absolute simplicity of expression."

But there was the changing light, and the actors were new to the set. There was an old camera that functioned jerkily. Then came days with the Moviola, cutting and editing these two scenes.

Then silence. Not a word from Fellini.

Collaborators and friends, however, were asking for news. Bertolucci asked; Franco Citti, already assigned to play the hero, asked.

Nothing—until Pier Paolo, though uninvited, decided to pay a call on Federiz.

"As I go in, Fellini also comes in by chance through the inner door. The Great Mystifier is unable to conceal, in the expression of his dark-rimmed eyes, his awareness that I am arriving unexpectedly and rather too early, but he gives me a welcoming hug. He is clean, smooth, healthy as a wild beast in a cage. He takes me into his office. And as he sits down, he immediately tells me that he wants to be frank with me (oh-oh!), and that the material he has seen, no, it hasn't convinced him."

They discussed the matter. Pasolini defended "the poverty, the carelessness, the crudeness, the clumsy and almost anonymous scholasticism" with which he had shot the scenes. It was his first time: there was the "broken-down" camera, not enough film; the actors were very inexperienced. Nothing "miraculous" had happened, but still it was "his" film. If he had to do those scenes all over again, he would do them in exactly the same way.

Too sure of himself and perhaps irritating, Pier Paolo did not give in an inch. "Like a grand and elegant bishop, Fellini then shifts the question to another plane"—the financial cost of the film. If it really wouldn't cost too much, they might try . . . "I realize that all this is a euphemism, an understatement, a chess move."

Actually nothing was to be done about it. Pier Paolo was to tell the whole story in a "diary" article in *Il Giorno* of October 16, 1960.

By now a break was brewing between Fellini and Pasolini. "It's much easier to quarrel than to agree to put the persistence of old affection to the test." The two wanted to make this experiment, and went to supper in a Chinese restaurant. "Fellini ordered the dishes with the precision of a magician. The supper—in that *Dolce vita* locale—was a real production. And Fellini used his regional technique—like Pascoli [who was also from Romagna]. I could have hugged him, with those big black-ringed eyes of his, those big flabby cheeks."

After supper, they went on talking on the esplanade in Ostia. It was an evening of confessions, about their mutual anxieties, death, people, the world. It all sounds like a film script, and yet it was all real.

Pier Paolo's urgent wish to make his film was real. His desperation was real. But also real was the impossibility of any help from Fellini. Federiz, a spaceship all set to be launched for the exploration of "the new," broke down on its first trial flight and never took off again.

Next morning, Mauro Bolognini came to see Pier Paolo at home. For Bolognini, Pier Paolo had been a valuable collaborator on various films, indeed the only one—for example in *Il bell' Antonio*—to suggest to him in his script the degree of melancholy, the heartbreak resulting from the absence of love.

On Pier Paolo's desk were the stills from his first set. Bolognini, as he examined them one by one, became enthusiastic. While Pier Paolo was trying to re-establish contact with Cervi and Jacovoni, Bolognini found the producer Alfredo Bini and persuaded him to take on *Accattone*.

Bini, "my contemporary from Gorizia / red-haired, hands in his pockets, / heavy as a paratrooper after mess-hall,"[4] was a friend to Pier Paolo—a tense friendship, even a difficult one. Pier Paolo was always grateful to him, and Bini was the producer for all of his films until *Oedipus Rex* in 1967.

The film, as they say, "took off." Franco Citti played Accattone, and physically the world of *Ragazzi di vita* came to be depicted in him and in his body—the real and doleful face of a shantytown dweller. The other "real" characters around him were Pier Paolo's "real" friends. Thus began a long series of films with the presence on the screen of well-known faces, from which the characters emerged. And Pier Paolo seemed always to be able to bring them out and situate them in the frescoes he composed with the Arriflex camera. Adriana Asti, Stefano D'Arrigo, Adele Cambria, and Elsa Morante appeared in *Accattone*.

Camera on the tripod, a few brief "dolly shots," the sound of plebeian voices "taken from the street"—the episodes stripped boldly and at the same time with rare elegance. When in September 1961 the film was shown at the Venice festival, it caused an uproar, and divided the critics and public. The government censors took action and banned it, "exceptionally" (as it said on the posters), to minors under eighteen.

Pasolini's sensitivity to cinematographic form seemed to have been trained by specific examples: Dreyer to be sure, Mizoguchi, Rossellini. Foregrounds prevailed over long shots and landscapes, frontality over the roving camera. The music was lifted from Bach's *Saint Matthew Passion*. And the final chorus of the *Passion*, imposed on the poverty of face and dress of the characters, kindled an intensity of emotion that the Italian cinema had not known since the days of *Ossessione*, *Open City*, and *Paisan*.

The way the film viewed the human body was upsetting to some— almost a violation. An unusual idea of beauty—Accattone and his friends were not beautiful according to cinema convention, nor had they been chosen in accordance with the expressionistic criterion that looks to long disheveled hair and livid faces for the declamatory presentation of social protest.

At the heart of Pasolini's images, and highly visible, there was an incontrovertible religious anguish. The emaciated, mortified bodies of the characters incarnated this anguish, and constituted its liturgy.

Accattone is not a film of political protest. Rather it is religious and existential. The overexposed whites, the unremitting Roman light— the intensity of the foregrounds is achieved over a time duration pushed to the limits of the tolerable. Accattone gazing at the Tiber, and the angel behind him like a kind of divine minister, evoke a sacred mystery and offer a meditation on the ever unrequited risk of life.

The film is the trajectory of an expectation, composed of progressive stations that gain significance in the dream sequence—a silent sequence in which Accattone contemplates his own death.

It is individual pain and torment that the film represents. Pasolini's cinema was to emerge pictorial.

With the serpentine sensibility of the sixteenth-century Mannerist painters, Pasolini combines an anomalous fury, a fury that is anti-humanist, anti-Renaissance, and profoundly rural Catholic, which might have been that of one artist who was immersed in the Renaissance but took a stand against it: Romanino. It is the Romanino of saints with gross, red, twisted feet, of sturdy, strong-limbed, mountaineer Christs. The film's singular, unconscious "obsessive experimentalism" is also like Romanino's.[5]

Stylistic obsession, experimental obsession. By now there can be no doubt about the quality of Pasolini's inspiration. After the formative period of apprenticeship—contained within the span of *Poesie a Casarsa*, the Italian materials of *L'usignolo*, the prose of *Amado mio*, and the preparatory sketches of *Il sogno di una cosa*—there is no more development or evolution. Time is suspended. Pasolini is driven to an overall, even simultaneous experimentation with all possible artistic techniques, those that best allow him, time after time, to pour out the aggressiveness of his own negative, self-destructive impulses.

To make films may have meant to him the "wish to emerge from the obsessive"[6]—but it was nothing more than a wish. He was a great mannerist, not out of an excess of disbelief and a secular spirit, but rather by neurotic determination, by his continual and unfulfilled search for a solution, whatever it might be, to his own anguished nature.

The anguish is expressed cinematographically in a form of severity, austerity, and visual pauperism that would seem to be opposed to the author's frantic sense of style. This "poor" use of style takes us back to the lyrical exhaustion of the poems following "The Ashes of

Gramsci." The world of the Roman shantytowns, the world of the subproletarian poor, is now that of the *finis historiae*, an apocalypse of the spirit.

Una vita violenta had recounted the possibility of a heroic and public solution of subproletarian existence. *Accattone* is despair in its pure state. The subproletariat becomes once again, as it had been in *Ragazzi di vita*, a transcendental idea—in the philosophical sense. The subproletariat was for Pasolini a category or a symbol of the mind in which a sense of drifting that could not be relinquished came to be mirrored, objectified, and enclosed.

AN "UNNATURAL SHOT"

"It happened in the Cinema Reale in Trastevere—seeing my name as scriptwriter for *La lunga notte del '43*, the audience murmured slightly, but with just enough malice and irony to bring the terror of lynching to my heart. And it's understandable—newsreels had been coming out all summer in which lackeys had been servilely photographing me and adding captions to their photographs just as servilely, with that vulgar, man-in-the-street humor in the presence of which Italian audiences are so defenseless. They have no other evidence about me except these servile allusions, delivered in pure bad faith."[7]

This took place in October 1960. Pasolini was living in despair, he was experiencing the effects of what he called "the sexual racism of the Italians." His lust and his shyness led him to know his fellows very well.

But his despair also partook of schizophrenia. The story of the murmuring in the Trastevere cinema was published in *Il Giorno* of Sunday, November 6, 1960, and takes up two pages. *Il Giorno*, a recently founded daily, was receptive to the moods of the changing Italy of neocapitalism. Though Pasolini suffered verbal attacks, and not only verbal ones, from one sector of public opinion, he was also successful in not letting himself be banished from the public limelight. The authority in his words was increasingly recognized.

Between 1956 and 1959 he had been poetry critic for *Il punto*, a political and cultural weekly that displayed considerable sensitivity to the problems of the new literature. For some months in 1960 he was film critic for *Reporter*, a short-lived weekly news magazine. His contributions to *Il Giorno* and such leftist dailies as *Paese-Sera*, and the Chianciano poetry prize in 1961 for the volume *La religione del mio tempo,* show that he was not isolated. In the early months of 1960 he and Moravia gave a series of lectures sponsored by the Associazione Culturale Italiana, in Turin, Milan, Rome, Naples, and Bari, on the novel, language, and dialect.

In late spring of the same year, on the occasion of the debate over the Strega prize at the Open Gate Club in Rome, he read a verse epistle entitled "In morte del realismo" (On the Death of Realism):

> Friends, Romans, countrymen, lend me your ears!*
> I come to bury Italian realism
> not to praise it . . .[8]

The epistle, modeled on Mark Antony's famous speech in *Julius Caesar,* denounces the "white socialism" of Carlo Cassola's fiction, "stylistic elegance," and "neopurism."

The epistle is a rhetorical manifesto, and also a message hurled at former literary friends as a demand for a final hearing:

> Dear friends, kind friends, I don't want
> to turn you against the official ideology:
> those who make use of the restoration
> of style are respectable writers . . .

This peroration in verse, read in a hesitant and at the same time hammering voice, created a stir. It was interpreted as an exhibitionist gesture, performed in the presence of a circle of intellectuals who in the previous year had preferred to give an award to *Il gattopardo* by Giuseppe Tomasi di Lampedusa, rather than *Una vita violenta.*

But Pier Paolo with his talent as a critic deflated the effects of such malicious gossip. Seen in perspective, the epistle is a summing up of the literature of realism, whose richness was on the verge of becoming a subject for polemics on the part of the new avant-garde. What had the "realism" of the decade just ended left behind as a legacy?

> Gadda's Pasticciaccio,
> that marvelous symbol of all
> creative mimicry: it leaves you also
> Moravia's fine and ruthless diagnoses,
> Levi's gentle sociology,

* The first line is in English in the original.—Tr.

Bassani's golden story, the creatures
of Arturo's Island,* a few young men
who hope for a future that will not be servile,
and a small Bolognese Officina.
And it leaves you Calvino. His prose,
French rather than Tuscan,
his imagination more Voltairean than
homegrown . . .

A "great hypothesis" was tottering, but certain books remained. The possibility had been offered of a linguistic koine—which would have meant the moral unification of a socially dispersed country. This possibility had been embodied in a style—it had been the style of a literature. But the world had changed, and the change threatened to drive literature back to its old role of handmaiden to official ideologies. No, the world was changing and hopes were fading.

He despaired at this retreat—but, despite his despair, Pasolini did not allow his creative energy to slacken. Mornings he worked furiously. He was working on a play, *Storia interiore*, an autobiographical dramatization of his postwar life, in which there are echoes from the first drafts of *Il sogno di una cosa*.[9] He worked on film subjects, on plans for a novel—they were called *Il rio della Grana, Storia burina, La mortaccia*. These are texts that try to recapture the material that had blazed so brightly in *Ragazzi di vita*—that world now lost in darkness, or else, as with *Accattone,* blinded by a light that "sank" in an "unnatural" tracking shot:

> Come on, Tonino, come on,
> set it at fifty, don't be afraid
> of the light sinking—let's take
> this unnatural shot![10]

The "faithful" Tonino was Tonino Delli Colli, director of photography for *Accattone* and almost all of Pasolini's other films. Delli Colli, a Roman short of stature and extremely nervous, with a slight nasal inflection in his voice, capable of uncontrollable rages, was very gentle with Pier Paolo. Glasses on his nose, he instantly caught his meaning. From him Pier Paolo learned the use of lenses, and on later occasions

* Giorgio Bassani's *Gli occhiali d'oro* was published by Einaudi in 1958, Elsa Morante's *L'isola di Arturo* by the same publisher in 1957.—Tr.

Tonino explained to him their modulations of expression. A few words, or even many, a great many if needed—at other times a mild entreaty by Pasolini, which could mean both reproach and at the same time a request for help—such were his relations with Tonino.

Thus the "Roman" world had been lost in darkness, and transformed into an aching prayer with *Accattone*. Pasolini worked doggedly in the morning at home, with eighteenth-century music—Bach and Vivaldi especially—on the phonograph. Or else he dictated into a tape recorder the diary entries to be printed in the newspaper. Devoured as he was by anxiety and rage, he produced an impressive quantity of written pages.

This anxiety, or rage, became a cinematographic style. The camera served to traverse the field of his anguish. And this anguish was resolved in a special form of painting.

What I have in my head as a vision, as a visual field, are the frescoes of Masaccio, of Giotto—who are the painters I love the most, along with certain Mannerists (for instance Pontormo). And I'm unable to conceive images, landscapes, compositions of figures outside of this initial fourteenth-century pictorial passion of mine, in which man stands at the center of every perspective. Therefore, when my images are in motion, it is a little as though the lens were moving on them as over a painting; I always conceive the background like the background of a painting, like a stage set, and for this reason I always attack it frontally . . .[11]

This "pictorial" quality makes us "feel" the backgrounds and figures of his films "as motionless and substantially in chiaroscuro." Shot against the light or bathed in white sunlight, these backgrounds and figures are signs of a completely funereal language.

THE CONSOLATION OF POVERTY

Already with his work as a scriptwriter, the cinema had altered, and to no small degree, Pier Paolo's financial situation. The scripts he turned out were successful, and he was sought after and well paid.

Ah, to emerge
from this prison of poverty!
To be free of the anxiety that makes
these ancient nights so marvelous!
There's something that unites one who knows anxiety

and one who doesn't know it: man's desires are humble.
Before anything else, a clean shirt![12]

A clean shirt, "good shoes," "serious clothes," "and a home, in a neighborhood / inhabited by people who don't make trouble."

This is the description of the *"private* longing to be rich"[13] that Pier Paolo felt. He fulfilled it against all the painful and degrading things he and his mother had suffered, first in the Piazza Costaguti, then in Rebibbia. Poverty, endured in its harshness in his youth—his father's low pay, his own low salary as a teacher—led him to think of his change of residence as a victory: an apartment, more decent than the one on Via Fonteiana, at Via Giacinto Carini 45, the same building where Bertolucci was living (this was in June 1959). Then came the purchase of a white Giulietta Alfa Romeo in 1961. This automobile gave him joy. Ingenuously—and perhaps he was right—he insisted that the shantytown boys, at the very sight of it, gave him a wink.

Pasolini was a modest and frugal man, and remained so even when his earnings were considerable. Money for him was not a vice or perversion. He did not pick up slum boys with bundles of ten-thousand-lira notes. Indeed he made a virtue of treating them to a pizza, a beer, a few thousand lire, and of being with them for simple erotic enjoyment.

He did not flaunt his economic security, but neither did he reject it. Due to his peasant origin, to which he was linked by Susanna, he was convinced that a good income was not to be despised but rather encouraged.

The change of residence meant buying new furnishings and getting rid of the Renaissance-style dining-room, Carlo Alberto's pride and joy, which had been transported almost in triumph from Casarsa to Via Fonteiana. Those dark pieces of furniture, with their inevitable lion-paw decorations, were shipped back to Casarsa. A few antique whims appeared in the apartment on Via Carini. Little more for the moment.

The real "consolation of poverty" was sex.

In the facility of love
the poor man feels like a man:
he builds his faith in life, to the point
of despising those who live another life.[14]

True "wealth" (the opening theme of *La religione del mio tempo*) was this. But for him sex, as we know, was the turning point of despair. In any case, the cinema, his work as a director, was also for Pier Paolo a side of his *"private* longing to be rich." He was able to look this longing in the face without moralizing. There was nothing in it to expiate.

SEX

One cannot grasp a profound sense of Pasolini's existence without realizing how heavily his demon weighed upon him—the torment that imprisoned him in the concept that there was no way out except by the blind alley of sensuality.

Pier Paolo was on familiar terms with his own senses, and on those terms he satisfied them. But to satisfy them did not placate the demon, which was tied to something else, more remote and deeply buried: the idea of father, of mother, and of power long consolidated by Italian rural life.

The rest of existence, for him, was to live it simply and freely—with biological freedom and simplicity.

He ate with a peasant's avidity and speed; he talked of essential things, unless he had to discuss theoretical and literary matters. His natural shyness could be quite loquacious. Beyond this there was his anguish, that wall against which his gentle nature continued to rend itself. He adopted the instruments of intelligence and culture to impede that rending, or to bring it to expression. But to win once was not enough—the game never reached a decision.

He appears in photographs of the early sixties, lean as always, with hollow cheeks, dressed in a proper bourgeois suit. He had begun wearing dark glasses because of his nearsightedness. His skin had become taut. An athletic leanness—and above his pronounced cheekbones and pointed chin, the ever flickering light of his eyes. When a boy on a motorbike passed him in the street, his whole face lit up.

Imbued with an endless despair, in his work he had a lightness that threatened to become indecent. In 1960, at Vittorio Gassman's request, he translated Aeschylus' *Oresteia* between winter and spring for the Teatro Popolare.

"What could I do, when I had only a few months in which to do the translation, and had moreover sacrilegiously to combine it with two or three consecutive film scripts?"[15]

The solution was to set a pre-existing Italian version, a French one, and an English one alongside the original. "How to translate? I already possessed an 'Italian,' and it was naturally that of *Le ceneri di Gramsci* (with a few expressive points left over from *L'usignolo della Chiesa Cattolica*); I knew (by instinct) that I would be able to make use of it."

The result is a text in which the sublime is turned into the "public" —the "desperate correction of any classicist temptation." The dialogue is flat, demonstrative.

Pasolini, in his Aeschylus translation, tries out the speech of his own future plays. The lyricism of the language flows from an essential quality already present, and is enriched by essayistic glosses. The *Oresteia* is seen as a victory of reason over instinct. "The irrational, represented by the Erinyes, must not be repressed (which anyway would be impossible), but simply held in check and dominated by reason, passion-producing and fertile." And again: "The existential uncertainty of primitive society persists as a category of existential anguish or fantasy in a developed society."

The victory of reason is filtered through a psychoanalytic idea: neurotic anxiety is unconscious irresolution, but the unconscious is also fantasy. What sort of experiment, then, was this hastily achieved translation?

All experiment aside, Pasolini's haste was an effect of despair—in some way to fill his life, silence the irrational, give voice to the imagination. This might be the path to health or the kindling of an uncertain light over the hope for health.

His "desperate vitality" came to fruition. His solitude—

I ran . . .
to commit, and repeat, till blood came,
the sweetest act of life,
all alone . . .[16]

—was certainly *also* a sexual solitude, and it was resolved and overcome in work. Solitary eroticism accompanies writing.

Beyond this maniacal writing fury stretched visions and landscapes —the archaic quality of Aeschylus as the anthropological prefiguration of some peasant Third World.

By now I've had everything I wanted:
I have even gone beyond
certain hopes . . .

I have been rational and I've been
irrational—to the end.
And now . . . ah, the desert deafened
by the wind, the marvelous and foul
African sun that illuminates the world.

Africa! My sole
alternative...............................
.... 17

The African sun, the sun over the desert and the *bidonvilles,* lit up
for him for the first time inside the camera filming *Accattone*—the
cinema his first Africa, his total "alternative."

In this shipwreck, this opposition to all reason, Pasolini felt himself to be "a force of the Past."

I wander through the Tuscolana like a madman,
along the Appia like a dog without a master.
Or I watch the dusks and mornings
over Rome, over the Ciociaria, over the world,
like the first acts of Post-history,
which I witness, for the privilege of recording them,
on the brink of some buried
age.[18]

THE TEMPTATIONS
OF THE CINEMA

His laughter was silent, he laughed with upraised eyes and open lips.
Adriana Asti and Laura Betti gave him something to laugh about.
The two actresses had been close friends. Then, during the
filming of *Accattone,* a rupture took place that forced their mutual
friends to dissemble and lie. If you were going to dinner with Adriana,
you couldn't mention it to Laura; if you were going to dinner with
Laura, you kept quiet about it with Adriana. Pier Paolo could go to
dinner with one or the other and not keep quiet—it was his privilege.

The break had been caused by Bernardo Bertolucci. Bernardo fell in
love with Adriana, and Laura, who claimed Bernardo as her discovery,
took it, so to speak, badly. Laura had plenty to say about both Adriana
and Bernardo—it was as though an epoch had suddenly ended. Pier

Paolo laughed about the whole business. He laughed about it with Alberto Arbasino and Goffredo Parise, both of whom were carrying tales back and forth between Adriana and Laura.

Adriana maintained a dignified reserve. Laura could not help obeying her own "jaguar" image, and those who got the worst of it were younger friends, friends of Bernardo, with whom she made endless scenes, insisting that they give him up, break off relations, cut him on the street, and so forth.

Meanwhile, Laura went on rehearsing her singing performances, her *Giri a vuoto*. She demanded song texts from Penna, but also from Ercole Patti, Fabio Mauri, and Sandro De Feo. De Feo, who perhaps had never written a line of poetry in his life, suffered a good deal from Laura's caprices. She would ask him for songs, he would write them, and regularly she threw them in the wastebasket. Nor did this stop her from asking him for them, nor him from writing them. Pier Paolo used to say that Laura was a torturer.

Seated at the piano in her apartment on Via del Babuino, the "jaguar" tried out the lyrics that had been offered her. She insisted on changes, and this led to stormy scenes and violent confrontations.

Didn't Moravia understand the requirements of musical meter? Laura, over everyone's protests and behind his back, altered his words.

Pier Paolo no longer frequented the houses "of ironical Roman ladies." By now Laura's house had become for him a necessary oasis. But his closest woman friend in those years was Elsa Morante.

What a pleasure; we meet almost every day, and to meet her gives me a feeling of celebration, as though each time we were returning from long journeys. We don't think about it, but deep down it's always a miracle to see one another. Elsa is sitting on the edge of the divan, upright, swathed in one of her undersea colors, with those eyes whose nearsightedness spreads a film of light haze around the pupils, the eyelids, and the stormy face. I see she is gentle this evening, beyond the territory of Angst: she too "quandoquidem dormitat": a light sleep, aggressive and blinking, like a cat. This evening she will not depart with her lance at rest, on the back of her spirited horse. For, I must say, almost every evening, in the arena of literary ideology, she unseats me: Boom! and I immediately find myself in the dust, unhorsed, with her there above me, over the smoking cloud, amid the azure and purple caparisons, amid the streaming plumes, sitting on the Breton horse and looking at me, still raging, with the first shadow of a smile that cleaves the violet haze of her eyes. This in matters of literary ideology. In other fields, she lets me not only straddle, but fly on the Hippogriff.[19]

It is true that this friendship with Elsa Morante helped Pasolini to consider with detachment the ideological drugs by which he was tempted. Sociology—the sociology that had infected his friends at *Officina* in Bologna—was not for him. The strictly aesthetic criterion that guided Elsa Morante in her judgments, her idea of an art wholly free from politics, but in no way divorced from the test of reality, caught Pasolini and convinced him to cling to the concepts of linguistics and literary morphology that he had learned in his youth.

But this is saying little about the substance of this fertile bond, in which life became an uninterrupted game, an uninterrupted story. Now that Pier Paolo had embarked on the path of the cinema, Elsa raised objections, objections strongly shared by Moravia. Pasolini ought not to say farewell to literature. Did it in fact mean a true farewell? Their objections and fears remained unchanged—and the future did nothing to lessen them.

Elsa and Moravia were severe critics of their friends' work—they could even seem ruthless. In both there was an almost monastic idea of the respect due to literature, if one was to bring it to terms with private feelings.[20]

Both had caught in Pasolini's work an insufficiency, or an organic problem that the cinema might be able to make up for—and in some way the cinema did make up for it. Over this they never tired of arguing.

Moravia, in reviewing *Accattone*, alluded to the question by reversing its terms:

In transferring the world of his novels to the screen, the Friulian writer had necessarily had to drop the ideological catharsis that might have deceived his inspiration and stick to pure representation. Let me say at once that this transfer has succeeded to perfection, so much so as to give rise to the suspicion that Pasolini's novels were an unconscious preparation for the cinema—meaning that his stubborn search for the physical and the authentic by means of dialect had necessarily to lead to relinquishing the ever metaphorical word for the image, which cannot be other than direct and immediate.[21]

Moravia was convinced that Pasolini was aiming at an aesthetic representation in which the division between nature and language would be abolished. Pasolini, in essence, was demanding the same thing of himself.

When he took up the Arriflex to film *Accattone*—strictly speaking, Pier Paolo became the "operator" for his own films from *Teorema* on;

he liked to shoot the imagined reality in a documentary fashion, by improvising—when for the first time he placed his eye to the camera, he was cultivating an idea, that of the "cinema of poetry" (at the time a polemical idea directed against the cinema of mere consumption), by which he wished almost to be driven to express himself, as by a breath of wind.

For the moment his crisis—the one that in some way led him to broaden his possibilities of expression in order to run the risks of life, or of vitalism, without defenses—for the moment this crisis was unapparent to him. For the moment, he achieved, at the crest of his energies, what the period demanded—to be a poet, writer, and *homme de lettres* boundlessly open to experience.

To Moravia, however, this gesture of taking up the movie camera meant a decision to run away from literature—and it was a decision that concerned not only Pasolini. After his work on *Accattone*, Bernardo Bertolucci began his first film, *La commare secca*—the subject a gift from Pier Paolo. Moravia, convinced of Bernardo's literary qualities, insisted that in another period of history a young man with the same talent would have decided to write a novel instead of making a film. And to the objection that Bernardo possessed an undeniable feeling for the cinema, Moravia's answer was: "A vocation is always the result of a personal relationship with one's culture. The culture of our time is cinematographic."

On the other hand, that moment, the beginning of the sixties, belonged to *auteur* or "poetry" cinema: Godard and Truffaut, the debut of Bertolucci himself, the arrival from America of such films as *The Connection*. Michelangelo Antonioni's *L'avventura* had appeared not long before *Accattone*. And there was Fellini, and later Elio Petri, and still later Franco Rosi.

The Italian cinema was working out formal and stylistic solutions that sought to restore the freshness that had been experienced immediately after the war. Rossellini was the master to whom Pasolini, Bertolucci, and the French directors looked back.

One aspect of the formalism of that moment was precisely the opposite of what is usually understood by formalism. The cinema reflected, or began to reflect on itself, to quote itself. It was hoping to break loose from the commercial syntax to which it had been excessively devoted. What was desired was a denuded cinema, cut to the bone—a cinema without words. This was the cinema of poetry divined by Pasolini. He found this path congenial, outside of literature, a stylistic and expressive search for living actuality. The cinema of that time was beginning to anticipate what cultural critics called the "postmodern age," an age in which the contemporary spirit was to destroy its own achievements, even its more recent and revolutionary ones, in order to keep up with the rapid pace of History.

Was it for this very reason that Pasolini was bidding a farewell to literature, just as his closest friends, Elsa and Moravia, feared? For him the cinema provided a kind of renewal of his blood circulation. The written word no longer carried the emphasis, the overwhelming necessity, that it had hitherto had for his inspiration.

Much as he might write, or justify himself by writing, it was the immediacy of life in itself that he wanted to capture, its pure poetic character. The slightly trembling frames in *Medea* or the *Decameron* physically express the sign of his hand, the visual possibility of his retina. Style tries to be life, life in its entirety—it seeks to coincide absolutely and religiously with life, with nothing in between. This was the approach of his "decadentism."

THE YEARS OF PERSECUTION

One to whom the authorities grant
no passport—while at the same time
the newspaper that should be the center

of his real life sees no merit
in some of his lines and censures them—
is the one they call a man without faith,

who doesn't conform and doesn't abjure:
it's therefore right that he find no place to live.
Life gets tired of one who endures.

Ah, my recidivist passions
forced to have no dwelling place![22]

Lines from 1962. Citizen of the world, "with no fixed abode." His own words censored: "I could/even go back to the marvelous phase/ of painting. I already smell my five or six/favorite colors giving off an acute perfume . . ." In Pasolini the violence of despair was released in a highly dramatic way.

For two or three years, during which he suffered almost daily attacks from the right-wing press, every sign of a change in customs was blamed on him. Pasolini fought against censorship in the cinema, against the support offered to the spirit of censorship by certain magistrates, whose false "naïveté" was the expression of a "hypocritical, provincial culture, mistaken to its roots."[23]

The persecution he experienced went through marked stages.

On the night of June 29–30, 1960, at almost one in the morning, Pier Paolo is returning home in his car. He is driving along the Corso Vittorio Emanuele. A whistle and a voice: "Hey, Pa'!" It is a boy from Trastevere known as "Il Tedesco" (the German), whom he often runs into in these parts. He is not alone, he has a friend with him—"Il Picchio" (the Woodpecker).

Pier Paolo is in his new Giulietta TI. The two congratulate him; laughing, they ask for a ride. "Just for five minutes, because I'm sleepy," he says. "Five minutes," they agree.

A spin through Largo Argentina, Corso Vittorio again, and Vicolo della Campanella—then Via di Panico. The heart of the quarter bordering on the back of the Chiesa Nuova—the quarter of the poet Belli, still a crime-ridden slum. It is a section of Rome that is all gesture and bravado, the Rome of pickpockets.

At the end of Via di Panico, at the corner of Via dei Coronari, people are in an uproar. A brawl.

As Pier Paolo tells it, "I put on the bright headlights and some old men and women appear, white as a bunch of bakers, half naked and in their underwear, who are running to and fro as though upset by this hellish quarrel. I go closer. A fight is going on between two youngsters and two old people, a man and a woman. They are hitting each other furiously, grabbing each other by the throat and shouting. It's a matter of a few seconds: Il Tedesco next to me yells, 'That's the Baron, I know him.' 'Let's get him out of here!' I say. It's obvious that the two of them have to be separated immediately . . ."[24]

At seven o'clock the next morning, Pasolini is awakened and escorted to the police station. He is alleged to have removed the instigator of a brawl from the reach of the police.

The brawl had broken out for the most childish reasons: someone made fun of a girl who was standing at a window complaining of having seen a cockroach; a Fiat '600 had driven off at breakneck speed, grazing two of the girl's friends with its open door. Insults and fist fights.

The newspapers—the right, and even the so-called independents—played up the episode. Their theme was life imitating art, the *ragazzi di vita* and their author joined in an embrace in which it was impossible to tell fact from fiction. The papers ended by urging Pasolini to "mind his own business" and "not go wandering after midnight through notorious streets of the city."

The trial was held on November 15, 1961. Pasolini was charged with aiding and abetting. The presiding judge asked him, "What were you doing in the street at that time of night?" Pasolini replied, "I was taking a drive to gather impressions about a neighborhood that I had decided to use as background for a literary work I had to write."

It was a defensive answer, one that reasserted that merging of life with art that was now *de rigueur* in speaking of him publicly—the trademark that reduced his person to an image. But to say these words must have seemed to Pier Paolo the most expeditious way to put an end to a disagreeable farce—with the additional fact that he was not averse to putting himself meticulously on record about persons and events.

On November 16 the court absolved him for "insufficient evidence." The verdict of the appeals court, on July 5, 1963, declared that from the juridical standpoint the brawl had not occurred. Pasolini was fully acquitted.[25]

The Anzio episode. It is July 10, 1960. The little port of Anzio—a promenade that fills up at seven in the evening with vacationers, children, fishermen. A row of houses set along the stone arc of the quay. Moored boats, a string of restaurants, glass booths with fresh fish displayed inside.

A boat cuts across the still water of the harbor—in it are some young boys. Other boys are watching the boat from the quay. Pasolini is said to have approached them: "Do you know them? How old are they?" The boys answer, "Twelve." "Still, they must have nice little cocks," Pier Paolo is supposed to have remarked.

Two journalists, having witnessed the scene from a distance—one of them seems to have been the father of one of the boys—informed the police.

A lawsuit followed—two parents filed a complaint, for "attempted corruption of minors," with the district attorney in Velletri. The latter forwarded it to the district attorney of Rome "in connection with other pending proceedings." The Roman district attorney sent it back, since the writ did not contain particulars "of the crime of corrupting minors," though possibly of the "offense of obscene language."

The proceedings were sent to the police magistrate of Anzio. The interrogation of the two boys turned out as follows: "We were leaning against the railing of the Marechiaro restaurant, a man came up to us, he looked at two kids who were in a boat, he asked us how old they were, as a joke I said twenty, he said, They've got small cocks. Then he said to us, And you, what are yours like? We didn't answer, I started laughing. Then he went away and two people came over to us and asked us what that guy had said, one of them said, We'll give you a hundred lire if you tell us everything! We told them. They told us to go to the police. We thought those two were cops."

On December 14, 1960, the suit was dismissed for lack of any "implication of crime as regards Pasolini Pier Paolo."[26]

Via di Panico, Anzio—the newspapers were full of news items and comments. "Pasolinian" became an adjective used by the press to indicate everything in Rome concerning the subproletariat, or low life and homosexuality in general.

The situation became still more inflamed when *Accattone* opened in the movie houses. The film had its premiere at the Cinema Barberini in Rome on November 23, 1961, four days after the end of the first trial over the Via di Panico incident.

A gang of youths, members of a neofascist organization calling itself "Nuova Europa," burst into the theater at seven o'clock on the evening of the premiere. They assaulted spectators, set off stink bombs in the orchestra, threw bottles of ink at the screen, and overturned seats.

Calm returned after half an hour. That same evening, for the last showing, the theater was filled with intellectuals and film people, as a gesture of solidarity. The film was greeted at its conclusion with long applause. Luchino Visconti embraced Pasolini. Pasolini, with a touch of boldness, declared to reporters, "If the fascists have it in for me, let them come to my house."

That November of 1961, however, harbored something fatal for Pier Paolo's life. On the thirtieth the Roman daily *Il Tempo*, "independent" but rightward leaning, published a full-page article: "Pier Paolo Pasolini Charged with Attempted Robbery of a Gas Station Attendant." The article was accompanied by a still from Carlo Lizzani's film *Il gobbo*—Pier Paolo, the actor, with a machine gun in his hand.

On November 18, Pier Paolo and Sergio Citti had been guests in Elsa De Giorgi's house in San Felice Circeo. The two were working on the script of *Mamma Roma*, the film that came after *Accattone*.

In the early afternoon, Pier Paolo went out alone for a drive in his car. He was wearing a tan reindeer jacket over his shoulders. He set out on the road leading from San Felice to the dunes and beach at Sabaudia. He stopped at a gas station.

> I went one day, like a fish out of the net,
> into the dry air
> in the vicinity of a promontory empty of souls, shimmering
>
> in the blue,
> and now I'll tell you what happened to me and how things really
>   went.
> I took a dry road that day,
> my hands equally dry and my brain dry, only my stomach,
> I tell you, was alive, like that promontory in the needless blue.
> All the myths had collapsed and rotted but at least on the
>   promontory
> someone lived.
> Urged on, in short, by my living belly and my nearsightedness,
> I drove in the dry sun,
> on a stretch of asphalt,
> between dry autumn bushes recalling the summer,
> toward a house standing alone in the sun,
> with lively patterns of old walls and old poles and old
> nets and old fences, blue and white
> —we're in Italy—where the mixture of sun and rain stank.
> There inside was a grim boy,
> wearing, I seem to recall, a smock, his hair
> long like a woman's,
> his skin pale and taut, a certain mad innocence in his eyes,
> like a stubborn saint, like a son who wants to be equal to his worthy
>   mother.
> In practice, I saw at once, a poor lunatic,
> whose ignorance gave him traditional certainties,
> transforming his cadaverous neurosis into the rigor
> of an obedient son identified with the fathers.
> What's your name, what do you do, do you go dancing, have you a
>   girl friend,
> do you earn enough money,
> these were the subjects with which I drew back like a dry fish
> from the first impulse of my old afternoon siesta lust.
> You have seen my Gospel,

you have seen the faces in my Gospel.
I could not have been mistaken, and sometimes decisions should
    have occurred
in a few minutes:
I've never been mistaken
because my lust and my shyness
have forced me to know my fellows well.
Him too I knew immediately,
the wretched possessed boy in the house besieged by the sun.
Winter was coming,
it was there in his face,
with its darkness and its silent houses, its chastity.
I withdrew.
But not in time for him not to feel, like a woman,
terror of a father unlike the fathers
who had set up the world for his obedience.[27]

The boy, whose name was Bernardino De Santis, reported a holdup
to the Circeo carabinieri.

He had been alone, in the gas station and bar, at three-thirty in the
afternoon. A stranger came in, wearing a black hat. He ordered a
Coca-Cola, and drank it. He asked him some "strange" questions:
how much he earned, if the motorcycle parked outside was his, if he
had a girl friend. Then he looked around, leaped to the door, put on
a pair of black gloves, took a black pistol from his pocket, and loaded
it with a "golden" bullet. Threateningly he said, "Don't move or I'll
shoot." He went back to the door and locked it from the inside, also
closing the shutters of another glass door. He came around behind
the bar.

Bernardino said he found himself with the pistol pointed at his
throat. With his left hand, the stranger tried to open the drawer of the
cash register: inside were two thousand lire. On the bar was a knife;
the boy seized it and struck the man's hand.

"We'll meet again," the latter is supposed to have said as he went
away.

Next day, on a street in San Felice, Bernardino recognized the
stranger at the wheel of a Giulietta. It was traced to Pasolini by the
number on the license plate.

On November 22, the carabinieri in Rome searched Pier Paolo's
house and automobile looking for the pistol.

Pier Paolo told his version—he was not believed. They believed in the black cowboy hat, the black pistol, the "golden" bullets. The right-wing newspapers believed these things, and gave the signal for a new onslaught of accusations and insinuations. They wrote, without pausing to ask questions, of the "Circeo robbery," and of "realism outdoing itself." The neofascist papers wondered why Pasolini was still "allowed to be at large."

Once again, during these days, at the opening of the Paolo Heusch film inspired by *Una vita violenta*, rightist youths at the Quattro Fontane cinema in Rome bullied the spectators and threw rotten eggs at the screen.

The trial was held at the tribunal in Latina on July 3, 1962. Pasolini was charged with armed robbery, illegally carrying a firearm, and failure to register a pistol (a pistol that no one had seen except Bernardino De Santis).

On June 21, 1962, an information agency, Stampa Internazionale Medica, had distributed a report on Pasolini ("confidential, not for publication") to the editors-in-chief of the newspapers. It had been drawn up on behalf of the civil plaintiff in the trial, and the author was Aldo Semerari, a professor of psychology at the University of Rome.

Professor Semerari asks himself: Is the accusation absurd? Is it absurd to think that Pasolini had had the intention of robbing a boy of two thousand lire? His answer is: "When we find ourselves faced with actions that are grossly incomprehensible on the psychological level, we must suspect that they are not the expression of a conscious capacity for self-determination with a purpose in view, but symptoms of a developing pathological process, or at least of an alteration in the congenital or acquired personality."

And again: "Pasolini is an instinctual psychopath, he is a sexual deviant, a homophile in the most absolute sense of the word." Semerari refers to the police report on the Ramuscello incident; he speaks of "skeptophilia,"* of a "highly insecure and extremely suggestible personality," of "a socially dangerous person."

The Semerari report is a good introduction to the atmosphere in which the trial was held; and it is surely surprising, after all these years, to think that there could have been a serious debate over an alleged holdup based on the story told by Bernardino De Santis—a

---

* As in the typewritten Semerari report, where it is followed, in parentheses, by "he had himself masturbated and masturbated himself in the presence of three boys." Presumably "scoptophilia" (or more correctly, "scopophilia")—sexual pleasure derived from looking.—Tr.

Pasolini's father Carlo Alberto on
the Adriatic shore in his youth,
and in his army uniform.

Pier Paolo and his mother
Susanna Colussi Pasolini.

Pier Paolo with his father
in Florence, and (below)
biking with friends, sum-
mer 1939.

Pier Paolo's younger brother Guido, who was killed in 1945, and Pier Paolo (second row, third from left) with his students at Valvasone, 1947.

Pier Paolo with Giorgio Bassani (right), with Elsa Morante (below left), and at a party with Alberto Moravia and others.

With the actress Laura Betti, 1970, and at a slum on the beach at Ostia.

Directing the *Decameron* (right), and making *Medea* with Maria Callas.

Pasolini in Times Square during a trip to New York, and with his mother and cousin Graziella Chiarcossi.

At home with three of his favorite actors: (left to right) Franco Citti, Ninetto Davoli, and Ettore Garofolo.

Jerry Bauer

Pasolini shooting *Canterbury Tales*,
and playing Chaucer in the same film.

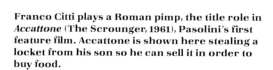

Franco Citti plays a Roman pimp, the title role in *Accattone* **(The Scrounger, 1961), Pasolini's first feature film. Accattone is shown here stealing a locket from his son so he can sell it in order to buy food.**

Mario Cipriani (above) as a
starving bit-part actor from the
Roman slums who is cast in the
role of the penitent thief crucified
beside Jesus in *La Ricotta*.

Uccellacci e Uccellini (Hawks and
Sparrows, 1966) stars the fabled
comedian Totò and the young
Ninetto Davoli in Pasolini's
"ideo-comic" parable of modern
Italian life.

Pasolini (center) at work on *The Gospel According to Saint Matthew* (1964), the film that brought him international acclaim as a director. Enrique Irazoqui (right) played Christ.

The entry into Jerusalem from *The Gospel*. Enzo Siciliano (second from left) is Simon in the film.

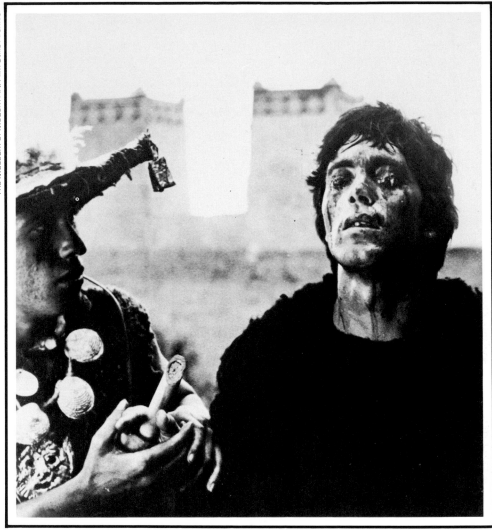

Oedipus Rex (1967). Franco Citti (above) as the blinded Oedipus, with Ninetto Davoli, and in *Porcile* (Pigsty, 1969).

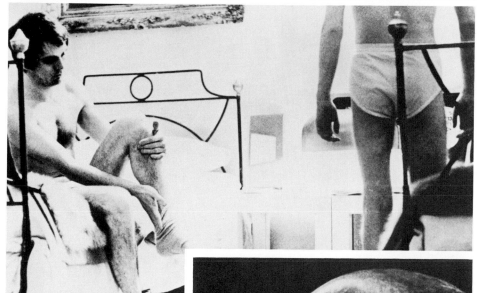

Terence Stamp (above left) as the mysterious stranger in *Teorema* (Theorem, 1968).

Ninetto Davoli in *Canterbury Tales* (1972), the second film in Pasolini's *Trilogy of Life*.

Pasolini as Giotto in the first of the *Trilogy* films, his 1971 adaptation of Boccaccio's *Decameron*.

Zumurrud (top), the reigning spirit of the luminous *Arabian Nights* (1974); Yunan (center) entering the underground chamber of a young prince whom he later murders; and the faithless Aziz (Ninetto Davoli) "making love" to Mad Budur.

Pasolini's dark adaptation from Sade, *Salò: The One Hundred and Twenty Days of Sodom* (1975), is set in Mussolini's post-liberation Republic of Salò.

story in which nothing is clear except the way in which a personal mythomania finds compensation in the culture of the comic strips.

But the debate was less over the holdup than over Pasolini's homosexuality. The lawyers for the prosecution spoke of it, bringing in Ramuscello and Anzio, mixing truth with suppositions, and supporting the latter with pages from *Ragazzi di vita* and *Una vita violenta*.

The judge asked Bernardino De Santis if Pasolini had made any proposals to him of which he felt ashamed to speak. De Santis replied, "He did not make me any sexual proposals, of any kind."

Then the judge asked Pasolini the reason for his questions to De Santis. "Because I had it in mind to make a film that would be set in that place. Those are questions I usually ask for the purpose of studying the subjects' reactions."

De Santis had answered truthfully, but he had been incapable of voicing what had unconsciously driven him to his absurd accusation: he had been incapable of speaking in court about his "terror of a father unlike the fathers," which he had felt that autumn afternoon in the presence of Pier Paolo, who was asking him about his girl and his motorcycle.

For his part, Pier Paolo took refuge behind the kind of words that some people expected of him: that he was studying actual life in order to invent it. It was a response that did not do justice to his truth, but it was the only possible one, the only justification that could put an end to the uninterrupted chain of speculations that seemed never to be lulled.

In the Latina courtroom, a sultry heat. Pier Paolo, dressed in white, is seated on a lictor-style chair of light wood. He is pale, his glasses on his nose. A carabiniere brigadier stands behind him. Pier Paolo listens, absorbed by the perorations of his accusers. He listens to the words of his defense lawyer, Francesco Carnelutti, a Christian Democrat who had previously taken on the defense of *Accattone*, when it had seemed that the film would not be shown in movie theaters because of the obstacles placed in its way by ministerial censorship.

Pier Paolo listens. From time to time he throws a glance toward the friends who have accompanied him this summer morning to Latina—they include Moravia, Adriana Asti, Laura Betti. In his eyes there is listlessness and fear, but incredulity as well.

The verdict takes for granted that he had it in mind to make a film and had acted out the holdup for purposes of "study," the study of human behavior and reactions. The attempted armed robbery is changed to "threatening with a weapon." The sentence is two weeks in jail, plus five days for illegally carrying a pistol, and a ten-thousand-lira fine for failure to register same. Naturally Pasolini is given a suspended sentence.

Those witnessing the trial came away with a deep-seated sense of unease concerning the administration of justice in Italy.

Did the judges convict Pasolini for simulated robbery?

In Moravia's words: "The judges realized that what De Santis was saying was pure madness, but they wanted to deliver a verdict of condemnation anyway, for the simple reason that Pier Paolo is a homosexual. In Italy there is no article in the legal code that views homosexuality as a crime. They have therefore contrived a loophole. It's a bizarre loophole, but for them it's enough."

There was a hearing in appeals court (July 13, 1963) and two appeals to the Supreme Court (March 1, 1965, and December 17, 1968). Pasolini was not acquitted unconditionally, but for "insufficient evidence."[28]

The question is, What really happened inside that "house standing alone in the sun"?

There were no sexual proposals—De Santis was clear on that point. Everything must have unfolded as recounted by Pier Paolo in his poem: the questions he asked, and his feelings as well. In his feelings there was "the living belly," there was his "old lust"—the same that had driven him to speak as he had done to the boys on the quay in Anzio. It was a lust that required verbalization, that at times could lead to some allusion, if the occasion allowed. Sometimes it may have been only a vocal inflection—but the "poor lunatic, whose ignorance gave him traditional certainties" must have noticed beyond it something that undermined just those certainties.

One might suggest that Pasolini's very kindness, exercised on a fragile and unstable person such as Bernardino De Santis must have been, could have violent results.

The point is thus not the reaction produced in De Santis by his conversation with Pier Paolo—this incident is parallel to what happened in Anzio—the point to be grasped is the exploitation of the episode by a portion of the press, and the interpretation given it by the carabinieri in their reports, and later by certain magistrates.

A climate of persecution. Hysteria grew around the public figure of Pasolini. And it is attested by certain episodes, negligible in themselves, but which, taken in connection with the Circeo affair, are expressions of this hysteria.

On October 25, 1961, a twenty-three-year-old elementary school teacher named Antonio Vece filed an accusation against Pier Paolo. He had supposedly been loaded into the now famous Giulietta TI, taken to the country, threatened with a pistol, knocked unconscious, and robbed of the manuscript of a novel entitled—alas!—*The Children of Sin.*

Two days later Vece retracted his whole story, and confessed that he was only seeking publicity for his own aspirations as a writer. He was charged with simulating a crime.

On February 24, 1962, Salvatore Pagliuca, a former Christian Democratic deputy from Muro Lucano, sued Pasolini and the producers of *Accattone.* A character in the film—a thief, pimp, and loafer—bore his name. Pagliuca demanded compensation for moral and material damages and the removal of his name from the soundtrack of the film.

The ex-deputy felt he had been mocked. He insisted that Pasolini had given his name to the character in order to harm him politically. He was thinking of running for the Senate in the next elections, and the voters might be influenced negatively by the film. Pagliuca failed to be elected in the political elections of 1963. In court he blamed Pasolini, at the same time imputing "to the defamatory campaign in his regard" various illnesses from which he was suffering, a sudden lack of interest in his work, and an equally sudden loss of interest in his family.

On February 22, 1965, the presiding magistrate ruled that it was impossible to confuse the lawyer Pagliuca with the character in *Accattone,* and therefore rejected the demand for payment of moral damages, but he ordered the name to be eliminated from the soundtrack of the film and sentenced Pasolini and the producers to pay material damages.

The episode sounds like something from a play by Pirandello or Eduardo De Filippo. The name Salvatore Pagliuca is extremely common in the regions of Campania and Lucania; the former deputy was not a person of such outstanding political importance, outside his local area, to justify a plan to belittle him like the one of which he claimed to be the victim. How can one help thinking, however, that the episode emerged from the climate of hysteria generated around Pasolini in those years?

In April 1962 there was another case of mythomania. A young Roman named Andrea Di Marco claimed to recognize himself in the person of Begalone, a character in *Ragazzi di vita*. He sued Pasolini for libel. Right-wing newspapers, especially *Il Tempo* in Rome, featured the story. They defended Di Marco's position as that of a person who did not wish to be confounded "with young criminals, and finds moreover that the rights of art are one thing, and the limitations of one who, being short of paints and brushes, adopts the camera to copy persons and things directly in order to write pure reportage, are another."[29]

One more painful confusion between art and life. The journalist in his unsigned article was unable to resist the temptation to make aesthetic judgments. But Di Marco withdrew his suit and nothing more was heard of it.

Again, with the release of *Mamma Roma*, Pasolini's second film, there was a repetition of intolerance.

The film was shown at the Twenty-third International Film Festival in Venice on August 31, 1962, and the lieutenant colonel in command of the local carabinieri post declared it to be obscene. The obscenity consisted in the use of the words "piss" and "shit," and the sound of farts on the soundtrack. The court, on September 5, judged the charge unfounded and refused to take action.

The press, of course, played up the incident. A few newspapers referred maliciously to "Pasolini and the pasolinids," guests at the Palazzo del Cinema at the Lido—the "pasolinids" being the actors "taken from life" who had had roles in the film.

Mamma Roma was built around Anna Magnani—homage to Rossellini, and to Visconti's *Bellissima*—with Magnani being seen as a cinematic object, a sort of prime exhibit that lent itself to the creation of a parable in which the desire of the subproletarian world to change its appearance would be implied. There shines through the film an illusion of petit-bourgeois redemption, and its consequent decay—death lurks in the background.

As Pasolini remarked, "The element that distinguishes this film from *Accattone* is a moral question not to be found in *Accattone*."[30] It is the same difference that separates *Ragazzi di vita* and *Una vita violenta*, with a corresponding difference in the results.

Mamma Roma, too, is spoiled by exemplarity and pedagogic zeal. The death of the young hero—played by Ettore Garofalo—a boy who dies in prison while tied to a concrete restraining bed—was suggested to Pasolini by an actual episode, the death in prison of the young Marcello Elisei. A blending of Masaccio, Mantegna's *Dead Christ*, and Caravaggesque light creates the pattern for the film image of this death. Society determines it, the responsibility for it is collective—it has roots both in the mythology of the consumer society and in the prison structure. A similar preordained determinism acts to flatten Pasolini's most original feeling—which had seen Accattone swept away and killed by a need for death, by a presence that inexplicably crushed all his resistance, making him the hero and at the same time the victim of his own existence.

A tragedy of maternal love, the son a lamb sacrificed to the ferocity of the world—it is not hard to find autobiographical hints in *Mamma Roma*. Already in *Accattone* this autobiographical tendency had taken an unaccustomed, Christological line. The myths of *L'usignolo*, stripped of their enchanted literary music, stamped on the howling world of the Roman shantytowns, and using the contrasted, highly pictorial black-and-white photography of Tonino Delli Colli, are brought to new life. From these myths the harrowing fable of the sacrifice rises abnormally to the surface—and it is the sacrifice of the life of the one who offers his own suffering as a lesson for all.

Pasolini progressively enriched his own personal myth in the image of Christ. The persecution of which he saw himself the object prefigured the rite of crucifixion. From *Accattone* and *Mamma Roma*, through *La ricotta*, there is a direct line to the *Gospel According to Saint Matthew*.

At the time he was working on the *Gospel*, Pier Paolo, in an interview, expressed himself on his own destiny with unequivocal words: "In the world in which I live I am rather the sheep in the midst of wolves. And it's been shown by what has happened in these years— I've been literally [*sic*] torn to pieces."[31]

September 22, 1962. The Roman premiere of *Mamma Roma* at the Quattro Fontane cinema. The last showing ended at one in the morning, and Pasolini was present. A group of university students, members of the far-right organizations Giovane Italia and Avanguardia Nazionale, attacked him in the theater lobby. Laura Betti and two actors in the film, Sergio Citti and Piero Morgia, were at Pasolini's side.

At the opening of one of my films, a fascist, a rather emaciated young man to tell the truth, publicly shouted an insult at me in the name of all his fine youth. I lost my patience (I regret it); I hit him and knocked him down. My friend Laura Betti was present, and therefore saw the whole scene "with her own eyes." I don't know what the newspapers that reported the episode thought they were doing by turning it around (accompanying it with false photographs), in such a way that I became the one who got hit. The thing has been repeated and has entered the public domain—to such an extent that Betti, in her aggressive naïveté, speaking of it to me, and though she had seen it "with her own eyes," said, "the Fascist who hit you" . . .[32]

Pier Paolo, that evening in the lobby of the Quattro Fontane, hit first. There was a brawl. The police cordoned off the theater, and took everyone to the station. A few days later, Laura Betti was attacked by unknown assailants in Via del Babuino.

In short, as the months went by, over and above the mythomania of some, it was the neofascist right that took it upon itself to use violence against Pasolini.

The trial for contempt of religion that accompanied the release of *Rogopag*, a film in episodes that included *La ricotta*, should be seen, however, in a different perspective.

In February 1962 the producer Roberto Amoroso had the idea for a film employing four directors, to be entitled *La vita è bella* (Life is Beautiful). He consulted Pasolini, who agreed and wrote the script of *La ricotta*. Amoroso rejected it, judging it indecent and offensive.

Alfredo Bini took over. The film he produced was entitled *Rogopag*, a cipher containing the names of the four authors who were to contribute to it: Rossellini, Godard, Pasolini, and Ugo Gregoretti.

Pasolini filmed *La ricotta* in the fall of 1962, on a hilly ridge in the countryside near the gates of Rome, a vague stretch of terrain between the Via Appia Nuova and the Via Appia Antica, near the Acqua Santa spring.

From that landscape of excavated tufa emerged his most singular film. Moravia, in his review, called it "brilliant." "I do not mean by this that it is perfect or wholly beautiful; but one can see in it the characteristics of brilliance, i.e., a certain quality of vitality that is astonishing and at the same time profound."[33]

A poem through images. The cinema as self-reference—the cinema caught in its own trappings, or cinema about cinema. But a cinema that voraciously utilizes painting and literature. A Crucifixion scene with the Deposition is being filmed, with the paintings of Pontormo and Rosso Fiorentino serving as artistic examples, while the director, played by Orson Welles, answers the questions of an interviewer with lines from the poetry of Pasolini himself:

I am a force of the Past.
My love lies only in tradition . . .

Intellectual autobiography and the experience of life—that Roman movie company and set, so neorealistically depicted in its sarcastic spontaneity—provide the crucible for the explosion of a highly singular metaphor.

"Get those crucified characters out of here"; "bring up the crosses"; "leave them nailed up there"; "cuckolds"; "silence"; the Magdalen who nonchalantly dances the cha-cha-cha in front of the cross; and Stracci, poor Stracci,* the extra playing one of the thieves, who eats so much ricotta during the break that he gets indigestion and literally dies, tied to the cross under the broiling sun. With all its cries and gestures, its bitter cruelty, this movie set is nothing but the temple overrun by the moneychangers. Poverty, suggests the author, only poverty with its pure and candid words, can redeem the faith.

The theme is complex and profoundly Christian. It does violence to the clericalism of any church. The blasphemy of the repeated cries— "get those crucified characters out of here"—is the sign of an ancient despair at not seeing the everlasting urgency of religion matched by the world.

Vulgar voices, vulgar orders—teeming confusion. Sudden breaks (the one in which Stracci's starving family furtively arrives, and the poor man, one of many in the ant heap of Cinecittà, gives them his own food ration). Everything becomes an element that goes to create a picture of "appalling sacredness."[34]

It is a picture in which Pasolini's cultural sensibility, and his irreversible need for desecration, for the purpose of making the Christian "credo" more concrete, achieve their greatest clarity of expression.

There is a glimmer of determinism in Stracci's death through hunger, a glimmer with an aura of irony. This is set against the disillusion, it too edged with irony, in which the director cloaks his responses to the interviewer: virulent accusations against the Italian

---

* The name means "Rags."—Tr.

bourgeoisie, the display of a "profound, secret, archaic Catholicism," that air of detachment and intellectual daring with which he speaks of death, a "pseudo problem for a Marxist."

Pasolini succeeded in making fun of himself, and in playing with the instruments of the cinema. He made his film with the elegance of a craftsman. This was the "brilliance" recognized by Moravia. The clerical party did not recognize any at all.

The film, on its release, had a cool and baffled reception. The reason, according to Moravia, lay in what Pasolini, "with naïve tactlessness," had put in the mouth of his director. "After all, he has the director declare in the interview, 'Italy has the most illiterate masses and the most ignorant bourgeoisie in Europe,' thereby offending the parties on the right as well as those on the left. Then, to make matters worse, Orson Welles states, 'The average man is a dangerous criminal, a monster. He is a racist, a colonialist, a defender of slavery, a mediocrity,' thereby offending everyone. The Italy of the past was really the country of man, in all his humanity; the Italy of today, on the other hand, is merely the country of the average man."

On March 1, 1963, the film was seized for the crime of insulting the religion of the state. The writ was signed by the acting public prosecutor, Giuseppe Di Gennaro.

On March 4 a debate was held at the Palazzo Marignoli, headquarters of the Italian press association, to demonstrate solidarity with Pasolini. Critics, directors, and writers expressed the fear that the courts were becoming the representatives of a schematic and reactionary religious viewpoint.

The case was not merely judicial. Not all Catholics shared the opinion of the acting prosecutor. The priests who taught at the Pontifical Gregorian University in Rome did not find the film insulting.

The hearing took place on March 6 and March 7. The center of the stage was occupied by Di Gennaro, self-appointed spokesman for a conception of faith that allowed no room for diversity. In his summation, he uttered the following words: "You will wonder why the Catholic press itself has not reacted with scorn to this man's insults. And you have good reason to wonder. The Catholics should have taken a stand . . . I am confident that your verdict will reawaken the dead and recall to life and dignity those churchgoing Catholics who have abdicated their culture for fear of being accused of conformism . . . Let Catholics beware of carrying the Trojan horse of Pasolini into the city of God."

The intention is clear, as well as the implied cultural ideas. Clearer still is Di Gennaro's psychology. "Here I stand, at the public prosecutor's bench, but in what guise? If a defendant is someone who is called to answer an accusation, well then I too am a defendant! It fully behooves me to be aware of the reality. By various voices, I stand unequivocally accused: attacker of freedom, liberticide, inquisitor! No more is needed to come to the realization that in this trial there are two defendants: Pier Paolo Pasolini and myself." The request to the judges is absolute: "If you convict Pasolini, you will be giving me your approval, but if you acquit him, then unavoidably you will be condemning my actions."[35]

Pasolini was held by the court to be "guilty of the crime with which he is charged," and sentenced to four months in prison. On May 6, 1964, the Appeals Court in Rome absolved him "because the act does not constitute a crime." This second judgment was revoked on February 24, 1967, by the Supreme Court "because the offense has been annulled through amnesty."

The 1963 trial, and the debate it aroused over film censorship and the articles of the Rocco code* still in force in Italy for offenses of this nature, give a picture of the cultural condition of the country.

The economic miracle had transformed the structures of production; the large cities in the North were changing their appearance; the construction of superhighways ensured that the countryside would be disfigured; the mass media, led by television, were in the process of expansion—all this above a core of rigid conceptions, above a morality so proud of its own immobility as to make the circulation of ideas extremely hazardous or disruptive.

In the new Italy there were margins of such abstraction and un-reality as to drive a nature like Pasolini's to the systematic exercise of provocation. He felt this destiny alive within him—but, of course, he did not take it lightly. He was well aware that what he was opposing to the ideas of Acting Prosecutor Di Gennaro was not what could be called a comparison of future and past, but rather a different conception of Christ.

The same can be said for the background of a country that was trying impartially to become enlightened in every possible way, while at the same time seeking to preserve—neurotically to preserve—the dross of the past, and to remain rooted in its own social frustrations.

---

* Fascist penal code devised by Arturo Rocco (1876–1942).—Tr.

"I am a force of the Past," wrote Pasolini. But because of this he did not want, as he had also written, to leave "to the priests the monopoly of Good." The culture of the rural parishes became enriched in him by a dynamic idea of history. But this dynamism was inextricably linked to the evangelical message of the "scandal."

Much more than literature, the cinema could be the vehicle of "scandal." The cinema, Pier Paolo was to say within a few years, is "language written from reality"—he was to say in 1966 that for him the cinema expressed nothing but "a hallucinated, childish, and pragmatic love for reality." Not only "pragmatic," but "religious in that it merges in some way, by analogy, with a sort of immense sexual fetishism. The world does not seem, for me, to be anything but a set of fathers and mothers, toward which I am totally drawn by a feeling of adoring respect, and by the need to violate such adoring respect through desecrations that are violent and scandalous as well."[36]

Fathers and mothers, sexual fetishism, scandal—all this is enclosed in an unbreakable cycle of passions cemented by neurosis, but which reason and poetic intuition nourish with expressive vitality, that "desperate vitality" that was the glow behind which Pasolini increasingly concealed his existence.

Having heard the verdict, that March morning in 1963, Pier Paolo returned home. The sun was hot—it was already spring.

For some months Graziella, the daughter of Annie Chiarcossi Naldini, had been living with him and Susanna. She had enrolled in the faculty of arts and letters at the University of Rome.

Susanna, informed of the verdict, became hysterical and fainted. It was a terrible moment. Pier Paolo was devastated—he called Moravia and begged him to come over to the house. Then he succeeded in locating Di Gennaro's telephone number and called him. Shouting into the phone, he blamed the prosecutor for his mother's emotional collapse.

That was the only time that Pier Paolo had an extreme reaction in the face of a court verdict. Susanna's tears and physical prostration had clouded his mind. His words for her were:

You are irreplaceable. That is why the life
you gave me is condemned to solitude.

And I don't want to be alone. I have a boundless hunger
for love, for the love of bodies without souls.

Because the soul is in you, you are you, but you
are my mother and your love is my servitude.

I spent my childhood as the slave of this high,
irremediable sense of an immense duty.

It was the only way to feel life,
the only color, the only form: now it is over.

We survive: and this is the confusion
of a life reborn outside reason.

I beg you, O, I beg you: do not wish to die.
I am here, alone, with you in a future April.[37]

CHAPTER 9

RECIDIVIST
PASSIONS

LE BELLE BANDIERE

Pier Paolo was experiencing years of crisis in his creative life, and it was hard to foresee any liberation in the future. And yet—and this was important to him—on June 4, 1960, at the invitation of Antonello Trombadori, he had begun a "dialogue with readers" in *Vie Nuove*, a popular Communist weekly. This collaboration, with occasional time out for his film work, lasted until September 30, 1965.

It was an intellectual commitment that Pasolini could meet with enthusiasm. Not only that, it was additional proof that the Communist Party was not handing him over to the persecution of his enemies.

On July 7, 1962, at the time of the court verdict on the Circeo affair, *Rinascita* wrote: "The truth is, and it is no laughing matter, that the responsibility for the real persecution to which Pier Paolo Pasolini has been subjected for some time, to the point where paradoxically the campaigns of the press have joined to his detriment with the powers of the state, must surely be sought in the shameful two-faced nature of bourgeois morality."

The Pasolini case was not a personal one. The violation of everyday morality that he committed—both consciously and unconsciously—raised the question of the civil rights of every individual. And this was a problem to which the left, Communists or not—and the Catholic left as well—seemed more sensitive in these years of innovation. The

Pasolini case was a sore point, and if his state of being "different" generated discomfort in public opinion, the recognition of it, of its legitimacy, became a moment of political liberation. The Communists, to be sure with some hesitation, were now able to make this theme their own, just as they had avoided it in 1949, at the time of the Ramuscello incident.

Readers wrote in and Pasolini answered, as writer and philosopher, film man and moralist, confessor and ideologue. They asked him for "his judgment on Hungarian literature and advice on whether or not to be baptized, his ideas on the problem of Latin or on a short story about miners, information on Soviet military strength and his evaluation of family laws in Italy, directions on how to join the Communist Party and the answer to some theoretical Marxist question, help in finding work and his opinion of a literary manuscript, suggestions for a way of life and a clarification of the Alto Adige dispute. There are also a few comrades (old or young) who reproach him, with old-fashioned but sincere moralism, for the 'sexual' material and 'dirty words' in his novels. Meanwhile, there is no lack of letters from occasional readers of the magazine or of Pasolini's works, shocked or furious right-thinking people, or echoes of little obscurantist journals full of malice, which point to him as a public corruptor, 'pornographer,' and blasphemous polemicist."[1]

Pier Paolo had words for everyone. Sometimes he inserted poems into his answers, like his "Poesia in forma di polemica," or the versified introduction to *Il rio della Grana*, the novel he had been working on for years since *Una vita violenta*. A portion of *Le belle bandiere* (The Beautiful Banners) was printed there in verse—banners of a hope that he felt was being weakened and dispersed under what he called "the violence of neocapitalism." He let his readers come into his workshop, without intimidating them.

Thus these responses, intellectual material in a state of incandescence, replete with a truth that gives itself over to doubts and contradictions without any fear of being used up, are actually a sign that though his heart was exhausted by anguish, hope, the flaming color of red banners, still shone in it.

What else did Piero Paolo write about in these columns? He wrote about himself. By now he had objectively become a public figure—perhaps also a figure with a positive face for those who asked his advice or scolded him affectionately. In any case, he was a public figure. He suffered from this, and spoke of it.

"The public part of my life . . . all that part of myself that does not belong to me, and which has become like a mask at the Nuovo Teatro dell'Arte—a monster that must be what the public wants it to be. Quixotically, I try to struggle against this fate that takes me out of myself, makes me a robot for the illustrated magazines, and then ends by being reflected back on me like an illness. But it seems that nothing can be done about it. Success is a horrible thing for one's moral and emotional life, and that's all there is to it."[2]

Or else: *Mamma Roma* is before the judgment of the public. There are brawls and accusations. Pasolini knows that his film is less success-ful than *Accattone*, he knows that the presence of Anna Magnani has pointed up the "errors" obviously committed. He is too involved in a reality that "is what it is" for this reality, once it has been represented, to tolerate the professionalism of a consummate actress. He writes: "It is forbidden to me, I don't say to make a mistake, but to expose myself at all. And if by chance there should be a little bit of persecution mania in this, it seems to me more than justified . . . It is clear that something unjust is happening, something elusive, as in all self-respecting Kafkaesque situations."[3]

They ask him why he feels himself to be "a force of the Past." His answer is: "Even my wildest experiments never depart from a deter-mining love for the great European and Italian tradition. We must take the monopoly of tradition away from the traditionalists. Only Marxists love the past. The bourgeoisie loves nothing, its rhetorical affirmations of love for the past are merely cynical and sacrilegious. And even in the best of cases, this love is decorative, or 'monumental' as Schopen-hauer says, certainly not historistic, that is to say real and capable of new history."[4]

When the questions touch upon his "religiosity," he specifies: "I don't believe in God. If then there survives in my works a Christian 'afflatus' of love for the things of the world and men—I mean an irrational, inspired love—I don't think I need be ashamed of it . . . And in whom would it not be found? I'm joking—but that there is a 'historically' Christian foundation in us is so obvious that there's no need to talk about it."[5]

This publicist activity is thus not marked by the anguish of terrible solitude. It almost seems, as one goes through it page by page, to be a rekindling of the will to life. And that is what it was. The notes for *Vie Nuove* were often dashed off hurriedly, but never absent-mindedly. Pasolini remains always informed, always alert.

As with the cinema, this too was a way of escaping the asceticism of literature. Pasolini never had anything to say against this asceticism, and one can suppose that he was still thinking of cultivating it, just as he had cultivated it in Friuli as an active militant for the Communist Party. But his creative sensibility obviously had need of strong fare, of a climate of aggressiveness and action by which he felt himself steadily renewed.

The writer of the dialogues with readers of *Vie Nuove* is the same one who was still becoming the theorist of a Gramscian idea: that of unifying consciousness through history. There is no doubt that he lived in torment over the laceration of his own consciousness. At the same time, there can be no doubt that he yearned for it to be made whole again. But was Pasolini aware that this reconciliation, or process of becoming whole, was impossible for him?

Pier Paolo was a man capable of gaiety, as his friends know. They know too that he went through whole weeks of silent gloom. He was stimulated by his meetings with Elsa Morante, his discussions with Moravia, or by certain wild and unabated quarrels with Laura Betti. These last could be furious and loaded with invective—Elsa Morante, on such occasions, would interrupt in exasperation, "If you two want to make love, stop doing it in words."

Anyway, Pier Paolo's everyday behavior was various and lively on the surface. The colloquy with his demon was harsh, continuous, and secret. Which means that, as he had written in "The Ashes of Gramsci," his awareness of the contradiction did not cease to torment him.

Was Pasolini then acting in bad faith by concentrating all his intellectual resources on the need to compose one's consciousness in the light of history?

In his writings for *Vie Nuove* there is the institutional bad faith that governs the relations between teacher and pupils. There is the estranged sound of paternalism, which, while expressing itself sincerely, makes clear to the listener the degree to which such sincerity, even by overstepping the bounds of modesty, does not belong to daily existence but to the exemplary universe of absolutes.

"Know then that I do not want to exert influence. If I should do so, it will be from time to time, through the possible strength of my arguments at *that given* moment, in *that given* circumstance—and above all through sincerity. The monstrous thing about the influential man is his making use of the sincerity, commitment, and total risk of his whole being through which he has been able to achieve influence, and which, it having been achieved, are mechanically reproduced in an a priori way." Thus wrote Pasolini in *Vie Nuove* on October 15, 1964, after less than a year's absence from the magazine. He had been traveling in search of locations and faces for the *Gospel According to Saint Matthew*; he had then shot the film, and had worked on it with such intensity and absorption as to leave him very little room for anything else.

He wrote this way, seeking "better to find the point where authority and sincerity coincide." But this point seemed to him to have been gained already through his own contradictions—"after all, I am protected by my contradictions" (words that follow shortly thereafter on the same page of *Vie Nuove*).

What is there to add? That he was conscious of being unable to avoid the incurable conflict between sincerity and bad faith except through the systematic practice of contradiction. This could already have been further proof of how far it was impossible for him to escape the vicious circle of existential bad faith.

Pier Paolo could also be accused of bad faith in smaller matters. This was the accusation leveled at him by Alfredo Bini during the harsh quarrel that was re-evoked in the lines of "E l'Africa?"—the poem on the myths of the father, which I have already had occasion to quote.

The court trial over *La ricotta* had ended badly. The producers found themselves in difficulty. Court gossip also attributed the verdict to a desire for revenge on the part of the judges, who had felt offended by a character in the film, the insolent interviewer of Orson Welles, named Pedoti. There had been a magistrate named Pedote from the prosecutor's office in Rome, who in questioning Pier Paolo during previous proceedings had behaved in a particularly insidious way.

Pier Paolo, perhaps inspired by the lingering case of Deputy Pagliuca, who was harassing him in those months, wanted jokingly to get even. He gave the name Pedote to the character in the script, then later changed it to Pedoti.

In his summation, Public Prosecutor Di Gennaro did not fail to point this out. Turning to the judges, he said, "Just think of the malice of introducing the character of Pedoti, who is Pedote in the script."

Bini had asked Pier Paolo to avoid the allusion, and Pier Paolo had paid no attention. When the guilty verdict was in, Bini's anger exploded.

In this case, however, it may not have been so much a question of bad faith as of the ironical delight in retorting to his opponents in which Pier Paolo persistently indulged.

This time the delight was costly. It cost him the chance to make the African film he had been planning, *Il padre selvaggio* (The Savage Father)—a script in which he had superimposed his old pedagogic passion on his growing passion for the Third World.

AFRICA! SOLE ALTERNATIVE . . .

Pier Paolo had uttered his first cry, his first invocation of Africa, in "Frammento alla morte," a poem written in 1960.

Beyond his rationalism, beyond his irrationalism—everything having been tried, "to the end"—there remained "the desert deafened / by the wind, the marvelous and foul / African sun that illuminates the world."

This was the first seed of a new hope. "Poor Italy," with its burden of particular, rural, Christian histories, was like Europe heading for shipwreck. What did the future hold?

In the sixties Pier Paolo began to travel systematically. It was the cinema adventure that led him to break out of his provincial "Italian" shell. His trips were usually occasioned by some pretext: an inspection tour, a landscape to be gone over inch by inch so as later to create it through the camera. Or else the showing of one of his films at an international festival.

On the other hand, the trip to India, in December 1960 and January 1961, was undertaken with no commitments. Pier Paolo and Moravia left together, and Elsa Morante joined them along the way. This was a trip to which Pier Paolo devoted a book, *L'odore dell'India*, in which he brought together the notes he had kept and had published in installments in *Il Giorno*.

Moravia has never had much patience with the Christmas and New Year's holidays in Italy, and this attitude leads him to avoid the air of festivity that infects Catholic and Protestant countries on those days. He takes refuge in Africa or the Orient, where Christmas either does not exist at all, or exists in forms that remain naïve and archaically barbaric. Pier Paolo joined him, and between them there was a journalistic contest. Moravia too published his notes, to which in his unflagging rationalism he gave the title *Un'idea dell'India*.

For Pier Paolo this trip was a recognition of himself, a recognition of the endless, swarming misery of the *bidonvilles* of Bombay and Calcutta as something known and ancient. Also the recognition in the gestures of the Indians of a familiar, or familiarly comprehensible, style.

The head goes up and down, as though slightly detached from the neck, and the shoulders too waver a little, with the gesture of a young girl who overcomes her modesty and fondly stands up. Seen at a distance, the Indian masses fix themselves in one's memory with that gesture of consent, and the childish and radiant smile in the eyes that accompanies it. Their religion is in that gesture.[6]

Poverty, its "odor," sweetish and dense—an intoxicating perfume for Pier Paolo. His travel notebook tells of intoxicated and odorous Indian nights, of dangerous nocturnal wandering in the company of boys, through dimly lighted alleyways, along arcades where the homeless curl up to sleep. "They are lying on the ground, against the columns, against the walls, against the door jambs. Their rags, waxy with filth, envelope them completely. Their sleep is so deep that they look like corpses wrapped in torn and fetid shrouds."[7]

The silence of the night is broken by melting dirges. Two young boys smile, "with their smiles of a solar whiteness at the bottom of their dark faces." Pier Paolo gives them a few rupees; one of them seizes his hand and kisses it. He leaves them, "as moved as a fool."[8]

Was this a journey toward the fevers of the Orient, similar perhaps to the one taken by the thirty-year-old Flaubert to Italy, Greece, Turkey, and Palestine? Or else similar to the other journey, meditative and creative, also made by Flaubert to Tunis at the time he conceived and wrote *Salammbô*? May not the *Gospel According to Saint Matthew*, but even more *Oedipus Rex, Medea*, and the *Arabian Nights*, be Pasolini's *Salammbô*?

In Flaubert there is the idea of a possible flight from the present, and there is the idea of the historical tapestry. In Pasolini the flight from the present involves, however, an adjustment of the past and its myths to the present.

Between Flaubert and Pasolini, in their experimentation with a psychological flight across geographical distance, both Freud and

Marx have intervened. For Pasolini, his trip to India was an occasion for an intoxication of the senses, but also for historical analysis.

"Let it be understood that, contrary to the legends, India has nothing mysterious about it. Basically we are dealing with a small country, with only four or five large cities, of which only one, Bombay, is worthy of the name; no industries, or almost none; very uniform and with simple stratifications and historical crystallizations. Essentially it is a question of an enormous agricultural subproletariat, frozen in its institutions for centuries by foreign domination, which has ensured that these institutions be preserved, and at the same time, due to so forced and unnatural a preservation, that they degenerate."[9]

Flaubert traveled in the direction of what was "different" and "unknown." In the world of the mass media, where one can have a remarkably precise idea of everything that exists, the "different" and the "unknown" are confronted for the sole purpose of winning them over to what one knows already, and denying them their reality.

In India Pasolini rediscovered the "agricultural subproletariat," its institutions having degenerated as a result of a "forced and unnatural preservation" caused by European imperialism. In India Pasolini again sought the sacredness of the human being attached to the soil. That human being is awaiting redemption, and he, in the presence of such expectation—a desperate expectation—is moved and loses himself. "One can lose one's way in the midst of this crowd of four hundred million souls, but lose it as in a puzzle, where with patience one can arrive at the end. The details are difficult, not the substance."[10] In India Pasolini was seized by an unquenchable desperation—it was to be a historical, social, and moral desperation.

From then on he made one journey after another. He went to Kenya in January 1961, and returned there a year later, passing through the Sudan. He spent the same months the next year in Ghana, Nigeria, and Guinea, and June and July in Israel and Jordan. It was at this time, 1963, that he planned to film the *Gospel* in the Third World, after having had to give up *Il padre selvaggio*.

He had the idea that "Negritude . . . will be the way."[11] One might say that in him an old cultural dream—exoticism—donned progressive clothes. And it was true—progressivism was followed closely in his heart by the decadent enigmas of forgetfulness and oblivion.

Do they accuse him of being a "populist"? He answers yes, he is. "If [one] uses the term populist in the sense that the word has now currently assumed, i.e., in the sense of 'a Marxist who loves the people with a love pre-existent to Marxism or partly outside it,' then . . . I could even accept the definition." But Pasolini takes pains to demonstrate that this love of his does not rule out a political view of things: "At this moment, when neocapitalism tends either to put the working-class elites to sleep (in a state of resignation that is by no means the evangelical one!) or else to make them become rigid in hard-line positions . . . it is obvious that the problem of the—immense—southern subproletariat is placed in a new light: a ripe and virgin mass, ready to be called to its historical function."[12]

The destiny of the Italian southern subproletariat is the same as that of the subproletariats of India and Africa—the performance of a historical function. And India and Africa are huge reservoirs of human energy. Therefore Africa became the "sole alternative."

Under the sign of that "alternative," there loomed in Pier Paolo's mind the face of a peasant and rebel Christ, a Christ who brings the *good news* but also wages war on Pharisees of every kind, and who destroys preconceptions with "force" and "meekness."

INSPECTION TOURS

The *Gospel According to Saint Matthew* took a long time to prepare, and its path was strewn with difficulties. It was not easy to "mount" the film. Alfredo Bini expended a great deal of energy, but it seemed from the beginning that the project was doomed to failure. It was a complex, costly film, which moreover aroused great suspicion among potential backers. How to present to public opinion a "Pasolinian" Christ?

The idea, in the eyes of many, was ambiguous and rash. But Pier Paolo's ambiguous rashness constituted a strength—he was capable of doing persuasive violence to his public. Now after the long series of court trials he had undergone, he saw himself forced to make a decisive step, one that by a surprise move would gain him the interest, if not the favor, of the more hostile part of the public.

The surprise was the *Gospel*. Pier Paolo was not to betray his natural culture; rather, he would restore it to its explicit truth. The accusations of blasphemy to which *La ricotta* had exposed him would, in the presence of his *Gospel*, show their clericalism and lack of foundation. The sentiment of his faith lay elsewhere.

"For myself, I am anticlerical (I'm certainly not afraid to say so!), but I know that in me there are two thousand years of Christianity. I with my ancestors built the Romanesque churches, and then the Gothic churches, and then the Baroque churches—they are my heritage, in content and style. It would be foolish for me to deny such a potent force in myself."[13]

This certainty, which is unmistakably anthropological and cultural, was to impart life to a restored mask. Pasolini's pedagogy became embodied in the supreme Mediterranean myth: Christ.

As I have said, the preparation of the film was slow and difficult. During the delays, Pier Paolo worked and went searching for locations. In the beginning, his Christ was an African, an expression of his need for an irresistible modernization of the myth. Christ was the true "savage father." But logic then suggested that only by scrupulously respecting historical truth would the film, appearing over Pasolini's name, gain the margin of acceptance that was hoped for. The landscape, therefore, had to be Palestine. But in a besieged Israel, in a permanent state of war, it was no simple matter to shoot a film, nor was it economically feasible.

Meanwhile, Pier Paolo had been working on something else: an early montage film, *La rabbia* (Rage), whose execution closely parallels *La ricotta*.

La rabbia originated in a clever scheme of the producer Gastone Ferrante, who thought of placing Giovanni Guareschi, exemplifying the facile indifference of the average man to social and political issues, alongside Pasolini, in a duet that in his view audiences were sure to find exciting. It would be a film in which the two of them, from their reciprocal points of view, would "comment" on the decade that had just ended.

Guareschi had been sent to prison for "aggravated and repeated slander" of Alcide De Gasperi. For Pasolini to place his name next to Guareschi's meant to go along with the arguments of his adversaries, to whom he himself, though of the left, was nothing but a figure of scandal.

Pier Paolo was thoughtless enough to consent to such an arrangement. When the whole film was ready and he screened it, he withdrew his approval and prevented its circulation—he called himself the victim of his own "naïveté." This produced attacks on him from all sides. As for his "naïveté," people again spoke, and indeed from the left, of bad faith, or of a double truth impossible to carry out:[14] Pasolini, they said, greets the new center-left government with verses dedicated to Pietro Nenni (this earned him attacks by the Communists).[15] Pasolini salutes the ecclesiastical revival embodied in John

XXIII. But he also makes a film with Guareschi, and only at the moment when it is about to be released to the public does he realize his mistake.

Pier Paolo had thought that the force of his words would be sufficient to cancel out Guareschi's vulgarity. This was his real, almost unforgivable "naïveté"—an intellectual presumption that was put to rout by the completed work. The medium, in McLuhan's words, coincided with the message. The film, whatever its content might have been, was summed up in the two paired names, and the hyphen that joined them.

What is *La rabbia*? A poem through images, a prose poem joined together by photographic exhibits. There is the 1956 crisis, Hungary and Suez. There are the great hopes of the early sixties: the papacy of Pope John, *détente*, Gagarin and his space flight. There are also the events of the "new prehistory": the martyrized face of Lumumba, the Algerian war, and the tortures practiced by the colonialists on innocent people seeking only civil and political liberty. At the end rises a poignant elegy for the death of Marilyn Monroe, symbol of a beauty now vanished from the world.

Those who saw the film disliked it for the underlying show of piety that colored its text—which was read on the soundtrack by Giorgio Bassani.

Pasolini countered the misfortune of *La rabbia* with a quite different undertaking, inspired by the French technique of *cinéma-vérité*: a film inquiry into the sexuality of the Italians. It was to be called *Cento paia di buoi* (A Hundred Pairs of Oxen), but later took the title of *Comizi d'amore*.

He raced all over Italy, movie camera and tape recorder in hand, asking people everywhere, from famous soccer players to unknown peasants in the Crotone region, what they thought about love and sex. The film is divided into sections, at the beginning of which questions are asked of Cesare Musatti and Alberto Moravia, or Giuseppe Ungaretti, and a group of three women journalists: Adele Cambria, Camilla Cederna, and Oriana Fallaci. The intellectuals comment, and the people speak, freely voicing their particular truths.

Comizi d'amore gives an unbiased picture of a changing Italy, and was a model for many later television documentaries. And yet what is striking is the presence on the screen of Pasolini himself—the film is his most dispassionate self-portrait. His stubborn pedagogy, his meekness that was violence and his violence that was meekness—the tone of insistence in his questions, his way of modulating them to suit his interlocutors, whether a mother, a recruit, a Sicilian youth, or two girls at a dance; then the unusual timbre of his voice, shielded behind a strict rationalism that seems not to be his. Unexpectedly, the film caught his physical appearance to perfection, the way he put on his glasses or wore his jacket draped over his shoulders.

For Alfredo Bini and Pier Paolo the film had a secret purpose: the opportunity to travel throughout Italy with an eye to filming the *Gospel* in one of its regions. From the producer's standpoint, this was the only way to overcome the staggering financial obstacles.

Crotone, Matera, Massafra—the locations for the *Gospel* were discovered in the course of this adventure.

There had been inspection tours in the Middle East as well,[16] these too filmed and arranged in a short documentary. But *Comizi d'amore* is also important as a photographic rendering of Italian faces and bodies, as visual experimentation with a human as well as scenic material that was to have its place, and not a secondary one, in the re-creation of the legend of Christ.

The Italian South, as though aesthetically destined for it, became the landscape of Judea and Galilee; the Lucanian peasants, scattered over the Sassi di Matera, were the crowd applauding Jesus of Nazareth's arrival in Jerusalem.

ACCORDING TO MATTHEW

A letter written by Pasolini in February 1963 to Lucio S. Caruso of the Pro Civitate Christiana of Assisi:

Dear Caruso, I should like to explain to you better, in writing, what I confusedly confided to you in conversation. The first time I visited all of you in Assisi, I found the Gospels at my bedside: your delightful and diabolical calculation! And indeed everything went as it was supposed to: I reread them after some twenty years (it was in 1940 or 1941, when as a boy I read them for the first time, and what came out of it was *L'usignolo della Chiesa Cattolica*. Later I read them only intermittently, a passage here, a passage there, as one does). That day, at your place, I read them from beginning to end, like a novel. And in the exaltation of reading—as you know, it's the most exalting thing one can read!—there came to me, among other things, the idea of making a film . . . As the days and later the weeks went by, this idea kept getting more overwhelming and exclusive. It threw in the shade all the other ideas for work I had in my head, it weakened and devitalized them. And it alone

remained, alive and thriving within me . . . My idea is this: to follow the *Gospel According to Saint Matthew** point by point, without making a script or adaptation of it. To translate it faithfully into images, following its story without any omissions or additions. The dialogue too should be strictly that of Saint Matthew, without even a single explanatory or connecting sentence, because no image or inserted word could ever attain the poetic heights of the text . . . To put it very simply and frankly, I don't believe that Christ is the son of God, because I am not a believer— at least not consciously. But I believe that Christ is divine: I believe, that is, that in him humanity is so lofty, strict, and ideal as to exceed the common terms of humanity. For this reason, I say "poetry"—an irrational instrument to express this irrational feeling of mine for Christ. I would like it if my film could be shown on Easter Sunday in all the parish cinemas in Italy and the world. This is why I need your assistance and support. I should not want my creative needs, my poetic inspiration, ever to run up against your sensitivity as believers. Because in that case I should never achieve my purpose of holding up again to everyone a life that is a model—albeit impossible to reach—for everyone.[17]

It had happened in October 1962. Pier Paolo, as a guest in Assisi of the Cittadella established by Don Giovanni Rossi, and while around him blazed, "muffled, extraneous, and basically hostile, the celebration for the Pope's arrival," read the Gospels—and felt "an immediate need to 'do something'—a terrible, almost physical energy."[18] The explanation he gives of this feeling is "aesthetic"—he felt overcome by that "increase in vitality" that the work of poetry (according to Bernard Berenson) arouses.

This was his immediate thought, and expressing it as he does, he does not quite deny that it may be a question of a poetical—and secular—stroke of lightning "on the road to Damascus."

Such an involvement in Jesus—irrationally, unconsciously—moved within him in two directions. On the one hand, his investment of himself—persecuted, brought to trial, also fired by an inscrutable need for expiation—in the figure of Christ. On the other, the re-creation on film, already hinted at in *La ricotta*, of "Christian" ideas and values that had accompanied him, as though on the sly, ever since the years of his adolescence and youth.

The letter to Caruso is wholly sincere, both in expressing the sense of his own personal, poetic religiosity, and in its request for help from

* "The distributors introduced 'Saint' into the title, against Pasolini's express wishes. The word 'joyful' (*lieta*) was also cut from the dedication to John XXIII."

the Pro Civitate Christiana. When the picture was finished and a *Vie Nuove* reader asked him polemically how he was able to combine Marxism and Christianity, Pier Paolo replied by citing Gramsci: "The religious idea does not constitute a reason for division in the working class, just as it does not constitute a reason for division in the bourgeois class. . . . This lack in the religious idea of motivations for division holds good in all cases. If it is legitimate for you to identify a historical moment of the Church with the exploiting class, this does not mean that you can always do so. . . . The Pope has removed the mitre from his head and given it to the poor, raising loud applause among all the advanced bishops and cardinals who think of the Church as the Church of the poor."[19]

Outside of the climate created by John XXIII and the Second Vatican Council—a climate that was still alive in the early days of Paul VI's pontificate—it is impossible to understand the motivations, not only individual but objective, that led to the realization of a film like the *Gospel According to Saint Matthew*.

Elsa Morante was enthusiastic about the project. Pier Paolo asked her to help in selecting music for the soundtrack and in the choice of faces.

Elsa, for her part, made a broad selection of records, from Bach and Mozart to such contemporaries as Leos Janácek, and submitted them to Pier Paolo. There were lengthy discussions.

Also long and tiring were the discussions over the actors. Some were found among intellectual friends, others in the shantytowns. Alfonso Gatto, Giorgio Agamben, Ferruccio Nuzzo, and Elsa's nephew Giacomo Morante appeared as some of the apostles; I too played one of them. Leonetti played Herod II; Rodolfo Wilcock, Caiaphas; Mario Socrate, John the Baptist; Elsa's brother Marcello Morante, Saint Joseph. Natalia Ginzburg portrayed Mary of Bethany, and in the scene in which she appeared, her husband was naturally played by her real husband, Gabriele Baldini.

It was more difficult to find the actor to play Christ, but he finally appeared in the person of Enrique Irazoqui, a Spanish student from Barcelona. Irazoqui was a student of economics, and had read *Ragazzi di vita* in translation; arriving in Rome on vacation, he wanted to meet the author and asked Pier Paolo for an appointment. Pier Paolo, who had even been thinking of offering the role to Yevgeny Yevtushenko, decided on Irazoqui the moment he set eyes on him. Some people said he looked as though he had stepped out of a canvas by El Greco, and that iconographically this was too remote from

Pasolini's visual style. But Pier Paolo was right—Enrique's penetrating gaze, darkened by a bridled anger, constituted the originality in Pasolini's conception of Christ.

Concrete assistance was accordingly given the film by the Pro Civitate Christiana of Assisi, to which, in November 1959, the papal brief of John XXIII had assigned the goal of "leading society back to the principles of the Gospels."

This assistance was an act of courage. Many, in the cinema world and in the Church, judged the enterprise insane. Controversy flared. The Cittadella in Assisi replied:

We have had an excellent impression of Pier Paolo Pasolini, as we have of everyone whom we have the good fortune to approach. Indeed in every human face we see reflected the wonderful face of the Lord. . . . To all those who tell us that Pasolini is not only an unbeliever but a sinner as well, we humbly reply that, even if true, this does not seem to us any reason to shut the door in his face and deny him the help he has asked us for. Jesus loved everyone but had a preference for publicans, sinners, thieves, and even poor creatures who had fallen into the most anguishing moral misery, such as the Magdalen, the woman taken in adultery, the woman of Samaria. To certain kinds of attacks we have not responded, since the Pro Civitate Christiana is not in the habit of engaging in controversy. We have, however, submissively observed that if all of us were truly Christian, on each human sore we would not pour vinegar but the oil of kindness. Jesus died to help everyone, to save everyone . . .[20]

To these "evangelical" reasons, others of a "practical" nature were added. A political and cultural principle was being diffused among Catholics: the use of the cinema, a use not propagandistic but evangelical. The resolutions of the Ecumenical Council stated that the mass media, "if properly used," would contribute "enormous benefits . . . to the human family." The Pro Civitate Christiana clarified the Council's reference: "Now the cinema can assume the role played in past centuries by the so-called 'Bible of the poor'—that is, large frescoes, sculptures, and in short all of sacred art."[21]

In a letter to Bini, in June 1963, Pier Paolo wrote:

From the religious standpoint, I, who have always tried to recover the characteristics of religiosity from my laicism, find validity in two ingenuously ontological facts: Christ's humanity is driven by such an inner strength, such an unquenchable thirst for knowledge and for verification of that knowledge, without fear of any scandal or any contradiction, that for it the metaphor "divine" almost ceases to be a metaphor and becomes ideally a reality. Furthermore, beauty for me is always a "moral beauty," but this beauty always comes to us indirectly, through poetry, or philosophy, or practice. The only case of "moral beauty" in my experience that is not indirect but immediate, in the pure state, is the Gospels.

As for my relation to the Gospels, it is a rather curious one. You perhaps know that, as a writer whose ideas were born from the Resistance, as a Marxist, etc., my ideological effort throughout the fifties was toward rationality, as opposed to the irrationalism of decadent literature (on which I was raised and which I loved so much). The idea of making a film on the Gospels, and the technical intuition that goes with it, are instead, I must confess, the fruit of a furious wave of irrationalism. I want to create a pure work of poetry, risking even the perils of aestheticism (Bach and Mozart as musical accompaniment; Piero della Francesca and in part Duccio for pictorial inspiration; the basically pre-historic and exotic reality of the Arab world as background and setting). All this once again calls my whole career as a writer dangerously into question, I know. But it would be a fine thing if, loving the Christ of Matthew as I do with all my heart, I should then be afraid to call something into question.[22]

The *Gospel According to Saint Matthew* represented a decisive process of creative discarding—the writer was going through the crisis of *Poesia in forma di rosa*. The irrational side of his sensibility was simultaneously besieged by two opposing urges, a demand for subjective testimony and for the obliteration of subjectivity in a transfiguring embrace with life.

Despite this, or by dint of it, he shared the conviction that the cinema was a potential "Bible of the poor"—and to this end he worked.

Pier Paolo went several times to Assisi. The laity of the Cittadella, and Don Giovanni Rossi himself, took an interest in his work. It was also being followed by two Jesuits from the Centro di San Fedele, and the theologian Romano Guardini, who expressed a systematic lack of confidence in the possibility of representing Jesus through an actor. The writer Stefan Andres was sometimes present at the discussions.

Filming of the *Gospel* began in early spring of 1964. The first frames shot were those of the baptism of Jesus—and the Jordan river was "found" between Orte and Viterbo, in a cleft hollowed out by a stream between stark and forbidding rocks. It was on that occasion that Pier Paolo discovered the tower of Chia, with which he literally fell in love. He decided to buy it, but it took him quite a number of years to do so. In Chia, amid the bold and pleasant landscape of upper

Lazio with its pervasive and archaic melancholy, Pier Paolo was to build a house for his periods of seclusion, beneath an isolated and seemingly inaccessible medieval ruin.

After the baptism, the next sequence to be filmed was the Mount of Olives, at a spot halfway up the hill between Hadrian's Villa and Tivoli. Then the troupe left for Matera and Crotone.

Pier Paolo did not ask the "actors" (and, unlike Franco Citti after *Accattone*, none of them were to become such) to perform. He asked only for their usual expression, whatever it might be. The frames were brief and mostly silent. We worked all day—Pier Paolo was tireless. He kept telling his actors not to worry: "The movie lens is truth serum. You'll come out as what you are, and that's all I care about."

The temptations of the devil were filmed on Mount Etna. The most difficult sequence was the one of the discourse on the Beatitudes. Finally, in the very last days of filming, Pier Paolo resolved it by a series of closeups of Irazoqui taken in the studio against a dark background, his face lighted in flashes—a solution that seemed to him extemporaneous and makeshift, and that instead, once the cutting was done, turned out to be highly original.

The choice of one face was symptomatic—that of Susanna to play the Madonna, convulsed by grief on Golgotha beneath the cross bearing her son. Pier Paolo "wrote," imagined, and visually created his own *Stabat Mater* for her. This choice was a declarative and loving gesture, but it also marks the expression of an archaic Christianity, almost unattainable by reason—to interpret the figure of Mary of Nazareth as the "unique" mother, identifiable only as one's own.

Pier Paolo spent the whole summer editing the film. On September 4, 1964, the *Gospel According to Saint Matthew* was presented at the Twenty-fourth International Film Festival in Venice. It was not a quiet evening. The fascists staged their usual uproar, hurling leaflets and insults at the spectators. They assaulted among others the painter Renato Guttuso and Paolo Valmarana, film critic for the Christian Democratic newspaper *Il Popolo*.

The showing of the film ended with long, warm applause.

Felice Chilanti wrote of the evening:

That evening, that occasion, saw the formation of an incredible point of intersection to which flowed various and opposed philosophies; irreconcilable political forces and interests found themselves so close together on that point as to merge, a little, among themselves. Only the fascists stood out distinctly; they were alone, and they spoke and gesticulated alone. At the end of the evening, even certain persons who did not speak alone no longer knew what to believe, nor how to think about it. The event that had taken place was—as we know—the showing of a film derived from the Gospels, announced as a faithful representation of that story and in the spirit of it, directed by a writer who a few hours before the showing had, in speaking with reporters, repeated that he was a Marxist and therefore also an atheist.

Among the individuals who turned out to be in difficult circumstances let us not forget the chief of police, who thought to deal with the conflicts and political and ideological contradictions of the event by tripling the number of policemen and carabinieri on duty in front of the Palazzo del Cinema. And so that evening even rich gentlemen in tuxedos and ladies in gala evening gowns, adorned with jewels and protected by fur coats, had, like the intellectuals, writers, critics, and actors, to file past the gaze of those armed guards, in the blinding light of the TV reflectors.[23]

Dedicated "to the dear, happy, familiar shade of John XXIII," the film was cited by the OCIC, the international Catholic cinema office. The citation explained: "The author, who is said not to share our faith, has given proof in his choice of texts and scenes of respect and delicacy. He has made a fine film, a Christian film that produces a profound impression."

Chilanti's words clarify the nature of the success achieved by Pasolini—a success that gained applause from opposed ideological and political camps. Only the fascists remained isolated. And Chilanti tells us that even they, when the showing was over, felt obliged to restrain themselves

Not everything was resolved during that evening in Venice, nor with the release of the *Gospel According to Saint Matthew*, but by now it was clear to all that the work of Pasolini, writer and director, was to be taken seriously, and involved problems of deep moral significance.

Pasolini is naïve, and at the same time highly unconventional. He is full of instincts and passions, and at the same time loaded with culture. He oozes with all the desires, and remembers at the same time all the books he has read, and he has read them all. . . . This is all right, and even this should cause no trouble. The trouble is simply that he makes no effort, but really none whatsoever, I don't say to achieve, but not even to set out in the direction of, a composition, a synthesis. The Peter and the Paul in him, it seems, can never merge into a single name. The two senses of religion, the natural and evolutive one (Peter) and the dogmatic one (Paul) seem, in him, destined for an agonizing perennial separation: agonizing because Pasolini's talent is very great and cannot but suffer from it; perennial because his unwillingness is equally great, or rather his absolute lack of will to overcome this fundamental Manicheism, and to seek, even from afar, even whimsically, some kind of unity.[24]

Mario Soldati, in reviewing the *Gospel*, thus singled out Pasolini's systematic contradictoriness. Let us say that the film's lyricism has roots in ambiguity, in superimposing little by little, frame by frame, reason on faith, using as a solvent a creatural idea of life—that idea of mortal suffering as seen and described by Spitzer and Auerbach in the early poetic romances of Europe. But this unabated paling of sentiment may have been the reason for doubt and even rejection by a part of the audience.

The rejection came from Franco Fortini, who wrote to Pier Paolo on October 19, 1964. He spoke of his identification with the film "beyond tears," but added:

This Pierpaolo-Jesus lacks the central point of Christianity, i.e., the necessity of the cross, and so is reduced to "humanism," to Christian socialism, in short to pastiche. Christ is not Salvatore Carnevale, nor Giordano Bruno or Fra Michele the Franciscan; or else he was, historically, but then he is not God, and one should say so.

What is Fortini's accusation? That Pier Paolo was trying to "have it both ways." And again:

I would urge you to be humble. . . . You enjoy the invective of this Jesus too much. It cannot (nor can I) help you. . . . I don't know if you'll understand the intention of this letter. I bear you a grudge, because your public life shows the signs of ugly and also clumsy calculation; I am angry, because of the objective (i.e., counterrevolutionary) evil that your public aspects have helped to create; I have the hope that you may contradict yourself to the point of wanting to contradict yourself no longer, the hope that you may, as that fellow said, "die (but really) and become." I prefer to entrust my affection to cold-blooded words. It's not enough, dear Pierpaolo, to scorn adulation; one must deserve it.

Fortini signed himself "your friend." To Pier Paolo it seemed that this friend was the victim of an irreducible "moralism," and that such moralism contained in itself conspicuous "counterrevolutionary" dangers.

But Fortini's letter clearly sets forth an attitude and a judgment, those of people who no longer cared to understand what in Pasolini was desperately essential and determining, "the thorn in the flesh"— that "thorn" without which, as Kierkegaard said, he would have been dead. And, in Pasolini, the "thorn," by analogy, was the reason for the crucifixion of his Christ.

THE REPUDIATION OF THE "RIDICULOUS DECADE"

Pasolini kept a poetic diary of these years, and he collected it in *Poesia in forma di rosa* (Poetry in the Form of a Rose). The book appeared in the stores in the late spring of 1964.

It was a diary broken up into narrated events in some parts, into expressions of ideology in others. There is the diary of the trial over *La ricotta*—its title is "Pietro II," the name of the last of the pontiffs according to legend, signifying the downfall of "true religion" under the blows of clericalism. There is the diary of *Mamma Roma*, with the title "Poesie mondane" (Worldly Poems), and of the tours of Israel and the Italian South for the *Gospel*. There is the "Progetto di opere future" (Plan for Future Works), and the testimony of a discussion with Leonetti and Calvino in "Poesia in forma di rosa." And, of course, still more.

Technically speaking, the tercet prevails in the first part, but disappears in the second. It is replaced by the loose hendecasyllable, then by rhythmic prose, and by geometric arrangements on the page in "Libro delle croci" (Book of Crosses) and "Nuova poesia in forma di rosa."

An angry and sorrowing tone hangs over it, and the prophecy is obscure, anguished. It is the feeling of life itself that here seems to be emaciated.

Life gets tired of one who endures.

Ah, my recidivist passions
forced to have no dwelling place!

Of these passions, sex is still inescapable:

I, dark with love, and all around me the chorus

of the happy, to whom reality is a friend.
They are legion. I cannot love just one.
Each has his new, his old

beauty, which belongs to all: dark
or blond, light or heavy, what I love in him
is the world. . . .[25]

The feeling for that kind of sex that is "pure sensuality," repeated in the "secret valleys of lust, / sadistic, masochistic," is a steady one—it is a sacred gesture. He does not seek the individual, he seeks "the enchantment of the species," "the rule whereby sons become fond fathers"—and they

little by little
have become stone monuments
thronging my solitude by the thousands.[26]

From sex to friendship: with the margins of existence blurred, his friends exchange faces and appear as players in a dreamlike "soccer match":

Giorgio running has the face of Carlo Levi,
propitious divinity, making an upset,
Giannetto has the hilarity of Moravia, the Moor
returning the ball is Vigorelli, when he gets mad or hugs you,
and Coen, and Alicata, and Elsa Morante, and the editors
of Paese Sera or Avanti!, and Libero Bigaretti,
they play with me, among the Trullo trees,
some defending, others on the offensive. Others,
with Pedalino in the orange jersey
or Ugo in last year's blue jeans faded in front,
are leaning against the honey-colored prison walls
of their houses, Benedetti, Debenedetti, Nenni,
Bertolucci with his face a little whitened by the sun
under the floppy brim of his hat, and the soft grin
of holy certainty of the uncertain.
And next to a sunlit garbage heap stands Ungaretti, laughing.
And the young ones, brothers and sisters to the Trullo youths,
Siciliano, Dacia, Garboli, Bertolucci *fils*; and, like Sordello,
disapproving and enamored, Citati. And who is that

on that plot of soil with a pink tin can and a yellow stump?
Baldini and Natalia. And within a courtyard cut
by light as in a Caravaggesque painter with no black tones, Longhi,
Anna Banti, with Gadda and Bassani. Roversi and Leonetti
and Fortini get off at the bus stop,
with greetings from Contini and some German sociologist . . .[27]

Friendships are not lost, but despair annihilates perception, sharpens the feeling of isolation, and in isolation the tragedy of error grows.

I've been wrong about everything.
He was wrong, frightened at the microphone,
with the overbearing uncertainty of the bad,

the gentle poet, that namesake of mine
who still bears my name.
He was called Egoism, Passion.

He was wrong, with his stammering bravura . . .[28]

The feeling of error, in this "skinny little Hercules of literature" (his words), becomes obsessive. But error about what? An error of historical judgment—and his individual despair grows ("a cry in heaven where my cradle rocked") as historical and social despair.

Not one of the problems of the fifties matters any more to Pasolini —he rejects "the livid moralists who have made of socialism an equally boring Catholicism." Ideology is "a drug." In short, his cry is: "I REPUDIATE THE RIDICULOUS DECADE!"[29]

In this despair, persecutions and trials no longer seem to count, except as confirmation. What counts is the certainty that the "industrial pact" cannot be "resisted":

Nothing can resist it: can't you see how weak
the defense of laymen friends or Communists
sounds against the vilest news reports?

Intelligence will never carry any weight, never,
in the judgment of this public opinion . . .[30]

Intelligence dies, and "irreality" devours space—physical and moral space. The "New Prehistory" appears threateningly on the other side —"it's about to die, / the idea of man that appears in the great mornings / of Italy or India, intent on his little task." Perhaps something else, in Italy, India, or Africa, will be able to be born and to produce an alternative, a cheerful hope. But this is a very brief, fleeting hope.

> Didn't you know? At the
> very same time as the Baroque of Neocapitalism
> the New Prehistory begins.[31]

No more hopes: the individual is ever more enclosed in his shell. The path of the future has no alternatives—it will be that of "opposition":

> The opposition of one who cannot
> *be loved by anyone, and can love no one,* and therefore
> tenders his love as a foregone
> no, the exercise of his political
> duty as the exercise of reason.[32]

"Crucified on his agonizing rationality," Pasolini, "consumed by puritanism," realizes that he has no other fate but that of an "aristocratic, and alas unpopular, opposition."

The first systematic appearance of the puritan, "pirate," and "heretic" writer—the future author of *Scritti corsari* and *Lettere luterane*—is in *Poesia in forma di rosa.*

What then was the source of his despair, since it went beyond mere personal limits?

There may also have been personal reasons. For example, the last literary controversies, those of the new avant-garde, epiphany of neocapitalism within the citadel of literature.

The polemics of the 63 Group, in support of an idea of literature that was wholly antirational and took no part in history, tended to push Pasolini back to the margins of Italian cultural life—along with Moravia, Cassola, and Bassani, all of them writers who had achieved their best work in the previous decade.

Pasolini—and he was not the only one—tried to regain his position. He made this attempt with Leonetti and Calvino (as attested by the colloquy explained in the poem that gives its title to the book *Poesia in forma di rosa*), and with Vittorini. Vittorini, through *Il Menabò*, was trying to break down the opposition between tradition and the avant-garde—he raised the possibility of a style which, while no longer humanistic, would be able to interpret the unexpected dynamics of the industrial world.

The idea shared by Leonetti, Calvino, and Pasolini was different, broader than Vittorini's. It was to combine with the work of *Il Menabò* whatever innovations had been achieved in European literature, and to transform the magazine into an international organ of culture and knowledge.

Ah, a system of signs
laughingly worked out with Leonetti and Calvino

at the usual stopover in the North.
Signs for deaf-mutes, with ideographs
once and for all international.[33]

The experiment occupied the whole seventh issue of *Il Menabò*, under the heading "Gulliver"—a single issue, with a wide variety of contributors.[34] But the result was unimpressive, too composite, divergent, like an anthology. And there was no sequel.

The new avant-garde had been proposing close ties with any European literature similar to itself. The "Gulliver" experiment, in some way rivaling it, showed that such ties could not be achieved merely by amassing names. And as a solution to the significant problems plaguing Italian literature, it must have seemed insignificant and disappointing to Pasolini.

What interested him were not such compilations, but, again like Gramsci, the reacquisition of history, its reappropriation and not in the abstract—i.e., Italian history, its morality and its anthropology, its politics and its poetry, brought together in a realistic synthesis. Such a task was belittled by the literary debate then in progress—historicism, now considered a dry fruit, incapable of renewal, was increasingly giving way to sociology. Pasolini, on the other hand, obscurely tended toward historicism, with the weapons of linguistics and an instinctive anthropology.

It was a forced intellectual solitude, into which he saw himself anxiously being driven. Pier Paolo experienced years of vague despair, and in this despair, one "error" stood out: not to have foreseen the apocalypse that lay ahead. This was one reason for his repudiation of "the ridiculous decade." And yet he had been a central figure of that decade.

But another basis for this despair should be sought. The new avant-garde also considered the decade just previous as "ridiculous." Alberto Arbasino, in articles published to acclaim in *Il Giorno*, pilloried "the dismal fifties," in his judgment years of waste and distraction, of unsuccessful interpretations and nearsighted critical assessments.

These questions were the usual ones that any literature raises when it tries to supplant another. In essence, Pasolini's interests lay elsewhere—his eye saw through the literary surface to scrutinize the social dynamics underneath.

The fifties had also been years of violent political discrimination, suffocating censorship, and intolerance. This intolerance had not developed in a single direction, on the part of the clerical party against the laity and Marxists. Rather, it had infected the overwhelming majority of Catholics, Communists, and laymen. Nevertheless, the themes of freedom had been defended by the left in its entirety, which included Catholics, Communists, and laymen.

It was in those very years of political darkness that people became aware that civil rights had to be tenaciously won and defended, and that the letter of the Constitution had to be tenaciously defended in order to be implemented.

For the growth of this awareness, the culture of those "dismal" years (Arbasino's adjective) was an active catalyst. If Italian culture, a broad alignment of men of letters, experienced a happy period, that period was written between 1948 and the beginning of the sixties. Pasolini repudiated it, but it was clear how much the hidden significance of that period was perpetuated as the face of the country changed.

The face of the country was turning ugly. The economic boom and the spread of the mass media were contributing to its barbarization. This was the striking aspect of the changes in progress. But these changes sowed different seeds—among other things, a collective, intangible sensitivization to problems of individual and social freedom.

Gross errors in political and economic planning—for which the nation was to pay a painful price in the seventies—ran parallel at that time to other decisions, almost as though the country were glowing with a hitherto unknown secular fervor. Such a modernization of the customs and habits of life seemed part and parcel of the success of the economic miracle, and the not merely aesthetic barbarization that went with it.

Pasolini heaped everything together in a negative judgment—he did not discriminate. By not discriminating, his mind included in the apocalypse both the ruling class, still inclined to exercise its privilege and will, and all those who did not belong to it and were slowly developing secular needs of freedom. In his imagination a few happy little islands remained exempt, the group of friends in the "soccer match," or a few Communists.

His pessimism thus ended in the "repudiation," the denunciation of an illusion, a utopia—and thereby of his own "error":

> Of the New
> Course of History
> — of which I know nothing — like
> one unauthorized to enter, a
> latecomer forever left outside —
> I understand only one thing . . .[35]

What remained? The "magma," "chance," and a "base petit-bourgeois whine":

> Thus
> I stripped a vain rose,
> the private rose of terror
> and sexuality, in the very years
> when I was required to be the partisan
> who neither confesses nor cries.[36]

What, finally, was the disillusionment? That the religion of the Churches he yearned for was betrayed. His maternal culture, a rural and Catholic culture (not the paternal one, bourgeois and after all decadent), prevented him from discerning in an Italy that was changing, albeit under contradictory guises, a laboratory of freedom.

"NINETTO IS A HERALD . . ."

For all his despair, there was in Pier Paolo considerable room for the joy of life. This joy became concrete in those years, when he met Ninetto Davoli.

In 1963 Ninetto was fifteen years old. The son of Calabrian peasants who had moved to Rome, he had lost all traces in his speech of his original Catanzaro dialect. His talk was Roman, shantytown Roman, inspired by the adulterated, composite dialect to which Pasolini had devoted so much attention.

In this young boy, with his slight and skinny build, pimples on his face, kinky hair, and incredibly "merry" eyes, there was a humanity that differed from the cynical and relaxed attitude that constituted the morality of the ordinary shantytown dweller.

In Ninetto, the histrionic and comic vitality of the Calabrian peasant boy was reborn—and it is a trait that has almost been lost, Calabrian peasants having by now become so few and far between.

Pier Paolo came to know Ninetto at the time he was preparing the *Gospel According to Saint Matthew*. Some lines dated 1965 tell how they met:

Look, here into the orchestra comes a madman, with soft
and merry eyes,
dressed like the Beatles.
While great thoughts and great actions
are implied in the relation of these rich people to the film spectacle,
made for him *too*, he, twirling one thin finger like a merry-go-
round horse,
writes his name "Ninetto"
on the back of the velvet seat (under a little long-eared nape
associated with rules of behavior and the idea of the free
bourgeoisie).
Ninetto is a herald,
and overcoming (with a sweet laugh
that blazes from his whole being
as in a Muslim or a Hindu)
his shyness,
he introduces himself as in an Areopagus
to speak of the Persians.
The Persians, he says, are massing on the frontiers.
But millions and millions of them have already peacefully
immigrated,
they are here, waiting for the No. 12, the No. 13, the No. 409 tram
of the Stefer line. What beautiful Persians!
God has just sketched them, in their youth,
like the Muslims or the Hindus:

they have the short lineaments of animals,
gaunt cheekbones, flattened or upturned little noses,
long long eyelashes, curly hair . . .[37]

Pier Paolo fell in love with him. He fell in love as a father, as a friend, sweeping away the tie of competitiveness that occasionally bound him to boys. It was an obsessive competitiveness, not enamored, only erotic, which he cherished for "the chorus of the happy, to whom reality is a friend." In that chorus, he did not single out faces, only bodies.

Ninetto, however, had a face, and a voice. His voice was raucous, his physicality pliant and emaciated. His histrionics had a melancholy tinge and conveyed from the depths an inexpressible emotional anxiety. Pier Paolo fell in love with all this.

Ninetto also embodied a myth: the myth of the Rome besieged by "Persians," by "barbarians," to the southeast of the urban belt, at the farthest ends of the Prenestino tram lines. This boy was an innocent "barbarian."

Again, the Third World at the gates, the Muslims, the Hindus. What did the future hold in store? In the barbarians, who were ingenuously so, Pasolini loved their raw, unconscious elegance. This elegance was an enchantment for his eyes, for his mannerist sensibility. His love for Ninetto was able to take on the tones of such aestheticism.

But the relationship was also open and direct. Ninetto liked the Beatles and the singer Adriano Celentano, bright-colored jerseys and mod boots. He enjoyed all the pop glitter that the consumer society scattered around itself like an alluring aura. Pier Paolo found himself caught up in this form of joy. He accompanied Ninetto to the Piper, the rock club of Rome, a discovery of the sixties, where cutting loose on the dance floor were not only young people of every variety and extraction, but even Moravia, Arbasino, Sandro De Feo, and Mario Pannunzio.

Did his passion for Ninetto interrupt Pier Paolo's compulsive nightly "cruising"? Did it draw him away from his lust for anonymous sex?

The perilous forays continued. Both in Rome and during the trips to Africa and the Middle East, Alfredo Bini and the production director, Eliseo Boschi, summoned more than once by a telephone call or by intuition, had to rush off and rescue Pier Paolo from this or that sinister adventure. And sometimes, in Rome as well as Africa, they found him injured and bleeding.[38]

Risk formed part of the erotic picture, as a challenge to his own courage, or a holy demand for punishment ("sadistic" and "masochistic" lust, as he wrote in *Poesia in forma di rosa*). His love for Ninetto was another matter. It was the truly loving compensation that Pier Paolo asked of himself after his nightly journey into the darkness.

Ninetto thus became the "herald" of joy, the incarnation of a peasant Ariel. He became so at once, on the set of the *Gospel*. Pier Paolo kept him at his side, a sort of Shakespearean fool, in whose innocence he noted the breath of a truth that was hidden from others.

Later Ninetto grew up and fell in love with girls. At first Pier Paolo was delighted, then he began to suffer. But with this we are already in the realm of another chapter.

CHAPTER 10

TEOREMA

THE NEW HOUSE

I go in search of the house of my burial,
making the rounds of the city like an inmate
of an asylum or rest home

out on a pass, with my face deformed
by fever, dry white skin and beard . . .[1]

The house, at Via Eufrate 9, was purchased in the spring of 1963. An apartment above street level, a terrace garden, wide French doors, a new building—a balustrade facing the Magliana valley, in the direction of the sea at Ostia; on the right, Rome with the cupola of Saint Peter's in the distance.

It was the EUR quarter, the most distant residential suburb, with quiet, tree-lined streets. The garden, the tranquillity, were dedicated to Susanna—the house was a gift to her.

By May 1963 the apartment was already furnished and inhabited. In furnishing it Pier Paolo was helped by his uncle the antiquary. But the choice, for example, of a nineteenth-century English lamp for the living room, a brass affair with several arms, led to much discussion among some of his friends, Moravia declaring reproachfully that Pier Paolo's taste, unerring on the film set—as in the case of *La ricotta*, where Pontormo and Rosso Fiorentino had been elegantly combined —was not likewise in his life.

Nevertheless, the lamp with its globes made a triumphal entry into the house on Via Eufrate, where it dominated the divans, the fireplace, and the bookcase for many years. It was solid in structure, a "bourgeois" object, as people said. Soon they stopped paying attention to it, and in time its presence even became reassuring.

The life of Pier Paolo, a director of slowly increasing fame, changed. It had already been changed by his travels abroad, as attested by *Poesia in forma di rosa*. The landscape of his poetry extends farther and farther—no longer Rome and its belt of shantytowns, but Africa, Israel, India: a horizon that includes "the Appian Ways / and the Centocelle airports of the world."

Hitherto Pier Paolo had lived in the traditional petit-bourgeois shell of the Italian writer—at first one's native province, then the metropolis, either Rome or Milan. But now he had taken to flying across continents, with all the coming and going associated with successful men.

The trail of success did not, however, eliminate his habits: suppers in trattorias, pickups in the shantytowns, his "little soccer matches."

Unlike most famous directors, he did not live surrounded by a group of followers. He lived alone, with Ninetto and Sergio Citti, at most, making up his entire entourage. At home, Graziella very quickly learned how to deal with would-be hangers-on and the like, though Pier Paolo was patient with them, and if the occasion required, generous.

His life at Susanna's side was enclosed in a myth, and in this myth loving trips together took their place. Sometimes in the summer Pier Paolo accompanied his mother to Casarsa to visit her sisters; other times he would take her for a vacation in the mountains—trips by car across Italy during the August holidays.

Susanna came to love the garden of the new house. She was to spend the years of her old age basking in the sunlight of Rome. But she refused to abandon herself to old age. She still retained from her youth the pleasure of a touch of lipstick on her lips, the care of her hair—which she dyed a slightly coppery chestnut.

Pier Paolo, hoping to rescue her from the passage of the years, wanted her to undergo Dr. Aslan's Gerovital treatment. Susanna agreed to everything as though it were a courtship—which, in a sense, it was.

DANTEAN PLANS AND DREAMS

Pier Paolo's fertile imagination planned new novels and films every day. He gave away subjects and titles for books to his friends.

Time and again he came back to ideas for novels, like *Il rio della Grana,* but it was still impossible for him to resuscitate the Roman world that had lapsed into darkness with *Una vita violenta.*

Traces of Roman dialect speech, mingled with the declarative requirements of film writing, appear in "Rital e raton."[2] The landscape has changed: Algeria, the guerrilla war of liberation, Paris; the world is the Third World. But the text clearly shows his elliptical elegance of style, under which Pier Paolo conceals the real difficulty of mastering a human and moral climate that is remote from him.

He devoted much thought, and frequently spoke of it, to a new version of the *Divine Comedy.* An ambitious project, to which he felt called by fate—some critics had compared his writing, for its linguistic richness, to Dante's poem.

Pier Paolo challenged himself to a contest with that model. He worked at this idea, and reworked it many times, from 1963 and 1965 until 1967. The result was a small sheaf of notes and prose fragments —only the first two "cantos" were completed. He himself readied it for the printer, adding some photographs in the appendix as a "yellowed iconography." *La Divina Mimesis*—this is the title of the text— was to come out in December 1975, several weeks after his death.

"I give these pages to the printers as a 'document,' but also to spite my 'enemies': in fact, by offering them one more reason to despise me, I offer them one more reason to go to hell." This in the 1975 "preface."

His enemies—a warning to them. The incompleteness of the text could have been for some a reason for satisfaction. His vindication was polemical—literary and polemical.

A critical retracing of the *Divine Comedy, La Divina Mimesis* is conceived as a journey. The first two cantos surprise the poet *"nel mezzo del cammin"*—they surprise him in the encounter with another self, a realized self, shamelessly happy, and driven by an acquired rationality. The other, the subject of the story, has lost all vital joy. Before his eyes he discovers the beasts that were driven out of the "common hiding places" of his soul, his own squandered unconscious.

The journey starts one Sunday morning in Rome, in an outlying cinema, where a celebration is being held for new members of the local Communist Party cell. In this celebration there is something dim and remote—the crisis of ideologies makes the assembly seem ritualistic. Over it hovers a spirit of renunciation, even if everything—compared to the past—looks identical: the smiles of the children and old people, the color of the flags. From here the journey through the Inferno begins. But what Inferno?

It is the Inferno of the consumer society, of neocapitalism. Neocapitalism's *Diktat* to literature is clear: that "commitment" be a meaningless word, that literature be an activity that resolves its own problem within itself. No more mirages of red flags. Let literature reduce its message to "obedience."

These fragmentary pages seem like the counterpart to the exasperated individualism of *Poesia in forma di rosa*. They are its gloss, they harmonize Pasolini's despair.

A "publisher's note" (i.e., by Pasolini himself), inserted in the middle of the fragments of Canto VII, explains the meaning of this despair. The "note" says that the author of the text is dead—he has left behind pages and notes of his work in desk drawers and in the "inside pouch of the door of his car." Some of these pages are incomprehensible; others are perfectly legible and dated. The task of the publisher (I repeat, Pasolini himself) is thereby facilitated: all he has had to do is collect the pages and arrange them in order by following the dates at the bottom.

Comment on the death of this simulated "author": "A macabre detail, but also—it must be admitted—moving, a note on graph paper (obviously torn from a pad), covered with a dozen scarcely legible lines, was found in the pocket of the jacket on his corpse (he was beaten to death with a stick last year in Palermo)."

These lines bear the date "1966 or '67." In 1965 a second gathering of the 63 Group had been held in Palermo, and it had been more polemical than ever toward the literature of the "ridiculous decade" and "commitment." Pasolini, who up to that point, and even despite direct attacks on him, had thought he would be able to maintain dialectical contacts with the new avant-garde, had had to take note of and accept his own "isolation."

In this "isolation," the poet had been killed, metaphorically beaten to death with a stick.[3]

It was from feeling himself isolated and rejected in this way that Pasolini suffered the "expiration of a certain purity and passion—what was left of the Resistance years, etc." By that *et cetera*—written in answer to a *Vie Nuove* reader—Pasolini indicated the burden of memories and remorse by which he was wracked.

True, these literary polemics were a reflection of something else. To the same *Vie Nuove* reader—it is June 3, 1965—he adds: "There can be no doubt that times have changed. Until a few years ago, there was a whole system of allusions and common references that made even a sentence, banal in itself or even rhetorical, significant. Now this series of allusions and references (in a word the ontology and eschatology of 'Hope') has faded away. That irrational quality that it implied has thus lost its vitality. One can no longer rely on that fund of strength, brotherhood, and exaltation that lies in a common political faith."[4]

The "crisis of ideologies," and a profound personal weariness:

The Revolution is nothing more than a feeling.[5]

At the height of these bitter reflections, Pasolini took a stand on his own, in "opposition" to everything and everybody. But feverish and ceaseless literary creativity, such as he had known up to that point, disappeared in him.

In a debate held at the Centro Sperimentale di Cinematografia in Rome on May 27, 1964, he is said to have confessed, "Talking relieves me a little of the desire to create. There was a book that by talking about it first, I completely got rid of, and now I don't think I'll ever write it."

With the autumn of 1965 his contributions to *Vie Nuove* ended. Pier Paolo claimed that he had become an "egoist," that he cared much more than before about what he could produce individually. The cinema absorbed him.

By now Pier Paolo's sense of being alive was inextricably bound up with his provocatory relationship with the public. His existence unfolded more and more openly. Irresistibly he ended by coinciding with his public image.

THE DEGRADATION OF LANGUAGE

Italy was changing and so was its language. "In short, one might say that the *centers for the creation, development, and unification of language are no longer the universities but the business firms. One* observes, for example, the enormous linguistic power of suggestion possessed by slogans in the 'language of advertising'."[6]

The monster of "mass expressivity" was born. Pasolini set out to analyze it.

Hitherto there had been no national language, except as a naïve and rhetorical aspiration—the aspiration of literature or of the universities. The mass media warped the tradition, and gave birth to a "sanctioned" language that might be called "standard Italian."

In the fifties, spoken Italian was "neorealist," it was Roman dialect, the language that was being diffused by the cinema. In the sixties, it was the North, with its heritage of well-developed technical languages —not with its dialects—that offered the model for a "sanctioned" language.

What will be the most important characteristics of this national Italian? Technological languages being international by formation and strictly functional by tendency, they will presumably contribute to Italian some typical habits of the more advanced Romance languages, with a strong emphasis on the communicative spirit, roughly in accordance with these three tendencies: 1) A certain bias in favor of the progressive sequence. . . . 2) The end of osmosis with Latin. . . . 3) The predominance of the communicative purpose over the expressive one.[7]

Pasolini had put forth these ideas in a lecture, "Nuove questioni linguistiche," published in *Rinascita* on December 26, 1964. It led to a debate, in which the first to respond were Alberto Moravia, Umberto Eco, and Andrea Barbato.

Pasolini was accused of having "stated the obvious" (a standard Italian can be said always to have existed, according to Moravia), or of having contrived the existence of a language that as yet did not exist.

The controversy shifted from the columns of *Rinascita* to *L'Espresso* during January 1965. In this weekly, on February 7, 1965, Pasolini responded that he did not wish to be the godfather of anything—he had merely recorded an event that was "much more profound and violent than an ordinary adjustment of society." The old "humanistic" bourgeoisie was disappearing, and its place was being taken by a new, "technocratic" bourgeoisie with a drive toward hegemony. "This bourgeoisie at the same time radiates economic, cultural, and therefore linguistic power."[8]

Pasolini was testifying to a phenomenon and conducting a diagnosis, he was not espousing a new language (as, not very subtly, his interlocutors insisted). "The new technological language of the bourgeoisie does not interest me in itself, personally I detest it, and my task as a writer is to oppose it, but not to ignore it. It is a real phenomenon."[9]

Other participants were Enrico Emanuelli in the *Corriere della Sera,* and Pietro Citati, who offered Pasolini supporting illustrations in the columns of *Il Giorno.* And in *Il Giorno,* in March 1965, Pier Paolo replied that what he was faced with was the "first cry" of an Italian that was, if not new, at least "different"—bureaucratizing, slangy, certainly "communicative," and risky to use.

The controversy went on for months, almost as a society game, or at least that was how it looked. But Pasolini, as though with a divining rod, had caught a prevailing trend. By not purifying itself in its contact with a civilization more efficient than the rural one, Italian was becoming barbarized. This was his way, through language, of foreseeing a future barbarization of customs.

Pasolini's lingering on the threshold of rural and Christian civilization, in accordance with the Italian secular tradition, had one compensation—he was able to perceive how much the social innovations that the country seemed to have taken up may have become rusted at birth and distorted.

In the fifties, Pier Paolo had breathed, and made his own, the anti-rationalist climate that, following on a more or less close understanding of Lukács's *Destruction of Reason,* hung suspended over Italian culture. To the requirements of irrationality and individuality, he had tried to give voice and response. His sensibility had also been swept away by Goya's "the sleep of reason produces monsters," even though in his heart of hearts he was able to see in post-Marxist schematism a more effective use of the instruments of reason. All the same, he had nourished a vaguely mystical conception of Marxism. For him, as for many others, Marxism was a genuine theology of history, a closed and providential system in which the torment of the irrational could be eliminated.

Caught up in the "crisis of ideologies," and with the arrival of a new time, Pier Paolo made room for the facts of existence. He wrote the despairing *Poesia in forma di rosa,* while living an intense and painful solitude. He declared that he had no language "in common" with others.

"Solitude" unexpectedly liberated him from all metaphysics. Ideology, one might say, is only the reflection of a collective ritual—once the one is dispersed, there remains no trace of the other. Pasolini seemed to become a methodologist. Linguistics and anthropology, with their experimental and intuitive criteria, reasserted their appeal. Even Marxism, in this framework, became methodology. With this we come to the essay "Dal laboratorio (Appunti *en poète* per una linguistica marxista)," his conclusive piece on the "new questions of language."[10]

"Dal laboratorio" limits itself to a journalistic approach—the writing is journalistic and to the point. This was already true of the articles written for daily and weekly periodicals. Pasolini would seem to have departed from his "wish for style," and now finds himself subject to the linguistic situation he is describing. It is thus in Pasolini himself that the reader verifies the lexical and syntactical disorder of the "new" Italian. He was later to say that he had "hypocritically"[11] dashed off these pages, conscious of his own "bad faith."

"The experiment is in progress, it's an open book."[12] What were the provisional conclusions?

From old Bertoni* to Lévi-Strauss and Hjelmslev, by way of Croce, Saussure, and Gramsci—in his anthropological examination, Pasolini observed the flight to the cities that took place during the second industrial revolution. It was the transformation of the rural and Third World *"pensée sauvage"* that he took to heart—how the archaic usages of language resisted or were added to the changes that economic acceleration imposed on human beings.

Again, it is the popular mind that Pasolini examined with clinical detachment.

Ninetto for the first time in his life sees snow (he is of Calabrian origin: he was too little to remember the snowfall of '57 in Rome, or perhaps had not yet come from Calabria). We have just arrived in Pescasseroli, and the broad stretches of snow have already made him rejoice with a pure surprise a little too childish for his age (he is sixteen). But with nightfall, the sky all of a sudden turns white, and as we emerge from the hotel to take a stroll in the deserted little village, the air becomes lively; by a strange optical effect, since the tiny snowflakes are falling toward the ground, they seem to be rising to the sky, but irregularly, because their fall is not continuous and a capricious mountain wind keeps them whirling. Looking up makes your head spin. It looks as though the whole sky is falling on us, dissolving in this happy and naughty feast of Apennine snow. Just imagine Ninetto. No sooner does he perceive this unheard-of occurrence, the sky dissolving on his head, and knowing no obstacles of good upbringing to the manifestation of his

* Giulio Bertoni, author of *Italia dialettale* (1925) and *Profilo linguistico d'Italia* (1940).—Tr.

feelings, than he abandons himself to a joy devoid of all modesty. Which has two phases, very rapid ones: first a kind of dance, with well-defined rhythmic breaks (I am reminded of the Denka, who beat the ground with their heels, and who in their turn made me think of Greek dances as one imagines them by reading the poets). He just barely performs this rhythm, suggests it, striking the ground with his heels and moving his knees up and down. The second phase is oral: it consists in a childish and orgiastic cry of joy that accompanies the heights and breaks of that rhythm: "Hé-eh, hé-eh, heeeeeeh." In short, a cry that cannot be reproduced in writing. A vocalization stemming from a recollection *that joins in an uninterrupted continuum* the Ninetto of today in Pescasseroli with the Ninetto of Calabria, a marginal area and preserver of Greek civilization, with the pre-Greek, purely barbarian Ninetto who beats time with his heels the way the prehistoric, naked Denka of the lower Sudan do today . . .[13]

The essay describes on the one hand, on the other polemicizes.

It polemicizes with structuralism, which it calls "geometry" and "formal projection."[14] It cannot be satisfactory to a poet and Marxist— to a poet because he is required to live in the magma of the world and to take possession of it; to a Marxist because into the magma he wants to introduce "order in both awareness and action," and both "are in rebellion against the wave of formalism and empiricism of the great European neocapitalist rebirth."[15]

So what are the conclusions? The systematic rejection of new illusions, whether from the new avant-garde (whatever its literary equivalent of the moment),[16] or from the propagandistic techniques by now in use, for example, in publishing.

Pasolini foresaw a ruinous future, a future fraught with social difficulties in which old and consolidated patterns, and ancient certainties ("democratic pacifism," for instance), would no longer make sense. In the flight from the countryside to the cities (a "linguistic" flight as well), he read sinister omens, the apocalyptic end of what he had loved most.

THE CROW

"An almost drugged sage, a lovable beatnik, a poet with nothing to lose, a character out of Elsa Morante, a Bobi Bazlen, a sublime and ridiculous Socrates, who stops at nothing, and is under an obligation never to tell lies, almost as though inspired by the Indian philosophers or Simone Weil. . . . The crow—a kind of irregular metaphor for the author."[17]

In 1965 Pasolini had the idea for a film, which he described as being "in prose": *Uccellacci e uccellini* (Hawks and Sparrows). The comic spirit transmuted the prose into poetry.

In the depths of Pasolini's despair an ancient virtue had taken root: patience. Pier Paolo was convinced that in the long run his ideas would be held in esteem, increasing esteem. He prophesied the apocalypse, convinced that his words would exorcise it. He was able to see himself comically as a talking cricket,* a cricket who foretells disaster and is also able to laugh at his own arrogance.

Here then was the crow—he gave him the voice of his close friend Francesco Leonetti. Heading the cast were Totò and Ninetto.

I spoke of despair—Ninetto's cheerfulness succeeded in diluting it. Through the very creation of *Hawks and Sparrows* one can measure the intensity of the relationship that bound Pier Paolo to Ninetto, and the symbolic values Pier Paolo invested in that relationship. It may seem either foolish or trite, of a trite romanticism, that Pier Paolo should have lent a great part of himself to the image of Ninetto. But this was, quite simply, the poetic force of his love.

He sees himself as a talking cricket, a querulous teacher and moralist, who can only come to a bad end. His truth cannot but become irritating in the long run. Plucked and roasted, the crow will end up in the stomachs of those he has chosen as objects for pedagogic treatment—Totò and Ninetto, respectively a new Don Quixote and Sancho Panza. But what happier destiny is there for a teacher goaded by a stubborn will to instruct than to be transformed into living nourishment for his pupils?

An "elegiac" and "funereal" happiness, it was to be called.[18] But any such tendency is subjected, in the course of *Hawks and Sparrows*, to a perpetual metamorphosis, a constant play of comic allusions. The theme of the film is classical, among the most classical in literature— the theme of the quest. Totò and Ninetto set out on the highroads of the world and of history in search of material and moral nourishment. They are, as I said, Don Quixote and Sancho Panza, but of course, since this is a film, they are also Charlie Chaplin. They represent the mildness and strength of the heart, and they are also faith, the Franciscan faith, purged of the rage and frenzy that had possessed the Christ of the *Gospel According to Saint Matthew*.

* The Talking Cricket, who becomes Pinocchio's conscience.—Tr.

On their journey, Totò and Ninetto meet an accomplice, the sententious crow, and he becomes the hero of the journey. The crow tries to teach them to look beyond appearances; he tries to teach them to know the world with reason as well as with the heart. He will not survive his destiny—the world gets the better of Totò's and Ninetto's naïveté; or else—ambiguity of metaphor!—reason, its task completed, can only let itself be digested by that naïveté.

The film has an abstract and intangible plot; the adventures are flimsy and symbolical, but they are saved by Totò's irresistible performance and the unequivocal vitality of Ninetto. What then is it through which the two characters travel? What is contained in their comical guises, and still more in the frantic croaking of the crow?

"Marxism grafted as an innocent norm, regeneration not however crazy but reasoned, over a flaw in the norm, over the trauma (nostalgia for life, detachment from it, solitude, poetry as compensation, the natural duty of passion, etc.). But the autobiographical element was manifested above all in the crow's type of Marxism. That is to say a Marxism open to all possible syncretisms and regressions, remaining firm on the more solid points of diagnosis and perspective."[19]

The two characters travel through "the crisis of ideologies," seeking, through the words of their author, or of the crow, a possible continuity, even if "irregular," with the world of fine hopes of the Resistance.

The crow looks on the proletarian mirth of Ninetto and Totò as a historical treasure not to be squandered or discarded. He also looks on the shantytowns as a place where regeneration is possible. The sacredness of history—here the sacredness of ideology is not extinguished. It supports the irony, as well as the comedy.

Is the journey therefore "elegiac" and "nostalgic"? Yes, in the sense that this elegy was the measure of Pasolini's smile. But the journey was also a fable, the Roman fabulist Phaedrus and La Fontaine being its godfathers. In the fable the rawness of Pasolini's despair found a moment of repose, if not of resolution.[20]

LIFE AND ILLNESS

"I'll never be able to forget that Italian society condemned me in its courtrooms."[21]

Despite the smile and the fable, Pasolini did not forget. He was also to add that he had made films "to repudiate with my tongue the coun-

try from which I have been on the verge of fleeing a hundred times."
His "opposition" by now is "on two fronts, against the petite bourgeoisie and against that mirror of it that is represented by a certain
conformism of the left."[22]

Despairing and tenacious, Pasolini did not, however, in his declared
solitude, hold back from cultural debate. He was increasingly caught
up in the cinema and now began to examine it theoretically.

Godard in France, Pasolini in Italy. From France came the critical
and semiological analyses in *Cahiers du Cinéma* by Roland Barthes
and Christian Metz.

In Rome a group of young cineasts had formed around a periodical,
Cinema e Film. They included Adriano Aprà, Luigi Faccini, and
Maurizio Ponzi. They directed their attention to a possible catalogue
of cinematographic language.

The Pesaro film festival, called to celebrate the "New Cinema,"
became the time and place at which these matters were brought
together and examined. It was organized by Lino Miccichè. In September 1965 a round-table discussion was held in Pesaro to coincide with
the showings. There Pasolini read his first film essay, "Il cinema di
poesia," using Antonioni, Bertolucci, Godard, Glauber Rocha, and
Milos Forman as examples.

The language of the cinema is "crude," lacking in definition, "irrational," "oneiric," "elementary," "barbaric." This language is "reality"
—the cinema of poetry is the total and immediate rendering of it.

Literature operates on a stabilized lexicon, but not the cinema.
"While the operation of the writer is an aesthetic creation, that of the
cinematographic author is first linguistic and then aesthetic."[23]

Roland Barthes was also present in Pesaro. He and Pier Paolo discussed at length the creation of a grammar of cinematographic images,
but at each meeting Barthes also insisted on the importance in a film
of the dynamics of the narration, the activation of logic whereby the
film "begins" and "ends," while tracing the curve of a destiny.

In the autumn of 1965 Pasolini placed great faith in a literary project,
the revival of *Nuovi Argomenti*, the magazine edited by Alberto
Carocci and Moravia—by 1963 its role of cultural-political mediator
had declined. Other magazines—*Quaderni piacentini*, for example—
had assumed that role by developing a leftist critical line toward the
policies of the Italian Communist Party.

The polemics of the new avant-garde had imposed a sudden black-
out on literature. Moravia conceived the idea for a revitalization of

Nuovi Argomenti, in which literature, creative literature, would play a decisive part.

Pasolini was enthusiastic about the project, and indeed hastened Moravia's decision by contacting Editori Riuniti, the Communist Party publishing house, in the hope that they would take over the printing and distribution of the periodical.

The deal was almost arranged when, acting on second thoughts— the fear that the party publisher would imperceptibly modify a literary magazine—Moravia and Pasolini turned to Livio Garzanti.

Garzanti agreed to print and distribute *Nuovi Argomenti*. He accepted the idea that the magazine might become an outlet for new writers, and expressed faith in Pasolini's talent for discovering them. For my part, I was offered the post of editorial secretary.

Pier Paolo no longer cared to adhere to a one-sided but consistent policy, as he had done with *Officina*. The policy of *Nuovi Argomenti* was to be much wider, based simply on quality. From all the manuscripts submitted, certain names stood out: Dario Bellezza, Giorgio Manacorda, Renzo Paris.

Among these, Bellezza, by the natural lyricism of his poems, was the most appealing to Pier Paolo. He was also amused by Bellezza's talent for wild gossip. Pier Paolo used to say that Bellezza was "his own priest," in an unconsciously comical form. This comic quality redeemed traces of the old *poète maudit* pose—it indicated a modern writer.

Bellezza had left his family, and it was hard for him to make ends meet. For a few years, in the late sixties and early seventies, Pier Paolo employed him to handle any of his correspondence that was not strictly personal. In this way, with his thick black hair, his heavy glasses on his nose, Bellezza earned a monthly stipend, and pittance though it was, it enabled him to write *Invettive e licenze*.

Literature, for Pasolini, was still present on the horizon. Soon he was to begin to write poems "to order," "on commission"—the first ones in *Trasumanar e organizzar* (To Transhumanize and Organize). In his imagination, "a new type of buffoon" was taking form—the poet, whose "purity" could also be "mystification." He was to write:

Mystification is lightness.

Sincerity is heavy and vulgar:
with it it is life that wins.

Instead, youth should win,
and by insolent and gracious effractions—patient ones,
because the young are patient, not the old.
Let the Falsetto return.

All this was suggested to me by the grace of the Eritreans.[24]

These lines, set down in the early months of 1969, sum up an
existential experience that had got underway at the time of *Hawks and
Sparrows*. The explicit experience of play, of masks—the holy nature
of the game and of the Nietzschean mask.

Pasolini never explicitly and consciously accepted Nietzsche. Nietzsche was to him what Lukács had declared him to be for a great many
of his readers: the negative and exemplary image of bourgeois irrationality. But some affinities often develop irresistibly. Beyond the face of
the scholar, was there not in Pier Paolo the disciple "of an unknown
god," or "a mystical and almost bacchic soul"? It was this inner quality
that made him speak of lightness. And was not "lightness" obligatory
for the disciple of Zarathustra?

"Lightness" in Pier Paolo also meant activity—feverish, exhausting,
creative activity. One March evening in 1966, during supper in a
restaurant near the Portico of Octavia in the Roman ghetto, he had
an ulcer attack. Moravia and Dacia Maraini were with him.

Pier Paolo had got up from the table to go to the toilet. Time went
by, a little too much time. Suddenly the door flew open and he fell
forward on the floor in a pool of blood, hemorrhaging copiously. Dacia
rushed to raise him up, and he fainted three times in her arms. As he
came to, he begged her, "Don't leave me, don't leave me." She bathed
his forehead—he looked dead.

With the help of the waiters, Dacia got him outside to the car. She
and Moravia took him to a private physician, who gave him an injec-
tion. Pier Paolo came to himself.

He had to stay in bed, immobilized, for about a month. When it
was over, he said to Giorgio Bocca, "Some mornings when I wake up
the thought of age is like a thunderbolt. The ulcer, a month in bed,
the sense of weakness, the treatments. For the first time, I felt old."[25]

He weighed 110 pounds—he kept strictly to his diet. He drank milk
and ate only bland food. For a few years, the usual suppers at Laura
Betti's adhered to a strict menu.

After two or three years Pier Paolo felt sufficiently recovered to go back to eating in the old way. But his illness, and the long and cautious convalescence, had marked his life. His words—"For the first time, I felt old"—were not careless ones.

Old age—he was being ironical, of course. At forty-four, Pasolini could not call himself "old." But solitude, the time inevitably spent thinking while lying in bed, led him to achieve that state of "lightness," of positive "mystification," to which he had already been "summoned" by the crow in *Hawks and Sparrows*. "Lightness" was an ironic weapon, an acquisition of freedom and maturity.

He went back to his friends, telling them, "In bed I wrote six tragedies." It was true: during that month he had blocked out the six texts that constitute his theatrical *oeuvre: Calderón, Pilade, Affabulazione, Porcile, Orgia, Bestia da stile.* He also made an outline of *Teorema.*

With the help of Moravia and Dacia, we had set up a theater for Italian writers in a cellar in downtown Rome, the Teatro del Porcospino on Via Belsiana—a small company led by Carlotta Barilli and Paolo Bonacelli, with Roberto Guicciardini as director.

For all its quarrels and conflicts, the theater kept going for two seasons. Guicciardini left, and his place was taken by other directors. Our chief hope was to provide a showcase for playwrights. We had long discussions in those months on how theater should be performed. Actors accused writers, writers accused actors. Pier Paolo maintained that the actors would never be able to free themselves from their traditional "affectations of speech." He said that his were closet plays and would never be "acted," and that he certainly would never entrust them to the Porcospino.

Which was how it turned out. After much hesitation, he printed *Pilade* and *Affabulazione* in *Nuovi Argomenti,* in 1967 and 1969, respectively.[26] These were transitional drafts. He was still thinking of setting the final seal to his plays in 1975. Only *Calderón,* published in book form in 1973, can be considered to have been completed by his hand.

As for the staging of these plays, on November 27, 1968, *Orgia* opened in Turin under his own direction. In the cast were Laura Betti, Luigi Mezzanotte, and Nelide Giammarco. He was driven toward this form of expression by a never assuaged feeling of discontent, or the need to find solutions that were not merely stylistic.

The holiness of existence, as it is manifested in the family unit and in the life of society—this was the theme of Pasolini's tragic *oeuvre,* outlined in that spring of 1966. He had the idea, already present in *Poesia in forma di rosa*, that neocapitalist "power," by violating historical moral values, was committing an irreversible outrage on society. Pasolini's intention was to give poetic and dramatic voice to the effects of this outrage.

The resulting suffering—social, existential—was represented as though it were an act of individual contrition carried out before the eyes of God and fate. Pasolini's dramatic works thus emerged, consecrated, soliloquizing, and offering no way out. And each of the six tragedies seemed to be a corollary of the others, revolving around the conflicting relations between fathers and sons, the political utopias of youth, the authoritarian dangers of mass civilization. The poetry disappears into an armor of didacticism, spreads imperturbably into pools of landscape painting. The characters, in their concerted voices, shatter their own vital existence while tasting it bit by bit.

Pasolini's cinema is no different, composed of one mosaic tile on another—one frame on another—and where life is represented as though on devotional tablets.

"I avoid long-shot sequences, because they are naturalistic, and therefore natural. My fetishistic love for the 'things' of the world keeps me from considering them as natural. It either consecrates or desecrates them with violence, one by one. It does not link them in a proper flow, it doesn't accept this flow. But it isolates and idolizes them, more or less intensely, one by one."[27]

Idolatry of the real—life loses itself in the *pragma*, the deed performed. Hence the imperative to run after it, to immerse oneself in it. In this there is deep intellectual pessimism, and deep mystical longing.

Geno Pampaloni, reviewing the essays collected in *Empirismo eretico*, circumscribed this pessimism and its religious counterpart: "Having lost the ideological and moral certainty of hegemonic Marxism, Pasolini's ideal is increasingly directed toward a pluralistic, spontaneous, libertarian world. His interests converge toward a general problematic or political center, no longer in the search for an order but for a meaning of life. In this religious space, he finds his truest accents. Like no other writer today, Pasolini succeeds in conveying to us the anguish, dismay, and misery of a period that, in dying, distractedly sets aside the same sufferings, hatreds, and regrets that have pierced it with dramatic light. From these pages, so often bristling and raging with formulas and theoretical subtleties, one derives above all a gently catastrophic sentiment, as of an intelligence overcome with pity."[28]

Religion—a particular relationship with reality. Such is Pasolini's thought, and the accent of his "pity." But in this religious feeling, transparent shadows of the past appeared—in the first place D'Annunzio, then the romantically re-evoked barbaric and buried civilizations. The example of Flaubert's *Salammbô* is not far off.

The visual pauperism of the *Gospel* might already have led one to imagine a Pasolini lost within the coils of myth, or of a past dreamed beyond history. The writing of the tragedies, the visual conception that governs them, confirms the supposition.

Nevertheless, in his evocation of psychological and moral archetypes, Pasolini uncovers forgotten material in himself—in that part of his ego that had languished since the years of his youth. His relationship with his father, his nostalgia for the image of him—Pasolini discovered the sacredness of a tie that he had hated for years. This is the specific theme of *Affabulazione,* perhaps the most tormented of this bundle of texts.

Illnesses of the body are said to be visible explosions of the invisible ills of the soul. At the somatic origin of Pier Paolo's ulcer lie inveterate constrictions of the heart, and perhaps the long silences broken by mute laughter, or by his writings and films. Certainly there were also the painful experiences of family life, his love for Susanna, the death of Guido, his rejection at the hands of Carlo Alberto.

This rejection long smoldered in his mind. His mind carefully followed its own motions—the slightest twitching was reason for examination. Then came his illness and convalescence. This examination, during the weeks spent in bed, must have become acutely accentuated, giving way to a feeling of maturity, to an ever advancing "old age." And the overbearing image of the father—a symbolic image, it should be emphasized—must have become clear in its outlines.

It should therefore come as no surprise that the father should appear as the central figure in the foreground of *Affabulazione,* or a decided nostalgia for him a support for society in *Pilade.*

In *Affabulazione,* the father seeks and demands a positive confrontation with the son. His despair arises from not finding any way out of such a confrontation except murder.

Cronos devours his own offspring. It is no accident that Pasolini, in retracing the steps of the myth in modern guise, should choose the viewpoint of Cronos.

So I, instead of
trying to kill my son
was trying to be killed!!
Doesn't that seem strange to you?
And he, instead of trying to kill me
—or letting himself be killed
willingly and resigned
like his obedient contemporaries—
wanted neither to kill me nor to let himself be killed!!!
. . .
He cared nothing about me,
or about any of the killings old and new
that bind a father and a son.
Therefore he was freed of it all . . .

But the Cronos fable was to have its effect on another film that was unfolding in Pasolini's imagination. Pasolini already saw bourgeois sons, stimulated by the euphoria of the neocapitalist boom, "freeing themselves of it all," transforming the feeling of freedom into indifference, denying the religious appeal of the myths around which psychology and history rotate. Cronos' despair mirrored, and to no small degree, the radical pessimism of the author of this new fable. What other hope could he cherish?

If this was the future, it was wholly unforeseeable. . . .
And the unforeseeable future that has armed my hand
is just this one, of the decade we are living.
It has made the past decline
and prematurely governs men.
Men live it with unawareness,
feeling it in reality rather as the death
of past values than as the birth of new ones.
This humiliates them, and makes them regress
to childish impiety.
This is what, in reality, has made me the murderer
of a spineless son, anachronistically
innocent (unless we are dealing with
an innocence anachronistically new).[29]

For the cinema, then, he made *Oedipus Rex* in 1967—a film of barbaric impasto, framed between two "Po valley" miniatures. The soft pastel colors of the prologue and epilogue, set in Lombardy in the early postwar period and in contemporary times—and in between, the jewel of a time that precedes history and which, as well by its ancient quality, provides a thrill of painful anticipation.

Oedipus Rex, and its twin tragedy of the mother, *Medea*, comprise Pasolini's true *Salammbô*, for their decorative pomp, highly concealed play of allusions, and formal elegance. But alongside this there coexists the idea, one that seems to have been suggested by Jung (or by Nietzsche?), by which the whole human succession of events would be contained, as in seed, in the archetypal symbols.

Writing about his film, Pasolini spoke of "aestheticism" and "humor," suggesting by his words a kind of ironical retreat. Even though present—and "he would seem to defeat Marx"—Freud is "inserted" in the film "as a dilettante might insert him." But the retreat is of the soul, or rather in the soul—the soul that hides the cruelest feelings.

Why Oedipus? Pier Paolo declares himself by now to be, "at the age of forty-five," beyond any Freudian and Marxist entanglement. He accepts his own condition as a "bourgeois" intellectual, with all its ambiguities and necessary legacies of the past. For this reason, in *Oedipus*, he is recounting "things from which he is by now remote."

Was he perhaps inspired by Sophocles' tragedy to explain the violence of his mother's ascendancy over him? "I have never dreamt of making love with my mother. Never even dreamt it."

On the other hand, there is the illumination of some lines that sound like an absent-minded, even needless confession: "Rather I have dreamt, if at all, of making love with my father (against the dresser in the miserable bedroom my brother and I shared as children), and perhaps also, I think, with my brother, and with many women of stone."[30]

On the lips of Pasolini himself is the explanation—concealed and despairing—of the urgency of the sacred in his imagination, that sacred quality that nested in the invisible sign of the paternal tree. It would seem scandalous to ask him to be any more explicit, or more clearsighted in self-knowledge.

Oedipus Rex was shown at the Twenty-eighth Venice Film Festival, in September 1967. Franco Citti was unconvincing as the hero; Silvana Mangano came through better as Jocasta, a totem figure of harsh, glittering topazes (indeed a "woman of stone"); and still more convincing was the Moroccan landscape chosen to represent ancient Thebes and its mountains.

Guido Piovene, in reviewing the film, defended its aestheticism, its

D'Annunzianism: "There are much worse things today than D'Annunzianism, and D'Annunzio is a much greater poet than most of the idols worshipped today by the critical and literary crowd. The same goes for aestheticism: there is certainly in Pasolini a considerable portion of stylistic aestheticism—all the better for him. . . ." Piovene's critical sagacity went further: "The ultimate point of arrival in Oedipus' search and blindness, one that is already implicit in the rest of Pasolini's work, is that human suffering is not fortuitous, nor bound in its more intimate and burning aspects to this or that historical cause, but existential, inevitable, bound up with blood and the destiny of blood, not historical but metahistorical, there where the great tragic myths have placed it."[31]

AMERICA, AMERICA

The Maserati 3500 GT—Pier Paolo had bought it second-hand for that summer of 1966. He spent a few days with Susanna vacationing at Piano d'Arta, in the Carnia region.

One might criticize him for the ostentation of a high-powered automobile. Pier Paolo had taken to dressing in a conspicuous way, almost as though to adapt himself to the fashionable "youthful" look—woolen sweaters with loud colors, leather pants, reindeer jackets, boots. With the seventies, he began dyeing his hair. He commented ironically on all this, and spoke of erotic necessity. It was his one fatuity.

On this little stage, an exorbitant, intrusive "pop" object, the Maserati was parked.

His trips took him to Czechoslovakia, Hungary, Rumania, and the United States. In the people's democracies of Eastern Europe, Pasolini became convinced of the obsolescence to which Marxism was condemned. In Czechoslovakia, Hungary, and Rumania, he met intellectuals: "Through them, through their anxiety, their malaise . . . I felt the anxiety, the malaise of those countries—the cause of which I think one can schematically and summarily point out in the fact that 'the revolution has not continued,' i.e., the state has not been decentralized, has not disappeared, and the workers in the factories are not really participants in and responsible for political power, but instead are dominated—does anyone by now not know and admit it?—by a bureaucracy that is revolutionary only in name."[32]

In October 1966 he made a brief trip to New York, his first to the United States. He was carried away by the atmosphere of change that one breathed in that city.

In America, even in my very brief stay, I lived many hours in the clandestine climate of struggle, of revolutionary urgency, of hope that belonged to the Europe of '44 and '45. In Europe everything is finished, in America you get the feeling that all is about to begin. I don't mean that in America there is civil war, and perhaps not even anything like it, nor do I care to prophesy it—nevertheless people are living there as on the eve of great things.[33]

New York was exciting to him—in interviews he expressed himself joyfully: "I'd like to be eighteen years old so as to be able to live a whole life over here."[34] But beyond this joy, he makes forceful distinctions:

Everything I saw, or thought I saw, stands out against a dark background—and one that for us is inconceivable at least to the extent of being inadmissible—i.e., against everyday American life, the life of conservatism, which unfolds in a silence much more intense than the "howls" reaching us from the Left.[35]

If in America one discovers "the most beautiful left to be seen," a left that is non-Communist but dominated by the "mysticism of democracy," the truth is that it is fighting against an Establishment as solid as granite. But it was this struggle, animated by "discontent," by "exaltation," that exhilarated Pier Paolo and convinced him that the revolution was still a living myth.

Two or three photographs of Pier Paolo, taken on Broadway, in Times Square. He had gone to New York on the occasion of its film festival, where *Hawks and Sparrows* was being shown.[36] Organized by Richard Roud, to parallel a similar event in London, the New York show was the showcase for all the "new" cinematography, formerly seen in Pesaro. Pier Paolo could hardly have failed to go—it marked the international launching of his films.

In the photos, he wears a light raincoat, beige corduroy jeans, and desert boots. His necktie flaps over his light-colored checkered shirt, and the chemical air of the city ruffles his hair. His face looks grim and fleshless.

He avoided social invitations. At night he ran off to Harlem, daring whatever there was to be dared, and laughing at those who advised him to be careful. He ran off to Greenwich Village, to Brooklyn.

One night in Harlem, I shook hands (but they shook my hand suspiciously, because I was white) with a group of young blacks wearing on their sweaters the sign of a panther—an extremist movement that is getting ready for a real armed struggle. . . . I accompanied a young black trade unionist who took me to visit the cell of his movement, a small movement, numbering only a few hundred members in Harlem, and which is combatting unemployment among blacks; he took me to the home of one of his comrades, a bricklayer who had been injured at work and who received us with a friendly smile, stretched out on his miserable bed, touched and overwhelmed by this forgotten partisan love of ours. I went up to a "bourgeois" apartment in the most sordid part of the Village, to hear the hysterical laughter and aberrant acrimony of an intellectual woman, married to a black, who shouted out her resentments against the American Old Left and the drug counterculture . . .[37]

What he tells is certainly only a small part of his adventures. The fascination of the city, its unusual beauty—Pier Paolo was swept away by an exhausting erotic euphoria. At the same time—since this was his way of knowledge—he was carried away by the moral fervor of the American dissent then in progress, by the discovery of a democracy of the spirit, something nonexistent in Italy.

His exaltation did not prevent him from making a careful scrutiny of the phenomenon called "America." In Italy, there was "pure curiosity" as well as "irony" over the American revolt against the consumer society. Pasolini instead wrote that "in the large American cities, those who drink, those who take drugs, those who refuse to integrate themselves into the secure workaday world, are committing something more than a series of old and established anarchistic acts—they are living a tragedy."[38]

Even New York, with its outlying slums, racial problem, and the humanity that washes up on its shores, is Third World: "Two or three generations have not been enough to transform to the depths the psychology of the huge masses of immigrants."[39] Pasolini did not forsake his methods of interpreting social life. He understood how much "the 'fear of losing presence' and the snobbery of his new citizenship prevented the American—this strange mixture, in concrete terms, of subproletarian and bourgeois deeply and honestly enclosed in its own bourgeois sense of loyalty—from reflecting on the idea he has of himself. Which thus remains 'false'." And yet, within such a social fabric, "class consciousness dawns . . . in situations that are entirely new and almost scandalous for Marxism . . . in pacifist and nonviolent demonstrations, governed . . . by an intelligent spirituality. Which is moreover, objectively, at least for me, a marvelous fact, and one that has made me fall in love with America. It is a vision of the world of people who have arrived, by roads that we consider mistaken—but which instead are historically what they are, i.e., the right ones—at the ripening of an idea of themselves as simple citizens (perhaps like the Athenians or the Romans?), holders of an honest and profound notion of democracy."[40]

What made Pier Paolo fall in love with the United States? The conviction—a projection if you like, but an honest one—that people there were arriving at a renewed conception of democracy, by embracing "the calvary of the blacks" and of all those who could be said to have been disinherited.

He was enamored by the struggle for civil and moral rights, the same struggle that in some way he had expressed in "The Ashes of Gramsci," and which now appeared to him to be winning in an entire country.

What he saw happening in America was not "revolution," perhaps it was the prelude to "civil war." And yet, the "newness" of America was supported by signs that for him were charged with vital energy— the signs of poetry. "Not since the old days of Machado have I read another poet in such a fraternal spirit as I have Ginsberg. And wasn't Kerouac's drunken passage through Italy marvelous in stirring up the irony, boredom, and disapproval of the stupid literati and vile Italian journalists?"[41]

Scattered through Pasolini's intelligence were nuggets of decadence —pleasure in vitality, a pleasure heightened at the sight of itself. Thus it did not matter if the Kerouac who had been dragged through Italy in that autumn of 1966 by the publicity department of a publishing house was a shambling ruin of himself, overcome by alcohol, mouthing words all too remote from his nature as a poet. Pier Paolo mistook the breakdown of physiological processes for creative vitality, and, in the solitude to which he was condemned, that was enough for him. Increasingly convinced that a poet and intellectual should shun the values of bourgeois society, he praised anything that appeared free from any sense of obligation. He would have loved to travel the paths of physical ecstasy, of a heightening of the senses, of free and abandoned pleasure. The trip to New York caused him to speak in the name of perennial youth, almost of an unhoped-for permutation of cells.

Having endured illness and convalescence, one can live by such flareups—and that was how Pier Paolo was trying to live.

But there was a further conviction in him, a philosophical conviction —he was discovering spontaneity; underneath his feeling of being ineradicably "bourgeois" and alone against the world, he discovered the explosive perdition of moral anarchism. Moreover, in his now consolidated rejection of literature—he no longer wished to be branded a "slave to style"—he yearned for a supreme, "sacred" wholeness.

The unpublished interview in verse, written in 1966 for a hypothetical New York reporter, offers an explanation:

> ... I should like only to live
> though being a poet
> because life is also expressed by itself alone.
> I should like to express myself with examples.
> To throw my body into the struggle.
> But if the actions of life are expressive,
> expression is also action.
> Not this expression of mine as a poet who renounces,
> who says only things,
> and uses language as you do, a poor direct instrument;
> but expression detached from things,
> signs made into music,
> poetry sung and obscure,
> expressing nothing if not itself,
> by a barbarous and choice idea that it is a mysterious sound
> in the oral signs of a language.
> I have left to my contemporaries as well as to the young
> this barbarous and choice illusion: and I speak to you brutally.
> And since I cannot turn back
> and pretend to be a barbarous boy,
> who thinks his own language the only one in the world,
> and in its syllables hears musical mysteries
> that only his countrymen, similar to him in character
> and literary madness, can hear
> —as a poet I'll be a poet of things.
> The actions of life will be only communicated,
> and they will be poetry,
> since, as I say, there's no other poetry but real action
> (you tremble only when you find it again

in poems, or in pages of prose,
when they evoke it perfectly).
I won't do this with joy.
I will always feel regret for that poetry
that is action itself, in its detachment from things,
in its music that expresses nothing
but its own dry and sublime passion for itself.
And so, I'll confide to you, before we part,
that I'd like to be a writer of music,
and live with instruments
inside the Viterbo tower that I haven't succeeded in buying,
in the most beautiful landscape in the world, where Ariosto
would go mad with joy at seeing himself re-created with such
innocence of oaks, hills, waters, and gullies,
and there compose music,
the only expressive action
perhaps as high and indefinable as the actions of reality.

Therefore, either music or action—"to throw my body into the struggle." His lack of faith in the mediating possibilities of literature is radical. Pasolini by now seems subjugated by the language of the cinema—or rather, he is subjugated by the idea of himself that has been developed from the language of the cinema. And he confesses that he no longer nourishes "illusions"—reality, the supreme good, remains beyond the grasp of words. Poetry is action itself—to affirm it there is no need to be afraid of "nature" or of "naturalism."

Indeed I go so far as to say: "If I want to express a railroad porter through cinematographic language, I take a real porter and reproduce him—body and voice."

Then Moravia laughs: "There, the cinema is naturalistic, as you see. It's naturalistic, it's naturalistic! But the cinema is image. And only by representing a silent porter (well) can you in some way create non-naturalistic cinema."

"Not at all," I say. "The cinema is 'semiologically' an audiovisual technique. That means the porter in flesh and blood and voice."

"A-ha, neorealism!" says Moravia.

"Yes, I, in creating cinema—not a film of mine—in creating cinema, if I have to express a porter, I express him by taking a real porter, with his face, his flesh, and the language by which he expresses himself."

"Oh, no, there you're wrong"—it's Bernardo Bertolucci speaking. "Why have a porter say what he says? You should take his mouth, but into his mouth you must put philosophical words (the way Godard does, of course)" ...[42]

The conversation is faithfully transcribed—and so many, endless discussions went the same way, with Moravia's laughter, Pier Paolo's didactic perseverance, and Bernardo Bertolucci, who, fascinated at the time by Godard, was pursuing a neoromantic dream.

But Pier Paolo, in the exercise of these subtle distinctions, saved himself from possible shipwreck in a form of wholly inflamed irrationalism. The cinema, the "written language of reality," by taking the place of literature, suggested to Pasolini a *theorem*, a sacred demonstrable meditation: that reality was itself and its mirror at the same time.

That is to say, is the ineffability of the real demonstrable in itself, if one does not presuppose in it a presence, or the visitation of the divine?

Involved, it would seem, in the great themes of European decadence, Pasolini was seeking—far indeed from the rigid Marxism of the fifties —instead of a new field of expression (he had already found it in the cinema), a different, or new truth in itself.

The visit to the United States had uplifted him—he would eventually find a way to throw his body into the struggle. For now he was aware of a burning need to sanctify his own cognitive experience. All his intuitive historical and sociological observations on American life, for all their clarity and richness, were put aside in favor of that need.

TEOREMA

A film, a book. The idea is meticulously expounded in the verse interview of 1966. The film was to have been set in New York, capital of the Western and bourgeois world.

It was the idea of a visit from God, who involves and overwhelms everyone—a visit that explains the sacredness of the real and renders it demonstrable. It was precisely the idea of a *theorem*.

Teorema was filmed in Milan, "the most European city in Italy," the one where the bourgeoisie has the most consistent and up-to-date look.

The bourgeoisie has changed some of its ideals, those of owning and preserving—now it wants to produce and consume. In this its unreality is complete: "horrible conventions, horrible principles, horrible duties, horrible democratism, horrible fascism, horrible objectivity, horrible smiles."[43] Pier Paolo thus depicted this bourgeoisie, and in all this horror he sought to unleash the miracle and carry out the "theorem."

Would the miracle show the needlessness of so much horror? The film ends with a howl—the howl is ambiguity, and it tempers feelings of liberation and appalling horror. The true miracle is that God appears, nothing else. And God appears in the guise of a beautiful and enigmatic youth, who carnally seduces a whole family: the industrialist father, the mother, two children, and the servant Emilia—and then disappears. His disappearance produces a crisis in all of them—the father will give his factory to the workers and strip naked on the platform of the central railroad station in Milan; the servant, absolute innocence and identification with the divine, will levitate as a saint in the sky, and a spring of holy water will gush from her grave.

The film was shot in the spring of 1968. Pasolini returned with his camera to the mellow luminosity of the Lombard landscape. And, if possible, this is the one film without cracks in its surface (those cracks that imparted strength and violence to the films of the "Roman" Pasolini).

The book was published in the same spring, before the film reached the screens. On the jacket flap, Pier Paolo wrote: "*Teorema* emerged, as though on a gold background, painted with the right hand, while with the left I worked to paint a large fresco (the film of the same name). In this ambiguous situation, I cannot honestly say which prevails: the literary or the film treatment. In truth, *Teorema* first emerged about three years ago as a play in verse; later it was transformed into a film, and simultaneously into the story from which the film is taken and which has been corrected by the film."[44]

A devotional painting, the "gold background"—the chastity of expression is linked to a pauperistic style by syntax and vocabulary. The present indicative makes the narration uniform—as always in a film treatment—and there are the summaries, the crude ellipses that mark the arrangement of scenes.

But the writer is in possession of too much manneristic expertness for his own good—the summaries and ellipses become, in his hands, the characteristic features of a "primitive," of a painter who indeed uses the "gold background" with holy reverence.

This reverence is, however, all things considered, slightly questionable. There is too much experience of culture in Pasolini. His feeling is and is not innate—it is a conquest, or actually a reconquest, if one thinks of the virginal aura surrounding *Poesie a Casarsa*. The Oscar

Wilde of the fairy tales was evoked by Cesare Garboli in connection with *Teorema*.[45]

Pasolini's "gold background" changes color in a revival of Pre-Raphaelite taste—a sublimated dream of innocence, in which eros becomes divine.

Teorema was received by the critics, with the exception of Garboli, as though it were a "treatment" and nothing else, a stratagem by an ex-novelist, with his eye to the viewfinder of his camera, but anxious to appear in the literary arena.

I have spoken of Pasolini's philosophical lack of faith in literature. *Teorema* emerged from literature, but it is its poetic testimony and not its product. These were the years in which the doctrine of the anti-novel, the antinarrative, held sway. The visual, cinematographic evidence of *Teorema* represents both the support and denial of that doctrine.

With *Teorema*, Pasolini decided to compete for the Strega prize, as he had done with *Ragazzi di vita* and *Una vita violenta*. He decided to do so with the same relish for challenge that he always enjoyed.

Pier Paolo by now was entirely remote from literary circles—whenever he wished, he directed caustic criticism at the literati. "The world of culture—in which I live by a literary vocation that every day reveals itself to be more alien to that society and that world—is the appointed place of stupidity, cowardice, and baseness. . . . Let's face it, I have remained isolated, to curl up with myself and the repugnance I feel in speaking, whether out of involvement or the lack of it."[46]

This all took place in the fateful spring of 1968.

For two years now, voices had been raised in opposition to literary prizes, on the part of the very same publishers who were sharing and debasing them. Politics came first.

The electorate for the Strega prize had expanded disproportionately and had lost its original, informal features.

An "air of competition" prevailed: all aims were held worthy, even the most innocuous. Given this state of things, the Strega prize was certainly not the one where the power of the cultural industry counted the most.

But the "air of competition" was mingled with the "air of youth" during that spring. For many it was an opportunity to give vent to long repressed or slumbering instincts and desires. Nothing was slumbering in Pasolini, certainly nothing that demanded an outlet against literature. The meaning of his "challenge" was directed elsewhere.

The first voting for the prize took place on June 18, as usual in the Bellonci home at Via Fratelli Ruspoli 2 in Rome. There was a rumor that the university students, acting on the urge to ridicule a culture afflicted with sclerosis, would stage a march on the assembled writers. But no march took place.

In the voting Alberto Bevilacqua's novel *L'occhio del gatto* came out first, followed by *Teorema*. Pasolini decided to withdraw from the contest, and Antonio Barolini, Cesare Zavattini, and Giulio Cattaneo, all of them contestants, decided likewise.

Meetings, powwows, telephone calls—weeks of heated debate in the little literary world of Rome. People took sides one way or another. Maria Bellonci tried her best to rally the dispersed. All in vain.

What was the reason for the dispersal? Everyone denounced the conspicuous lack of scruple with which the supporters of Bevilacqua's novel had gone about collecting votes. Pasolini too had written some letters to friends, asking for their support and votes—but this was part of the traditional game of the Strega.

The real dispersal had to do with the literary worth of *L'occhio del gatto*. Its skill was not in question so much as its necessity, its poetic value. *L'occhio del gatto* was judged as an example of that decline of literature and fiction caused by some publishing houses in pursuit of best sellers.

People were saying: let the publishers play their game, but that doesn't mean the Strega voters must go along. Therein lay the root of Pasolini's challenge.

Pasolini, by participating in the prize and then withdrawing from it, was challenging the weak judgment of a number of Italian literary critics—those who had welcomed Bevilacqua's novel with praise as unmindful as it was enthusiastic.

And again: the reasons for the challenge were anything but accidental. The explanation is to be sought in the unequivocal words written by Pier Paolo two years earlier in the essay "La fine dell' avanguardia":

The action—in a certain way necessary—committed by the avant-garde for the reconsideration and subversion of literary values that were being codified, has ended, of course, by having counterproductive results (about which anyway I care nothing—I am merely confirming something)—i.e., the paper bomb made to explode by the avant-gardists under the little codified fort of literary values has allowed a fine little group of second-rate literati to swarm through the breach (Berto, Bevilacqua, the worthy Prisco, etc.), so that Italian literature has receded to the minor league. But that's quite all right since that is its truth, and therefore one will have to be grateful to the avant-garde for having in its way re-established it.[47]

A vein of harsh irony—and ironically Pasolini exploded his own paper bomb in the quiet salon of the Strega prize, in order once again to verify the "truth" of a literature.

On the evening of July 4, 1968, the final balloting was held in the Ninfeo of the Villa Giulia. Alberto Bevilacqua's *L'occhio del gatto* won with 127 votes, as against 117 blank ballots.

Some of the voters, interviewed on television, directed coarse insults at Pasolini.

Even Piero Dallamano, a few days earlier, had spoken critically: "Let's be honest—this protest over the Strega has broken out at a time when protests are the fashion. Nor are they all innocent lambs, those finalists who withdraw while the race is in progress, denouncing in loud voices (without, however, ever naming him) to the jury and public the errors of the winner who is crossing the finish line. Poor Bevilacqua!"[48]

Pasolini had no intention of victimizing anyone—there was in him, as always, the highly ambiguous desire for "evangelical scandal," by which a situation, even the most futile, was carried to the point of truthful disclosure.

The controversy went on for some time. Gossip had it that Pasolini, because of his absence from the literary scene, had planned to re-enter it with the uproar of a "total confrontation of institutions." The Strega prize in his eyes did not represent any "institution" whatsoever—at most it represented "the triumph of the awful marriage between the respectable literary man and the respectable lady of the good salon."[49]

He was accused of going too far—if that was all the importance he gave the prize, then why participate in it? The question fell once more within the framework of an ethic of responsibility, but why should Pasolini feel himself obliged to respond to this ethic?

Teorema was presented at the Twenty-ninth Venice Film Festival in September 1968. In Venice, too, the atmosphere was one of violent competition. Luigi Chiarini, president of the festival, had invited the film to be shown.

"At first I had decided to send the film to the Festival because Chiarini had promised me that it would be a festival without prizes and without police, and that the cinema element would be maintained, all things that have not happened. It is for this reason that I've withdrawn *Teorema*"[50]—this was Pier Paolo's response to the invitation.

The film was nevertheless shown for the film critics on the morning of September 4. At the beginning of the showing, Pasolini asked those present to leave the hall to protest against Chiarini, who was essentially defending the status quo of the festival.

It was a turbulent festival, with young people and cineastes holding sit-ins. Police intervention was not averted, nor could it be. This led to protests and counterprotests.

In any case, the specialized audience did not desert the showing of *Teorema*. It was followed by an improvised press conference in the gardens of the Grand Hotel des Bains at the Lido. Pier Paolo was accused of "turning somersaults"—he raised opposition and at the same time found a way of not offending the obligations contracted with his producer; he was saving his soul by the confrontation without losing sight of the box-office.

Pasolini overturned these accusations with proper dialectics—he accepted his own ambiguities. He retorted that it was important to have forced the festival to be what it was, one of producers and not of authors. His dexterity, in the end, was convincing.

Teorema was disconcerting because of its content. A combination of eros and religiosity—it was the first time that a completely nude male body, that of the protagonist Terence Stamp, had appeared on the screen in a film that disavowed pornography.

Insistent questions were raised on this point. Pasolini's provocation was judged "commercial." Politics and permissive morality—as was obligatory in that season—exchanged roles. By this nudity, Pasolini meant to express the sacredness of the body—to "cite" it in its immediate reality. The scandal of the nude served to show how intolerable was the sight of the genuine in itself—the body is divine, and that was all. It is ritual epiphany—in the presence of its explicitness the tragedy is unleashed.

The psychodrama did not remain confined to intellectual circles. On September 3, 1968, the public prosecutor's office in Rome ordered the confiscation of *Teorema* for obscenity.

In Venice, the film had received an award from the Office Catholique International du Cinéma, as previously had the *Gospel*. Laura Betti had won the Volpi Cup as best actress.

Despite this recognition by the OCIC, the *Osservatore Romano* of September 13 wrote: "The disturbing metaphor purporting to represent the problem of an encounter with a reality intended as the symbol of a transcendence is undermined at the roots by Freudian and Marxist consciousness. . . . The mysterious guest is not the image that liberates and frees man from his existential torments, from his limitations and impurities, but is almost a demon."

At the trial, which was held in Venice in November 1968, Pasolini defended himself by clarifying the relation between the authentic and the inauthentic that the film implies. He explained the irruption of the divine into the everyday world, and the philosophical role of eros in existential crises. The trial ended with acquittal—the film was judged to be a work of poetry.

Had the "theorem," at this point, been demonstrated? Had the reality of the divine coincided with its representation? I do not believe it is possible to give a positive answer to these questions. Pasolini had perhaps demonstrated a single point: he had shown how much his cinema was really the epiphany of "an immense sexual fetishism." His "hallucinated, childish, pragmatic love for reality" had remained stationary, stripping the polished body of Terence Stamp and suggesting that this body was sacred.

Having abandoned ideology, Pasolini, in his feeling for the sacred, discovered pure autobiographical symbols. The upsetting arrival of the unknown youth in the bourgeois household marked the projection of a destiny that he wished were his—simply and religiously his—he the mysterious messenger, bearer of a celestial and neglected eros, offended by the vulgar aggressiveness of the affluent society. But the fable of the film did not go beyond this suggestion, and the "theorem" remained a statement rather than a demonstration.

CHAPTER 11

REPUDIATION
AND UTOPIA

NINETEEN SIXTY-EIGHT

A juggernaut was rolling across Europe, its wheels setting off the bombs that lay in its path. Tear-gas fumes rose; policemen defended themselves behind plastic shields. The barricades were old, the costumes futuristic. The ancient wind of revolt blew in heavy gusts through Turin, Rome, Berlin, and Paris where the students were shouting, "*L'imagination au pouvoir!*"

The youthful blast by which Europe was convulsed in the year 1968 seemed like a regeneration. Permissiveness was the banner. Not that the world did not need permissiveness. But it needed to reappropriate certain things. Freudianism had urged the individual to reappropriate his own body, but social groups would have to reappropriate their own history. This task, and this obligation, in a society that outlawed all traditions by lumping them together as obscurantist, remained to be evaluated for what they were—necessary steps for man's survival.

Each student revolt—in France, in Germany, in Italy—took place in a particular context. The permissive society, common denominator of the affluent society, hoping to remain immune to any justified criticism of itself, had sought to turn back the clock. Political motives, formulated along the lines of a vengeful conservatism, were being successfully imposed. The new fever showed itself for what it was—

a youthful sickness that if not properly treated, carried with it considerable dangers.

Italy was thus in grave danger. But the "Italian case"—then only dawning—was a complex one. The demands of its student movement were for real participation in the life of the country by the younger generations; reduction of the discretionary power traditionally invested in the ruling classes. This meant, on the purely political level, the encouragement of an effective policy of reform.

The economic boom, the miracle of the sixties, had immediately shown its "poor" side, its inability to change an unbalanced country (north and south, the old cancerous question), and its lack of balance was having troublesome social and moral effects (internal emigration of unheard-of proportions, impoverishment of agricultural resources).

The justifiable reasons for political dissent were overturned, distorted by their lack of cultural content. The theatricality of the revolt, its appearance within a pop context—the manifestos, the mythologized images, counted more than ideas—foiled and dissolved any rational cultural plan. And there was a desperate demand for a different culture. But this demand, like a wave that peters out on the sand, was to be extinguished on the enigmatic and ascetic lips of Ho Chi Minh, or still more on the handsome face of Che Guevara.

A new romanticism was born. It seemed that the children of the Italian bourgeoisie, petit bourgeois as far as its wealth was concerned, could think of nothing else but concocting the figure of a new Santorre di Santarosa, the nineteenth-century Italian patriot and martyr, through the photos of this lightly bearded Christ. The photo went all over the world, for each to read as he would. It was not important to know something about this hero; it was enough to know that he was a martyr, and that martyrs wore such beards and such expressions on their faces.

The Italian '68, born in the universities—the Palazzo Fontana in Turin, the School of Architecture in the Valle Giulia in Rome—demanded that culture examine itself, but imposed its own conclusions on that examination. The political criterion that cultural activity must "serve the people" was re-established. This formula, initially, had no other meaning but an aesthetic one, an aestheticism turned upside down. It did not take long to reveal itself as a Stalinist revival. The Italian petite bourgeoisie was transforming its recent ideas of permissiveness into repression.

Little groups of youngsters appeared in the homes of a number of

Roman intellectuals—they called themselves "birds." They chirped like birds, sacked the refrigerators, on principle refused to speak, soiled the walls, and abused the dogs and cats. In the end, their invasion, which probably claimed to be a "celebration," a spontaneous celebration, displayed the doltish, inexpressive face of violence—they were impelled by an instinctive and disagreeable *squadrismo*.

They were not expressing any sort of happiness. On the contrary, they were filled with a rage that precluded expression. What were the roots of this rage? Perhaps they lay in a generalization of needs and desires, borrowed from ideological propositions rather than the necessities of life. This rage, this borrowing, were strengthened by a social order whereby their demands, whatever they might be, were immediately propelled down the inclined plane of consumerism. No response could satisfy them, since it was immediately consumed on its appearance.

The roots of this rage lay also in the physiology of society. The unchecked growth of urban agglomerates, the transformation of the universities into mere containers for intellectual apprentices, promoted forms of massification with completely new aspects—a massification that fueled existential and social crises. What practical outlet was being prepared, for example, for all those apprentices crammed into the various university faculties?

From this standpoint, the Italian '68 resembled no other. If it was dominated, as elsewhere, by anti-institutional tendencies and by a critique of every supposed form of authoritarianism, the underlying social question was a specific one, and scant attention was paid to it by those who should have done so.

The political parties and the government showed that they were not alert to the situation. People talked of a general revolt of sons against fathers—a periodic generational manifestation. But there was no attempt to understand the dangerous—socially dangerous—sense in which the widespread feelings of frustration could have taken root in the collective psychology.

Revolt, not revolution. Such a distinction had a certain validity—but, on the side of the revolt, one could see positive indications of a release of rage of which, like a bleeding, not only Italy but Western civilization had an urgent need.

In the political parties, even the Marxist ones, which more than others should have been culturally sensitive to the dangers implicit in the concept of "revolt" (as opposed to "revolution"), libertarianism was taken as such, without stopping to realize that anarchic euphoria, even with generous gestures, could cover regressive tendencies. In the long run, those tendencies came to the fore, and made room for interpretations that completely reduced Leninism to the connotation of violence and its programmatic and experimental employment.

The design—deliberate, obscure (it is not easy to decipher it, since surface and depths had unfathomable connections)—was the methodical petit-bourgeois one of weakening the political importance of the proletariat and its parties, to the extent of appropriating their language and exploiting their ideology.

Among the Communists, as elsewhere, there was acquiescence, or acceptance. "Without doubt, in '68, during what was called the year of the students, there was confusion almost everywhere, and I recognize that not even we were completely immune to it. In other words, our mistake, when confronted with that youthful eruption was to judge it too positively, without realizing that the working class was extraneous to such phenomena, especially when they gave rise to instances of degradation, intolerance, and actual violence."[1] These words by Giorgio Amendola, pronounced ten years later, clearly suggest the problem that the whole Communist Party was inclined to ignore.

The failure of the "Prague spring" constituted a blow to the conscience of Western Communists equal to if not more serious than the one inflicted in 1956 by the autumn of Budapest. Soviet reasons of state acted to liquidate all hopes for "national roads to socialism." In the Western Communist parties the reaction was to emphasize the libertarian spirit—but it is one thing to practice that spirit in Prague, another to test it in Rome or Paris. As for Rome, one ought not to forget one characteristic of the Italian petit bourgeois—he, with his unrelinquishable values, is "ubiquitous," as Paolo Sylos Labini has written.

"On the more cultured levels of the petite bourgeoisie there can frequently be some who feel solidarity with the workers, not so much for economic reasons as for ideal reasons of social progress; and then one can see why there are persons who even support measures that are harmful to their own immediate economic interests. The choice of petit-bourgeois individuals who dedicate themselves to political or trade-union life may be determined by ideal motivations, but it can also be (and simultaneously) determined by the more or less conscious consideration that by going over to the workers they can become leaders, while by turning toward the upper bourgeoisie they would become minor officials."[2]

Sylos Labini seems to be describing that generation of sons of priests, of noncommissioned officers, of merchants, of decadent aristocrats, of urbanized peasants described by Trotsky—the Russian students of over a century ago who, amid dense ideological clouds, gave birth to revolutionary nihilism with the idea of taking the fortunes of the country into their own hands.

This social discontent, with its demands for a change of generations, could have been redeemed only by cautious political choices. But the ruling class of the country showed no farsightedness. The parties, the Christian Democrats, Communists, and Socialists, found themselves split down the middle, moved by the wish not to fail in the spirit of renewal—the accelerating appeal of the young people—and at the same time by the need to keep anything from changing.

The flame of revolt was an illusion for the left, and a large portion of the intellectual class let itself be drawn into that fire. University students burned their textbooks and set up "counter-courses" on the Vietnam war. An eagerness for wholeness never before so broadly felt seemed to be running in the minds of youth.

There was considerable turmoil, but what eventually exploded was what Alberto Ronchey has called the "experimental revolution." This "new type" of revolution was carried out "in accordance with variants not foreseen by Marx and Gramsci or anyone else." Its characteristic was fragmentation: "As in industrial production, the various operations are parceled out. As in experimental literature, time is decomposed. As in the cinema and the visual arts, one sees bursts of images that are then reconstructed. As in experimental music, every hierarchy of sound is abolished. But in fact, from '68–'69 on there took place the systematic and gradual destruction of all political or economic authority, of the decision-making management responsible for factories and rates of production, for schools, administrative bodies, important services, and the information or acculturation media, while the legislature actually deliberated without any sure or foreseeable object."[3]

This "fragmentation" meant volatizing any conclusive goal—there was no unifying image of society. The revolt was shipwrecked by one of the most obvious traps that the petit-bourgeois spirit was accustomed to place in action: corporatism.

The trade-union battles of the autumn of 1969—these too justified by hardened and painful de facto situations—were vitiated by a lack of balance between private consumption and public expenditures. Corporatism, even draped in a red flag, made any real revolutionary perspective unlikely. For mass psychology, the policy of "sacrifices" turned out to be offensive, and of course it was offensive for all those who could not keep silent over the tax evasion practiced by the wealthy classes, the flight of capital abroad. The question arose: who pays for the sacrifices?

Only the legislature could have resolved so many conflicting pressures in a positive way. But the legislature only wrangled and did nothing, and the result was a state of increasing turmoil.

In December 1969, with the massacre at the Banca Nazionale dell' Agricoltura in Milan's Piazza Fontana, the long and sinister period of destabilization began.

Among its ambiguities, the year 1968 signified the need for a broad participation by the masses in the life of the state. Against this demand a hostile design was set in motion, at first under the colors of the far right, then of the clandestine left, the implications of which are still not clear today. Massacres and attacks, assassinations and dramatic political compromises—such was the high price of a new Italy.

Pasolini suffered from these collective ambiguities. He had decided to be both rational and irrational, and had institutionalized within himself the freedom to be contradictory. He had experienced in broad daylight how much his ego was "divided," both in its public face and in its private one.

Prepared to contradict himself, prepared to take a radical stand against all political or ethical preconceptions, Pier Paolo grasped the regressive, petit-bourgeois content of the '68 "revolt."

"When I was a boy, at the most delicate moment of my life, the bourgeoisie excluded me, it put me on its list of outcasts, of those who were different, and I cannot forget it. It has left me with a sense of injury, and indeed of evil, the same as a black from Harlem must feel when he walks along Fifth Avenue. Having been driven from the centers of cities, the fact that I found consolation on their outskirts is hardly a pure coincidence."[4]

He wrote these words and dedicated them to the year 1968. The feeling of "evil" had made him very sensitive in noticing where the repressed charge of intolerance and disunity cultivated by the bourgeoisie and petit bourgeoisie lay hidden.

Far in advance of a great many others, Pasolini divined that the Italian student revolt of May '68 had nothing to do with the Maoist cultural revolution by which it was supposedly inspired, but was a disguised revolt of the bourgeoisie against itself.

DEAR STUDENTS . . .

A beautiful early springtime morning—March 1, 1968, in Rome. Almost haphazardly, serious clashes between police and university students took place on the avenues of the Valle Giulia. An onslaught of jeeps, the discharge of tear gas—the ramps leading to Via Antonio Gramsci, where the School of Architecture is located, were the scene of an actual battle. Reports of it spread in the city as of an incredible event—and it was true. That March morning rightfully became part of the mythology of '68.

On the spur of the moment, Pasolini wrote some verses—he called them "bad verses," churned out for polemical purposes, a tract. He had prepared them for *Nuovi Argomenti*. The magazine was making a critical effort to keep up with events. It had commented in its first issue of the year on what had taken place in Turin and on the "cultural" polemics of *Quaderni Piacentini*; with its next issue, it proceeded to an analysis of what had happened in Rome.[5]

A preview of Pasolini's verses came out in *Espresso*. Even though only a sampling (and this led Pier Paolo to protest), the verses kindled a debate.[6]

The title of the tract was *Il PCI ai giovani!!* (The Communist Party to Youth!!*).[7]

It's sad. The polemics against
the party were all over in the first half
of the last decade. You're late, kids.

In question was not only the harsh and unresolved confrontation between young people and the Communist Party, but the political and social content of the "revolt."

When yesterday in the Valle Giulia you came to blows
with the cops,

* In the sense, ironically, of "Power to the people!"—i.e., that youth should take over the Communist Party.—Tr.

I sympathized with the cops!
Because the cops are sons of the poor.
They come from the outskirts, whether peasant or urban.

In these declarative and unlyrical words lay the fuse for a fire. In the polemics of the left the police had always been considered the arm of repression. The police were the uniform they wore, and the uniform was a clear signal.

Pasolini, almost in an outburst of anger, laid bare psychology, anthropology, and history. For him, policemen, "sons of the poor," belonged to the dispersed galaxy of the "wretched of the earth" of whom Frantz Fanon had written. Those cops were the sons of a poor subproletariat, disinherited by bourgeois society *within* the police force.

And then, look how they dress them: like clowns,
with that rough fabric that stinks of food rations,
orderly rooms, and crowds. Worst of all, of course,
is the psychological state to which they're reduced
(for some forty thousand lire a month):
with no more smiles,
with no more friendship with the world,
separated,
excluded (in an exclusion that has no equal);
humiliated by the loss of their quality as men
for that of cops (being hated makes one hate).
They're twenty years old, your age, dear boys and girls.

On the other hand, who were the students? "Spoiled kids," inspired by "sacred hooliganism (of choice Risorgimental / tradition)"—they were "the rich" who had "beaten"—"though from the side / of reason" —"the poor."

This was the dispute, set forth in the pages of an illustrated weekly, that ignited the gunpowder. Vittorio Foa and Johannes Agnoli reproached Pasolini for having revived arguments of a "fascist and middle-of-the-road kind."[8] The students, in debates, prolonged the controversy for years; and such was Pasolini's obstinacy, his insistence on sticking to his guns, that many people retained the schematic conviction which the text—and nothing more offensive to poetry had ever been read in verse—had gone to support.

Pasolini's conviction was something else—he had started out with the same thought that had underlain his diatribes against the new avant-garde. The new avant-garde had imparted a practical look to its own polemics by taking as its target an allegedly hardened literary Establishment—it too had taken as its position the struggle between generations. Pasolini had already responded to this that the true assumption of power was not conducted through the editorial offices of publishing houses or through university departments—it was conducted over history, over the moral contents of a literature, over creative forms of expression.

This time, Pasolini extended the argument to politics. His exhortation to the students ran:

Stop thinking about your rights,
stop demanding power.
A redeemed bourgeois must give up all his rights,
and banish from his soul, once and for all,
the idea of power. All that is liberalism: leave it
to Bob Kennedy.

In this idea of "power," or of its destruction—as of a paralyzing psychological inheritance—lay the sting of the tract. If there was a "power" to take over, it was that "of a party that is nevertheless in opposition."

Even if disheveled, by the authority of gentlemen
in double-breasted suits, bowling enthusiasts, lovers of litotes,
bourgeois gentlemen contemporary with your stupid fathers,

the Communist Party at least had "as its theoretical objective the destruction of the State."

The conflict between generations was carried back by Pasolini to its pivot, the dreadful conceit whose purpose is not "liberation from the chains of capitalism," but a naked substitution of pawns on the chessboard of the bourgeois economy.

Pasolini's invitation—the PCI to youth!!—was dialectical: it shifted the goals to a different level, while keeping in mind that "breeding will tell," and the bourgeois will not change by changing his clothes, mind, and strategy.

The police were not considered as a guarantee of constitutional order, but as the expression of a repressive power—an index of the distance between the real country and the state. This is how they were considered at the time among the same leftist parties that were simultaneously offering their support to the Constitution.

The police as a "fascist" residue in the state. For Walter Benjamin, too, they had had an "ignominious" aspect—in them "the separation between violence that enforces and violence that preserves the law" was to be "suppressed." For Benjamin, the state itself, "whether out of impotence, or out of immanent connections with some juridical arrangement," finds itself at their mercy. The reasons of security that allow the police to intervene, when and how they like, ensure, in Benjamin's judgment, that the state will witness the failure of the "empirical purposes" that it sets itself.[9]

This is a conception that pertains to prewar images of the state—those that encouraged and allowed the various fascisms that dominated Europe from the twenties until the Second World War.

Everything had changed, however—and changed in Italy. Benjamin's conception of police violence was integrated with ideas that contemplated the political and anthropological changes in progress.

When Pasolini pointed out that the conflict between students and police was one between two bands, which, archaically and as a poet, he called the "rich" and the "poor," he was developing an argument in favor of a viewpoint informed by social dynamics and not entrapped by idols of the forum.

I speak of changes in progress—and these were the dark years of the attempted coups, of which certain police authorities were suspected. It remained that the policemen themselves, "sons of the poor," coming from the outskirts, and among the "wretched of the earth," did not fit the pattern, and this was because the economic boom, with its errors and successes, had broken every pattern before the critical intellect could grasp it.

Pasolini was convinced that the bourgeoisie was trying to be "transhumanized"—this is the implied theme of Teorema. It is also the theme of the verse tract Il PCI ai giovani!! But such intentions—in times of one-sided pronouncements, deliberately devoid of nuances—were difficult to clarify. And even if they were clarified—Pasolini, again in L'Espresso, wrote: "This is the reason I provoke young people: they are presumably the last generation to see workers and peasants; the next generation will see nothing around it but bourgeois entropy"[10]—there was no wish to understand them.

HIS BODY INTO THE STRUGGLE

Toward "bourgeois entropy"—a dreadful assent to customs and morality from which one had to escape, from which it was urgent to be saved, and to say everything possible to save oneself, even at the cost of being at first misunderstood. Pasolini scornfully embraced the fate of being misunderstood.

An inconvenient guest, a "disturber of the peace"[11]—such was Pasolini on the horizon of Italian culture. In these years he felt an overriding need for a tauter colloquy with public opinion.

His conflict-ridden relations with the "public" became chronic defiance. The Vatican had protested the award to *Teorema* from the OCIC. Pasolini's films were increasingly to challenge the public and the censors with the "body's reasons," understood as the ultimate reasons of the spirit. The nude body that had fleetingly appeared in *Teorema* was the prelude to the repeatedly displayed nudes in the *Trilogy of Life*.

The times of John XXIII had passed. Pasolini had planned a film on Saint Paul. Despite the help they had given him on the *Gospel*, the Catholics this time refused to cooperate. The film remained on paper.

"With the simple strength of his religious message, Saint Paul in revolutionary fashion demolished a type of society founded on class violence, imperialism, and above all slavery. And so it is clear that for the Roman aristocracy and the various collaborationist ruling classes, one can substitute by analogy the present bourgeois class that has the capital in its hands, while for the humble and downtrodden should be substituted, by analogy, the advanced bourgeois elements, the workers, and the subproletarians of today."[12]

His programmatic opposition to "everything and everybody," and his isolation, had brought Pasolini's psychagogic tendencies to extreme pitch—prophecy by now was merged with action. The spirit of '68, in defiance of rejection and suspicion, had infected Pier Paolo—especially his actions.

Action could be "cinema," but still more it could be words. "Disturber of the peace" was an appropriate definition. And Pasolini threw "his body into the struggle."

The decision was an obvious and natural one—it was a decision that had been taken ever since the years in Friuli. His body and his words were one. But if in the beginning, the synthesis was realized in poetry, now the word was stripped of all literary blandishment and was to try to become simply "political." The example of Saint Paul, seen as a preacher on both sides of the Atlantic, pastor of the spirit in the midst of a violent technological society, was to be mirrored for the next few years in the pages of the *Corriere della Sera* by Pasolini as "pirate" and "heretic."

From the beginning, this "pirate" is "Gracchus," the "new type of buffoon":

> This buffoon talks big. True,
> he writes in the same style I do.
> He needs applause from youthful hands,
> and is therefore forced to talk bigger than they.
> But the content of demagoguery is demagoguery.
> And: every demagoguery is every other demagoguery.
> In opposition, I *know*, and now *want*, every word to be useless.
> I'll throw this manuscript (in words only)
> into Lake Victoria, let's say in a Coca-Cola bottle . . .[13]

He began writing a column for the weekly *Tempo Illustrato*. It was entitled "Il Caos" (Chaos), a miscellany of thoughts, dialogues with readers, bits of film and literary criticism, notes on customs and politics.

The first appeared on August 6, 1968; the column ran until January 24, 1970. The tone was a personal one. "I've talked too much about myself," Pier Paolo was to write at the end of the first year. But talking "too much" about himself was inevitable—it was his style of "preaching."

"For a trip to the moon, how many regressions on earth." Pasolini talks politics by drawing a moral—this is the temptation, the snare of his linguistics, his anthropology. But even if he is caught up in moral issues, Pier Paolo does not turn away from an obligation toward "little daily battles." " 'Il Caos' is a front for little daily battles."[14]

"AFRAID OF ME?"

Pasolini's film work was proceeding without letup. *La sequenza del fiore di carta* (Sequence of the Paper Flower), an episode in *Amore e rabbia* (1967). *Porcile* (Pigpen) and *Medea* in 1969; and in 1968 and 1969, respectively, *Appunti per un film sull'India* (Notes for a Film on India) and *Appunti per una Orestiade africana* (Notes for an African Orestia).

"Difference" is the theme of *Porcile*, which alternates two complementary stories—the Germany of today, and a mystical, Spanish, fifteenth-century fable. The common denominator is cannibalism. In the fable, a young man kills his father, and in a fever of expiation turns bandit and continues to kill in order to feed himself. In the "German" episode, the perspective is reversed. Instead of making love with humans, the hero gives himself over to loving swine. He makes love to pigs and the pigs devour him.

Pasolini's mannerism enriched itself from other models—the cinema of Mizoguchi, the cinema of Jean-Marie Straub. *Porcile* is a film about historical and social catastrophe—Pasolini took as his models two directors of catastrophe films, remote in their style and agelessness.

Tragic and ritual solemnity—*Porcile* contains the literary inspiration and combined rhetoric of ahistoricity and contemporaneity. Not only that, it contains a crudely Oedipal message, the killing of the father, by no means accidentally placed in counterpoint—as in a case from *Psychopathia Sexualis*—with zoophilia.

Medea, on the other hand, exploits the decorative, D'Annunzian, barbaric style of *Oedipus Rex.* Pasolini had convinced himself that a writer could only have "a sacred relationship with objects." With haunted precision, he confessed: "I don't succeed in seeing nature with naturalness."[15] *Medea* reflects a view that has lost spontaneity. By now the writer still hidden in Pier Paolo was increasingly crystallizing his own relationship with reality through the movie camera.

Appunti per una Orestiade africana: a trip to Tanzania and Uganda. Pasolini made the documentary for Italian television. It was sponsored by Angelo Romanò, his friend from *Officina* days, who in the meantime had become a TV program director. Pier Paolo traveled with camera in hand. He searched black Africa, singled out characters and places, and combined contemporary material (wars, revolts, massacres)—he improvised a shred of story.

When the film was finished, Moravia asked himself: "Why has Pasolini abandoned the realism of his novels and early films?" His answer was: "Perhaps Pasolini has tried to avoid forced interpretations, forged by the practical necessities of political action, by shifting himself to a more ambiguous level." And again: "The simplest explanation is that in Pasolini the intermediary of culture is now a poetic necessity."[16] Which is to say that in Pasolini's inspiration reality had lost its clout—and culture remained.

The cascade of jewels that clothes Medea—a grim and animal sensuality. The Furies—the Furies dominate Medea's mind, just as they dominated the mind of Electra in *Pilade*. But what are the Furies? The Furies, in the *Orestiade africana*, were the monstrous, anthropomorphic roots of the giant trees of the black continent. Medea suggests these configurations by her load of gems and semiprecious stones, of black and bristling garments.

Medea and Jason—the harsh, dark maternity of Medea, the open and elegant virility of Jason. Jason is civilization, he is the Centaur's pupil. And the Centaur trains him to culture: "All is holy, all is holy, all is holy. There is nothing natural in nature, my boy, keep that in mind. When nature seems natural to you, all is over—and something else will begin. No more sky, no more sea!"[17] Medea embodies pre-history, where one lives by the senses alone, and where nature is a bundle of dark and inexplicable forces. Medea's culture is magic.

In seeing the film, one wondered with which of the characters Pasolini identified. With the Centaur? With Jason the heedless youth, with the Jason who dances happily among friends under the bright walls of Pisa's Piazza dei Miracoli, where many sequences were filmed? Or with the desperate mask of Medea? The double nature of Pier Paolo's psychology harbored in itself the Centaur and Medea—complementary poles of the ideal, open and tragic, physical beauty of Jason.

In Medea, in her despair, Pasolini represented his own cultural despair, but he sealed it in myth, imbued it with the unreality that belongs to decadent visual art. It was his taste for *bricolage* that triumphed, triumphed in the choice of landscapes—Turkey and the island of Grado—and in the Early Christian cells frescoed with crude Byzantine images, and Pisa. Along with this, the creation of cannibal rites, and the creation of Hellenic customs. Then the face and magnetic presence of Maria Callas.

Maria Callas had been predictably identified with the role of Medea ever since her performance, in 1953 at La Scala, of Luigi Cherubini's *Medea*, conducted by Leonard Bernstein. Pier Paolo scoffed at opera, and made fun of its fans. He used to say sarcastically, "It's queenish to carry on about the opera." He loved eighteenth-century music, and that of the nineteenth century seemed not to interest him. The name of Maria Callas, for the role of Medea, was suggested to him by Franco Rossellini, assistant producer of the film.

Callas, as a tragic actress, possessed an exceptional instinct for the stage and for the liturgy of gesture that accompanies the voice. This instinct had been "worked on" and perfected under Luchino Visconti's direction. Visconti's productions of *La Vestale, La Traviata,* and *La Sonnambula* brought Callas to the peak of her expressive potential.

There were both artistic and box-office reasons for choosing her. Maria Callas, having given up the stage, was still a dazzling name for the public. Pier Paolo chose her, and his Medea accompanied him toward the infernal gods of opera and song:

> bringing with you that odor from beyond the tomb,
> you sing arias composed by Verdi that have turned blood-red
> and the experience of it (without a word being uttered)
> teaches sweetness, true sweetness.[18]

From the meeting between the two, author and stage figure, emerged the legend of a love affair. Photographs in the illustrated weeklies—they were photographed kissing each other on the lips, probably at some airport. Pier Paolo accompanied Maria on a vacation to the Greek islands—the Greece of the "colonels." (And he had written a poem about Panagoulis.) He accompanied her to Paris—she came to Rome. With Moravia and Dacia, the two of them made a trip to Africa between December 1970 and January 1971. He called her: "Little bird with the powerful voice of an eagle / a trembling eagle."[19]

The great tragedienne, the difficult artist who had held Milan in her grip by her "calculations" as well as by her inimitable bravura, was now sweetly ingenuous—almost a girl, at the age of forty-six. Her mysterious delicacy fascinated Pier Paolo—the spell exercised on him by femininity, especially if he perceived in it the echo of the symbolical Mother, repressed and kept at the margins of urban and civilized life.

His friendship with Maria confirmed in his mind the correctness of his intuition—her ingenuousness, that of "a young girl thirsting for bloodless massacres,"[20] was the reflection of an unconscious eroticism, of something "repressed" and only released in song. He drew her picture many times, and enjoyed coloring the drawings with coffee grounds, oil, vinegar, and wine. (Victor Hugo also used to draw, using such substances as tobacco.)

Ninetto and Pier Paolo were still close. Ninetto was doing his military service at that time, in Trieste, and Pier Paolo would go to see him, sometimes in desperation. Maria seemed to doubt the depth of the relationship between them, and Pier Paolo may have taken advantage of Ninetto's absence to play on her doubts. Maria went to the house on Via Eufrate; she met Susanna and Graziella. There were long telephone calls from Paris. In Paris Pier Paolo listened to music with her, and came to understand that the music of Verdi was something immensely different from what he had thought.

Then both of them surrendered to the insurmountable nature of a loving friendship.

One of Pier Paolo's poems testifies to the impossibility of crossing that threshold. The title is "Timor di me?" (Afraid of Me?), a title from Verdi, words written for Leonora in *Il Trovatore* by Salvatore Cammarano. It is the moment when Leonora, under the tower where Manrico is held prisoner one "dark night," mourns her lost "rosy-winged love." The feeling of darkness, the mysterious vital determination, the passion wholly hidden in the secret cells of the heart—all this Maria Callas was able to sing in an astonishing voice and with keen feminine sensibility.

> Oh, a terrible fear.
> Happiness explodes
> against those panes over the darkness.
> But this happiness, which makes you sing *in voce*,
> is a return from death.[21]

Woman, for Pier Paolo, represents a "chthonic reappearance"—a reappearance from a journey to places he has never been. The woman returns with news, the news of the "void in the cosmos."

> Who is there, in that COSMIC VOID,
> whom you carry in your desires and know?
> It is the father, yes, he!
> Do you think I know him? Oh, how wrong you are,
> how naïvely you take for granted what is not so at all;
> you base your whole discourse, here resumed by singing,
> on this assumption, which for you is a humble one,
> not knowing instead how arrogant it is,
> bearing within it the signs of the majority's mortal will—

One evening in Paris ("Paris stands out behind your shoulders with a low sky / and pattern of black branches") Pier Paolo read in Maria a request for love, love between woman and man. He read there the customary, ancient, womanly request: that the man be "father." Pier Paolo could not respond to that request. Psychologically, what to her was "certain," was not so to him at all. Within him, his image of the "father" was a "cosmic void."

> You smile at the Father—
> that person about whom I have no information,
> whom I frequented in a dream that I obviously don't remember.

And yet, for that image ("that person . . .") he had felt in life an acute, fierce, and unconfessed nostalgia—so acute and fierce that it had been, as we know, a reason for trauma.

And so, to Maria's probable request—a request wholly contained in the gift of her singing ("You give, you scatter gifts, you have the need to give")—Pier Paolo could answer with a smile:

> I pretend to receive;
> I thank you, sincerely grateful.
> But the weak fleeting smile
> is not of timidity;
> it is dismay, more terrible, much more terrible
> than having a separate body in the realms of being—
> whether it is a sin
> whether it is only an accident: but in place of the Other
> for me there is a void in the cosmos
> a void in the cosmos
> and from there you sing.

His smile was meant to be the sign of his "dismay." His trauma, or his homosexuality, allowed him no adventures but the crude ones he had known.

His friendship with Maria Callas was not thereby extinguished—with a different scenario, it seems that Pier Paolo had uttered in verse the words written by letter to Silvana Mauri in 1950. The poem offered him the possibility of enclosing his secret in a symbol—a rapid sign, in this new, wholly functional poetic language: the word "father." And he adds, as though for irony:

> strange that from that monster of authority
> should come also sweetness
> if nothing else as resignation and brief victory.

The telephone calls from Paris became less frequent, as did Maria's visits to Rome. Laura Betti had become jealous. The rule of her "kitchen" was threatened.

Laura would sometimes declare that "her man" was free to stray if he wanted to. She accused Callas of being unworthy of the aura surrounding her.

One evening Pier Paolo returned to dine at Laura's, bringing her a brightly colored embroidered silk shawl. An atonement present, said Laura—husbands always come home to be forgiven, and they're always smart enough to bring a present. With Laura, Pier Paolo did not suffer from having "a separate body"—their relationship was maintained by Laura "in rivalry." Laura countered Pier Paolo with her own loves, her own "boys"—an eros, that is, in no way "repressed," but rather displayed ostentatiously, to the point of shamelessness.

Maria Callas, on the other hand, showed Pier Paolo what "fear" of a woman meant.

"THIS SO CHASTE LOVE OF OURS"

The loving friendship with Maria Callas became less important in Pier Paolo's heart because of a violent emotional crisis occurring at this time.

Oh, Ninarieddo, do you remember that dream
we've spoken about so often?
I was in the car, and drove off alone, with the seat
beside me empty, and you ran after me;
alongside the still half-open door,
anxiously and stubbornly running, you cried
with a little childish sob in your voice:
"Hey, Pa', will you take me with you? Will you pay my way?"
It was the journey of life, and so only in a dream
did you dare to reveal yourself and ask something from me.
You know very well that that dream is part of reality,
and the one who spoke those words was not a dreamed Ninetto.
It's so true that when we speak of it you blush.
Last evening, in Arezzo, in the silence of the night,
while the sentry closed the gate behind you
with the chain, and you were about to disappear,

with your flashing and comic smile, you said to me—"Thanks!"
"Thanks," Ninè? It's the first time you've said it to me.
And indeed you realize it, and correct yourself, without losing face
(something you're a master of), joking:
"Thanks for the ride." The journey that you wanted
me to pay for was, I repeat, the journey of life:
it was in that dream of three or four years ago that I decided
what it was that my equivocal love for freedom was contrary to.
When now you thank me for the ride . . . My God,
while you're in the clink, I fearfully take
an airplane for a far-off place. I'm insatiable for our life,
because only one thing in the world can never be exhausted.[22]

The poem—beautiful and the only serene love poem written by
Pasolini—is dated September 2, 1969. Ninetto was in the army. A
turning point in their relationship—it was almost as though the
separation, the fleeting reunions, had rooted their feelings in a fitful
necessity for which there was no remedy.

But Ninetto was growing up, and his psychological needs were beginning to strain his loyalty to Pier Paolo. He wanted to take "the
journey of life" with Pier Paolo, but at the same time he wanted his
own life freely to run its course.

Sex between them was a thing of the past. Eroticism had been
shifted to that everyday life that the departing automobile, the *empty
seat*, the *half-open door*, the *anxious and stubborn running*, so felici-
tously represented in the transition from dream to poetry.

It was the sublimation of homoeroticism, but also the stabilization
of a male friendship, a friendship in which the relationship could
never be between equals because of the difference in age. Pier Paolo
did not represent a "father" to Ninetto—or else he did so in a wholly
unexpected way. There was no noticeable psychological dependence
in Ninetto. There was an ingenuous need for independence. Pier
Paolo encouraged in him the expression of the old, inherited peasant
morality, but also the expansion of every possible vitality. They
appeared equal—if equality between them had ever been possible.

There was no equality, because Pier Paolo was suffering the oncoming
shadows of age. He was afraid that youth was deserting him—he
suffered because his hair was thinning and turning gray. He made up

for it by his way of dressing, increasingly under the spell of youthful fashions. He was helped by the leanness of his body.

His face was pale and fleshless, his look always more wounded. He had trouble with his teeth, and went several times to Merano to have them treated. But all this was the dust of life.

He had gone to the Aslan Clinic in Rumania to take the Gerovital treatment in the spring of 1971. He took Moravia and Ninetto with him. Ninetto was chasing girls, and Pier Paolo was beginning to worry.

It was not a question of sexual jealousy. Ninetto was off on an independent journey of his own through life. Girls fulfilled the meaning of that flight. It was this that accounted for Pier Paolo's suffering—a suffering that derived from the realization that Ninetto was now a man, and that life would take on a new inconstancy.

In Rumania Pier Paolo wrote the script for the *Canterbury Tales*. When he went to England to shoot the film, the crisis broke.

It was while shooting the film in Bath—and of course Ninetto, as always, was one of the actors—Pier Paolo realized that an unavoidable separation was in the offing. It was certainly not a physical separation but an emotional one, and for this reason doubly dramatic.

When Ninetto told him that he was going to get married, Pier Paolo's despair was uncontainable. He wanted to die.

That August he began writing the despairing sonnet sequence, *L'hobby del sonetto*.

The pleasure of classical composition, with meter and rhyme tending to adjust themselves with precision, came back to Pier Paolo. But the form then turned out to be violated, torn asunder by a thirst for destruction that scattered words and emotions. Pier Paolo here uses the formal *"voi"*; the object of love is called, in the vocative, "my Lord." These sonnets express a torment in loving that recalls the sonnets of Shakespeare. The whole sequence—well over a hundred sonnets, between drafts and revisions, and a pile of corrections that makes them difficult to read—the whole can be interpreted as a long ballad on the agony of love caused by a "vile" betrayal. In addition to the Shakespeare of the *Sonnets*, one might draw a useful comparison with the Oscar Wilde of the *Ballad of Reading Gaol*.

The need to die, to hang himself "from a tree in the garden" with a "faithful and reassuring cord." "I am a rag of a man"—"a dog that curls up / to lick its wounds." No reproaches or accusations: "I want no excuses for my dishonor":

it being by now my inveterate
custom, I masturbate, within the burned-out
windings of the sweat-covered bed.

One solution: that "she," the girl, might die—a death that would serve only for an exercise of disrespect. For the rest, no other solution. "Eight years" of love have been lost. In this exacerbated reprimand in verse, *pace* ("peace") rhymes with *brace* ("embers").
Is it the thorn of sex that heightens such revulsion?

It's not a matter of sex, as you know,
but of a love which like death has clutching hands.

Sex has been a "bit of seed"—"the bit of seed we both saw / in our first meetings long ago." It has been nature that has transformed sex into love, irreparably sublimated it, the "laughing" nature of this "Lord" who is now a betrayer:

What you are is nearly the Inexpressible.

Love is perhaps entirely "inexpressible." Put to the test of life, this love object, often called by "the pet names" given "to the mother"— "I squeezed your hand as though it were hers"—seems "deaf," his face "puffy" and disfigured because devoid of laughter. And yet, amid these truths, love blazes more violently—"you never lacked dignity."
Finally the painful recognition comes—it is not "jealousy over the girl" that provokes these tortured cries, but a feeling of violation, a solitary and for that reason more exasperating feeling. The poet who writes *L'hobby del sonetto* discovers, almost like Proust, that his agony suffers from itself and nothing else—it is its powerlessness to emerge from the shell of the psyche. But this drives him almost insane with grief.
Pier Paolo confided this grief to his friends—he spoke of it endlessly, in exacerbated words. It seems that at the same time he was indulging in severely masochistic erotic practices. In the previous years, his human "communion" with Ninetto had reached a state of happiness. A large canvas painted in 1969—Pier Paolo's return to an old artistic passion—for Laura Betti's new house (she had moved from Via del Babuino to Via di Montoro) shows this clearly: Ninetto's curls are the sign of joy. Thus, in a portrait of Laura, the curly head

of the "herald" in profile against the background, in the manner of Chagall, repeats the symbol of a Shakespearean "joy." It stood for an equilibrium achieved. Life was to break it.

Elsa Morante became impatient with Pier Paolo's heartbroken rage. She accused him of selfishness. This caused a chill in their friendship. Elsa said that Pier Paolo did not really love Ninetto. Someone who loves desires the happiness of the beloved.

It's true that love should be holy,
Elsa was right, and one should want nothing
but the happiness of the one who is loved. But it's also true
that there is no right not matched by a duty.

Pier Paolo discovered that his feelings of love had no outlet, but he was also afraid of a future solitude. This solitude might be filled by the presence—loving and not erotic—of the "angel," the "herald." This presence was a "duty."

Elsa has certainly not understood that
I might die; or that I was so weak as to wish
to be consoled, or treated like a madman.

Pasolini did not listen to arguments about his "selfishness." He unwillingly accepted the fact that Ninetto might get married and have children—as he did. On the other hand, Ninetto, as it turned out, did not come and go in his existence—that was to remain what it was. The marriage did not represent the rupture of a companionship that by now was something quite different from any erotic one.

In Pier Paolo, almost childishly, one incredulity persisted:

it escapes me,
the reason for so much fury in your mind
against this so chaste love of ours.

The "chaste" love was to remain intact in Ninetto's heart, and Pier Paolo understood this. But he certainly did not understand it immediately.

Meanwhile Pier Paolo's erotic life went elsewhere, more and more. He said so in a sonnet, with corrections marked on the manuscript, and in saying it foreshadowed the landscape that was to be that of the last night of his life:

It was almost two in the morning—the wind
streamed through Piazza dei Cinquecento
as in a church—there wasn't even any refuse,
the only life at that hour—on the grass

prowled the last two or three boys,
neither Romans nor rustics, in search of the usual
thousand lire, but as though without cocks—
I talked to one of them in the car—

a fascist, poor kid, and I struggled
to touch his desperate heart.
You arrived in your car

and honked; next to you sat a horrible
young individual; stolen goods
dangled in the window; where had you come from and where were
    you going?

Anyway Pier Paolo accepted the marriage—Ninetto was to have a
wife and a "nest," a "petit-bourgeois" nest:

I on the other hand live the reality
reserved for the different who have no alternative
but to wish well to those who love.

With Ninetto's marriage, Pier Paolo accepted something in himself
that he would have preferred not to accept: his vagabond emotional
existence. It was to this that he had been furiously refusing to submit.

CULTURAL DESPAIR
AND POLITICS

The solitude suffered by Pasolini was also, of course, cultural.

The moment came when his fame as a film director seemed to
eclipse his authority as a writer. He conceived films of fantasy, and
purely novelistic ones. He thought that the *Decameron*, the *Canterbury Tales*, and the *Arabian Nights* would be, as they were, a light-hearted outlet for his desire to tell stories. He was to take on in his
own style these three masterpieces of medieval, European, and Medi-

terranean narrative in order to reconceive the moments in which man—the new man, the juncture between archaic peasant ideals and humanistic values—had discovered himself as the moral agent of his own destiny.

The *Trilogy* was intended as a fairy-tale canvas—a canvas in the "flamboyant" style, swarming with human circumstances interwoven among themselves, and all of them carried off by a beneficent and smiling touch of fate.

The years 1971, 1972, and 1974 are the dates of the three films— Pasolini's real box-office successes. The ear of the literary man, pupil of Spitzer and Contini, and the eye of the art historian, pupil of Roberto Longhi, quick to catch the sound and images of reality under the transparent veils of the languages of art, were no small help to the film director.

A great decorator, in frames lightly sprinkled with the golden dust of a diffuse aestheticism, Pasolini revealed unusual shrewdness as a showman. Into his tapestries he wove patterns of unsimulated sexuality, explicit male and female nudity. He showed the male organ in erection, and often of such size as to quadruple the scandal. And scandal meant success.

Freedom of the body, the body as language—Pasolini aligned himself with the most reckless experiments in psychiatry, whether of the Freudian school or not. The so-called "themes of desire" seemed to be his. The total visualization of eros and its most secret symbols appeared in these films as the sum of calculation and play, of show-business shrewdness and moralistic provocation. The director, in premeditated progression, was aiming to present himself—by sweetening the pill with poetry—as the therapist for the most hardened collective inhibitions. Denunciations and court trials rained down on him. The charge of obscenity over an *auteur* film had become so frequent in Italy as to be part of the publicity ritual of its release. The *Trilogy of Life* passed unscathed through this ordeal of humiliation.[23] Art triumphed over pornography, and Pasolini achieved a utopia.

What utopia? That of showing how all of existence is catalyzed by an idea of youth, of physical vitality that develops outside the norm, in an innocent and uncontaminated landscape. This is the utopia of those who do not recognize impediments and taboos to erotic life.

Writing of the *Arabian Nights*, Moravia saw a connection between Pasolini's "peasant" utopia and this other utopia, which he called "homosexual." He asked himself: "What is the relation between the nostalgia of the genuine peasant and homosexuality? It seems clear in seeing the *Arabian Nights* that the relation consists in a certain idea of youth. Peasant civilization has been the youth of yesterday's world —homosexuality is the youth of today's world. Thus, in a surprising way, peasant civilization and homosexuality become identified."[24]

Running through this identification was the sign of the now widespread ideal of permissiveness. Pasolini's characters smiled. They smiled in the *Decameron* and showed their bad teeth—but they also smiled, with a health that brimmed with undefiled beauty, in the *Arabian Nights*.

It was a smile that was to be extinguished in itself. Italian life was to show such persistent shadows as to dissipate any dream, any utopia. Permissiveness, in reality, manifested itself to Pasolini's eyes and intellect as a cancerous monstrosity. But Pier Paolo, beyond the pessimistic certainties that he increasingly entertained, allowed himself the dream when his camera was in his hands.

The repudiation of it was harsh. The language of the body to which he had given life brought him horror. Having completed the *Trilogy*, he composed its elegy—his "hatred" in the presence of the "sex organs of the new Italian young people and children,"[25] "human refuse." It was "the collapse of the present," which implied "the collapse of the past."

Despair was systematic in Pasolini's mind.

His body in action—the psychological crisis of presence drove him toward vital solutions. With the cinema he had sought to heal the first wounds he had received. The theorizing of the cinema as the "written language of reality" had offered itself to resolve the conflict in which his sensibility and intelligence had risked final collapse. Then the cinema had devoured him with its obvious production requirements. The *Trilogy of Life* corresponded both to those requirements and to cultural ones, not only of pure creation but, as I said, of collective therapy.

All this was not enough. Pasolini's life demanded that its private wounds be healed in public and with the public. It demanded a struggle.

Il PCI ai giovani!! was the first gesture of struggle. Then came his participation, as a cineaste among cineastes, in the demonstrations against the Venice Film Festival of 1968.

The occupation of the Palazzo del Cinema in Venice earned him a court trial on October 11, 1969. His codefendants were Cesare

Zavattini, Lionello Massobrio, Marco Ferreri, Alfredo Angeli, Francesco Maselli, and Filippo De Luigi. In a photograph—all of them lined up in magistrate's court in Venice—Pier Paolo's hand is pressed to his chin, his eyes fixed on the floor. The seven were acquitted because "the acts ascribed [to them] do not constitute a crime."

In "Il Caos," *à propos* of the Venice festival and the clash between police and demonstrators, he published on September 21, 1968, an open letter of denunciation to Prime Minister Giovanni Leone. Leone answered him publicly, stating that "no brutality or violence" had been perpetrated in Venice.

On October 5, again in his column in *Tempo Illustrato*, Pasolini retorted: "I have an absolute belief in your good faith. . . . But you must also believe in my good faith. I was present that night. And *with my own eyes* I saw the violence of the police."

This was the first step in a confrontation with the political authorities that Pasolini, from that moment on, was to carry bitterly forward for the last seven years of his life. Not an abstract, or intellectual, confrontation, but one over specific details.

Again—his body into the struggle, and not only against the representatives of power. In his reply to Giovanni Leone's letter, he writes: "I know: awareness of one's rights—by now I've said it many times, and I'll never tire of repeating it—can become aggressive and terroristic. Never fear: I will not cease to struggle, as best I can, even against the 'fascism of the left.' "

This expression, "fascism of the left," provoked stinging accusations. But Pasolini's intuition had by then already understood what transmutations were taking place, and with what consequences, in one portion of rebellious youth, both those of a Communist persuasion, and those of a Catholic one, among the members of the Associazione Cattolica dei Lavoratori Italiani.

In his column, "Il Caos," on September 28, 1968, he had explained what lay at the root of this "fascism of the left," and there he foresaw the birth of terrorism. "So many Catholics, in becoming Communists, bring with them Faith and Hope, while neglecting, without even realizing it, Charity. This is how fascism of the left is born."

The country, as the younger generations were attesting, was demanding a different way of conducting public life. At the same time, it rejected any reappropriation of history and tradition. It rejected everything, symbolically burning every book and custom.

If young Catholics were lacking in Charity, Faith was changing into fideism, into violent blindness. Freedom is a paradox governed by the ascertaining of its limits, in the dialectic of rights with duties— duty flows from historical awareness.

Pasolini lived all this obscurely in conflict, but he had a clear image of it in his mind. He indulged in controversy with the newspaper *Lotta continua*, but he lent his name to it as editor so that it could appear on the newsstands—no editor of the extraparliamentary paper was listed at the time in the register of publicists, as required by press laws, in the capacity of *"direttore responsabile."* Therefore, when the fifth supplement of the periodical, entitled *Proletari in divisa* (Proletarians in Uniform), came out, Pasolini was held responsible and charged in a report sent by the Turin police on May 27, 1971, to the public prosecutor's office. The reason was "the highly polemical content concerning the armed forces."[26]

The trial, suspended by the Court of Assizes in Turin, was never held.

For this mode of behavior, public opinion accused him of "ambiguity." Pasolini responded in an interview with Jean-Michel Gardair: "I can no longer believe in revolution, but I can't help being on the side of the young people who are fighting for it. It's already an illusion to write poetry, and yet I go on writing it, even if for me poetry is no longer that wonderful classical myth that heightened my adolescence. . . . I no longer believe in dialectics and contradictions, but in pure opposition. . . . All the same, I'm increasingly fascinated by that exemplary combination, achieved by saints like Saint Paul, of the active and contemplative life."[27]

The failure of the revolution, the illusion of writing poetry—here lay the roots of Pasolini's complex, systematic cultural despair. In this way he marked his own solitude—the solitude was transformed into anger, then into aggressive polemics. A kamikaze joy, sacrificial and provocatory, was steadily growing in him. The offer of his own body to the struggle was meant to be—and was—a publicly agonizing one.

THE "RESTORATION OF THE LEFT"

Without ever having compromised itself, but with great skill,
great and powerful skill,

the Communist Party again protects us like a beloved mother hen.
Nor do I mind. A little security in so much risk is human.
Thus, with their tails a bit between their legs
after all their pride, the young people return to the CLN,*

against the repression, they say, by bad power:
every union conceals a postponement to the future, and thus a
    weakness . . .[28]

In every election, Pasolini declared his support for the Communist Party, and *l'Unità* printed it. His relations with the party, however, remained uncertain, and below the surface hostile.

I have always opposed the PCI with devotion, awaiting
an answer to my objections. So as to proceed dialectically!
This answer has never come: a fraternal polemic
has been mistaken for a blasphemous one.[29]

"A beloved mother hen"—the revolutionary ideal had lost vigor. The spirit of the "revolt" contained more than one bourgeois lie: The "Bourgeoisie" (Pasolini's nominalism allowed itself these capital letters), in the span of a few years, had dampened all the fireworks.

There was the resurrection of the Trade Unions,
which carried forward into the empty space that had opened
the great masses of workers with their class consciousness.[30]

Because of this, "the old prestige of the Communist Parties was restored." Was this "restoration" a "new spring"?
The Communist Party was visibly gaining support among the middle classes—right-wing terrorism, which kept repeating its attacks, helped to consolidate on the left a feeling of defense and constitutional legitimacy.

The road remained strewn with corpses and wounded
who hobbled along behind,
but were recognizable by their hair
and crowded together as in concentration camps . . .[31]

---

* Committee for National Liberation, from the time of the Second World War.—Tr.

In the face of the success that the Communist Party was gaining, Pasolini maintained an attitude of ironical detachment. It was clear to him, however, that beyond the party's "conservatism," a dark pool of ambiguities lay still further to the left.

"L'ortodossia" (these lines are dated April 15, 1970):

> . . . it was about *il manifesto* that I was to speak to you
> (as you asked me to).
> The heretic, then, did not seek his heresy with disinterested love:
> he didn't even dream of it!
> He countered seriousness with seriousness;
> sought again the original purity of thought.
> He struggled, in reality, for the real orthodoxy.
> He fought against habits and their deviations.
> Much as I (I, impure) go back in thought,
> I find nothing but revolts
> led by a secret anxiety for order.
> Orthodoxy smoldered in the depths of the revolt,
> opposing itself to the acolytes who had yielded to history
> and its necessities.
> The authors of *il manifesto* were thus undaunted,
> but to create new certainty, new defenses for those who—[32]

Pasolini was not seeking ambiguities but "impurities," the mirror of his own "impure I"—that impurity that signified the understanding of history "and its necessities." The suspicion is this—Pier Paolo may well have had it at the back of his mind—that the "beloved mother hen," the party, in its apparently tired wisdom, knew better how to disobey than all those who opposed it with heretical fury.

His having taken *il manifesto* as an example is not surprising. This publication represented the spearhead of the ranks of Marxist heretics at the beginning of the seventies. All the others, scattered but active fringe groups, had the faces of rabid students of order, of strenuous conservatives of a buried past—they appeared to him as neo-Zhdanovists from the standpoint of culture, and as "fascists of the left" from the standpoint of practice. Some others were "the barbarians," and although

> . . . as for me, I'll continue (in the first person, of course)
> to have a poetic idea of the barbarians
> that makes life marvelous for me,[33]

in them were the signs, the indications, of the approaching apocalypse.

THE "UNFORTUNATE
GENERATION"

Solitude: one must be very strong
to love solitude; one must have good legs
and uncommon resistance; one mustn't risk
colds, influenza, or sore throat; one mustn't be afraid
of muggers or murderers; if one has to walk
the whole afternoon or even all evening,
one must be able to do so without realizing it; there's no place to sit;
especially in winter; with the wind blowing over the wet grass,
and with big stones amid the damp and muddy refuse;
there's really no comfort, no doubt about it,
beyond that of having before one a whole day and night
with no duties or limits of any kind.
Sex is a pretext . . .[34]

Pasolini did not reject his intellectual solitude, nor did he suffer from it. Rather it was the result of deep suffering.

After the controversies that exploded in 1968 over the Strega prize and *Teorema*, he was called a "pornographer" over the *Decameron*, the *Canterbury Tales*, and the *Arabian Nights*.

In the *Decameron* and *Canterbury* Pasolini appeared on the screen, an illuminated self-portrait amid the throng of characters, almost in the corner of the fresco, the artist surprised at his work—Giotto in the first film, Chaucer in the second. Ironically making fun of himself, in the pleasure of his disguise, Pier Paolo accentuated on the screen what he attempted to erase in life: his fifty years. He was enjoying himself—the joy of the *Trilogy* was the brightest flash of his happiness.

Poetry was an illusion. And yet Pasolini went on writing prolifically.

I cease to be an original poet, its price is a lack
of freedom: a stylistic system is too exclusive.
I adopt tested literary models, in order to be freer.
For practical reasons, of course.[35]

"The practical purpose" of his poetry went even further—ever more urgent, with no letup, the need to "intervene"—an intervention shouted from solitude.

Pride led him to demand of himself the relinquishing of all constraining erudition of style. He eliminated the hendecasyllable, and wrenched the line into the rhythm of speech. He aligned his free strophes according to the extemporaneous breaks that occur in speaking—more than one of his poems reads like an improvised public speech.

But his reliance on these breaks, these jumps in logic, turned out to be a subtle stratagem—Pasolini instituted a personal code of writing endowed with an inner, almost too obvious, communicative dynamism.

He wrote, but he thought he was writing in a "literary void."

Voids, in literature, follow periods of fullness—this present void was produced "by the failure of the negation-literature of the new avant-garde and by the action-literature of the student movement." Such "failures" bring about other things: "during a cultural void, one has a sudden luxuriance of existence." Existence, the rejection of any intellectual intermediary, in appearing as pure mobility, is essentially immobility. "With the young people (who have not experienced hermeticism, or neorealism, or the literature of commitment, or the new avant-garde) one sets up a dialogue that becomes more difficult every day. Having become Byzantines by themselves, they seem ever further from the truth—since their *inexperience* coexists with a curious, precocious, and rather monstrous *experience*."

What had happened with these young people? That they, with the ideas for which they had become spokesmen, and denying themselves any dialectic with the past, were not refilling the present "void" with something new, but encouraging the restoration of the old content which seemed to have been swallowed up.[36]

To explore the reasoning of Pasolini's mind in the years immediately following 1968, and retrace the torturous line of his despair, means to throw light on one of his profound convictions:

O unfortunate generation!
What will happen tomorrow, if this ruling class—
when they were under fire for the first time
they didn't know the poetry of tradition
it gave them a rough time because without
a realistic smile it was inaccessible to them
and even for that little they did know, they had to demonstrate
that, yes, they wanted to know it but with detachment, outside
   the game.

   In the lines bearing the title "Poesia della tradizione,"[37] this conviction, or this obsession, is clear—the break in historical and cultural
continuity had generated monsters. It had generated nihilism—the
rejection of the past, a blind and raging rejection within which the
Italian middle class seemed to have burned itself out.

What had happened in the country's vitals?
   "The growth of the class of subordinate intellectual workers does
not succeed in occurring in the form of technicians who place themselves in crucial positions of production thereby ensuring its development. . . . The great mass of children of the independent petite
bourgeoisie that throngs to the university understands at a certain
point that it has set out to become an elite, or at least to remain middle
class, and instead is faced with the specter of intellectual unemployment and social decline. It is in this framework that the tragedy-revolt
of '68 ripens. In the attempt to define its own class position, this class
in decline will seek to identify itself with the industrial proletariat.
Herein lies the fundamental difference between the situation in Italy
and the one in the United States or Germany or France. It is not the
proletariat trying to become middle class, it is the latter, threatened,
that seizes hold of the proletariat and supports it in its revolt."[38] One
might add that in its support, this middle class, this petite bourgeoisie,
furnished the proletariat with an old and vanishing set of anarchist
ideals, on which it was easy to graft the spiral of terrorism.

   O unfortunate generation!
   that in the winter of '70 used fantastic overcoats and shawls

Pasolini's lines continue,

   you came into the world, which is large and yet so simple,
   and there found those who laughed at tradition,
   and you took this falsely ribald irony literally,
   erecting youthful barriers against the dominant class of the past
   youth passes quickly; O unfortunate generation.

It was a generation that had yielded to the allurements of false
teachers—the accusation is leveled against the "falsely ribald" irony
of the new avant-garde. But this generation was still more unfortunate

in having yielded, youthfully and unconsciously, to the world against which it also fought "with zeal":

> it was what tried to cast discredit on history—its own;
> it was what wanted to sweep away the past—its own;
> O unfortunate generation, and you obeyed by disobeying!

What is the fate of these young people? They had shed no tears— "intellectual" tears, "owing to pure reason"—either for "an octave of the Cinquecento" or for "the shrines of their ancestors."

> the class struggle cradled you and kept you from crying:
> rigid against everything that did not smell of good sentiments
> and desperate aggressiveness . . .

A betrayal had been perpetrated by these young people,

> for love of the worker: but no one asks a worker
> not to be basically a worker
> workers don't weep in front of masterpieces
> but they don't perpetrate betrayals that lead to blackmail
> and therefore to unhappiness
> O unfortunate generation
> you'll weep, but lifeless tears
> because you may not even be able to go back
> to what, not having had it, you haven't even lost . . .

Blackmail and unhappiness. Pasolini was not among those who, carried away by the aggressiveness of the young, theorized the "suicide" of the man of letters and the poet. Literature, to him, was not a sin or a fault for which amends had to be made.

In this it was possible to verify the distance of the secretly Christian and Catholic writer that he was from the unconscious Catholicism that was acting in so many. Pasolini's Christianity was tinged with a Pauline glow, with oracular clairvoyance—with anthropological sensitivity acquired on the terrain of experience. Far from the idea of being a "mediator" and settling quarrels as a Catholic, anomaly became ever more conspicuous in him: anomaly and contradictoriness.

He seemed to become the slave of cortical reactions, of a compulsion to contradict. On the other hand, no one grasped better than he what consequences such a vast loss of historical awareness would have in Italy.

I, getting old, saw your heads filled with sorrow
where a confused idea whirled, an absolute certainty,
a conceit of heroes destined not to die—
O unfortunate children, who saw at arm's reach
a wonderful victory that didn't exist!

LITERARY "UNREALITY"

In February 1971, Pasolini published his last book of poems, *Trasumanar e organizzar*. The critics paid such scant and fleeting attention to it that he decided to review it himself.[39] In his review he spoke of himself, pedantically and ironically, in the third person.

He divided the book into three sections: "a private diary"; "the collection of lyrics for a woman named Maria" (the poems for Callas); and a third, "wholly political" section. "His nostalgia for a mode of being that belongs to the past (and which sometimes imparts to Pasolini almost a shy and awkward reactionary vehemence) and will never be restored, and for a final victory of evil, is transformed into a kind of cosmic pity for those younger brothers destined to live from now on existentially, by values that to Pasolini seem intolerable."

The sting of the article comes, as usual, in the tail, with the last lines: in the volume there may be "falsity, insincerity, awkwardness," but not "unreality." "Speaking generally (and relying on the reader to understand), one might say that Pasolini loves reality; but still speaking generally, one might also say that Pasolini does not love— with a love equally total and profound—truth: perhaps because, as he says (*Nuovi Argomenti*, April 1971), 'the love of truth ends by destroying everything, since there is nothing true.' Might we then conclude by stating that this refusal to know, to seek, to want the truth, any truth (any nonrelative one, since Pasolini continually and quixotically fights for partial truths), this Oedipal terror of coming to know and admit, is what determines the strange and unhappy fortune of this book, and probably of all Pasolini's work?"

It is a question with no answer. Oedipal fear is the most unexpected revelation of the article, the point of critical acknowledgment. The rejected "nonrelative" truth produced the risky discourse of a poetry confused in its contingency, in its stream of reproach. The larger truth, though unknown, lay elsewhere: perhaps in faith.

So *Trasumanar e organizzar* was published almost in silence. The publisher himself, still Livio Garzanti, had come to believe less in his author. For many, this bundle of poems constituted a sortie by a survivor.

In literary society, Pier Paolo continued to have very few friends. And yet he wanted to maintain his presence in its midst, if only through writing. He resumed his activity as a critic.[40]

In 1971 Eugenio Montale's *Satura* was published. Pasolini reviewed it for *Nuovi Argomenti*. Unlike others, he stressed the ideological line in this complex volume. The form of the book seemed to him ironical and deliberately "unpoetical." "Knowing that the *unpoetic quality* and the *content* of *Satura* pertain to its form . . . it does not seem to me that a reader who responds to deeds with deeds, to ideas with ideas, can in any way consider himself a transgressor."[41]

This response, by Pasolini "the reader," was:

All of *Satura* is basically an anti-Marxist tract. But if it were only that, I would limit myself to taking note of it (called into question by its satirical tone). If I disapprove of it, it is rather because Montale has tried to ignore the fact that bourgeois pragmatics, as well as Marxist praxis, is also founded on the illusion of *time*, and that the bourgeoisie, like the Communists, do nothing but talk about "tomorrow." If the "better world" (of this cursed tomorrow) is a promise of opposition, it is also an assurance of power.

But unlike Marxism, Montale does not, as a satirical poet, "free" himself from power. Indeed, he achieves a kind of identification of power with nature.

His book is based wholly on the naturalness of power . . .

Montale in turn replied. He replied in verse, calling Pasolini by the name "Malvolio."

Pasolini had spoken of "cowardice," of ideal cowardice. Montale's lines read:

This violent burst of charity
falling on our heads
is a final imposture.

It can never be said to begin "at home"*
as they taught us at Berlitz; never
will it turn up in primers.

And certainly not from you, Malvolio, or from your gang,
not from wailing trumpets, not from one who makes of it
a second skin that he then sloughs off.

Charity belongs to no one . . .

And again, in another poem entitled "Lettera a Malvolio":

It has never been a question of my fleeing, Malvolio,
nor even of a flair for sniffing out the worst
a thousand miles away. This is a virtue
that you possess and I don't envy you, also
because it would do me no good.
                              No,
it wasn't ever a question of fleeing
but only of taking up
a respectable distance.

It wasn't very difficult at first,
when there was a clear separation,
horror on one side and decency,
oh just a very little decency,
on the other. No, it wasn't difficult,
it sufficed to slip away, fade out,
make oneself invisible,
perhaps be so. But later.

But later when the stables were emptied,
honor and indecency locked in a tight embrace
established the permanent oxymoron
and it was no longer a question
of fleeing and taking shelter. It was the hour
of conceptual phocomelia
and the crooked was straight, on everything else
derision or silence.

* In English in original.—Tr.

It was your hour and it's not over.
With what agility you've mixed
historical materialism and evangelical pauperism,
pornography and redemption, nausea for the odor
of truffles, the money that came to you.
No, you're not wrong, Malvolio, the science of the heart
is still unborn, each invents it as he likes.
But let's not talk about fleeing . . .⁴²

These were scorching accusations, especially where Montale connected Pasolini's intellectual "agility" with an interest in the box-office.

Pasolini retorted with a series of epigrams:

The impure to the pure
I have no gang, Montale, I'm alone.

I don't reproach you for having been
afraid, I reproach you for having made excuses for it.

I may want evil [*mal voglio*]; but my own.

She has darkened your mind, your somewhat too Italian
Dark Muse.

Besides I'm not astute:
usually it's the fearful who are astute.

Italian household gods
In inventing a nickname for me
the only disappointed hopes, as far as poetry is concerned,
would be Jakobson's:
you've made yourself the spokesman for the bourgeoisie,
with Saragat and the Devil at your back.

Evangelical pauperism (?)
Ah, Montale,
with your mumbling
you practically reported me to the tax collector.

Between poets
All I had left was a single eye
and you put it out with a toothpick;
but I've always known you by the name of Οὖτις*
and so I can only accuse Οὖτις.[43]

Bitterness oversteps its bounds with Pasolini's reply to Montale, and his despair becomes, if possible, more deeply rooted than ever.

In May 1972, on behalf of the Associazione Culturale Italiana, Pier Paolo gave lectures in Turin, Milan, and Rome. He began: "First of all, I must say that I do not find myself in a happy moment of my intellectual life. I have a vague feeling, for example, that my words here lack both originality and authority."

In an interview for *Il Mondo*, he said, "I now live outside literary society. I no longer vote in the Strega. I am voluntarily on the sidelines. Literature, in its social aspect, does not interest me very much. . . . As for the silence around me, it only seems to me a symptom of incompetence, cowardice, or simply hatred."

Even years before, the critics had seemed to "hate" him. "It was a vague racial hatred, the kind felt for all those who are different, whether Jews or homosexuals. This hatred was lumped with a more specific one, or rather one specifically belonging to intellectual games: the hatred that is directed at anyone who refuses to be identified by an exact signboard. Hatred was everywhere, while I was avoiding definitions. . . . Yesterday's hatred was the hatred of the subculture. Today's hatred is the same thing, decanted into culture."[44]

What emerged was the figure of the persecuted writer, the face of Pasolini's personal myth. Did this myth have any new justification?

Youthful "blackmail" was having an effect on many. Pasolini knew it. He felt alone and "desperately unreal"—he maintained this in the publisher's note that he added to the volume of essays *Empirismo eretico* in the spring of 1972. Of this "unreality," he wrote: "The author makes a virtue of it, corresponding to the scorn he feels for his critic colleagues—almost all of them—whose inglorious white heads and dishonored graying ones lie prone before the inhumanity of the worst of the new generation."

---

* I.e., "Nobody," the "name" used by Odysseus in his dealings with the Cyclops.—Tr.

The physical image of solitude: the Chia tower, so long desired, was finally purchased in November 1970. Pier Paolo used to shut himself up in it, sometimes accompanied by Ninetto, sometimes alone. The tower—the remains of a medieval castle protected by an outer wall on which stands a second, uninhabitable tower—very high and visible from afar, rises on a buttress at the juncture of two gullies, at the bottom of which two streams converge.

North of the Cimini Mountains, sheltered by a small hill along the road that leads from Viterbo to Orte, the tower looks like an architectural setting designed for a sequence from the *Decameron* or the *Canterbury Tales*. Behind the wall, the outermost one on the rocky spur, a concrete and glass block was fitted out, with rooms laid out one after another, in which two people at most could live.

There Pier Paolo, in the love he had for this place, would have liked to be buried. In a nearby field he had a cabin built of light wood —one large, well-lighted room. He said it would be his painter's studio. He often spoke of going back to painting, and Laura Betti kept a room with a private entrance for him in her house on Via di Montoro, so that he could use it as a studio whenever he wished.

Nothing came of the idea. His refuge in Chia was used instead for other work. In the summer of 1972 Pier Paolo began to retire there frequently, to write a new novel that promised to run to two thousand pages. He said very little about the contents of the book, but he did say that in it he would draw his most authentic self-portrait, adding that this book would also be a portrait of contemporary Italy—probably the Italy of the "austerity" brought about by the Yom Kippur War and the oil embargo.

Petrolio was the first title written on the first page, later replaced by *Vas*. It is a notebook of over five hundred pages jumbled with corrections, intercalated by jotted and incomprehensible notes. A chaotic procedure. If the design of the two thousand pages was vivid in Pier Paolo's mind, as fate would have it barely a quarter of them were written, a dimly perceptible quarter wracked by second thoughts.

The solitude of Chia, and the mirroring glass of the windows, vast as walls, seem to have suggested the metaphor of the double. The book contains the actions of a character doubled like a playing card— a young intellectual placed in parallel with a second self. It is a Dostoevskian trick—the positive perfectly reversed in the negative—

and this mirroring proceeds so that the one character is transformed into the other, while at the same time both transform their masculinity into a desperate femininity.

The doubling of the ego is not alien to the spirit of Pasolini's fiction —it belongs to Pasolini the story-teller in the Italian language, the one to be seen in the unpublished Friulian pages, the rough drafts of *Il sogno di una cosa*, and in those of *La Divina Mimesis*. But in *Vas* all is different. The distance between these last pages and the others can be measured by the fury that intoxicates them. The writer seems to be attacking, within a clot of hostile material, an emotion that protests against the light and flees—perhaps eluding him.

This duplication of the ego—or its doubling—proliferates in adventures that are dreams to be deciphered: a party at the Quirinal Palace, for example, where political and literary figures mingle. A modest reality is expanded, inflated beyond possibility and its meaning is obscure. The reader, in going through these pages, has the feeling of penetrating a secret that does not wish to be violated—a novelist's workshop unexpectedly thrown open. You hold your breath as you enter.

The most successful pages, of an artistic mastery that breathes a sound of mourning, are the erotic ones. Never had Pasolini depicted the mystery of his sexuality in such a total and direct way. The "generic and numerical" Petrarchism about which Gadda in his curiosity had joked, had—one can here check the evidence of it— some truth. And in a night scene, in a field on the outskirts, as always hazy and scrubby, with all the many *ragazzi di vita* who offer themselves for fellatio by the double and feminized hero, as in a ritual that heals the wounds in the soul while at the same time reopening them, one is able to see how much tormented human experience is gathered here in all its reality—and it is the reality of an anguish that has no name.

Erotic passion in Pier Paolo was recidivist and was carried on with nightmarish obsessiveness—a repetitive rhythm that made his life crudely identical to itself. On the other hand, this life was what he loved most—a boon, an unattainable dream to which, in these very years, along with the cinema, he freely devoted his imagination. How can one fail to notice, however, in even the lightest and happiest sequences of the *Trilogy*, signs of a tormenting fury, and in the bodies chosen—except for the young people in the *Arabian Nights*—in the smiles that often break over their sadly decayed teeth, the pain of one who does not succeed in believing that existence differs in any way from a horrible wound?

Existence was also sin in Pasolini—a sin that it was impossible not to commit, and which had sex as its stage.

In an interview with a French monthly periodical, he had let it be written: "I love life fiercely, desperately. And I believe that this fierceness, this desperation will carry me to the end. . . . Love of life for me has become a more tenacious vice than cocaine. I devour my existence with an insatiable appetite. How will it all end? I don't know. . . . I am scandalous. I am so to the extent to which I stretch a cord, an umbilical cord, in fact, between the sacred and the profane."[45]

What is the last threshold of possible scandal?

A photographer, Dino Pedriali, has told of spending two days with Pasolini in Chia, in mid-October 1975.

Pier Paolo had himself photographed naked, from outside the windows of his bedroom. It seems to be night outside, and inside the tower there is a raw electric light. Pasolini is supposed to have told Pedriali that the photographs would be used as inserts in the novel he was working on.

Vas is an unknown quantity. But in the photographs, his lean body, with the muscles of a soccer player, is not. Half reclining on a light-colored bedspread, or standing next to a chest of drawers, Pier Paolo leafs through a book, and in his physical presence there is no scandal. Rather there is, in the stubborn way he holds the book in his hands, indifference to the act, and a form of substantial modesty that thwarts any inference.

The scandal is to be read instead in the pages of *Vas* where the enervation of oral intercourse is celebrated. It is the scandal that bursts forth from confessions, from the projection into words of what our bodies and sensibilities unconsciously contain. This was the scandal that boomeranged on the heart and passion of Pasolini.

In *Vas* there is perhaps another unforeseeable "scandal"—a wish for intellectual, psychological, and moral change, which seems to dominate the last years of Pier Paolo's life. In these unfinished pages there is not only a writer who reveals the urgency of an artistic adventure whose results he cannot foretell—there is also a man who dissects and amputates the wounds by which he is possessed, and who is tortured by the need to investigate their tragic origin.

Pier Paolo's knowledge of himself was surprising in its lucidity—so surprising as to seem enigmatic. His "division," his psychological doubling, his manifest contradictoriness were all known to him. He was capable of making a virtue of it: "One can cheat in everything except style. . . . Consistency is inhumanity, it is a language for fanatical monks, not for men. . . . Seriousness is a quality for those who have no other qualities."[46]

Nevertheless, he may have arrived at a point that required reconciliation. To strip his soul—perhaps his body—naked, to reconstruct in words and images the ruling obsessions by which his existence was oppressed, may have signified the supreme revulsion.

Life gets tired of one who endures.

Ah, my recidivist passions
forced to have no dwelling place!

The cinema by now had resolved, and by a wide margin, all his economic problems, and had given him widespread international notoriety. Literature, on the other hand, seemed definitely to have relegated him to the sidelines. At this time, Pier Paolo conceived the necessity for a change—therefore the ultimate scandal.

The change might have come about through a reflection, even a festering one, of his own most secret image. Would *Vas* have achieved this goal? Was this the hidden plan of his two thousand pages?

The unfinished notebook suggests a *Bildungsroman*. But there is no support for this hypothesis.

POSTSCRIPT TO THE PRECEDING PARAGRAPHS

Pasolini believed in social regeneration, believed in it like another Gioachino da Fiore.* But he also believed in it like a politician who gauges his convictions in accordance with the fluctuations of contingencies.

---

* Or Joachim of Floris—twelfth-century Italian mystic and Cistercian monk, who divided time into three stages: of the Father, of the Son, and of the Holy Spirit. He prophesied that the last would begin around 1260.—Tr.

The refined poet, brought up on the French decadents and the Italian hermetic school of the thirties, hoped to recover from the historical wounds of the soul by transforming the ethical and psychological aim of his poetry into a practical and political one. This poet, in the course of his journey, underwent radical changes—he became a political man, and a man of the cinema.

The practical aim. Pasolini prophesied—and allowed himself to make pronouncements and recantations. He entrusted his conduct to contradiction, certain that the truth of feeling, *hic et nunc*, was reason for salvation.

Had he not perhaps prophesied that the "blue-eyed Alìs," the youths of the Third World, would invade the old Western world and destroy its history by violence?

> ... They will destroy Rome
> and on its ruins
> lay the seed
> of Ancient History.
> Then with the Pope and all the sacraments
> they'll go like gypsies
> up toward the West and North
> with the red banners
> of Trotsky in the wind ...[47]

The words leave no room for doubt—the whole volume of *Poesia in forma di rosa* was shot through with this dark and at the same time cheerful certainty. The events of '68 overturned the prophecy, and Pasolini disowned it.

"Why do I disown this prophecy? Because then I was alone and ridiculous in making it, and today it has become common property. But that doesn't mean that I wish presumptuously to attribute to myself the monopoly of certain ideas and the prerogative of being enamored of them. No, I mean that this prophecy was the right one at the time but only insofar as it was mistaken. It was a vital and fruitful caprice of political passion, a conscious and desired reversal of future common sense."[48]

So the intellectual, the man of letters, consciously lied. For what purpose?

"How then to account for the fact that this hope that was placed in the revolutionary potential of the peasants of the Third World is now mistaken? Because it is no longer seen in revolutionary perspective. The students in fact are bourgeois. They would like to exorcise the poor and preindustrial peasant world, evoke it as a metahistorical entity, and put themselves in front of it like an apocalyptic guide. To make the Revolution? No, to make Civil War."

The Revolution, the red revolution of the disinherited, was in decline. It had been the great myth of Pier Paolo's life, the myth that seemed to redeem him from the ancient and endured religion of his peasant forbears. And yet this myth had foundered in the calm sea of neocapitalism. For one who had adorned the myth with the ambiguous and graceful images of decadent poetry, and then with the violence of a highly active life, this foundering was morally as well as politically repulsive.

The myth was disappearing—the last children of the bourgeoisie were appropriating it for themselves and disfiguring it. The myth was becoming "matter-of-fact." How to lead it back to originality? How to rediscover in the poor and disinherited of the world the prophetic mission of social regeneration?

The "old, knowledgeable Communist mole" remained to measure by a slow metronome the tempo of social development, but it too was working out reformist strategies, and extinguishing the shimmering fire of the myth in plans calculated with too much patience.

"At this point, in spite of themselves, and even clinging to their old error, the Communists who criticized me some years ago were right at the time, when all this was not fashionable. The peasants can make the Revolution, but *in concrete situations*—indeed, in practice they are always the ones who make it, with the impoverished workers (in Russia, China, Cuba, Algeria, Vietnam), but these are national revolutions, not international ones, and they are born of a national hunger. The workers are international, but not the peasants—they are universal."

These words were spoken by Pier Paolo to Ferdinando Camon in 1968. There is no trace of disappointment in them. But the frankness with which the "error" is confessed may have been a prelude to more frankness, to the wish to look at things with the lens of distance and to discover even in the strategy of the "old Communist mole" a consistent truth.

It seemed that Pasolini was thinking of throwing away some of his inveterate convictions. It seemed he was thinking of regenerating himself.

Another example, another trace, perhaps a fleeting one, of this wish. In the autumn of 1969 all the poems of Ungaretti were collected in a single volume. Ungaretti, as we know, had been the poet most lovingly read by the young Pasolini. What impression did the forty-seven-year-old Pasolini derive from rereading the poet he had loved in his youth? "As for responses, I got nothing out of it."[49]

The judgment is a harsh one. But it is immediately softened and modulated: the poetry of Ungaretti is "poetry of a total innocence," which, "like all true innocence, is shameless." It is "chaotic, equivocal, childish, ambiguous, demoniacal, ingenuous, immature, incomplete"; it is "like a roguish eye whose light cannot be extinguished by any sort of good upbringing." These are words that uphold what they deny.

Still, the judgment is iconoclastic—or perhaps it is a profoundly autobiographical judgment. Pasolini is speaking of his own unrealized, equivocal, and incomplete poetry, and seeking comfort in the visible defects of the master. It is the kind of comfort that one asks for, with a pinch of irony, while feeling the sting of bitterness, because one would like to be different, immeasurably different, from what one is.

Nineteen sixty-eight had left its load of repressed truths and drugged intellectualism. The bourgeoisie, still the protagonist of history, had created new "metahistorical myths, banners of absoluteness."[50] Pasolini had the understanding to grasp what was happening: he confessed past lies, and spoke lightly of his culpable instances of levity.

In the cultural panorama in which he moved he glimpsed sins more serious than his own:

Among educated men there was not one who had the courage to raise his voice in protest. The risk of unpopularity was more fearful than the old risk of truth. Besides, even specialized culture was worthy of its time; by now its internal organization was definitely pragmatic, intellectual products were products in their essence, like things or facts: bets won or lost. Bad faith was ideologized as an element of the way to be cultured or even a poet. "Groups"—they themselves psychologically and physically similar to a bourgeoisie that had seemed to be finished forever—made "literary power" their declared or direct goal, not only without shame, but even simultaneously carrying out a moralistic, terroristic, and blackmailing function, deduced, with unheard-of cheek, from a pathetically defeated leftism.

The only reality that throbbed with the rhythm and breathlessness of truth was the—flaunted—one of production, of the defense of the currency, of the maintenance of institutions essential to the new power, and these were certainly not the schools or hospitals . . .

This is a page from *Vas*. The perspective of '68 has been reduced to the effects it has had on the life of culture. Pasolini loved to run "the old risk of truth," but he suffered from certain personal ambiguities. He had raised his voice "in protest" (*Il PCI ai giovani!!*), but in the cinema his urge to let the pure language of the body speak had declined into unrelated "permissive" illustration. He ideologized "bad faith," insisting that only in this way could judgment adapt itself to experience.

Because of this, the lucidity with which he expresses himself, melancholy and distant as a historian, shows still better his wish for intellectual withdrawal.

To change, and to run as much as possible "the old risk of truth." But in what way—here is the question—in what way "to throw his body into the struggle"?

THE WRITER AS PIRATE

Ninetto was married at the beginning of 1973. For Pier Paolo writing poetry was no longer what it once had been. *Trasumanar e organizzar* was a satirical, polemical, and wildly autobiographical book. *L'hobby del sonetto* rooted the poet in the violence of private passions.

His old cultural passions had lost the meaning they had once had. When someone tried to bring them up, he would answer with resentful harshness. He responded in this way to Enzo Golino in an interview on dialect:

Go back to dialect? What for?—it's a minor issue that has no connection with reality. If once again today people are talking about dialect in films, if a few farces in dialect are broadcast on television, if popular songs seem to be rediscovering our folklore heritage, the fact is irrelevant—it has to do with the superstructure, not the structure of society. Dialect and the world that expressed it no longer exist, people don't speak, don't want to, and can't speak in dialect.[51]

But don't they speak dialect in his films, in the *Decameron*, the *Canterbury Tales*?

Of course, because in my films I show a vanished life, people and places from a historical pocket outside of time, an archaic fossil. At the time I made *Accattone, Mamma Roma,* and even *Hawks and Sparrows,* this ancient world existed—but then it was swept away, and from the age of innocence we passed to the age of corruption.

Consumer civilization had destroyed the "ancient world." Ideology was transformed into moralism, and "Pauline" fury got the upper hand.

In that same year, 1973, Pier Paolo became increasingly impatient with his publisher. He was dissatisfied with the way *Trasumanar e organizzar, Empirismo eretico,* and *Calderón,* the tragedy published in the fall, had been distributed and promoted by the publishing house. Basically, his dissatisfaction had more to do with himself than others. His literary talent had become dulled—or if not dulled, it corresponded less objectively to the expectations of his readers. Pasolini's existence rebelled at the feeling of being confined again to private, merely individual limits.

Pier Paolo wished to break his contract with Livio Garzanti, while taking care not to break with him personally. He seized the opportunity from chance developments of no importance—that Garzanti, for instance, was about to publish a novelist not up to the publisher's previous standards. These were pretexts, on which he even commented ironically. The fact was that he wanted a new connection. He accepted the offer of Giulio Einaudi.

Having denied any function to dialect, he set about writing a sort of palinode to *La meglio gioventù,* in a rediscovered Romance tongue. He turned his old enthusiasm for the world of the "little homeland" upside down into "gloomy enthusiasm."

The dedication to *Poesie a Casarsa* had read:

Fontana di aga dal me país.
A no è aga pí fres-cia che tal me país.
Fontana di rustic amòur.

———

(Fountain of water in my village.
There is no fresher water than in my village.
Fountain of rustic love.)

The corresponding dedication in the new book reads:

Fontana di aga di un país no me.
A no è aga pí vecia che ta chel país.
Fontana di amòur par nissún.

––––––––––

(Fountain of water in a village not mine.
There is no staler water than in this village.
Fountain of love for nobody.[52])

A retraction—and a "repudiation." The volume, with the title *La nuova gioventù*, was published by Einaudi in the late spring of 1975. It too was largely ignored by the critics and the public. Pasolini realized that it had not done him much good to abandon the publisher of his successes—he regretted having done so, and hoped to be able to go back to him. But that spring he was no longer a suffering Christ excluded from the society of the living, the faded painting of a rural *maestà*. That spring he was an inflamed Paul of Tarsus, who was composing his "letters to the Romans," filled with accusations and dark premonitions.

The repudiation of dialect had become a repudiation of the *Trilogy of Life*. Pier Paolo had cancelled or postponed other cinema plans in order to film with meticulous care *Salò o le 120 giornate di Sodoma*. His vitality and joy had taken on a deep shade of mourning.

A change had occurred. Or else there had been an unexpected strengthening of his qualities—the qualities that at the end of the fifties had made him an indispensable questioner of all of Italian society. He was now writing a political column for the front page of the *Corriere della Sera*.

Pasolini rejected the "reformism" of the new Communist policy, but at the same time he rejected the "barbarous" and petit-bourgeois "extremism" of the dissenters on the far left.

Crisis had overtaken Western democratic society, most cruelly the Italians after 1968. The more the official line of the Communist parties approached, in concrete terms, the parliamentary ideal (and this was what it intended to revive), the more those who felt themselves physiologically cheated of "revolution" rose up against this line. And again the more Pasolini stressed his own solitude.

This solitude spoke—not in verse, nor in a dialogue with readers, as had been the case with both *Vie Nuove* and *Tempo Illustrato*.

Solitude meant not setting himself "against everything and everybody," but placing himself in the position of a "reactionary of the left."

It was a difficult position to hold. His targets were the consumer society, the Christian Democratic exercise of power, permissiveness in the young, the official line of the Communists. Fluid material. It was a matter of provoking, by surprise, one controversy or another: now showing support for those who contested the Communist Party from the left, now espousing arguments that might even appear welcome to the right. It was a matter of making the viewpoint unrecognizable in the immediate sense—making it a "pirate" viewpoint, so that it would be impossible for anyone to claim it as his own.

In 1972 Piero Ottone succeeded Giovanni Spadolini as editor of the *Corriere della Sera*. Ottone's intuition suggested to him that the upheaval in Italian society after 1968 required the expression of the most diverse opinions. The large newspapers were losing their inveterate "semi-official" function, institutionalized during the twenty years of fascism, and which afterwards had deteriorated only slightly. They were the connection between the real country and political power.

The *Corriere della Sera* set up an "Open Tribune" column, and thereby provided unusually stimulating opportunities for public debate. Hitherto the Milanese daily had never violated the moderate tone of the Lombard and Italian bourgeoisie. The new "Open Tribune" served to violate it, and sponsored individual expression of thought as an indispensable element in the dialectics of politics.

D'Annunzio, too, had written for the *Corriere della Sera*—verse or proclamations inspired by an overheated interventionalism, with the war of 1915 at the gates. The Italian bourgeoisie needed to be galvanized.

Pasolini, who spoke out of his own solitude, forswore the effects of any such galvanization. His role as the "inconvenient guest" of literature and Italian culture reached its height.

"Open Tribune" gives us an opportunity to stress a fact that in any case has taken on considerable importance in the "new Corriere," namely the first contribution by Pier Paolo Pasolini on January 7, 1973. How did you come to publish this writer, detested by so much of the Establishment and sometimes not held in an "odor of sanctity" by parties on the left?

We came to do so precisely in our search for less conformist and less traditional voices. I have said that we believe in the circulation of ideas: who can promote the circulation of ideas if not the intellectuals, who are the first artificers of ideas in society? Pasolini's contributions found a vast response, first of all because Pasolini was in a period of favor during those months. We helped to ensure that the Italian public would notice his articles by placing them on the front page.[53]

These are the words of Piero Ottone.

Pasolini's first contribution to the *Corriere della Sera* appeared on its second page on January 7, 1973, with the title "Contro i capelli lunghi" (Against Long Hair): "I understood that the language of long hair no longer expressed 'things' of the left, but expressed something equivocal, Left-Right." A "discourse" on the anthropological mutation of the Italians, and not only the Italians, had been opened.

"Long hair says, in its inarticulate and obsessed language of non-verbal signs, in its hooligan iconicity, the 'things' of television or of commercials for products."[54]

In 1973 Pasolini's presence in the *Corriere* was anything but frequent—only three articles.

The second piece was also published in "Open Tribune," on May 17 —its title was "Il folle slogan dei jeans Jesus" (The Crazy Slogan of Jesus Jeans).[55] The third, "Sfida ai dirigenti della television" (Challenge to the Television Executives),[56] appeared as a third-page literary essay on December 9, 1973. In treating it this way, the editors shortened the distance that Pasolini wanted visibly maintained for his contribution.

Pier Paolo was writing for the *Corriere*—his first article had aroused irony and dissent. His gesture shattered old patterns of behavior. On the other hand, the paper's traditional readers saw in this collaboration a change of conduct that they found severely provoking.

The dynamism of Italian society was expressing itself in those years in violence and laceration: from the rise of terrorism (the conviction that it was the "strategy of tension" gained currency at this time) to the extremely diversified seething of public opinion.

It was in this framework that the divorce referendum was announced for May 13, 1974. The victory of the "no" votes, which opened Italian legislation to a concept of marriage that was not exclusively religious, was the most exciting moment in the secularization of the country.*

* The referendum was worded in such a way that those opposed to divorce were to vote "yes," those favoring it "no."—Tr.

Pasolini with his front-page articles was to have a catalytic effect at this moment.

"In 1968 and the years that followed, the reasons for agitating, for struggling, for shouting, were profoundly right, but historically opportunistic. The student revolt emerged from one day to the next. There were no real and objective reasons for agitating (except perhaps the thought that the revolution was to be now or never—but that is an abstract and romantic thought). Furthermore, for the masses, consumerism, prosperity, and the hedonistic ideology of power were the real historical novelty. On the other hand, today there are objective reasons for a total commitment. The state of emergency involves the masses—indeed, especially the masses."

This was Pasolini's thought in March 1974. The "nonpolitical" intellectual found himself involved in the "duty" of political intervention.

There were two reasons for the state of emergency. The first: fascist terrorist attacks. The second: "to bring up again the subject of the 'historical compromise,'"* since it "offers itself as a help to those in power in maintaining order."[57]

Pasolini's design was to use the *Corriere della Sera* for purposes of "struggle." More than one person was to object that he, in his turn, was used by the newspaper.

The objection makes no sense. The newspaper edited in those years by Piero Ottone could not call itself the expression of a class in power or of preconstituted interests. Mirrored in it, Pasolini "read" a disfigured society, different and in the process of becoming—different as compared with any preconceived and deep-seated vision. Pasolini shunned orthodoxy rooted in the logic of ideological confrontation. That confrontation had collapsed, and the kind of newspaper that Piero Ottone was orchestrating through the contributions of the most culturally varied intellectuals testified to that collapse.

There were contractual agreements between Pasolini and the ownership of the *Corriere* in early June 1974. Pasolini went to Milan for a showing of the *Arabian Nights*, and on that occasion met with Giulia Maria Crespi, who represented the publishers (and whom he already

---

* The arrangement, proposed in the early seventies but never carried out, by which Communists and Christian Democrats would join in governing the country.—Tr.

knew, having used her villa on the Ticino as the setting for part of *Teorema*), and with Gaspare Barbiellini Amidei. An understanding was reached.[58] On June 10, 1974, the paper published on the front page, though under the heading "Open Tribune," the article entitled "Gli italiani non sono più quelli" (The Italians Aren't What They Used To Be). It was the signal for polemics.

I said that the divorce referendum represented the highest moment of secularization for the overwhelming majority of Italians. Many were convinced of this. Pasolini was certainly convinced that the preponderance of "no" votes was a "victory." But he analyzed the quality of that "victory." And his analysis turned out to be a provocation.

The "no" vote has undoubtedly been a victory. But the real indication it gives is that of a "mutation" of Italian culture, which is moving away as much from traditional fascism as from socialist progressivism.[59]

It was a victory obtained through the diffusion, in all classes of Italian society, of the values "of consumption and of consequent modernistic tolerance of the American kind." Peasant and early-industrial Italy was being dissolved. The void it left would "probably" be filled "by a complete bourgeoisification." Not even the Communists appeared capable of halting this process. A "cultural ratification" was in progress that involved everyone: "masses and bourgeoisie, workers and subproletarians. The social context has changed in the sense of being extremely unified."

The conclusion, which called forth a violent denial from his readers, was: "The matrix that generates all Italians is now the same. There is no longer any appreciable difference—beyond political choice as a dead pattern to be filled by gesticulating—between any fascist Italian citizen and any antifascist Italian citizen."

For Pasolini, fascism itself had changed, to the point of being its "purely nominalistic" definition. Had not many fascists voted "no" on the divorce referendum?

The most insidious argument in the article, the one that required very careful reflection, was where it was said that antifascism, as a political choice, was now a "dead pattern."

There was a severe reaction on the part of the Communists. In *l'Unità* of June 12, 1974, Maurizio Ferrara accused Pasolini of irrationalism and aestheticism. Pasolini was said to have distorted Italian society to fit his unconscious image of the world. Similar arguments were expounded by Franco Ferrarotti in *Paese-Sera* of June 14.

To read these articles suggests that Pasolini had come to the point of wildly contradicting himself, or to unveiling some secret nature of his own. With the perspective of time, one must say that he had not changed his conviction since the years of his political and intellectual apprenticeship. His point was to break with demagogic convictions, with accredited principles. This had happened in Friuli, and likewise in 1956.

If Pier Paolo was at fault on this occasion—a resounding occasion— it was in not completely clarifying the extent to which historical continuity, as a determined motive in anthropological analysis, had pressed him to insist.

There was in him a moralistic characteristic—his anthropology and his semiology of collective forms of behavior possessed, so to speak, an unconscious. It was an enraged, vindictive unconscious, and its psychological reality obliterated the actual truth. And yet he succeeded in pointing out multiple responsibilities.

The sins and responsibilities of intellectuals and politicians. The responsibility for fascist outrages fell, for example, on the entire left: "We have done nothing to keep the fascists from existing. We have only condemned them, gratifying our consciences by our indignation —and the louder and more petulant the indignation, the more tranquil the conscience. In reality, we have behaved with the fascists (I speak especially of the young ones) in a racist way—that is, we have hastily and unmercifully tried to believe that they were racially predestined to be fascists."

LETTERS TO THE ROMANS

Yet there was something new in the articles that Pasolini was publishing in the *Corriere della Sera* and other newspapers that year. This new element did not consist in his dreaming of a hypothetical "golden age"—an age that could have been represented by the fascist "Italietta."* It was something less easily grasped.

It would seem that those engaging in controversy with him needed

* Diminutive epithet used to disparage the Italy of the fascist period for its provinciality.—Tr.

to superimpose a target on him—one suggesting a pamphleteer's nostalgia for a politically and morally vanished past. Both Maurizio Ferrara and Italo Calvino accused him of "nostalgia," and they were not the only ones to do so.

I mourn the "Italietta"? But then you haven't read a single line from *Le ceneri di Gramsci* or *Calderón*, you haven't read a single line from my novels, you haven't seen a single frame from my films, you know nothing about me! Because everything I am and have done *excludes* by its nature any mourning on my part for the Italietta. Unless you consider me radically changed—something that forms part of the miracle-minded psychology of the Italians, but which just for that reason seems to me unworthy of you.

This was how Pier Paolo responded to Calvino, in an open letter in *Paese-Sera* on July 8. On June 18, questioned by *Il Messaggero*, Calvino had stressed the "nostalgic" quality of Pasolini's anthropological analysis. On what was the misunderstanding over "nostalgia" based? On the fact that Pasolini had spoken of the "boundless prenational and preindustrial peasant world," which had been preserved intact up until the years of the economic miracle. The people of that world were not living in a *golden age*, but in a bitter *age of bread* (Pasolini was borrowing an image from Felice Chilanti):

That is to say they were consumers of extremely necessary goods. And it was perhaps this that made their poor and precarious lives extremely necessary. While it is clear that superfluous goods make life superfluous. . . . Anyway whether or not I mourn this peasant world remains my own business. This in no way keeps me from exercising my criticism on the present world *as it is*—indeed, all the more lucidly the more I am detached from it, and the more I agree only stoically to live in it.[60]

Pasolini considered this "necessity" of poor and precarious existence as a value—a value not to be strengthened but not to be squandered. A value with which to create history. The ideal content of these multiple sorties was not something new in him—he was right to remind his critics of what he had written in poetry and prose, and put on the screen.

And yet, I repeat, there was something new—and it was surprising. It was that "state of grace" of which Piero Ottone has since spoken. It was something essentially new stylistically. Pasolini was now achieving the "practical goal" of poetry through a prose strong in content.

Writing for the newspapers seemed a negligible activity, but it was not. The need for a change, to explore a new area of relations, justified the result. But its roots went deeper—into the severity of thought, the repudiation of the surrounding world, in which Pasolini was involved in those years.

He agreed to live in the world "only stoically"—and by suggesting to himself a moral distance from it, he felt almost obsessed by the urgency of informing everyone of his own state of mind. His detachment did not prevent him from cultivating the hope of eventual future changes. In bringing together this personal disparity, he achieved success.

"Front-page intellectuals" became an ironical and even disparaging slogan. Among the others, Pasolini's name was the most conspicuous, the one around which major disputes developed. Moravia, Calvino, Fortini, Umberto Eco, Giorgio Bocca, Natalia Ginzburg—a great many felt called upon to answer him. For all of them, Pasolini found stinging replies, with unflagging polemical energy.

Despite controversies that were expanding like an oil slick, Pier Paolo did not let himself be conditioned by them, for he had a thematic project in mind. It would seem that he deduced his arguments one from another, as his chain of interlocutors grew.

The first articles, on the anthropological transformation, and the disappearance of the fascism-antifascism conflict, attacked the consumer society in a general way. In this phase the old theme of the "little homelands" repeatedly appears:

No country has possessed like ours such a quantity of "particular and real cultures," such a quantity of "little homelands," such a quantity of dialect worlds—no country, I say, in which there was later such an overwhelming "development." In the other large countries there had already previously been impressive "acculturations," on which the final and definitive one, that of consumption, is superimposed with a certain logic . . .[61]

But here is the "Christian" tactic. That in the face of the consumer society the Church should have the courage to divest itself completely of all temporal claims:

The Church might be the guide, grandiose but not authoritarian, for all those who reject (and a Marxist is speaking, precisely as a Marxist) the power of the new consumer society, which is completely irreligious, totalitarian, violent, falsely tolerant—indeed, more repressive than ever—corrupting, and degrading (never has Marx's statement that capitalism transforms human dignity into exchange goods made more sense than today). It is this refusal that the Church could therefore symbolize by returning to its origins, i.e., to opposition and revolt. Either do this or accept a power that no longer wants it—that is, commit suicide.[62]

The prophesying became increasingly visible, and in it the existential wound displayed livid hues:

The fortunate nominalism of the sociologists seems to exhaust itself within their circle. I live in the world of things and invent as best I can the way to name them. Certainly if I try to "describe" the terrible look of a whole new generation, which has suffered every kind of imbalance owing to a stupid and dreadful development, and I try to "describe" it in "this" youth, in "this" worker, I am not understood—because to the sociologist and to the professional politician nothing about "this" youth and "this" worker counts personally. To me, on the other hand, personally is the only thing that counts.[63]

The second phase had to do with abortion and sex. The Radical Party, which led the fight on the divorce referendum, raised the possibility of a series of new referendums to modify anything that hindered the exercise of civil rights. The liberalization of abortion, an essential aspect of the struggle for women's freedom, was the first item on the Radical agenda. Pasolini argued with the proponents of abortion.

I am traumatized by the legalization of abortion, because like many I consider it a legalization of homicide. In dreams and everyday behavior— something common to all men—I live my prenatal life, my happy immersion in the maternal fluids, and I know that there I existed . . .[64]

The number of new referendums (then nine) proposed by the Radicals was to grow over the years, and Parliament was to take action on most of them, including the regulation of abortion. Meanwhile, for Pasolini, the abortion theme served to raise the issue of the function of sexuality.

I know . . . that the majority is, potentially, all for the legalization of abortion. . . . Legalized abortion is in fact—no doubt about it—an enormous convenience for the majority. Especially because it would make coitus—heterosexual coupling—easier, and there would practically no longer be any obstacles to it. But by whom has this freedom of coitus of the "couple" as conceived by the majority—this wonderful permissiveness on its behalf—been tacitly desired, tacitly promulgated, and tacitly made to become part, in a now irreversible way, of people's habits? By the powers of consumption, by the new fascism . . .

The new fascism, impalpable as an erosion that moves in the depths of society without showing the extent to which it rots and pulverizes, "has taken possession" of all the "liberal and progressive" demands for freedom and has routed them—"it has changed their nature."

Sexual freedom, "given" by the authorities, produces "neurosis"— it is an "induced" and "imposed" facility that has created a new racism, a mass "ready to blackmail, crush, and lynch minorities." This leads to a new intolerance—"crude, violent, disgraceful." "Along with its poverty, the Italian people does not even care to remember its 'real' tolerance."

In this scenario, marriage has become "a funeral rite." And existence is "funereal" in a world that imposes the mechanical happiness of coitus on the couple.

Pasolini concluded: "My extremely reasonable opinion . . . is this: instead of struggling on the level of abortion against the society that repressively condemns abortion, one should struggle against this society on the level of the cause of abortion, i.e., on the level of coitus"—popularize a series of " 'real' liberalizations having precisely to do with coitus (and therefore its effects): contraceptives, pills, different techniques of making love, a modern morality of sexual honor, etc."

A real declaration on sex. Once again Pasolini was commenting on "permissiveness." The design was clear, or rather could clearly be discerned underneath his arguments. Christian respect for the sacredness of life did not keep him from having a "liberal" conception of eroticism.

But this was not the subject of the controversy, and his opponents did not debate with him on this point. In reading Pasolini's text one discovers an underground libertine fire—the ease (and this is something really "new") with which he mentions homosexuality.

Heterosexual coitus, "induced" by permissiveness, would wipe out in the Italians an ancient tolerance—the one that made lower-class youths available for homosexual relations without prejudice to their heterosexuality. Homosexuality, as an actual contraceptive possibility, ran like a watermark through Pier Paolo's words, and he did not scruple to make ironical use of this idea. If pro-abortion arguments included that of regulating the birth rate to put a limit to overpopulation, he insinuated:

it is the heterosexual relationship that would appear to be a danger to the species, while the homosexual one represents its security.

People said that Pasolini was thinking of resolving the problem of abortion with deviance; that the root of his polemics, and the idea of anthropological change, sprang from the reduced mercenary availability of *ragazzi di vita* in times of economic prosperity. They kept repeating that the problems he was raising were entirely "personal" and "private."

Pasolini the polemicist did not free himself from his psychological bonds. It was through them that he drew conclusions.

On January 30, 1975, he replied to Moravia:

I'm well aware that you're pragmatically for accepting the *status quo*, but I, who am an idealist, am not. "Consumerism exists and what can you do about it?" you seem to be trying to tell me. And now let me answer you: for you consumerism exists and that's all, it doesn't affect you except, as they say, morally, while from the practical standpoint it affects you the same way it affects everybody. Your inner personal life is safe from it. On the other hand, not so for me. As a citizen I'm affected by it like you, and like you I suffer a violence from it that offends me (and in this we're brothers, we can think together of a common exile); but as a person (as you know very well), I'm infinitely more involved than you. Consumerism consists indeed in a real anthropological cataclysm, and I *live*, existentially, that cataclysm, which, at least for now, is pure degradation. I live it in my days, in the forms of my existence, *in my body*. Since my bourgeois social life is exhausted in work, my social life depends entirely on what people are. I say "people" advisedly, meaning society, the people, the masses at the moment they come existentially (and let's hope only visually) in contact with me. It is from this existential, direct, concrete, dramatic, *physical* experience that all my ideological statements emerge in conclusion. As anthropological transformation (for the moment degradation) of disappointment, rage, *taedium vitae*, acedia, and finally, as idealistic revolt, as rejection of the *status quo*.[65]

The libertine fire was sparked by his *taedium vitae*; the anguished *physical* reasons led to anthropological divination. Existence, with its tragic quality, was not denied—Pier Paolo entirely accepted its consequences. His "ideological statements" did not thereby have less grip on the facts.

Pasolini legitimized deviance, but he legitimized it as an instrument of awareness. His "social" life was reduced to a thin strip of ground, on which he fought his intellectual and moral struggle. He had no other space.

His old nightly "cruising" was now nothing but a way of testing the correctness of his own conclusions, reinforcing the painful *taedium vitae* that had taken him by the throat. Pier Paolo lived his repudiations intensely, and "repudiation" is the word that recurs with impressive frequency in the polemical writings of this last year.

A theological rage was flaring up in him, a theological need for change.

In 1974, having completed the *Trilogy of Life*, he turned to his idea for a film about Saint Paul. He rewrote the script for it—his articles are likewise "Letters" to the Romans, Corinthians, Philippians, and Ephesians.

"For we wrestle not against flesh and blood, but against principalities, against powers, against the rulers of the darkness of this world, against spiritual wickedness in high places"—so wrote the Apostle (Eph. 6:12). And it was against the effects of "power" on flesh and blood that Pasolini struggled, torn by the certainty that evil is a destiny from which it is difficult to separate oneself.

An apostolate. The confrontation of sanctity and actuality—the concreteness of the divine against the abstractness of what historicity accepts as contingent.

"Paul demolished in a revolutionary way, with the simple strength of his religious message, a type of society founded on class violence, imperialism, and above all slavery."[66] Pasolini likens this to his own message, invests himself with it, and takes it on himself completely.

A pastoral precept is quoted in the script: "This know also, that in the last days perilous times shall come. For men shall be lovers of their own slaves, covetous, boasters, proud, blasphemers, disobedient to parents, unthankful, unholy, without natural affection, trucebreakers, false accusers, incontinent, fierce, despisers of those that are good, traitors, heady, highminded, lovers of pleasures more than lovers of God; having a form of godliness, but denying the power thereof."[67]

The third phase of Pasolini's polemics takes as its target precisely those "having a form of godliness, but denying the power thereof"—

the Christian Democratic political class. We are at the end of 1974 and in the first months of 1975.

> I know.
> I know the names of those responsible for what is called the *golpe** (and which in reality is a series of *golpes* instituted as a system for the protection of power).
> I know the names of those responsible for the massacre in Milan on December 12, 1969.
> I know the names of those responsible for the massacres in Brescia and Bologna in the first months of 1974. . . .
> I know all these names and I know all the incidents (attacks on institutions, massacres) of which they are guilty.
> I know. But I have no proof. I don't even have clues.
> I know because I am an intellectual, a writer . . .[68]

Pasolini stated that he "knew." This was a way of practicing politics—it was, as he corrected himself, the way of the "intellectual courage of truth."

> The intellectual courage of truth and political practice are two irreconcilable things in Italy.[69]

An inept political class, which has created an irremediable power vacuum in the country—a political class that knows how to extend the list of good things it thinks it has accomplished without realizing that this list is "pure nominalism," and "does not care, almost as though it were not its business, about the human, cultural, and political effects"[70] that the changes have produced.

Yes, the country has changed—a country where before there were "fireflies," and where now the "fireflies" have disappeared. The "firefly" metaphor marked for Pasolini the turning point of the "Christian Democratic regime."

> In the early sixties, due to the pollution of the air, and above all, in the countryside, due to the pollution of the water (the blue rivers and transparent millstreams), the fireflies began to disappear. The phenomenon was an instantaneous and striking one. After a few years there were no more fireflies . . .[71]

> Before the fireflies: the old values of the agrarian and early-capitalist world, which had been upheld by fascism, go on resisting

* I.e., "coup."—Tr.

the Christian Democrats in power. After the fireflies: the old values "suddenly no longer count." They are replaced by the " 'values' of a new type of civilization, totally 'other' with respect to peasant and early-industrial civilization"—it is this that unifies the country but at the same time traumatizes it. There is only one precedent for this violent cultural ratification: "Germany before Hitler."[72]

The Christian Democratic political class, if only so as not to lose its power, wickedly does not record the changes that have taken place. But the changes are there.

It was impossible for the Italians to react worse than they have to such a historical trauma. They have become in a few years (especially in the center and south) a degenerate, ridiculous, monstrous, criminal people. You have only to go out in the street to realize this. But, of course, to realize the changes in people, you must love them. I, unfortunately, have loved this Italian people: both outside the patterns of power (indeed in desperate opposition to them), and outside populist and humanitarian patterns. It was a real love, rooted in my mode of being. I have therefore seen "with my senses" the forced behavior of consumerist power re-create and deform the consciousness of the Italian people to the point of irreversible degradation.[73]

The Christian Democratic politicians are guilty of this "degradation," and their guilt is even more serious because unconscious. "The Christian Democratic Party . . . has not realized that it has become, almost overnight, nothing but a surviving instrument of formal power, through which a new and real power has destroyed the country."[74]

In this degraded country, there is an island "of salvation," the Communist Party.

The Italian Communist Party is a clean country in a dirty country, an honest country in a dishonest one, an intelligent country in an idiotic one, a cultured country in an ignorant one, a humanistic country in a consumerist one . . .

And yet,

the division of the country into two countries, one sunk up to its neck in degradation and degeneration, the other intact and uncompromised, cannot be a reason for peace and constructiveness.[75]

The solution: to eliminate this disparity, a "trial" is needed. In the summer of 1975 Pasolini thought that the Christian Democratic leaders should be put on "trial" ("a penal trial, in a courtroom,"[76] from which the defendants would emerge "handcuffed between carabinieri"[77]).

In what did the guilt of these men consist?

It does not consist in their immorality (which exists), but in an error of political interpretation in judging themselves and the power in whose service they have placed themselves—an error of political interpretation that has had quite disastrous consequences in the life of our country.[78]

An error of "political interpretation" of their own role and destiny. The betrayal of the true faith, the betrayal of humanism. These were the real sins of the Christian Democrats.

Pasolini prophesied—his style had taken on increasingly visible liturgical cadences. While the polemical battle was joined—and his opponents became such political commentators as Leo Valiani, Giorgio Galli, and Luigi Firpo—Pier Paolo seemed completely invested with the prophetic role. He stated that his was the "fantasy of a moralist,"[79] but in it he saw how urgent it was to deliver the country from the "tragic" and "ridiculous" fate it had embraced.

The "penal trial" of the Christian Democratic ruling class was to have "the form, meaning, and importance of a Synthesis,"[80] as he called it. It is urgent—he said—that this take place for the salvation of the "democratic game."

On June 15, 1975, in the local elections, the left gained a sizable increase in votes. There was a notable increase for the Communist Party. After that date, Pasolini maintained that the moment had arrived when Italian citizens should know, and know "in the pure spirit of the Stoa."[81]

The Italians "want to know," even if their questions are not yet formulated "with sufficient clarity," what is "the human 'condition' . . . in which they have been forced to live almost as though by a natural cataclysm"; what is "the 'new culture'—in the anthropological sense— in which they live as though in a dream: a leveling, degrading, vulgar culture"; what is "the 'new type of power' by which this culture is produced, since clerico-fascist power has declined"; what is "the 'new mode of production,'" if it "does not produce, for the first time in history, 'unchangeable social relations'—that is, removed from and denied, once and for all, every possible form of 'distinction.'" Without knowing all this, "one cannot govern"—or one governs in the manner of the Christian Democrats, locked "in the labyrinth of their Palace of Madmen."[82]

In September and October of 1975 Pasolini drew up "his" plan of reform: the immediate abolition of compulsory high school and of television.[83] This abolition meant cutting the Evil to its roots—preventing contagion, weaning a whole country from the pollution to which it had been subjected.

In these months any "nostalgic" perspective seemed to vanish from Pier Paolo's words. Perhaps he was about to realize the true change in his life, much more radical than when he had dedicated himself to the cinema. Active political life, as an intellectual's "right and duty," might have been able to claim him in ways more exclusive than in the past.

Meanwhile his relations with the Communist Party had changed. Some Communist intellectuals continued to have heated arguments with him. The leaders of the party's Youth Federation, on the other hand, became his privileged interlocutors.[84]

On September 24, 1975, in Rome, Pasolini participated in a demonstration that the Youth Federation had organized on the Pincio. The theme discussed was "permissiveness" and drugs—Pasolini saw in permissiveness and drugs the agents of criminality.

We must admit once and for all the failure of tolerance. It has been, of course, a false tolerance, and it has been one of the major causes of the degeneration of masses of young people.[85]

There was widespread debate in the Communist Youth Federation on the forms of social derailment that had struck the younger generations in Italy. The importance of the facts of daily existence as against ideological rigidity was emphasized.

Pasolini's profession of Marxism, and his "moralism" (an ever more substantial moralism, in whose fire burned elements from the conceptual avalanche of the social sciences), could turn out to be stimulating, and deeply so, for anyone seeking to give his own political passion a language that was not the one inherited from the remote fifties.

By now '68 was, for many young people, only a memory, the point of departure for a political adventure that needed to be subjected to critical analysis.

Pasolini was offering cues for such an analysis. His rejection of "false tolerance," of unrelated permissiveness, subjected one of the most compelling imperatives of '68 to revision. With regard to it, "one must act, in judging, *by consequence and not a priori* (the progressive *a priori* valid up until some ten years ago)."[86]

The young Communists, in the schools and factories, knew that received criteria of judgment, received ways of conducting politics, slogans or catchwords, by now were of little use. Pasolini's flaming words, his constant appeal to a culture that confronted Italian problems in a nonaffirmative way, while at the same time rejecting the coded language of the "Palazzo," the official seat of power, carried enormous weight.

Pier Paolo's popularity was growing—and it grew precisely because, in denying trust to professional politicians, he vigorously upheld the urgency of an ideal redemption.

> Politicians are difficult to reclaim for such an operation . . . today it seems that only Platonic (I add: Marxist) intellectuals—even devoid of information, but certainly devoid of interests and complicity—have some probability of intuitively grasping the meaning of what is really happening —naturally, however, provided that this intuition of theirs is translated— literally translated—by scientists, Platonists themselves, into the terms of the only science whose reality is as objectively certain as that of Nature, i.e., Political Economy.[87]

These are the last words of Pasolini's last article published during his life, in *Il Mondo* on October 30, 1975. The last words of his "Pauline" letters.

They were the words of his utopia, which certainly does not perfectly emerge. But its outlines can be seen clearly. The country, its history, had to be reclaimed culturally before anything could be done on the practical or political level.

Pasolini was right in accusing the Christian Democratic ruling class of historical unawareness—something different, more profound and complex, than if he had simply accused it of ineptitude.

He watched the flow of life with long-range perspective, and set down his thoughts with compelling speed.

True, his polemics rested on a paleo-Christian conception of Evil. This was combined with an oratorical aspiration toward Marxist social regeneration (he had been an attentive reader of Gramsci, and had grasped the concreteness of his thought).

This idea of Evil—a sort of original sin of the modern world, which seemed to apply itself only to a barbarous use of very delicate instruments of knowledge—this idea kept him from understanding the positive dynamics of the social alternatives that the new enlightenment, for all its deficiencies, was elaborating.

Pasolini was a radar mechanism in constant operation. Simultaneously, line by line in his articles, he caught the controversial arguments of the ecologists and the Jacobin extremists, the radicals with flowers in their mouths and the believers in the sacredness of the human person, those who upheld the formal efficacy of state institutions and those who wanted to destroy the state in the name of some deadly nihilist scheme. To these intuitions he gave a language that was persuasive and dramatic, passionate and vibrant. It was a language that brought literature closer to life, and rediscovered its painful existential meaning.

From this emerged his legend—especially among the young people who followed him in the debates. He gave much of himself in those meetings, much of his pedagogic fervor, and what he expressed was a strange mixture of resentment and dedication, improvising, or awkwardly reading aloud from the typewritten sheets that he pulled from his pocket.

On his face he had the desperate strength of a smile, and when he noticed the same anguish in an interlocutor, he spoke to him—and said so—as to a "companion in misfortune." And he was certain that his suffering, the most bitter event of that last year of his life, had at that moment found a way of being mirrored and allayed.

"HABITS, THESE SISTERS OF TRAGEDY"[88]

His last years—his love for the Chia tower.

In the village of Chia he had met a boy, the son of peasants—a curly-haired youth with a pimpled face, almost a new Ninetto. His name was Claudio Tròccoli—Pier Paolo called him Troccoletto. He was a shy and silent boy. Pier Paolo took him to Rome a few times. It is on his face, an extreme expression of innocence, that *Salò* ends—the frame with the two boys dancing.

His old habits had not withered. Though now with less frequency, at eleven in the evening he would still get up from the table where he was having supper with friends and disappear into the tunnel of his night.

Sunday supper at Laura Betti's—where they ate elaborate potato soufflés—was an exception. Pier Paolo, like the others, went home when it was time to go to bed.

At Laura's house there were frequent discussions on feminism and the women's "revolt," with Laura dissenting or agreeing, as the case might be. Pier Paolo, as always, enjoyed himself immensely.

In addition to the suppers, there were vacations at the seashore. Moravia rented a summer house on the dunes at Sabaudia. This beach, still unspoiled and extending like a long scythe blade under the green Circeo cliff, had been discovered by a painter friend, Lorenzo Tornabuoni.

Pier Paolo spent a few weeks in Moravia's house. Laura also rented a villa, not on the dunes, but at the quarry on the promontory, with a view all the way to Ponza. Pier Paolo divided his time between ultraviolet rays on the cliff and relaxing on the sands at Sabaudia.

There too he pursued his nocturnal "habits." He would go to Nettuno, where he had friends among the pupils at the police school. He used to say that they were "very sweet" boys, sons of the old Italian South.

In Sabaudia, in August 1973, he and Dacia Maraini wrote the script for the *Arabian Nights*.

Working at the sea was his way of taking a vacation. Later he joined Susanna in the mountains, and in September was back in Rome, taken up by the countless simultaneous commitments of his life.

Having finished the *Trilogy*, he planned his Saint Paul film, as I said. But at the end of 1973, he had confided a different project to Enzo Golino:

Yes, in the film I'll make after I finish the *Arabian Nights*. The protagonists will be two Neapolitans, and I should like Eduardo De Filippo to play one of them. The film begins in Naples and covers a long journey in which this pair of Neapolitans meets a lot of Neapolitans traveling around the world. . . . Naples has remained the true large dialect city. The adjustment to models from the center, to rules imposed from above on language and behavior, is only superficial. For centuries the Neapolitans have been adapting themselves mimetically to whoever is over them . . .[89]

The project, for which there remains a seventy-five-page "treatment" with some handwritten corrections, bears the title *Porno-Teo-Kolossal*. The protagonists were to be Eduardo and Ninetto. A repeat in the seventies of *Hawks and Sparrows,* the film is an imaginary journey through three symbolic cities, Sodom (Rome), Gomorrah (Milan), Numantia (Paris), and ending up in Ur (the Indian East).

The two characters follow the bewitching directions of a comet, which guides them to the discovery of new "good news," and the stages that they must necessarily cover (the three cities) depict, respectively, senseless permissiveness, violent revolt against any diversity, and neocapitalist fascism in power.

For "stoic" irony, Pasolini represented himself in the figure of a wise, naïve old man, detached and aware, marked by the exquisite aristocracy of intelligence possessed only by true men of the people. Eduardo De Filippo's role in *Porno-Teo-Kolossal* was to be that of a poet who pursues utopia in the sky of his soul—a political and religious utopia surrounded by a smiling aura.

The *Porno-Teo-Kolossal* project was postponed. Instead, from the early months of 1975 to late spring, Pasolini filmed *Salò or the 120 Days of Sodom* in a villa near Mantua.

Sergio Citti and Pupi Avati had collaborated on the script. Rumors circulated that the erotic scenes in the film were played with complete truth by the actors—lubricity, sado-masochism, scandal. The nakedness is visible, as is the crudity of the situations. But also visible is the chocolate that plays an excremental role in the coprophagy scenes.

No film, if the director is famous and the subject one that gives rise to gossip, can escape rumors—they are the business of the publicity department. It is a way of keeping alive that sense of the marvelous on which the film industry feeds. The subject of *Salò* had more than its share of reasons for the most unbridled gossip.

For his part, Pier Paolo, in the more harrowing scenes, incited the actors with the subtle sarcasms of which he was capable. To force an adult heterosexual to kiss a boy passionately on the lips (both of them were nonprofessional actors) was a game for him, but at the same time the expression of his deep-seated conviction that everyone, and not simply unconsciously, harbors in himself conspicuous areas of homosexuality, repressed only because of the social obligation to do so.

During the months in Mantua, he wrote the unfinished pedagogical treatise entitled *Gennariello,* in weekly installments for *Il Mondo.*

Gennariello was to be his *Émile*—the epiphany of his furious pedagogism. To a "Neapolitan," or in any case southern, boy—one therefore historically prepared to suffer the violence of power—he taught the way to save himself, to live in contemporary society and at

the same time resist its corrupting influence. Repudiation, utopia—
and hope. He was cultivating this hope.

Meanwhile, not many kilometers away, in the countryside around
Parma, Bernardo Bertolucci was filming *1900*.

Pier Paolo had disliked *Last Tango in Paris*, and had said so in no
uncertain terms. He saw it as a sellout by Bertolucci to commercial
cinema. Friction and rivalry had destroyed the old rapport between
teacher and pupil. For some time now Pier Paolo and Bernardo had
been avoiding each other. Now they found themselves neighbors, both
engaged in work. Laura Betti was in the cast of *1900*. The two films
were being produced by Alberto Grimaldi. Nico Naldini was present
on both sets for working reasons. The two troupes challenged each
other to a soccer game. Pier Paolo played.

The two friends made peace and embraced.

Pier Paolo completed the shooting quickly, and spent the summer
cutting and editing the film. A few years before, he and Moravia had
bought a plot of land on the Sabaudia dunes. It included a half-
finished house, which they finished building and divided in two. That
summer the house was ready. Moravia spent his vacation there; Susanna
and Graziella occupied their half. With Graziella was Vincenzo
Cerami, the student from the Ciampino school—he had written a
novel and was writing poetry.

Salò was ready at the end of October.

Pier Paolo had almost reached an agreement with Eduardo De
Filippo for *Porno-Teo-Kolossal*. Nevertheless, he had spoken to some
of his friends about the need to loosen his ties with the cinema—he
was talking of finishing the novel he was writing.[90] In his wish to
change, which had even become insistent, Pier Paolo seemed to be
besieged by his habits—and by now the cinema was a habit too.

A collection of his poems was published in Sweden. In the last
week in October 1975 he left for Stockholm. During that month he
had made a trip to Paris; he was editing the French dialogue for *Salò*.

Salò or the 120 Days of Sodom is a sort of critical essay for images.
The theme of the essay, in which Sade's posthumous novel is taken
up as an intellectual provocation, is the Nazi-fascist concentration-
camp mentality as an instigator of violence. But its themes are also
the transgression of sex and death.

In the titles, printed as was Pasolini's custom in Bodoni type on a white background, appears a caption reading "Essential Bibliography." It lists works on Sade by Barthes, Klossowski, Blanchot, and others. The author of the film shows that he has gone through and made use in his own work of the essential conclusions of certain interpreters of Sade. First among all of them: that the writings of Sade are one of the major monuments to nominalism. Sade puts in the mouths of his characters speeches of endless verbosity and stories of a programmatic abstractness. And yet this lavish expenditure of words and speeches has a precise purpose: to reduce the action of the novel to ritual and symbol.

Salò is steeped in Sadean ritualism and symbolism. The characters in *Les 120 journées de Sodome* perform their actions on the printed page in the manner of actors, while never embodying them. There thus occurs a calculated separation between what they say and what they do. Pasolini aims deliberately at this separation, this "theatrical alienation," for which Brecht had been the theorist.

Salò, a "Brechtian" film, a "critical" film, a ritualistic film, opens with images of the Po countryside—the Nazi-fascists are rounding up young people. The tones are soft and like watercolor, muted or rendered bluish by the mist. We are at the *Introit* of the ceremony— the ceremony will begin once the roundup has been thoroughly completed.

Four gentlemen and four female storytellers shut themselves up in a Neoclassical villa in order to carry out in 120 days the regulations of a horrific code.

Power is anarchy, says Pasolini—power would like to abolish history and overcome nature. History and nature can be abolished and over-come through sex.

The chronicle of human events suggests that during the Republic of Salò, under the rule of the Nazis, such a total and radical abuse of power may have been carried out. Here then, in the film, at the prompting of Sade, the metaphor of this apocalypse is made explicit.

The inferno of pain and suffering is shown, organized in a closed structure over the foundations of the successive stories that the female celebrants contrive with odious delight in the Hall of Orgies. The celebrants recite, and the gentlemen will try to adapt themselves to their words by using as objects the girls and boys sequestered from the neighboring countryside.

Nude bodies livid in the cold—these bodies that Pasolini shows us in *Salò* are without the poor and chaste splendor of the *Trilogy of Life*. They are bodies gray in color, certainly beautiful, well proportioned, but annihilated, their beauty canceled by the hell into which they have been kidnapped.

Their passivity as victims is petrifying—since, being victims, they cannot help weaving a poisonously consenting relationship with their executioners. What is frightening is their wavering between consent and refusal. The—highly regulated—anarchy of the situation ensures that in feeling themselves sometimes free, they delude themselves into thinking that they can offer their loving devotion to someone in full freedom.

At that point, the irrationality of power acts, forcing them to engage in the foulest practices, including coprophagy—until the "final solution," when all of them are killed.

The four gentlemen take turns in observing the scene of the massacre from a window of the villa with binoculars, which they sometimes reverse to furnish what is being seen—in miniature—with an aesthetic frame.

A harsh surrender to the inevitable—even though the final message of the film, the dance performed by two boys (two boys of the fascist guard, free to be themselves in the midst of the horror), suggests an uncertain trickle of hope.

But what hope? Going along with Georges Bataille, one might say that in this film the knowledge of death arouses no more dread than being born. Pasolini, "pirate" and "heretic," seems in *Salò* to nourish in his heart nothing but the mysticism of annihilation—and he gives it plastic visualization with polished bits of detail.

The vitality, the bursts of erotic laughter—the most brilliant features of the *Arabian Nights*—seem to have vanished from Pasolini's view; or rather they seem to have been brought back to the calculated, sometimes melodramatic, ritual of a *Grand-Messe des Morts*. Eros, in the *Arabian Nights*, had truly been love; in *Salò* it is hate. Was this perhaps a dialectical juxtaposition?

It has been said, and it is true, that in *Salò* "Pasolini makes use of Sade to unmask Pasolini,"[91] but the unmasking takes on the tone of an unconditional surrender—and eros, once laid bare, becomes sin.

This was the sin to be purged, the sin about which Paul of Tarsus wrote his most tormented words—a sin that in Pasolini's mind seems to rise from the obscure anguish of youth and to be mirrored in what he called "anthropological genocide."

The despair contained in the political tracts is added to the despair in the "erotic" pages of *Vas*, and expands into a program on the screen of *Salò*. The hope that had emerged at various moments in these years, the utopian relish for foreseeing good—all is dismembered by the siege of incalculable Evil.

Even *Salò* contains a utopia, which, though wearing the guise of the forties, is projected into the future—it is dark foreknowledge.

The fox-trot performed by the two boys at the end offers little or no salvation. The Erinyes seemed to demand mourning and death in Pasolini's heart.

True, he no longer felt the joy of eros; true, his anguish was incapable of keeping silent about it. His repudiation of the bodies and sex organs of the *ragazzi di vita* was not the result of intellectual mannerism.

The river of time had overflowed images and ideals. Susanna was already showing signs of physical decline. Pier Paolo would take her in his arms, and whisper to her all the tenderness of his passion, but her eyes distilled a dazed look of old age.

That summer of 1975, on the terrace of the house in Sabaudia, Susanna, between flashes of kindled sensibility, sat alone, and no one could tell what old fantasies she was murmuring to the sea.

These were the months of a sad twilight. The joy of eros had gone dark in Pier Paolo's heart, and this meant discouragement and defeat.

But he did not yield the smallest portion of his vitality to this destiny. He made plans, he worked, concealing his anguish and despair under the magnitude of his undertakings. He was planning a different everyday life for himself—for the winter, he said, he would like to attend concerts and again listen to music systematically. Then there was always the idea of going back to painting, and in any case going back to being a novelist.

But his habits, like his passions, were recidivist. Lately, in his nightly prowling, he had been physically attacked, and had found himself on familiar terms with criminality. He ascribed these things to the disordered state of Italian society—for himself he had no fear. Refusing to harbor fear was part of his heroic, personal destiny.

So he left for Stockholm on Sunday, October 26. In the course of the week, he went from Stockholm to Paris, again to work on the French version of *Salò*. He returned to Rome on October 31. On Saturday, November 1, he had lunch at home—Susanna had cooked for him. He decided to have supper that evening with Ninetto.

The meal at the Pommidoro, near San Lorenzo. The final night of his life sees him disappear in the Giulia GT. His last words are the customary ones, of good-bye—the same as any evening. In what happened later, Pier Paolo is silent—he is the silent form glimpsed through the lines of a confession made to the carabinieri by a murderous "Gennariello."

Habits and passions won out, in the poet, over each repudiation, each utopia. Pier Paolo by now was a disfigured corpse that the dawn of November 2, 1975, slowly disclosed by a fade-in (as it is called in cinema jargon) on the hazy terrain of the Ostia seaplane basin.

THE WILL TO LIVE

Did Pasolini ask to die? Was his murder a suicide by proxy?

In the prologue of this book, I asked myself the meaning of the inevitability in which Pier Paolo's death was enclosed—the co-incidence of landscape and imagination, the outcome of a destiny that seemed to calculate its own trajectory to a hair's breadth. I spoke of "chilling fatality."

Pasolini's life would seem to explain everything—his "cruising," night after night, seems to contain irrefutable confirmation that he predisposed himself daily to punishment; it would mean he complied with the call of a deadly eros. Pasolini is supposed to have sought death in the darkness of the night—until finally death was offered to him at the hands of Pelosi, or of others believed to be with him.

Old, contradictory repugnance in the presence of his own eros. Pasolini lived in the torment of not being able to give it what it demanded of him. And the demand was obscure, indeed dark and nocturnal. It was an eros that did not demand incest, and not even the fantasy of incest—perhaps it required punishment for the absence of this fantasy. Simultaneously, it required compensation for everything that signified nostalgia for the loved, hated, and lost father.

Hence, the boys—

They are legion. I cannot love just one . . .[1]

Each with his beauty, his eternity—each the lure of annihilation, of an impossible sublimation. All this is not arbitrary induction. Pasolini "confessed" himself in his poems, unstintingly.

Here I am in the dim light of an old April,
on my knees to confess
completely, to the point of death . . .[2]

But what significance should one attribute to this act of throwing himself weeping on the ground?

Confession. If we were to go over in our minds all the complex meanings that the act of confessing has made explicit in the Catholic tradition, we should have to evoke in our imaginations the most dreadful sufferings of the ego. It is the wounded, divided ego that, by confessing on its knees, that is to say crouching that much closer to the earth (the mother), tries, by the awful undertaking of verbalization, to vanquish all its schizophrenia and collect its scattered limbs. It is the will to be cured, since sin is sickness, a highly particular sickness, whose cure consists in its very utterance.

But can the utterance of sin realistically disclose to the sinner the open fields of health? The Catholic (and Christian) says that it can. And there is no need at this point to insist on Pasolini's Christian inspiration.

Pasolini throws himself on the ground; he confesses:

Then . . . ah, my only happiness is in the sun . . .[3]

The utterance of the sin was liberating for him, but it did not set him free.

"I have made the first and most painful step in the dark and muddy labyrinth of my confessions. It is not what is criminal that is most difficult to say, it is what is ridiculous and shameful. From now on I am sure of myself; after what I have just dared to say, nothing can hold me back any longer."[4] Thus Jean-Jacques Rousseau in his *Confessions*.

The "ridiculous" and "shameful." Jean-Jacques confessed the moment in which he had stumbled on his own masochism—the astonished pleasure that he had felt in being chastised by Mademoiselle Lambercier. Rousseau does not believe in the mere utterance of sin, he believes in the cognitive strength of "confession." Rousseau was a layman. But he too, in confessing, lifts himself to the idea of an incommensurable state of his own of being "different," he being the only depository of truth. Pasolini, in the act of confessing his sin, does likewise—in him grows "inadmissable" ardor:

I must defend
this enormity of desperate tenderness
that, like the world, I received in being born.[5]

Confession of the sin thus becomes a celebration of ecstasy. If the ecstasy were to be missing—"better death / than to renounce it!"[6] His repudiation constituted renunciation—therefore, "better death."

All would seem to be explained. Pasolini would seem to have been crucified in the reconciliation of the opposites in which he lived. Every inference would be silenced. Death is an absolution of existence, an immediate settlement of what was formless and confused. In this case, what had once appeared contradictory would acquire a tragic composure.

But everything concerning Pasolini still does not escape being an oxymoron, the rhetorical figure that indicates conflict and disparity. The Appeals Court sentence in the Pelosi trial, signed on December 4, 1976, by Ferdinando Zucconi Galli Fonseca, reconstructs the night at the seaplane basin by placing Pasolini and "Pino the Frog" as the sole protagonists in the affair—one against the other.

After examining in detail the evidence offered for the participation of third parties in the crime (the orthopedic sole and the sweater found in the Giulia GT, the prints of rubber-soled shoes left on the soccer field, the scant traces of blood on Pelosi, the presence of blood-stains on the roof of the car, and the rest), the sentence concludes: "That these elements can be explained by the hypothesis of the participation of several persons cannot be doubted; that they are certain and incontrovertible clues is to be denied." Indeed, the sole lay under the seat, and Graziella Chiarcossi, in cleaning the automobile, might have overlooked it; the sweater could have been left by someone in the course of the day of November 1 (Pier Paolo had gone out that afternoon alone); the prints of the rubber-soled shoes on the ground at the seaplane basin may have belonged to persons who had been there in the hours prior to the murder; the traces of blood on Pelosi were scarce because the boy had attacked Pasolini first and taken him by surprise; the bloodstains on the roof of the car could have come from a stick flying in the air. Each proof, in short, is matched by a counterproof.

On one point the new verdict insists: the unreliability of the story told by the young murderer. Pelosi is lying. This is proved by his malice aforethought—it proves that he did not commit "a gratuitous and irresponsible act." He was perfectly well aware of who Pasolini was and of what might happen in the encounter with him.

The sentence also dispels the hypothesis of a sadistic, or in any case aggressive, attitude on the part of Pasolini: "The court notes that if one examines [Pelosi's] story in depth, even with no attempt to keep in mind its mass of incongruities, in whatever way the attack itself was manifested, one finds nothing to make one believe that the defendant's sexual freedom or his physical integrity had been truly endangered or could have seemed to him seriously threatened. Even if Pasolini may have demanded something that Pelosi, perhaps out of a change of heart or last-minute disgust, did not wish to agree to, no attempt at the violent subjection of the boy to his wishes emerges from the story."

Pelosi said that Pasolini tried to do violence to him with a stake. The verdict objects that, if the gesture "was carried out as an abnormal form of approach or means of excitation, it would not have been repeated nor accompanied by the attempt to lower the boy's trousers by force, since Pelosi would not have needed to resist it or to react violently."

At the conclusion of these analyses, and having to provide a motivation for the crime, the appeals sentence speaks instead of "unclear circumstances," in which the events, taken together, can be said to have unfolded; and it ends by stating the "impossibility of identifying the motive for the crime."

Pelosi has killed, but he does not say why he has killed, nor does his behavior explain it. So it is legitimate, as though to set the wheel of destiny again in motion, that in the search for some motive or other, the ambush hypothesis should reappear and justify itself, overcoming the aura of doubt that surrounds it. But even in this case (what was the motive for the ambush?), there is no satisfaction to be had—conflict and disparity regain the upper hand.

If the facts are silent, psychology may help to explain them.

"The motives for the attack could be many and we do not know them. But Pasolini's death, in its psychological reality, which is the only one that counts, was surely provoked by the murderer's hatred for himself and by his identification with Pasolini at the moment of the crime. By killing Pasolini, the murderer wanted to punish himself; the homicide was thus a kind of dissociated and objective suicide." This is Moravia's idea.[7]

The suicide by proxy would, therefore, have been committed by Pelosi on Pasolini. It is a persuasive idea—many murders of homosexuals, perpetrated by sexual mercenaries, are primed by this logic.

Nevertheless we do not know what set off the bloodthirsty seizure in Pelosi. The agreement as to money had been concluded. The terms were clear. It is probable that on Pasolini's part a request was put forward, perhaps in the form of provocation—using the stake. At that moment, with a series of misunderstandings converging in a gesture, the more sinister load of fatality may have built up.

Did Pasolini's gesture conceal a form of masochism? Did it conceal a challenge to the death? Was the urge to suicide by proxy present in him too? The wheel of possibilities keeps spinning and changing color, and will continue to do so until other facts, thus far unknown to us, arrive to tell us the truth of what happened. But I repeat what I wrote: it is the reality of this death that matters, not its truth.

The human and literary events in Pasolini's life suggest that he must have found himself facing his murderer armed with a courage unknown to others.

What was the nature of this courage? Rossana Rossanda maintains that had he emerged alive from that night of horror, Pasolini would have been "on the side of the seventeen-year-old who beat him to death. Cursing him, but with him. And so on until the next, inevitable, perhaps foreseen and feared occasion for death."[8]

Pasolini knew that the reasons for the lives and deaths of men are historical and not fortuitous—this was a form of cognitive courage that was not alien to him. Nor was the Christian *pietas* by which Rossana Rossanda sees him nourished alien to him. It was a *pietas* made complex and explosive by his Marxist convictions.

The courage of which I am speaking, however, is existential and not cultural. To live his life outrageously, to the ultimate risk—this was Pasolini's courage. He outraged his own existence as a renowned intellectual by laying himself open to all contradictions and denying to his person any image of good behavior. The unmotivated and the shameful seemed to be his domain—and so they were, however things may have gone, on the field at the seaplane basin.

At the same time, he did not deny his words the inevitability of a moral message, the severity of their own rational rigor. His destiny as one "accursed" was continually compromised by the demands of reason.

All this signified scorn for all conventions, and scorn also for the ultimate convention of keeping oneself alive by protecting oneself.

His "bad faith"—Pasolini often made use of a screen of "masks." The mask of the "nightingale," or of Christ spat on and mocked; the mask of the "crow," or of the raving Don Quixote of ideas; the mask of Saint Paul. They were masks that suggested collective salvation. Pasolini's own deep-seated, unresolved contradiction emerged from the fact that he was certain, incontrovertibly and despairingly certain, of being unable to save anyone—not even himself. For this reason, his words of hope, every time they were uttered, had a faint and wistful sound.

Thus Pasolini did not ask of life a suicide by proxy. He looked at death with the courage of one who does not look beyond his own destiny. He was a profoundly religious man, but in his religion the vocative "God" was absent. "Transcendence," with him, was an unvoiced word. His religiosity was animated by "Dantean" pride; he did not contemplate the values of being a faithful son and submitting to the divine—with the divine his relationship was one of challenge. Conversely, the divine, when it took the face of its "creature," transported him, reduced him to himself—but not as the son.

The "mask" he used most often was that of denying in his soul every aspect of the son by taking on the mask of the "teacher." Only such an investiture gave him the strength to endure "martyrdom"— a martyrdom that, on the other hand, he was able to evoke, provoke, and catalyze with rare and pernicious intuition.

This martyrdom, however—here was his "bad faith"—helped him to sharpen his thought, to render it paradoxical, and bring it to a dazzling brilliance. And this thought could also be contradictory and destructive. But it, and it alone, was in his judgment the path by which to reach the harsh and difficult places where we can utter the cruelest truths about ourselves.

At the point when he decided on politics, and decided to "throw his body into the struggle," Pasolini remained irrevocably an artist. He wished to give his words the fire of action, but what tormented him were the ghosts of his sick conscience. He was not a decadent who liked to obliterate himself in action. Even a novelist like Joseph Conrad could write: "Action is consolatory. It is the enemy of thought and the friend of flattering illusions."

Pasolini did not scorn ideas—indeed, he pursued them, he worked them up to white heat. His language was woven from the rational vocabularies of psychoanalysis and Marxism. Still there is no doubt that both the cinema and the journalistic writings of his last years take on the color of action—they possessed the impact of animated objects, hurled against overwhelming difficulties.

If we go back to the memory of his early years, when we discovered him intoxicated and uplifted by the more intense aromas of pure literature—the poems of Foscolo, the *amor de loinh*, the seductive appeal of Gide—we can see that Pier Paolo at that time was as if dead. Though he was undeniably talented, and a highly sensitive poet, writing was a disease of which existence did not succeed in curing him. His feeling of reality was diverted into an unlawful and sensual embrace with life. Pier Paolo divined that salvation would come to him by a considered reliance on action.

He was helped by historical contingencies: the intellectual fervor of the postwar years, the passion not to squander the small heritage of culture that remained undamaged under the ruins of fascism, the hope for a future of social justice. In short, Gramsci's message came to Pasolini's aid.

His accursed state, the strangling ties with the physical, the annihilating battles of the flesh—all this was later overcome within him, or quieted, by the dream of Christian pedagogy. The tradition of the "little homelands" was mingled in his mind with that of the "little parishes." In the equilibrium of all this, he lived the happy creative season of the nineteen-fifties. Then came the unexpected change.

Pasolini had put his faith in the objectivity of history—his inner life was rooted in a dialectical link with the collectivity. He lived by the understanding that had been created between culture and politics on the side of the left—to that understanding he gave a symbolic significance.

In his troubled relations with the Communist Party, he was never led to question that significance. Indeed, he fought strenuously to keep it alive and renew its content.

I don't think Pasolini had a concrete idea of what the "dictatorship of the proletariat" was. In his mind, socialism and communism were superimposed on each other as a happy entity in which human sufferings, and the historical sufferings of a nation, would find relief.

He was a utopian—but he did not hesitate to rend this utopianism for the inescapable demands of eros. From there sprang his originality —he was not afraid of his own demon.

The sudden arrival of the crisis of ideologies, the disfigurement of the world of "little homelands" or "little parishes," deprived him of a source of nourishment that had been very fruitful for him.

To give visual plasticity to the fruits of his anthropological and poetic imagination, he was driven to take up the cinema, "the written language of reality." The cinema suggested to him the idea of being able to celebrate a mystical cognitive rite. The cinema could be the new "Bible of the poor."

The incurable disease of literature would be still more happily overcome. But by now every equilibrium was broken. The poet had entered into the realm of illusions, of grandiose and epic gestures.

The epos required battles, struggles—they were struggles and battles directed at reintegrating, by demonstrating, a faded state of grace. Pasolini seemed to act in accordance with the Nietzschean imperative: "*Not yet enough!* It is not yet enough to demonstrate a thing, one must seduce men to it, or else raise them up to it. Therefore the sage must learn to *speak* his wisdom, and often in such a way that it *sounds* like madness!"[9]

There rings in Pasolini's words the echo of philosophic madness. His arguments are not functional, either for the political right or left —even though he remains faithful to the perspective of the left.

Not yet enough! Pasolini devoted himself to prophecy, and his prophesying became his weapon in a controversy that agitated Italian public opinion for almost two years.

The subtle poet of *L'usignolo* was now raising arguments that struck at those responsible for public affairs. He summoned them to a reckoning, to a "trial."

Underlying his prophecies, there was in Pasolini a realistic perception of what had happened in Italy from the sixties on.

This frantically manneristic writer—and of a baroque mannerism, a lover of asymmetry, of tormented versifications of topical matter, who made of his style a shining example of the forbidden, who delighted in a "poetics of regression" in order to break the gilded trappings of twentieth-century academicism, and who re-evoked the great heroes of Greek tragedy (in the theater and in the cinema) not out of an addiction to neoclassicism but to give voice, with agonizing nostalgia, to passions and sentiments that had been extinguished— this writer, and film director, seemed to have descended into the political arena for a harsh scrutiny of facts.

The polemics over Italian misgovernment during the years of the economic boom still centers on questions that were clear to Pasolini's eyes: the harm provoked by social disequilibrium, the impoverishment of the agricultural heritage, the pollution of the coasts, the loss of water resources, the highly dangerous effects of internal emigration, the overcrowded atmosphere of the urban agglomerates—all this was obvious to him.

But it was a clarity that dimmed. Because of the magnitude of the problem, he did not succeed in considering other aspects of the "Italian case" in a proper light. He was unable to consider as a positive factor of development the quadrupling of the national income. The very readiness of the Italians to give up their years of poverty seemed to him a misfortune.

This blindness—a blindness of which he availed himself in prophesying—ensured that he would participate in the irrational and "anti-industrial" climate that was encouraged by the crisis of 1968.

The school system was exploding, and unemployable intellectuals were multiplying. Pasolini saw clearly the distortions in political management that had primed this explosive pattern. Belts of Third World *bidonvilles* around the large city agglomerates—Pasolini knew first-hand what reservoirs of violence they were.

What was lacking in so much clarity?

There were many enigmas in him. The most visible of them concerned the writer's nature—all too delicate, all too vulnerable, to the point where one might say it ought to be manifested secretly and not in violent clashes with the public, as happened in his case. In explanation of this enigma, I would say that Pasolini let his delicacy and vulnerability be violated, in a generous thirst for life.

Another enigma, whereby his need for reason was overcome by his psychagogic impulse and shipwrecked, can be explained by stressing how much he lacked a pragmatic culture. I am speaking of philosophical empiricism—but empiricism for Pasolini was a sin of secularism. Therefore he rejected it.

Wholly a man of his time, he chose to live in the enemy camp, launching polemics and accusations, pushing his intolerable personal situation to the point of paradox, and not troubling himself about anything else. For this reason his clarity of intellect became clouded, and the weight of ideology heavy.

He was more an orator than a politician, and he did not liberate himself from the confinement of his psychological realities. He would have liked to be free of them, and he made assiduous efforts in that direction, when he tried, for "irony," to become like a "stoic" sage, capable of saving men by virtue of his cold example, by virtue of the austere practices by which he had saved himself. But his austerity did not partake of coldness, and was only a hypothesis of life.

The weight of ideology. This was the heritage of the fifties, which hung on in Pasolini and led him to judge the complex cultural unification that had taken place in the country as deplorable "assent." At this he hurled his rage. His "madness" claimed to look beyond the minute comparisons between means and ends, between resources and "theories of needs" or "of desires." Prosperity seemed to him a vehicle of unhappiness. He became a victim of moralism.

Abuse of ideology, rejection of any philosophy of experience, the risk of falling into the irrational—these are peculiarly Italian characteristics, and in Pasolini they rose to incandescence. By that incandescence his enigmas are outshone.

Much as he seems perfectly at one with a certain Italian spirit, all of a sudden Pasolini goes beyond it and finds himself at odds with it.

> . . . I will arrive at the end without
> having had in my life
> the essential test, the experience
>
> that unites men, and gives them
> such a sweetly defined idea
> of fraternity at least in the acts of love!
>
> Like a blind man: from whom something
> will escape in death that coincides
> with life itself . . .[10]

His individuality ended by gaining the upper hand over all other considerations, arousing torment and injury, and activating the pain of the old and secret wound. To this, and to the erosion of experience, Pasolini subjected every triumph of intelligence, of morality, of form.

The grip of the irrational acted on him in these ways, the difficult and unexamined ways of the unconscious.

In a bundle of papers dating to 1969 or 1970, a drawing has been found—his only "abstract" drawing. The sheet has been folded in four—the same as the sheets on which he drew his portraits of Maria Callas, tinted with wine, vinegar, and coffee. On this sheet, in each section, a line is repeated diagonally, which might stand for lips or hills or a bird in flight. The repetition is obsessive, but framed in the different squares the obsessiveness seems assuaged, reduced to reflection.

At the bottom, in the center of the sheet—a sheet of what is called "transfer paper"—Pier Paolo wrote: "The world doesn't want me any more and doesn't know it."

The height of pride—or the height of despair? Pasolini was governed by a sensibility of survival. This impure feeling was sparked in him every time the attack of reality, direct or indirect as it appeared to him, became more painful. Perhaps his death was his courageous way of asking the world to "know" him, even when it no longer "wanted" him.

NOTES

Prologue: The Ostia Seaplane Basin

1. In the course of the trial it was stated that the car was indeed "jointly owned," but that each of the three owners had duplicate keys.
2. Alberto Arbasino, "Troppe coincidenze nella morte di Pasolini," *Corriere della Sera* (November 5, 1975).
3. Pier Paolo Pasolini, *Lettere luterane* (Turin, 1977), pp. 8–9.
4. Ibid., pp. 16–17. The *Gennariello* treatise was published in weekly installments in *Il Mondo* from March 6, 1975, to June 5 of the same year, and cut for typographic reasons. The only proper text is the one contained in the volume cited above.
5. *Lettere luterane*, op. cit., p. 73.
6. Alberto Moravia, "Come in una violenta sequenza di 'Accattone,' " *Corriere della Sera* (November 4, 1975).

PART ONE

Tal cour di un frut

1. Pier Paolo Pasolini, *Le poesie* (Milan, 1975), pp. 670–72 passim.
2. Ibid., p. 193.
3. Ibid., p. 573.
4. Dacia Maraini, *E tu chi eri?* (Milan, 1973), pp. 259–69.
5. Pier Paolo Pasolini, *Empirismo eretico* (Milan, 1972). On page 72 the episode is told in full. There we also read: "During that period in Belluno, from three years of age to three and a half, I felt the first pangs of sexual love, identical with the ones that I was to feel till now (terribly acute

between sixteen and thirty): that terrible and anxious sweetness that takes hold of the guts and consumes them, burns them, twists them, like a hot, melting gust of wind in the presence of the love object. All I remember of that object, I think, are the legs—and precisely the hollow behind the knees with the tendons taut. . . ."

6. Pier Paolo Pasolini, *Affabulazione, Pilade* (Milan, 1977), p. 124. The italics are Pasolini's.
7. Ibid., p. 129. Here too the italics are his.

The Time of the Analogical

1. Franco Farolfi, "Un ricordo," in *Nuovi Argomenti* (January–March 1976), pp. 85–88.
2. Pier Paolo Pasolini, "Lettere a Franco Farolfi," in *Nuovi Argomenti,* op. cit., p. 21.
3. Ibid., p. 6.
4. Pier Paolo Pasolini, *Lettere agli amici (1941–1945)* (Milan, 1976), p. 7.
5. Ibid., pp. 15–16.
6. Giacomo Leopardi, *Zibaldone*, 3837–38.
7. *Lettere agli amici*, op. cit., pp. 29–31.
8. "Lettere a Franco Farolfi," op. cit., p. 12.
9. Pier Paolo Pasolini, "Al lettore nuovo," in *Poesie* (Milan, 1970), p. 6.
10. Ibid.
11. Luciano Serra, Preface to *Lettere agli amici*, op. cit., p. xi.
12. Cf. for everything regarding the magazine: *Pasolini e "Il Setaccio,"* ed. Mario Ricci (Bologna, 1977).
13. In the text "Al lettore nuovo," in *Poesie*, op. cit., Pasolini indicates the year 1937. Rinaldi, in "Pasolini o dello stato di 'guerriglia permanente,'" *Salvo imprevisti* (January–April 1976), p. 1, corrects the date to the school year 1938–39.
14. "Lettere a Franco Farolfi," op. cit., p. 12.
15. Ibid., p. 21.
16. *Lettere agli amici*, op. cit., pp. 17–18
17. Ibid., pp. 33–34.
18. "Al lettore nuovo," in *Poesie*, op. cit., p. 7.
19. Preface to *Lettere agli amici*, op. cit., pp. xi–xii.
20. *Empirismo eretico*, op. cit., pp. 62–63.
21. *Botteghe Osure*, VIII, pp. 405–36.
22. The third person singular should not deceive; this is still a quotation from "I parlanti," *Botteghe Oscure*, op. cit., p. 450.
23. *Le poesie*, op. cit., p. 467.
24. Alberto Asor-Rosa, *Scrittori e popolo* (Rome, 1966), p. 73.
25. *Le poesie*, op. cit., pp. 454–56.
26. The quotation in this chapter from *Poesie a Casarsa* (whose title, by the way, seems to me modeled on *Morto ai paesi* by Alfonso Gatto) belongs to the 1942 edition of the volume. Later on, both in *Tal cour di un frut* (Udine, 1953), which contains a new version of "La domenica uliva,"

and *La meglio gioventù* (Florence, 1954), Pasolini had recourse to a more simplified transcription of the dialect, a dialect less difficult in sonority.

The "Pure Light" of the Resistance

1. "Al lettore nuovo," in *Poesie*, op. cit., p. 8.
2. Cf. *Lettere agli amici*, op. cit., p. 37.
3. "Al lettore nuovo," in *Poesie*, op. cit., p. 9.
4. Pier Paolo Pasolini, *I turcs tal Friùl* (Udine, 1976), afterword by Andreina Ciceri, p. 59.
5. *Le poesie*, op. cit., p. 217.
6. *Passione e ideologia*, Milan, 1960, pp. 136–37.
7. *La meglio gioventù* (Florence, 1954), p. 149, and *La nuova gioventù* (Turin, 1975), p. 157.
8. "This was the only way [for the author of *Poesie a Casarsa*] to know if at the origins of his sensuality there was an impediment to a form of knowledge directed from the inside outward, from below to above—the effusion, the pure and blinding heat of adolescence; if a screen had fallen between him and the world toward which he felt such a violent, childish curiosity. Being unable to take possession of it by psychologically normal and rational methods, he could not help but immerse himself in it again, go back, retrace that path to a point whose phase of happiness coincided with the enchanting landscape of Casarsa, with a rustic life made epic by a mournful charge of nostalgia. Knowledge was equivalent to expression. And here was the linguistic rupture, the return to a language closer to the world." Cf. *Passione e ideologia*, op. cit., p. 137.
9. Ibid., p. 198.
10. Ibid., p. 196.
11. *La Panarie* (May–December 1949).
12. *Lettere agli amici*, op. cit., p. 36.
13. Ibid., p. 38: "Look, ask Calcaterra, if you can, whether with my situation he could accept a thesis on 'Giovanni Pascoli' [January 26, 1944]."
14. Ibid., pp. 39–40.
15. Ibid., pp. 41–42.
16. *Le poesie*, op. cit., pp. 206–7. The couplet goes on: "on the March grass in innocent sunlight." Also in the sixth episode of *La ricchezza* it says that Guido departed "on a silent morning in March." This is a retrospective error in dating. Such errors are frequent in Pasolini. In this case, not only does all the evidence agree that it was May, but it is obvious from the letters to Luciano Serra.
17. *Lettere agli amici*, op. cit., pp. 43–44.
18. *Le poesie*, op. cit., p. 196.
19. *Passione e ideologia*, op. cit., p. 134.
20. *L'Osoppo e la "questione slavo-garibaldina"* (Trieste, 1951), pp. 49–54.
21. Recent, and useful, is that of Marco Cesselli, *Porzûs: due volti della Resistenza* (Milan, 1975).
22. Cf. M. Cesselli, *Porzûs: due volti della Resistenza*, ibid., pp. 101–3.

23. *Lettere agli amici,* op. cit., p. 43.
24. *Le poesie,* op. cit., 196–97.
25. Confirmation of this supposition: the letter to Serra, already cited, of August 21, which speaks of Guido's "enthusiasm" as the cause of his death. Pier Paolo seems almost tormented by this idea in these months.

Friulian Epos

1. "I parlanti," in *Botteghe Oscure,* op. cit., pp. 422–23.
2. Mario Lizzero, today a Communist deputy, has written about a meeting he had with Pasolini in early 1946 at the Communist Federation in Udine (*Confronto* [December 1975]): "He spoke to me with deep bitterness and sorrow over the tragedy of his mother following the death of his brother, Guido Alberto, the partisan 'Ermes.' He said that I, as a commissar of the Garibaldi divisions, was just the person he wanted to ask as to how a crime like the one committed at Porzûs could ever have happened. A wrong that could never be forgiven, he said, because of the unjust death of his brother Guido and all the others who fell at Porzûs. Partisans against partisans, how could we have done such a thing? . . . We talked for a long time. It was hard to know what to say at that moment. I said frankly that we were quite capable of judging, even in the framework in which that terrible incident had occurred, in a troubled and difficult area during a very hard struggle not devoid of errors, and perhaps inevitable besides, what fearful guilt had fallen on us Garibaldini due to the grievous incident at Porzûs. I told him our judgment on that incident. About the responsibilities of a few people, especially the commander of the GAP units. I also told him, however, that we were fully aware of the fact that, while understanding his sorrow, his mother's, and that of all the relatives of Porzûs, we would be brought to trial for that incident and an attempt would be made to use it for political ends within the framework of the anti-Communist campaign. But in any case, of course, the tragic reality of that disastrous incident remained. In later years, in 1948, I think, we spoke of it again, then again in 1952 and 1953 in Rome, this last time in Piazza del Gesù, shortly after a Christian Democratic spokesman had tried once again to persuade Pasolini to attend the trial over the Porzûs incident, and had received as always a negative reply. For Pasolini always retained, along with his sorrow and that of his mother for the death of 'Ermes,' the conviction that a great sin, a crime, had been committed at Porzûs, one that could not be forgiven. But he never wished to take part in the trials for that incident, because he was aware, as he kept saying, that it was not justice that was being sought there but a political operation with reactionary, conservative aims, which had nothing to do with himself or his brother."
3. The last issue of *Il Stroligut,* with the heading "Quaderno romanzo n. 3," bears the date JUNE MCMXLVII. The critical contributions are written in Italian; Pasolini reprints the articles he had written for *Libertà* on autonomy; hospitality is given to an anthology of Catalan poets; and there is a selection of Friulians—Naldini, Bortotto, Cantarutti, Tonuti Spagnol, and De Gironcoli. Despite the breadth of its contents, the issue lacks the

aggressive creativity of the previous ones. No more were to follow, and the activity of the *Academiuta* died out.

4. To the interest his articles aroused even among writers still unknown, this letter from Elio Pagliarani, sent from Viserba on March 27, 1947, to Giovanna Bemporad, bears witness: "Speaking of *Fiera letteraria*, I've read a *fine* article—bulging a little too much with quotations, to tell the truth— by P. Pasolini on inspiration, and so in accordance with my ideas (even a mention of Bo's reprehensible definition of poetry as absence, with which I've been dealing) as to please and anger me at the same time (so there— I thought—an important future article of mine gone up in smoke). Nevertheless, I warmly congratulate P. P. Pasolini."

5. The little volume also contains "Il testamento Coran," later included in the definitive edition of *La meglio gioventù*, the poetic utterance of a young peasant hanged by the Nazis immediately after having savored love for the first time. *Un incant thentha pretho*, reads one line: "a priceless enchantment," this being the epic-lyric synthesis to which Pasolini entrusted his own truth: the ego submerged by the waves of life, and barely noticeable in the impalpable outlines of form.

6. *Le poesie*, op. cit., pp. 53–63.

7. Now in *Rinascita* (November 4, 1977), p. 48.

8. As in the case of his judgment on Vittorini's *Politecnico*. Pasolini devotes a few words to *Politecnico* in his speech: the magazine has encouraged a literature of social consciousness, it has been nourished by the Resistance, but it is not " 'new' in that linguistically it is still a product of literary forms, albeit of the highest, but from our point of view negative." There is a tinge of opaque Marxist determinism in that "negative"—only an allusion, and fortunately immediately allowed to drop.

9. Pier Paolo Pasolini, "Opinioni sul latino," in *L'Illustrazione italiana* (May 1959), p. 62.

10. The two poems, with three others, were published in *Confronto*, op. cit. They are accompanied by a note stating that they were rediscovered in a notebook belonging to Francesco Scodellaro, a former pupil of Pasolini's and today a teacher in San Martino al Tagliamento. Pasolini had improvised them in class at his students' request, dedicating them to their home villages. We also owe to Scodellaro a "Ricordo del prof. Pasolini," written with Mariannina Lenarduzzi, in *Pasolini in Friuli* (Udine, 1976), p. 144. The same volume (various authors) reprints the quoted poems.

11. Andrea Zanzotto, "Per una pedagogia?" in *Nuovi Argomenti* (January– March 1976), pp. 47–51.

12. Among them one finds these two tercets, already indicative of the spirit of *L'usignolo della Chiesa Cattolica*: "Tremble, boy. / The shadows are closing in / on your village. / Ah, what sorrow / to catch you naked / within my range."

13. In a later working phase, in the early fifties, the loose sheaf of chapters took the title *I giorni del lodo De Gasperi*.

14. Cf. the "Paolo e Baruch" section of *L'usignolo della Chiesa Cattolica*.

15. In the unpublished collection of verse *Diari*, among the texts dated 1948, there is a prose poem entitled "L'unica divinità," which reads: "Mirror

against mirror the mysteries are mirrored to the end of space and time, in the heart of a boy who does not know his mystery. I am dying because I have submitted too many times. I am dying alone with my mania. I am dying in the odor of a latrine of my childhood, but linked forever to life by a wasp that kindles in the air the gold of Summer."

16. Cf. the speech at the First Congress of the Communist Provincial Federation of Pordenone, now in *Rinascita* (November 4, 1977), op. cit.
17. *Ritratti su misura*, ed. Elio Filippo Accrocca (Venice, 1960), p. 321.
18. *Le poesie*, op. cit., p. 255.
19. Baudelaire, *Oeuvres Complètes*, II (Paris, 1975), p. 677: "La femme est le contraire du Dandy. . . . La femme est *naturelle*, c'est-à-dire abominable."
20. This is how Pasolini entitles a long poem of 1948, one strophe of which appears as the first of "Le primule," in *L'usignolo*.
21. The text of the letter is quoted by Ferdinando Bandini in *Pasolini: cronaca giudiziaria, persecuzione, morte*, ed. Laura Betti (Milan, 1977), pp. 48–54.

As in a Novel

1. It is a letter difficult to date, written October 25, 1947 or 1948.
2. *Pasolini: cronaca giudiziario, persecuzione, morte*, op. cit., p. 46.
3. Ibid., p. 45. The letter is postmarked October 31, but was certainly written the evening of the 29th, on the morning of which *l'Unità* had published the notification of expulsion
4. "Al lettore nuovo," in *Poesie*, op. cit., p. 9.
5. *Le poesie*, op. cit., pp. 219–20.
6. Pietro Citati, *Il tè del cappellaio matto* (Milan, 1972), p. 227.
7. For all quotations from *L'usignolo della Chiesa Cattolica*, cf. the edition published in Milan, 1958.

PART TWO

The Discovery of Rome

1. Cesare Garboli, "Ricordo di Longhi," in *Nuovi Argomenti* (April–June 1970), p. 36.
2. In a letter to Luciano Serra from Rome, presumably in the earliest months of 1950—a letter quoted in the stage production *I campi del Friuli: leggendo e rileggendo Pasolini*, arranged by Roberto Roversi, 1978—Pasolini wrote: "Dear Luciano, I've received an incredible letter from you, incredible because I thought you knew I was in Rome, having fled from Casarsa with my mother about a month ago. In fact, before leaving, I had written you a note to let you know—the thing could also have ended very badly. And actually it is ending badly. My mother is working as a servant. I can't find work, I feel alone, useless, in awful shape. For the moment my uncle is supporting me. Our escape from Casarsa is due to

the fact that my father had become unbearable—he would have been the death of my mother. In fact, I now conceal from her my suicidal frame of mind—she has recovered so well that she seems to me to have gone back to the old days in Bologna. . . ."

3. Pier Paolo Pasolini, *Roma 1950, diario* (Milan, 1960), p. 40ff.
4. Almost all the "Roman" literary pieces published in 1950 and 1951 in the newspapers mentioned above were later, along with the scattered pages written in those and later years, collected in Pier Paolo Pasolini, *Alì dagli occhi azzurri* (Milan, 1965), especially pp. 5–102.
5. On the manneristic nature of this early "Roman" Pasolini, cf. Marco Vallora, "Alì dagli occhi impuri," in *BN* (January–April 1976), pp. 156–204.
6. Cf. "Un poeta e Dio," in *Passione e ideologia*, op. cit., pp. 354–73.
7. If an influence of Gadda can be found in Pasolini, it is in "Giubileo (relitto di romanzo umoristico)," a title that illustrates the meeting point between the two writers· the attempt at "humor" exercised on a character of petit-bourgeois extraction—an area frequently explored by Gadda. Cf. *Alì dagli occhi azzurri*, op. cit., pp. 53–63.
8. *Pasolini: cronaca giudiziaria, persecuzione, morte*, op. cit., pp. 52–53.
9. Pier Paolo Pasolini, "Gli 'Appunti' di Sandro Penna," *Il Popolo di Roma* (September 28, 1950).
10. Pier Paolo Pasolini, "La capanna indiana," *Il Giornale* (August 18, 1951).
11. Cf. Antonio Gramsci, *Quaderni dal carcere*, ed. V. Gerratana (Turin, 1975), II, p. 1384.
12. *Alì dagli occhi azzurri*, op. cit., pp. 80–88.
13. Letter also transcribed in part in *Pasolini: cronaca giudiziaria, persecuzione, morte*, op. cit., pp. 58–59.
14. The anthologies were included in the "La Fenice" series of the Guanda publishers in Parma. The series was edited by Attilio Bertolucci.
15. *Le poesie*, op. cit., pp. 23–31.
16. Pier Paolo Pasolini, *Sonetto primaverile (1953)* (Milan, 1960), p. 38 passim.
17. *Le poesie*, op. cit., pp. 161–62.
18. Ibid., pp. 103–4.

The Poet of "The Ashes of Gramsci"

1. *Pasolini: cronaca giudiziaria, persecuzione, morte*, op. cit., pp. 63–68.
2. Now in Carlo Salinari, *Preludio e fine del realismo in Italia* (Naples, 1967), pp. 55–59 passim.
3. An exception, among literati loyal to the Communists, was Niccolò Gallo, who in expressing his dissent in *Il lavoro* from Salinari and others such as Gaetano Trombatore, wrote that *Ragazzi di vita* was "important above all for the attempt, and a largely successful one, made by Pasolini to transfer the representation of a harsh and scorching reality onto a plane of cultural and moral reflection" (now in Niccolò Gallo, *Scritti letterari* [Milan, 1975], pp. 138–39).
4. Now in P. Citati, *Il tè del cappellaio matto*, op. cit., p. 230.

5. On the meeting with the Citti brothers: Pier Paolo Pasolini, *Mamma Roma* (Milan, 1962), pp. 134–37.
6. From 1957 to 1961, until he began his preparations for *Accattone*, Pasolini served his cinema apprenticeship by working on eleven film scripts. His contribution is sometimes highly visible in the choice of striking titles in the vein of *Ragazza di vita*—i.e., *La notte brava*, or *La giornata balorda*. Besides *Le notti di Cabiria*, the films are: *Marisa la civetta* by Mauro Bolognini (1957), *Giovani mariti* by Mauro Bolognini (1958), *La notte brava* by Mauro Bolognini (1959), *Morte di un amico* by Franco Rossi (1960), *Il bell'Antonio* by Mauro Bolognini (1960), *La giornata balorda* by Mauro Bolognini (1960), *Il carro armato dell '8 settembre* by Gianni Puccini (1960), *La lunga notte del '43* by Florestano Vancini (1960), *La cantata delle marane* by Cecilia Mangini (1960), and *La ragazza in vetrina* by Luciano Emmer (1961).
7. Elio Filippo Accrocca, "Che cosa fanno gli scrittori italiani: 10 domande a Pier Paolo Pasolini," *La fiera letteraria* (June 30, 1957).
8. For everything concerning the Bolognese periodical, cf. Gian Carlo Ferretti, *"Officina": cultura, letteratura e politica negli Anni Cinquanta* (Turin, 1975).
9. Francesco Leonetti, "Il decadentismo come problema contemporaneo," *Officina* (April 1956), p. 223.
10. G. C. Ferretti, *"Officina,"* op. cit., pp. 472–73.
11. Pier Paolo Pasolini, "La libertà stilistica," in *Officina* (June 1957), p. 345; now in *Passione e ideologia*, op. cit., p. 489.
12. Edoardo Sanguineti, "Una polemica in prosa," *Officina* (November 1957), pp. 452–57.
13. *Le poesie*, op. cit., p. 260.
14. Ibid., p. 277.
15. G. C. Ferretti, *"Officina,"* op. cit., pp. 110–11.
16. Cf. what Geno Pampaloni has written on the subject, "La saga degli Olivetti," *Il Giornale Nuovo* (May 31, 1978).
17. *Le poesie*, op. cit., p. 258.
18. G. C. Ferretti, *"Officina,"* op cit., p. 458.
19. Ibid., pp. 454–55.
20. *Ritratti su misura*, ed. E. F. Accrocca, op. cit., p. 321.
21. Ibid.
22. *Le poesie*, op. cit., p. 267.
23. This is the first line of a poem by Ferretti, entitled "Lode d'un amico poeta." Cf. Massimo Ferretti, *Allergia* (Milan, 1963), p. 36.
24. The friendship between Pasolini and Ferretti lasted a long time. It came to an end in 1965 when Ferretti published his third book, an experimental novel entitled *Il Gazzarra*. The influence of Gozzi having vanished from his poems, Ferretti was anxiously trying other forms of expression. Pasolini, in a long article entitled "Lettura in forma di giornale del 'Gazzara'" (*Nuovi Argomenti* [January–March 1967], pp. 167–80), discussed the limits of the kind of experimentation in which Ferretti was indulging—he judged the book "a subject that leads nowhere." This was enough to bring about an eclipse in their friendship.

25. Cf. Pier Paolo Pasolini, "La lunga strada di sabbia," *Successo* (July-August-September 1959).
26. Cf. *Pasolini: cronaca giudiziaria, persecuzione, morte*, op. cit., pp. 101–6.
27. These are words contained in autobiographical verses written in 1966, on the occasion of his trip to the United States—unpolished lines, tortured by second thoughts, found among his unpublished papers.
28. *Ritratti su misura*, ed. E. F. Accrocca, op. cit., p. 321.
29. Roberto De Monticelli, " 'Non ho campanile,' dice Pier Paolo Pasolini," *Il Giorno* (December 16, 1958).
30. *Le poesie*, op. cit., p. 72.
31. Cesare Garboli, *La stanza separata* (Milan, 1969), pp. 11–18.
32. These are the opening lines of "The Ashes of Gramsci." Cf. *Le Poesie*, op. cit., p. 67ff.
33. P. Citati, *Il tè del cappellaio matto*, op. cit., p. 228.
34. *Le poesie*, op. cit., pp. 233–34.
35. Giorgio Amendola, *Il rinnovamento del PCI*, interview by Renato Nicolai (Rome, 1978), pp. 140–41.
36. Ibid.
37. This is the poem that Sanguineti, with his "Polemica in prosa," written later, tried to parody in *Officina*.
38. Pier Paolo Pasolini, "La posizione," *Officina* (April 1956), p. 250.
39. Cf. "Maramaldi e Ferrucci," *Il contemporaneo* (June 9, 1956), lead article contained in the column "Il Caffè," and attributed to Carlo Salinari; P. P. Pasolini, "Lettera al direttore," ibid., June 23, 1956; P. P. Pasolini, Italo Calvino, and Carlo Salinari, "Lettere al direttore," ibid., June 30, 1956. Salinari, among other things, went so far as to scold Pasolini for his "character," "as peevish as a little boy."
40. Now in C. Salinari, *Preludo e fine del realismo in Italia*, op. cit., p. 145.
41. Gaetano Trombatore, literary critic and uncle of Antonello Trombadori, had been one of the Marxists most stubbornly opposed to Pasolini's writings and ideas.
42. *Le poesie*, op. cit., pp. 117–25.
43. In September 1958, Pasolini accepted an invitation from the Union of Soviet Writers for a poetry congress in Moscow. It echoes in *La religione del mio tempo*: the crowd in Red Square on a night of "pious pallor"— "that immense pit / on which the stars shine nearby." There is the picture of a crowd that plays "with simple and emotional joy." "Lines of men" form a ring around some girl, taking her "roughly and affectionately by the hand" (*Le poesie*, op. cit., pp. 225–27).

 What struck Pasolini in the Soviet Union was the festive and rural appearance of the people—the people enjoying its "innocent," religious happiness in the shadow of the gilded cupolas of Saint Basil, monument to a lifeless past. Little more. His curiosity about the socialist world did not go beyond this impression.
44. Cf. *Il punto* (November 14, 1959): the account by Gianni Rocca of the Crotone prize in the year it was won by *Una vita violenta*. Rocca reports some of Pasolini's remarks: "I don't want to be a literary case. I don't want to be reduced to a pure subject of current events and journalistic

superficiality. I know very well that if this is tried there is a reason for it. Only the secondary aspects of my work, such as language or the crudeness that exists in my reality, are brought to the fore. An elegant way for not lingering instead over the social question, which for me, in my aims as an artist, is more important."

45. *Le poesie*, op. cit., p. 235.
46. Ibid., pp. 214–15.
47. Ibid., p. 238.
48. Ibid., p. 241.
49. Ibid., p. 242.
50. Ibid., pp. 243–44.

Cinema

1. C. Garboli, *La stanza separata*, op. cit., p. 18.
2. Massimo D'Avack, *Cinema e letteratura* (Rome, 1964), p. 111.
3. Cf., for this and the following quotations from the "diary" of *Accattone*, Pier Paolo Pasolini, *Accattone* (Rome, 1961), pp. 1–15 passim.
4. *Il padre selvaggio*, op. cit., p. 60.
5. Cf. Pasolini's remarks in the course of a discussion held in Brescia for an exhibition of Romanino's paintings, in Balducci, Dell'Acqua, Guttuso, Pasolini, Piovene, Russoli, *L'arte del Romanino e il nostro tempo* (Brescia, 1976). The discussion took place on September 7, 1965.
6. Daisy Martini, "L'Accattone di Pier Paolo Pasolini," *Cinema nuovo* (March-April 1961).
7. *Accattone*, op. cit., p. 7.
8. *Le poesie*, op. cit., pp 283–89.
9. This text never reached the stage, nor was it printed. A reworking of it was performed—its title was *Nel '46*—at the Teatro dei Satiri in Rome, April 1965, directed by Sergio Graziani.
10. *Le poesie*, op. cit., p. 337.
11. Pier Paolo Pasolini, *Mamma Roma* (Milan, 1962), p. 145.
12. *Le poesie*, op. cit., p. 180.
13. Thus wrote Pasolini in a letter to Antonello Trombadori, published in *Il contemporaneo* (August 21, 1957).
14. *Le poesie*, op. cit., p. 179.
15. Pier Paolo Pasolini, "Lettera del traduttore," in Eschilo [Aeschylus], *Orestiade* (Turin, 1960), with texts by G. Thomson, V. Gassman, T. Otto, R. Bianchi Bandinelli, L. Zorzi, L. Lucignani, C. Stanislavski, pp. 1–3. The performance was staged on May 19, 1960, at the Greek Theater in Syracuse, direction by Vittorio Gassman, settings and costumes by Teo Otto, music by Angelo Musco, and with the assistance of Mathilda Beauvoir's Vodu Ballet of Haiti. Another experiment in translation for the theater, this time into the glow of Roman dialect, was that of Plautus' *Miles Gloriosus*, which Pasolini prepared in 1963 for Franco Enriquez under the title *Il Vantone* (cf. Pier Paolo Pasolini, *Il Vantone di Plauto* [Milan, 1963]).
16. *Le poesie*, op. cit., p. 455.

17. Ibid., pp. 304–5.
18. Ibid., p. 344.
19. *Accattone*, op. cit., p. 14.
20. Cf. Andrea Barbato's remarks on the subject in "Nomi e cognomi," *La Stampa* (March 4, 1978).
21. Alberto Moravia, "Immagini al posto d'onore," *L'Espresso* (October 1, 1961).
22. *Le poesie*, op. cit., p. 350.
23. Pier Paolo Pasolini, "Dialoghi con Pasolini," *Vie Nuove* (November 26, 1960).
24. Pier Paolo Pasolini, "La mia avventura a Panico," *Paese-Sera* (July 4, 1960).
25. *Pasolini: cronaca giudiziaria, persecuzione, morte*, op. cit., pp. 111–19.
26. Ibid., pp. 109–10.
27. This is how the incident is told in the unpublished and aforementioned autobiographical verses of 1966.
28. For the reconstruction of the whole trial, cf. *Pasolini: cronaca giudiziaria, persecuzione, morte*, op. cit., pp. 119–33.
29. Unsigned, "Si riconosce in un romanzo di Pasolini e denuncia lo scrittore per diffamazione," *Il Tempo* (April 11, 1962).
30. Nino Ferrero, " 'Mamma Roma,' ovvero, dalla responsabilità individuale alla responsabilità collettiva," in *Filmcritica* (September 1962).
31. Unsigned, " 'Cerco il Cristo fra i poveri,' " *Italia-Notizie* (November 20, 1963).
32. *Empirismo eretico*, op. cit., p. 30.
33. Alberto Moravia, "L'uomo medio sotto i bisturi," *L'Espresso* (March 3, 1963).
34. Adelio Ferrero, *Il cinema di P. P. Pasolini* (Venice, 1977), p. 45.
35. *Pasolini: cronaca giudiziaria, persecuzione, morte*, op. cit., pp. 162–63.
36. Originally in *Cinema e Film* (winter 1966–67); now in *Empirismo eretico*, op. cit., p. 233.
37. *Le poesie*, op. cit., p. 347.

Recidivist Passions

1. Gian Carlo Ferretti, Introduction to Pier Paolo Pasolini, *Le belle bandiere* (Milan, 1977), p. 21.
2. Ibid., p. 219.
3. Ibid., p. 228.
4. Ibid., p. 234.
5. Ibid., p. 239.
6. Pier Paolo Pasolini, *L'odore dell'India* (Milan, 1962), p. 43.
7. Ibid., p. 24.
8. Ibid.
9. Ibid., pp. 79–80.
10. Ibid.
11. *Le poesie*, op. cit., p. 336.
12. *Le belle bandiere*, op. cit., p. 159.
13. Ibid., p. 170.

14. Cf. Franco Monicelli, "Rabbia e ingenuità," *Paese-Sera* (April 19, 1963), which contains, among other things, the following: "I will write . . . of the naïveté of Pier Paolo Pasolini, who accepts a producer's proposal to make half a film the other half of which will be made by a fascist, the former editor of a humorous fascist newspaper, who went to jail (and stayed there for a year) for aggravated and continual defamation and slander of De Gasperi, a man we opposed but who was an honorable man; I will write of the naïveté of this forty-two-year-old crusader for our defenseless and virgin literature who does not know who this all too well-known fascist is with whom they propose to have him link arms . . . and who only after the release of the film whose execution they have shared in, realizes his gross mistake and writes letters to the newspapers to justify himself, declaring that he will withdraw his name posthaste from the credits."

15. Pier Paolo Pasolini, "Nenni (1960)," *Avanti!* (December 31, 1961).

16. It was at this time that Pasolini "understood" Israel and the life of siege its people were leading. Cf. *Le poesie*, op. cit., pp. 492–93: "While leaning on the hood of the car / obscure sign of the apprentice, insincere / seeker of God's places, / there comes, behind a pair of camels, / to the honking of horns of the cars / of the ruling myths, a young Arab, / with blue jeans and a white jersey, / his hands on his narrow hips / at the belt—with its big buckle / under his navel, and his crotch / slung low, as though a troubled burden / —a boy from Quarticciolo. / With silver teeth. He has / the same face as us Jews. / But in ours, ah, not only is there / never rage, nor hate, but not even / the possibility of rage and hate. / But he's got it. Just as he's a man. / His existential certainty / sweetly throws the cruelty of the race in the faces / of us Jews, or rather Israelis, / who with the incapacity of the myths, / squeeze our weapons in our hands, wanting / finally for the violence of reason / to know the humility of rage and hate."

17. Pier Paolo Pasolini, *Il Vangelo secondo Matteo* (Milan, 1964), pp. 16–17.

18. Ibid., p. 14.

19. *Le belle bandiere*, op cit., p. 265.

20. *Il Vangelo secondo Matteo*, op. cit., p. 265.

21. Ibid., p. 266.

22. Ibid., p. 20.

23. Felice Chilanti, "La serata veneziana di Matteo e Pasolini," *Paese-Sera* (September 22, 1964).

24. Mario Soldati, "Il 'Vangelo' di Pasolini," *L'Europeo* (November 23, 1964); now in *Da Spettatore* (Milan, 1973), pp. 170–79.

25. *Le poesie*, op. cit., p. 355.

26. Ibid., p. 444.

27. Ibid., p. 398.

28. Ibid., p. 371.

29. Ibid., p. 439.

30. Ibid., p. 333.

31. Ibid., p. 432.

32. Ibid., p. 530.

33. Ibid., p. 372.

34. The others included Roland Barthes, Maurice Blanchot, Hans M. Enzensberger, Uwe Johnson, Martin Walser, Marguerite Duras, Jean Starobinski, Claude Ollier, Günter Grass, Jean Genet. Pasolini published "Appunti per un poema popolare" in it.
35. *Le poesie*, op. cit., p. 473.
36. Ibid., p. 475.
37. The lines are included in the "Avvertenza" of *Alì dagli occhi azzurri*, op. cit., pp. 515–16, where Ninetto is also thanked for "his unintentional linguistic contributions and above all for his joy."
38. Cf. Alfredo Bini, "I primi passi del regista Pasolini," *L'Europeo* (November 28, 1975).

Teorema

1. *Le poesie*, op. cit., p. 348.
2. *Alì dagli occhi azzurri*, op. cit., pp. 494–513.
3. When these lines were read posthumously, some gave them a prophetic interpretation. Pasolini was supposed to have foreseen his own death, beaten with a stick next to his automobile. The present writer instead sought a literal interpretation—they dealt with a residue of literary controversy, supported also by a photograph (included in the "Iconografia ingiallita") showing some representatives of the 63 Group at a conference. This interpretation (cf. Enzo Siciliano, "L'inferno postumo di Pasolini," *Il Mondo* [December 25, 1975]) has been adopted by Gian Carlo Ferretti in *Pasolini, L'universo orrendo* (Rome, 1976), p. 53, and in his preface to *Le belle bandiere*, op. cit., pp. 15–16; and by Luigi Malerba in "Ce mal-aimé qui aimait le scandale," *Le point de l'épée* (1976), pp. 56–57.
4. *Le belle bandiere*, op. cit., p. 343.
5. *Le poesie*, op. cit., p. 531.
6. *Empirismo eretico*, op. cit., p. 22.
7. Ibid., pp. 25–26.
8. Ibid., p. 29.
9. Ibid.
10. Ibid., pp. 55–81.
11. Ibid., p. 53.
12. Ibid.
13. Ibid., pp. 73–74.
14. Ibid., p. 80.
15. Ibid., p. 81.
16. Ibid., pp. 85–107 ("Intervento sul discorso libero indiretto"), and pp. 119–25 ("La fine dell'avanguardia").
17. Pier Paolo Pasolini, *Uccellacci e uccellini* (Milan, 1966), p. 57.
18. A. Ferrero, *Il cinema di P. P. Pasolini*, op. cit., p. 71.
19. *Uccellacci e uccellini*, op. cit., p. 58.
20. Two film episodes, filmed in 1966 and 1967, are also fables: *La terra vista dalla luna* (The Earth Seen from the Moon) and *Che cosa sono le nuvole?* (What Are Clouds?). Totò and Ninetto are again the protagonists. Both contain, in a reduced and subtle way, the theme of *La Divina Mimesis* and *Uccellacci e uccellini*: men move toward the future, abandon-

ing the old instruments of reason. Will innocence and candor survive in them? How to nourish hope for the future? For now, the questions remain unanswered.

21. Pier Paolo Pasolini, statement on the Sinyavsky-Daniel case, *Il Giorno* (February 17, 1966).
22. Giorgio Bocca, "L'arrabbiato sono io," *Il Giorno* (July 19, 1966).
23. *Empirismo eretico*, op. cit., p. 174.
24. *Le poesie*, op. cit., p. 608.
25. G. Bocca, *Il Giorno* (July 19, 1966), op. cit.
26. Cf. respectively *Nuovi Argomenti* (July–December 1967), and *Nuovi Argomenti* (July–September 1969).
27. *Empirismo eretico*, op. cit., p. 235.
28. Geno Pampaloni, "Vince la pietà" (*Corriere della Sera*, August 27, 1972).
29. *Affabulazione, Pilade*, op. cit., pp. 111–12.
30. Pier Paolo Pasolini, *Edipo re* (Milan, 1967), pp. 11–15 passim.
31. Guido Piovene, "Fino in fondo nel sangue nel buio," *La fiera letteraria* (September 14, 1967).
32. *Empirismo eretico*, op. cit., p. 148.
33. Ibid., p. 149.
34. Oriana Fallaci, "Un marxista a New York," *L'Europeo* (October 13, 1966).
35. *Empirismo eretico*, op. cit., p. 150.
36. The film had also been shown at the Montreal festival at the end of the previous July, and Pasolini had made a brief trip there.
37. *Empirismo eretico*, op. cit., p. 149.
38. Ibid., p. 150.
39. Ibid., p. 151.
40. Ibid., pp. 152–53.
41. Ibid., p. 154.
42. Ibid., p. 252.
43. Camilla Cederna, "Tra le braccia dell'arcangelo," *L'Espresso* (April 21, 1968).
44. Pier Paolo Pasolini, *Teorema* (Milan, 1968), jacket cover. As for the "about three years ago," read "two," one of Pasolini's errors in dating.
45. C. Garboli, *La stanza separata*, op. cit., p. 266.
46. *Empirismo eretico*, op. cit., p. 154.
47. Ibid., pp. 136–37.
48. Quoted in Maria Bellonci, *Come in un racconto gli anni del Premio Strega* (Milan, 1971), p. 103.
49. Pier Paolo Pasolini, "Il Caos," *Tempo Illustrato* (August 20, 1968).
50. "Il regista invita il pubblico di non vedere la sua pellicola," *La Stampa* (September 5, 1968). G. Gh. (Gigi Ghirotti).

Repudiation and Utopia

1. Arturo Colombo, "Anche noi sbagliammo nel '68," *Corriere della Sera* (April 12, 1978).
2. Paolo Sylos Labini, *Saggio sulle classi sociali* (Bari, 1976), p. 61.
3. Alberto Ronchey, *Accadde in Italia, 1968–1977* (Milan, 1977), pp. 5–6.

4. *Empirismo eretico*, op. cit., p. 162.

5. Cf. in *Nuovi Argomenti* (January–March 1968), the texts, unsigned but written by Alberto Moravia, entitled "Napalm LDT" and "Da non leggere," and "Il rifiuto dei libri a Palazzo Fontana" by Enzo Siciliano. Cf. all the signed texts by P. P. Pasolini in *Nuovi Argomenti* (April–June 1968), and "Impegno e integrazione" by Alberto Moravia, "Lettera a Pasolini" by Enzo Siciliano, and "Roma: Le due linee del Movimento Studentesco" by Giorgio Manacorda.

6. Cf. *L'Espresso* (June 16, 1968).

7. *Empirismo eretico*, op. cit., pp. 155 and ff.

8. Cf. *L'Espresso* (June 23, 1968, and June 30, 1968).

9. Walter Benjamin, *Angelus Novus* (Turin, 1962), pp. 14–15.

10. Now in *Empirismo eretico*, op. cit., p. 162.

11. The expression is Umberto Cerroni's. Cf. his politico-philosophical notebook, *Carte della crisi* (Rome, 1978), especially pp. 49 and 65–66.

12. Pier Paolo Pasolini, *San Paolo* (Turin, 1977), pp. 6–7.

13. *Le poesie*, op. cit., p. 601.

14. "Il Caos," *Tempo Illustrato* (October 18, 1969).

15. Piero Sanavio, " 'Porcile' o no, tiriamo le somme su Pasolini," *Il Dramma* (September 12, 1969).

16. Alberto Moravia, "Oreste a 30° all'ombra," *L'Espresso* (February 14, 1971).

17. Pier Paolo Pasolini, *Medea* (Milan, 1970), p. 92.

18. *Le poesie*, p. 719.

19. Ibid.

20. Ibid.

21. Ibid., pp. 717–18.

22. Ibid., p. 637.

23. More than thirty complaints were filed against the *Decameron* between late September and November 1971. Even though it had been placed in circulation by decree of the examining magistrate in Trento, it was confiscated by order of the district attorneys' offices of Sulmona and Ancona. *The Canterbury Tales* was confiscated on October 7, 1972; it was ordered released on January 9, 1973; and confiscated again by order of the public prosecutor's office in Teramo on March 19, 1973. The Supreme Court annulled this decree on April 2, 1973: two days later the public prosecutor's office in Benevento issued another confiscation order. This raised a question of constitutional law. The Constitutional Court met to deliberate the issue on March 27, 1975. A complaint was filed against *Arabian Nights* on June 27, 1974, and the complaint was shelved by decision of the examining magistrate in Milan on August 5, 1974. Cf. *Pasolini: cronaca giudiziaria, persecuzione, morte*, op. cit., pp. 180–207.

24. Alberto Moravia, "Dall'Oriente a Salò," in *Nuovi Argomenti* (January–March 1976), pp. 93–95.

25. *Lettere luterane*, op. cit., pp. 72–73.

26. Cf. *Pasolini: cronaca giudiziaria, persecuzione, morte*, op. cit., pp. 177–79.

27. Jean-Michel Gardair, "Entretien avec Pier Paolo Pasolini," *Le Monde* (February 26, 1971).

28. *Le poesie*, op. cit., p. 677.
29. Ibid., p. 621.
30. Ibid., p. 678.
31. Ibid., p. 680.
32. Ibid., p. 698.
33. Ibid., p. 699.
34. Ibid., p. 652.
35. Ibid., p. 616.
36. Pier Paolo Pasolini, "Che cos'è un vuoto letterario," in *Nuovi Argomenti* (January–March 1971), pp. 7–10.
37. *Le poesie*, op. cit., pp. 670–72.
38. Francesco Alberoni, "Crisi di identità della gente borghese," *Corriere della Sera* (October 17, 1975).
39. Pier Paolo Pasolini, "Pasolini recensisce Pasolini," *Il Giorno* (June 3, 1971).
40. Pasolini wrote about books during the year 1971 for *Nuovi Argomenti*. On November 26, 1972, in *Tempo Illustrato*, he started a weekly column of literary criticism, which continued until January 10, 1975.
41. Pier Paolo Pasolini, "Satura," *Nuovi Argomenti* (January–March 1971), pp. 17–20.
42. Eugenio Montale, "Diario del '71," *L'Espresso* (December 19, 1971); now in *Diario del '71 e del '72* (Milan, 1973), pp. 32 and 61–62.
43. Pier Paolo Pasolini, "Οὖτις," *Nuovi Argomenti* (May–June 1972), pp. 149–50.
44. Quoted in Enzo Siciliano, "L'odiato Pasolini," *Il Mondo* (July 14, 1972).
45. Louis Valentin, "Tête-à-tête avec Pier Paolo Pasolini," *Lui* (April 1970).
46. "Il Caos," *Tempo Illustrato* (December 19, 1969).
47. *Le poesie*, op. cit., p. 421.
48. In Ferdinando Camon, *Il mestiere di scrittore* (Milan, 1973), p. 121.
49. "Il Caos," *Tempo Illustrato* (December 13, 1969).
50. In F. Camon, *Il mestiere di scrittore,* op. cit., p. 119.
51. Enzo Golino, *Letteratura e classi sociali* (Bari, 1976), p 108. This interview with Pasolini was first published in *Il Giorno* (December 29, 1973).
52. *La nuova gioventù*, op. cit., p. 167.
53. Piero Ottone, *Intervista sul giornalismo italiano*, ed. Paolo Murialdi (Bari, 1978), pp. 112–13.
54. Now with the title "Il 'discorso' dei capelli," the article is included in Pier Paolo Pasolini, *Scritti corsari* (Milan, 1975), pp. 9–16.
55. Ibid., pp. 17–23.
56. Ibid., pp. 31–34.
57. Ibid., pp. 36–37, from a text that appeared first in *Il Dramma* (March 1974).
58. His collaboration with the *Corriere della Sera* also allowed Pasolini to write literary criticism, pursuing in its pages the themes he had already worked out in *Tempo Illustrato*. Pier Paolo had the idea for a column to be called "Che fare?" in which he would deal with literature, to begin at the end of 1975.
59. *Scritti corsari*, op. cit., pp. 50–56.

60. Ibid., pp. 64–69.
61. Ibid., p. 93.
62. Ibid., p. 101.
63. Ibid., p. 94.
64. Ibid., p. 123ff.
65. Ibid., pp. 134–35.
66. *San Paolo*, op. cit., pp. 5–8 passim.
67. Ibid., p. 161.
68. *Scritti corsari*, op. cit., pp. 111–12.
69. Ibid., p. 114.
70. Ibid., p. 172.
71. Ibid., p. 161.
72. Ibid., p. 164.
73. Ibid.
74. Ibid., p. 173.
75. Ibid., pp. 114–15.
76. *Lettere luterane*, op. cit., p. 112. In the weeks following March 16, 1978, the day on which Aldo Moro, chairman of the Christian Democratic party, was kidnapped by the Red Brigades, public opinion recalled what Pasolini had written about a "trial" to be brought against the Christian Democratic political leaders. The Red Brigades members, in their "communiqués," spoke of a "trial" of Moro that was being held in the inaccessible "people's prison." It was suggested that Pasolini might be responsible, and in no uncertain way, for what was tragically unfolding. The formal aspect aside (Pasolini had spoken of a "regular" trial), it was the institutional framework within a socialist perspective that was intended and reinforced by his words (cf. Giorgio Galli, "Non era questo il processo voluto da Pasolini," *La Repubblica* [March 28, 1978]). Because of its symbolic importance, the "regularity" and public nature of the trial were what was closest to Pasolini's heart—therein lay its legitimacy.
77. Ibid., p. 122.
78. Ibid., p. 115.
79. Ibid., p. 148.
80. Ibid.
81. Ibid., p. 148.
82. Ibid.
83. Ibid., p. 169.
84. This happened after the articles on the divorce referendum. The leaders of the Communist Youth Federation of Rome, Gianni Borgna and Goffredo Bettini, decided on a meeting with Pasolini. This decision brought about a split within the party, which was later healed by Giorgio Napolitano, then in charge of cultural matters. Napolitano gave the signal for the "confrontation" with Pasolini. And in June 1974, Pier Paolo met with the young Communists during a public debate in the Villa Borghese.
85. *Lettere luterane*, op. cit., p. 168.
86. Ibid.
87. Ibid., p. 184.
88. *Le poesie*, op. cit., p. 747.

89. E. Golino, *Letteratura e classi sociali*, op. cit., p. 112.
90. Cf. what Paolo Volponi has written in (various authors) *Perché Pasolini* (Florence, 1978), pp. 25–26.
91. Franco Cordelli, "Per 'Salò-Sade,'" in *Nuovi Argomenti* (January–March 1976), pp. 89–92.

Epilogue: The Will to Live

1. *Le poesie*, op. cit., p. 355.
2. Ibid., p. 353.
3. Ibid.
4. Jean-Jacques Rousseau, *Les Confessions*, I (Paris, 1934), p. 18.
5. *Le poesie*, op. cit., p. 356.
6. Ibid.
7. A. Moravia, "Come in una violenta sequenza di 'Accattone,'" op. cit.
8. Rossana Rossanda, "In morte di Pasolini," *il manifesto* (November 4, 1975).
9. Friedrich Nietzsche, *Aurora e Frammenti postumi* (1879–1881), ed. Giorgio Colli and Mazzino Montinari, Italian translation by Ferruccio Masini and Mazzino Montinari (Milan, 1964), p. 193.
10. *Le poesie*, op. cit., p. 361.

CHRONOLOGICAL LIST OF PUBLISHED WORKS OF PIER PAOLO PASOLINI

Poesie a Casarsa, Libreria Antiquaria Mario Landi, Bologna, 1942.

Poesie, Stamperia Primon, San Vito al Tagliamento, 1945.

I Pianti, Pubblicazioni dell'Academiuta, Casarsa, 1946.

Dov'è la mia patria, with thirteen drawings by Giuseppe Zigaina, Pubblicazioni dell'Academiuta, Casarsa, 1949.

"I parlanti" (1948), in *Botteghe Oscure*, VIII, Rome, 1951.

Poesia dialettale del Novecento, with translations at the foot of the page by Mario Dell'Arco and Pier Paolo Pasolini, Guanda, Parma, 1952.

Tal cour di un frut, Edizioni "Friuli," Tricesimo, 1953.

Dal "diario" (1945–1947), Salvatore Sciascia, Caltanissetta, 1954.

La meglio gioventù, Sansoni, Florence, 1954.

Il canto popolare, La Meridiana, Milan, 1954.

Canzoniere italiano, anthology of popular poetry edited by Pier Paolo Pasolini, Guanda, Bologna, 1955.

Ragazzi di vita, Garzanti, Milan, 1955.

Le ceneri di Gramsci, Garzanti, Milan, 1957.

L'usignolo della Chiesa Cattolica, Longanesi, Milan, 1958.

Una vita violenta, Garzanti, Milan, 1959.

Passione e ideologia (1948–1958), Garzanti, Milan, 1960.

Eschilo [Aeschylus], *Orestiade*, translation by Pier Paolo Pasolini, Edit. Urbinate, Urbino, 1960 (reprinted by Einaudi, Turin, 1960).

Donne di Roma, Il Saggiatore, Milan, 1960.

Giro a vuoto, Le canzoni di Laura Betti, with various authors, Scheiwiller, Milan, 1960.

Roma 1950, diario, All'insegna del pesce d'oro, Milan, 1960.

Sonetto primaverile (1953), All'insegna del pesce d'oro, Milan, 1960.

La religione del mio tempo, Garzanti, Milan, 1961.

Accattone, F.M., Rome, 1961.

L'odore dell'India, Longanesi, Milan, 1962.

Mamma Roma, Rizzoli, Milan, 1962.

Il sogno di una cosa, Garzanti, Milan, 1962.

La violenza, 24 drawings by Attardi, Calabria, Farulli, Gianquinto, Guccione, Guerreschi, Guttuso, Vespignani, presented by A. De Guercio, D. Micacchi, and D. Morosini, with 12 ballads by Pier Paolo Pasolini, Editori Riuniti, Rome, 1962.

Il Vantone di Plauto, Garzanti, Milan, 1963.

Poesia in forma di rosa, Garzanti, Milan, 1964.

Il Vangelo secondo Matteo, Garzanti, Milan, 1964.

Poesie dimenticate, Società Filologica Friulana, Udine, 1965.

Alì dagli occhi azzurri, Garzanti, Milan, 1965.

Potentissima Signora, canzoni e dialoghi per Laura Betti, with various authors, Longanesi, Milan, 1965.

Uccellacci e uccellini, Garzanti, Milan, 1966.

Edipo re, Garzanti, Milan, 1967.

Teorema, Garzanti, Milan, 1968.

Medea, Garzanti, Milan, 1970.

Ostia, un film di Sergio Citti, subject and script by Sergio Citti and Pier Paolo Pasolini, Garzanti, Milan, 1970.

Poesie, selection chosen by the author, Garzanti, Milan, 1970.

Trasumanar e organizzar, Garzanti, Milan, 1971.

Empirismo eretico, Garzanti, Milan, 1972.

Calderón, Garzanti, Milan, 1973.

Il padre selvaggio, Einaudi, Turin, 1975.

Scritti corsari, Garzanti, Milan, 1975.

La nuova gioventù, Einaudi, Turin, 1975.

Trilogia della vita, ed. Giorgio Gattei, Cappelli, Bologna, 1975.

La Divina Mimesis, Einaudi, Turin, 1975.

Le poesie [*Le ceneri di Gramsci, La religione del mio tempo, Poesie in forma di rosa, Trasumanar e organizzar, Poesie inedite* (1950–1951)], Garzanti, Milan, 1975.

"Volgar' eloquio," ed. A. Piromalli and D. Scarfoglio, Athena, Naples, 1976.

L'arte del Romanino e il nostro tempo, with various authors, Grafoedizioni, Brescia, 1976.

I turcs tal Friùl, ed. Luigi Ciceri, "Forum Julii," Doretti, Udine, 1976.

Lettere agli amici (*1941–1945*), ed. Luciano Serra, Guanda, Milan, 1976.

Pasolini in Friuli, 1943–1949, with various authors, Arti Grafiche Friulane, Udine, 1976.

Lettere luterane, Einaudi, Turin, 1977.

Affabulazione, Pilade, Garzanti, Milan, 1977.

Le belle bandiere, Dialoghi 1960–65, ed. Gian Carlo Ferretti, Editori Riuniti, Rome, 1977.

San Paolo, Einaudi, Turin, 1977.

Pasolini e "Il Setaccio" 1942–43, with various authors, ed. Mario Ricci, Cappelli, Bologna, 1977.

I disegni, 1941–1975, ed. Giuseppe Zigaina, Scheiwiller, Milan, 1978.

INDEX

ABOUT THE AUTHOR

One of Italy's leading critics, Enzo Siciliano
was born in Rome in 1934, where he still lives.
Literary critic for Italy's leading newspaper,
the *Corriere della Sera* of Milan, he is also
editor, with Alberto Moravia and Attilio
Bertolucci, of Italy's most distinguished cultural
review, *Nuovi Argomenti*, of which his friend
Pasolini was a founder.

Apart from the biography of Pasolini, which
was a major best seller in Italy and was acclaimed
in Germany, Siciliano has also published a study
of Puccini, as well as several novels and
story collections.

ABOUT THE TRANSLATOR

John Shepley is a translator and writer whose
stories have appeared in magazines in the
United States and Italy.